Home Again, Home Again, Jiggity, Jig

HOME AGAIN, HOME AGAIN, JIGGITY, JIG

SUSIE STONE

Copyright © 2017 by Susie Stone.

Library of Congress Control Number:		2017900142
ISBN:	Hardcover	978-1-5245-7452-9
	Softcover	978-1-5245-7453-6
	eBook	978-1-5245-7454-3

All rights reserved. No part of this book may be reproduced or transmitted in any form or by any means, electronic or mechanical, including photocopying, recording, or by any information storage and retrieval system, without permission in writing from the copyright owner.

Front cover design by Arthur Chidlovski. Used with permission.

Print information available on the last page.

Rev. date: 03/13/2017

To order additional copies of this book, contact:
Xlibris
1-888-795-4274
www.Xlibris.com
Orders@Xlibris.com
752119

CONTENTS

Chapter 1   Going Home 1

Chapter 2   I Have Ancestors? 26

Chapter 3   My Life Begins..64

Chapter 4   Meet Viola and E.P. 83

Chapter 5   The House Across the Street 92

Chapter 6   Et tu, Brute? 101

Chapter 7   School Days..108

Chapter 8   A Change in Residence 115

Chapter 9   Nein on the Coat..124

Chapter 10 Traveling With The Beelers..............................128

Chapter 11 What Dreams Are Made Of…...........................130

Chapter 12 King Kong Lives! 144

Chapter 13 Arrival of Mr. Big Man 154

Chapter 14 Doctor! He's Not Even A Nurse 161

Chapter 15 A Christmas Story...167

Chapter 16 War Comes To Town 176

Chapter 17 Tickling Those Ivory Keys 182

Chapter 18 Oh, Dem Golden Slippers 189

Chapter 19 Meeting the Mick 192

Chapter 20 I Don't Think We're In Kansas 198

Chapter 21 Polio 205

Chapter 22 Houdini Who?..211

Chapter 23 A Two-Legged Table..219

Chapter 24 Visiting Neighbors 227

Chapter 25 Busy Days 236

Chapter 26 Honor The Veterans 245

Chapter 27 Every Home Needs A Television 253

Chapter 28 Grandma Clayton..263

Chapter 29 Election Day...267

Chapter 30 Under The Big Top..271

Chapter 31 Mary, Mary...283
Chapter 32 I'm Called Little Buttercup 291
Chapter 33 Tantrum For Two......................................299
Chapter 34 Arizona Bound 304
Chapter 35 A Kiss Is Just A Kiss 312
Chapter 36 "Oh, Say Can You See…".........................322
Chapter 37 Elvis Has Left The Building.......................329
Chapter 38 Gorgeous George......................................334
Chapter 39 Pellet With The Poison
            In The Vessel With The Pestle.....................338
Chapter 40 We Are All Rainbows.................................341
Chapter 41 Strictly Robbery...348
Chapter 42 Driving With Miss Daisy............................360
Chapter 43 Truman, Can You Spare A Dime? 366
Chapter 44 Graduation 371
Chapter 45 College Bound...374

Dedication

When Momma and I would return home from a drive or wherever we had been, she would drive our blue Cadillac into the parking spot in front of our clock shop, turn off the ignition, and as she pulled out the keys, she would turn to me and say, "Home again, home again, jiggity, jig." We would both laugh.

This book is lovingly dedicated to my mother, Lela Priscilla Clayton Stone.

Thank you for the memories.

Lela Priscilla Clayton Stone

My mother, Lela, is pictured in her favorite black two piece suit with a long-sleeved white silk blouse. Her favorite accessory for this ensemble was always her string of pearls. This suit was mainly worn for special occasions, especially our trips to Joplin for a movie and dinner.

Betty, my sister, and I gave Momma a rhinestone star shaped pin for Christmas when I was four years old. Momma would sometimes add the pin to her suit to wear with the pearls.

I always thought she looked so very lovely.

Today, this picture is framed and sits lovingly by my daughter's desk at work. Momma would have been thrilled by that notion.

"But why had he always felt so strongly the magnetic pull of home, why had he thought so much about it and remembered it with such blazing accuracy, if it did not matter, and if this little town, and the immortal hills around it, was not the only home he had on earth? He did not know. All that he knew was that the years flow by like water, and that one day men come home again."

— Thomas Wolfe, You Can't Go Home Again

Chapter 1

Going Home

The dream comes lightly to me at early morning. I am walking up the street to my family home. It is early dusk, and there are no cars or people, other than me, in the dream. I can see my home standing just before me, waiting. I walk up the two steps in front of the shop, open the large screen door, and enter my father's clock shop. The only sounds I hear are the many clocks on the wall ticking. I see a cigarette burning as it sits dangerously on the tip of the ashtray. I walk through the shop down the hallway and turn right into the kitchen. All is quiet in the room as I turn to the left again and walk through the living room and into my childhood bedroom. I see my old iron bed with all the floral curls and blossoms. White with a colorful quilt lying on top, the bed looks comforting and warm. My room has an old white dresser and matching chest with a cedar hope chest placed at the foot of the bed. I stand and listen to the walls as if they could speak to me of past years. The old house is quiet and still as if waiting to welcome an old friend. I know that this visitor is myself, and I smile with delight at being home again. When I awake a few minutes later, I find that my face is wet as if I had been crying.

I know this dream has been lately replaying in my mind because I am feeling mixed emotions. I have not been home for some twenty years or more, and I have missed the older, past days of my youth. Now in these past days I have found a longing in my heart to return to my own home, or shall I say my own hometown, to see if I can relive my own memories of those past years. Yet I find that returning home comes to

1

me as a tough decision to make. On the one hand, I am excited to see my cousins, Janice and Doug, and their family. They are essentially the last of my family or relatives.

On the other hand, I am dreading my return. My mother had died some twenty years ago, and I had left Monett, my hometown, dusting the dust off my feet, so to speak, in an angry huff vowing to never, ever return. I had packed up my clothes, a few items that had belonged to my mother, grabbed Melissa, my daughter, by hand and walked out of the door, out of my home, and drove away from Monett. In those following days, I never even looked back.

I had not relented even when my heart had ached to be back among my old childhood neighbors and friends. I longed to call out their names to say hello and greet them with years of affections. I longed to see familiar homes and faces. Later, there were many times during my divorce when I wanted so much to reach for family members to receive comfort and security. It would have been so comforting to be able to have someone back home who cared about Melissa and me. But I didn't have the courage to reach for my father and ask for his help. I was too proud and too angry at all I had strived to escape from. I had succeeded to leave all behind, and now I had to pay for it.

All this brought me back to the reality of the fact that I had finally decided to go home for a week or so to visit. Arthur and I had made plans. I had called my cousin Janice and was set to spend the visit at her home. We had not seen each other for twenty-some years, and it was all sounding exciting. At least, one person or place still called to me to return. We were excited and I was nervous. As I packed our suitcases for the trip, I felt an old song slipping through my mind: "Going Home." Maybe you remember this song? I first heard it in the wonderful old movie *The Snake Pit* with Olivia DeHaviland. In this movie, Olivia portrays a woman who suffers a mental breakdown and at the end of the movie, having won her battle, she is going home. The song "Going Home" was played at that time, and I always loved the simplicity and comfort of that song. As I packed our bags, I was needing some of that old country comfort, and so I was humming and alternating quietly singing various lines to the old song: "I am going home . . ."

"Lots of folk gathered there, all the friends I knew.
All the friends I knew, I'm just going home . . . ."

So now we were on the trip to my home—Arthur, my husband, and me. As we sat down in the seats of our airplane, adjusting the seat buckles and settling down for the flight home, my mind swarmed with images of the past. I smiled at Arthur and told him it was exciting to be taking this trip. He returned my smile as he thought of the new journey. It was an adventure to him. To me, the trip seemed like a ponderous journey into the past. My mind was racing through images as if I were watching a slideshow. Images jumped back and forth from present to past as I saw my home, my father and mother, friends, various locations in Monett, all in my mind. These images were playing on the wall of my brain. No sounds, just images whizzing by in my mind as I attempted to act normal behavior at the beginning of the flight home. These pictures were a pain: a smile, a tear, a heartbeat.

Because Arthur had never seen the Midwestern states, we decided to fly from Winthrop, Massachusetts, to St. Louis, Missouri, and from there, we could take a bus to Springfield, Missouri. There Janice and Doug, her husband, could pick us up and continue the journey on to Pierce City, where they lived, just outside of Monett, Missouri. So on this appointed day in May, 1999, we were now on the second leg of the journey, in a bus, traveling from St. Louis to Springfield, Missouri. Sitting in front of the bus, I leaned back on the headrest and looked around me at the landscape we were traveling through. I remembered the drive well from when I had lived in St. Louis teaching and would drive home to Monett, Missouri, for holidays and summer. It all looked pretty much the same as those younger days. Farmers looked like they had the very same cows and horses out in the fields eating grass from the last time I had been home some twenty years ago. Nothing seemed to have changed in this landscape. Also, the many little towns on the route going home seemed to have the same diner stops and gas stations as those past years had shown. It all looked about the same to me.

When we arrived at Springfield, Missouri, the bus was driven into the parking lot so we could all descend and gather our various luggage. I could see Janice and family waving to us. It was exciting to finally see a family member once again. I had never met Janice's husband Doug, and they had never met Arthur. Their son Nathan was present.

Arthur and I descended from the bus and hugged and greeted Janice and Doug and Nathan. Janice's other son Justin and his family would be by the house later, and we would meet them. It was so exciting to see each other and be able to talk. Soon we were just chatting and laughing together as if we had never been apart. It felt good to see my family members again, someone I remembered from so many years ago. We packed the suitcases into their waiting car and squished in together to continue the homeward trip on to Pierce City, while driving through Monett for a quick glimpse. It seemed we were all talking at once in the car, laughing and talking about our journey so far. As we got closer to home, Janice began to point out things to me that had probably changed since I had last been home. I was startled at what I was beginning to see.

Monett had changed. What had been a quiet highway, lying on the outskirts of Monett, was now a busy shopping and eating area on both sides of the lanes. The area was filled with cars, trucks, and people. I was amazed to see all this activity in what had been my sleepy little town when I had left. I struggled to recognize and take in all this activity where once there had only been farms and cows. As I tried to locate my memories and take in all the new locations, the first thing I looked for was my beloved Lakeland Restaurant, where I had worked summers during my college years. To my surprise, it was now a Mexican restaurant with piñatas, papier mache parrots, and sombreros hanging from the restaurant's ceilings. There were smells of refried beans and various spices rafting through the front shop. The aromatic smells filled the dining area. The offered menu smelled good as one entered, but it was different from what I had remembered from my days in Lakeland. I spoke to the owner and told him I had worked there when it was a family restaurant. He smiled and told me to look around. Upon going through the sliding doors at the end of the coffee shop, I discovered that the dining room had now become a video game room. I was amazed to see all the blinking lights and hear the sounds in what had been the solemn and decorated dining room. Even though the food smelled good, I felt it was time to leave. I was saddened to find a different place from what I had remembered. I wanted to see all my old friends still working there and greeting me as if the past twenty years had not even gone by. I had thought in my mind that all would stay the same. I was now learning that those thoughts were greatly wrong. Nothing had stayed the same. Standing there, I could still hear echoes of voices from the past, with laughter and chatter from the customers. I could smell the steaks sizzling from yesteryear and Dale ringing the bell for the waitress to come get the order while it was hot. But none of those

Lakeland Restaurant

I found this nostalgic picture of Lakeland Restaurant from the late 1960s-1970s. Elinore and Floyd VanDerhoef (we always called him Van) owned and operated this lovely restaurant, Lakeland, during the years I was in college. I worked there from 1962-1965. I would come home on weekends and work every shift I could get to make monies to spend during the week.

I also worked there all summer during these years. Elinore hired most of their wait staff from college students home for the summer which made for great friends and a super working atmosphere. We girls all became fast friends and have even remained friends to each other to this day through emails and Facebook. I was always amazed I kept my job because of my many accidents - spilling food or drinks on customers, or dropping plates of food.

I cannot begin to tell you of all the accidents I incurred in that restaurant during my working hours.

But, Elinore persevered and kept giving me more chances. I really appreciated the VanDerhoef family for those days of employment. It was an excellent opportunity.

aromas or sounds were still there. It was interesting to now see the difference in decoration and style. I had remembered Lakeland with an elegant dining room and quiet décor while now I was seeing the lovely Lakeland restaurant through a different character. It wasn't bad—just not what I had remembered and hoped to see. I was feeling nostalgic for my own memories. As I had said earlier, one can't go home again, and this trip was slowly proving it to me in many ways.

It all made me remember when I was a small child. As night fell, and it was time to go to bed, I would place my little dollies in the dolly bed and cover them to their chin by the blanket. I would then admonish each one with a kiss on their forehead that I was going to bed but that I would be back in the morning to wake each one up. I skipped off to my own bed as I knew I would be there in the morning to wake each one up to play. Well, when I had left Monett and kissed it good-bye, despite my promise I would be back, I had not returned, and I now found that unlike my little dollies, Monett had not waited faithfully for me. The people, the stores, and the general appearance of the whole area of Monett had changed. It had all gone on to grow without me.

We all gathered back into Janice's car and drove through the other shopping area and looked at the many stores that had been added. Then we turned around and headed back into Monett to drive down Broadway. It looked like Broadway to me, but I couldn't be sure because the stores had changed so much. There had been many changes with new owners and what was sold in the store. Some of the old standards had now retired or closed. Some had gone out of business. The little town was of another era. Also, five percent of the population of Monett was now Mexican, and the downtown stores were beginning to show more items in selection and décor of their interest, such as food and other shopping items. A few of the stores were now owned or operated by Mexicans. There were empty and boarded over shops. The populace seemed to have shrunk and were not shopping locally as much as before. Local people now had more access to cars so that they could drive to larger towns for their shopping. They claimed the larger stores offered cheaper prices and more choices. Whatever. I missed seeing all the local stores from my yesteryear.

Over on the right, I saw where the J.C. Penney's store was still opened. I had loved to go in there as a child in the late 1940s to shop with my mother. I would just stand and watch the business of the clerks

Downtown Monett

Downtown Monett as I remember from my years living there - 1942 -1965. I find great joy looking at this picture because it really depicts the Monett downtown as I remember it from my childhood. Our home was located up one block on Bond Street so we could easily take a walk downtown to do any shopping needed.

Mainly, I just walked down those streets of Monett and looked in the shop windows to make my wishlist for a certain item - a new coat or dress, shoes, or a toy from the Main Variety.

Townspeople were friendly and always greeted each other. Many stopped to chat about recent developments in their lives.

There was a peaceful and comfortable setting to enjoy while shopping.

On Saturday afternoons, Momma and I would often walk down to the Main Variety store and treat ourselves to twenty-five cents worth of orange slices or some chocolate delight. Sometimes we would really splurge and buy a fifty cent bag of hot mixed nuts.

We also enjoyed browsing through the packages of embroidery kits in the Main Variety and purchasing kits to sew later during the evenings at home.

working in the store. It was like being inside a huge spider's web. There were no cash registers on the first floor for payments. The whole first floor showed the merchandise, and various sales clerks were in locations to assist. When customers purchased items from J.C. Penney stores with balconies, such as the one in Monett, downtown, the sales clerk would take the customer's money and place it with a bill of sale, inside a closed container attached to a cable line. This was called a "cash carrier." The carrier would then be cabled up to the balcony overlooking the sales floor, where another associate would retrieve the cash before sending the container back down with a receipt and correct change. There were no cash registers nor any money collected on the first floor, or sales floor. Instead, the clerks would write a receipt for a purchase, collect the monies to pay for the item, and place the two things into a small black cash carrier that was attached to wires leading up to the second floor where the cashiers worked. The assistant on the second floor would make change and then place the box back on the wire and send it whirring back down to the person selling the item. It was fascinating to stand and watch these many little black boxes whirring up across the ceiling to the person on the second floor and then whirring back down to the first floor for settlement with the shopper. What a blur of activity there was to watch—imagine all these little boxes zooming along, back and forth, speeding along over small, almost transparent cable lines, first floor to second floor and vice versa. Quickly zooming along. It was fascinating to stand and watch these many little black boxes whirring up across the ceiling to the person on the second floor and then whirring back down to the first floor for settlement with the shopper. I could stand for hours and watch this happening. On the top floor, in the balcony, there was always one very stern older woman standing resolutely in the balcony watching as boxes flew up and down. She was always keeping an eagle eye firmly on the girls as they made change and returned the change to the customer. I was sure that not even one tiny iota of an item could miss her eyes. She was like an eagle. In the 1950s, this was all replaced by cash registers at locations on the first floor. I missed those "cash carriers."

Also, Saturdays downtown had always been interesting to watch during the day with the arrival of farmers and their families to shop. They would get their chores done early and then head into town for various errands to accomplish. The old cars and trucks would arrive

Home Again, Home Again, Jiggity, Jig

early in the morning with the womenfolk spreading out through the town to shop and chat. The menfolk would be coming into town to wait and visit together as their wives shopped in the stores and purchased needed grocery items. The farmers would gather at the local feed shop down by the Greyhound Bus Station or stand by the lampposts in the center of town. There they would gather wearing their denim overalls, shirts, boots and old straw hats or aged felt hats, tattered and worn by the elements of the years. These hats seldom left the farmer's head, and each person exhibited what was called a farmer's tan. Each farmer was tanned or red on the neck and face where the hat did not offer shade. If they took off their hat, their head would be exposed as pale on top. The head was pale because it was usually covered by hats in the daytime sun. Often, as they talked, one of the farmers would turn his head aside and spit a wad of tobacco juice on the street gutter. The wives would appear in simple cotton housedresses and often, as not, a small hat on their head. The women would often be carrying parcels they had purchased. Walking over to their various parking spots, the women would place the packages in the back of the old Ford truck so their hands were free to go do some more shopping. Many would go "window shopping" as they called it. Money was scarce in those days, no credit cards designed yet, so one spent only what monies one had to spend. Farmers stood beside the local bank there on the main street. They would come to deposit their "egg money" or withdraw monies to shop and pay with. Today, the street was mostly empty, no farmers or wives on the corner talking. People were passing by each other and on their way to manage some errand they might have. No longer was there the corner pharmacy where one could enter and sit at the booths or on the stools at the counter. There the jukebox would be loudly playing while people sat and enjoyed a malted or a banana split. My own favorite was a cherry coke. This refreshing delight was a soft drink and ice with a squirt of cherry juice added. This was great to quench the thirst.

Standing there in the center of downtown, looking down the street, I could just see Moss Market, still there in Monett and thriving. Mr. Moss had accomplished much with the beginning of his store from small wooden carts where he sold fresh fruit and vegetables. When Moss Market had been built, it was a needed addition to our town. Years later, in the 1970s, other markets had come into Monett and had lured my mother and Aunt Rena away from Moss Market because of the stamps

Moss Market

Here is Moss Market as I remembered it while I lived in Monett. You could go there any time and get an item that you needed. Many times, after getting off from work at the summer drive-in, Momma and I would drive here and park in the lot and I would go in and get us each a cold Dr. Pepper in bottle form to sit and drink while we relaxed. There was always someone that we knew going in or coming out for us to say hello to. It was just always a busy place and seemed to be a center of the hub of activity.

It was truly a Monett fixture at the time.

the grocery stores gave to their customers. For each amount of groceries one customer would buy, a value of stamps to save and place into books were given to them by the store. When the stamp books were filled, the customer could submit these collected and stamped books for items available in the store. Momma kept her completed books in a shoebox hidden under the bed until redemption time for some gifts for me. Actually, I recall that my mother presented to Chuck and me, at my wedding, a complete place settings for eight of lovely white china. These lovely patterned dishes were my special dishes for companies and holidays. She also gave me a complete eight place settings of my everyday dishes, Blue Willow, with matching blue glasses. Every dish available in the eight place settings had been saved for through these grocery stamps and presented to me from Momma. My aunt Rena gave me a complete set of silverware for eight to be used for every day. She had also saved her stamps from the store to obtain the items. I loved the dishes and the idea that Momma was able to obtain all these beautiful gifts for me through her own steadfastness savings and determination. It was a proud moment for her when she presented me with the place settings of dishes. If one had spent monies in a store for these items, it would have been a very expensive shopping. But Momma had been able to accomplish this without spending any monies. Momma was proud she had been able to accomplish such a task. I was proud of her also.

A little further down from the Moss Market, across the street from a gasoline station, was our favorite diner. Salads were their specialty. I don't think I ever ate anything other than their fantastic salads at the Black Kettle. The restaurant was located in a small white building, where one entered to find a dining room with a bar. Then when you ordered your Black Kettle Salad, you were in for a treat. A salad served with chucks of roast beef and cheese and fresh slices of rye bread and butter was mighty good eating. The dressing on the salad seemed to be what completed the taste. To this day, I don't believe I have ever eaten a salad as good as the Black Kettle. Momma, and I would meet there for lunch on Saturdays or an evening late after work. A cold mug of beer rounded out the meal perfectly.

I was happy to see the Black Kettle was still there and open so that we could once more delight in their salad before returning home. Janice had promised that we would treat Arthur to the famous salads. And to my excitement, Aunt Rena would be able to join us.

A block down from the Black Kettle Restaurant was a small, rather dingy-looking bar. I was always amazed that the fellow town members allowed the bar to be open right there in the town, among the other shops, such as the clothing stores and diners. But it was open day and night and seemed to keep a pretty dedicated number of customers. I had never been in this bar—it was too dark and scary to me. But on this particular day I was remembering, I almost once had to go into the bar. In the story, it was a Sunday morning, around 10:30 a.m. I was to work the lunch crowd that morning at Lakeland, and I had overslept. I was desperately rushing around to get dressed and on the way to Lakeland to work. I was sure Elinor would be furious that I was late. Momma was gone on an errand and would not be returning in time to take me to work. So Dad called me a taxi. The cab arrived quickly, and I slipped into the backseat readjusting my hair and gathering my purse and apron and putting on my tennis shoes as the cab pulled off to my destination. After putting on my shoes, I sat up and looked in the front seat. I saw a young man driving the cab and a younger woman sitting in the middle of the cab. She turned around and said a giggly hello to me. I responded hello back to her. The cab had turned down left from my house and was soon on the main street of Monett heading through the center and out to my work, Lakeland, or so I thought. Suddenly, without any warning, the cab turned and proceeded to stop in front of the small little dark bar there on Broadway, among all the other stores and shops. The cab driver parked the car, pulled out the keys, and turned to smile at me. "Me and my gal will be back in about ten to fifteen minutes," he explained and began to get out of the cab.

Startled, I yelled, "What?" in my most incredulous voice. I asked the driver what he was doing as I watched the girl also get out of the cab and walk over to join him on the sidewalk. The driver leaned into my window and said, "Now this is my first date with my little sugar here, and I promised to take her for a beer. We are going to run in here and have a nice cold beer, and then we will be right out and take you on to the Lakeland Restaurant." Again, I shouted, "What?" too dumbstruck to be able to tell my brain any other word to speak. "Listen, Mr. Cab Driver," I hollered, "I have to get to work. I am late already."

"Don't worry, little lady, we will be back in ten to fifteen minutes latest, I promise." And with that, he winked at me, grabbed his new girlfriend by the waist, and off they went into this small dark bar to have a cold beer while I waited out in the hot cab, sitting and fuming in the backseat, beginning to sweat and get uncomfortable.

I flopped back onto the backseat and sat and waited, staring at my watch as the second hand traveled brightly around the clock face. Time was not moving slowly, and I had to get to work. Elinor did not tolerate lateness. Ever. I had just about decided to go into the dark, dank bar where no electric lightbulb had ever seen light, when out walked the cab driver and his gal, arm in arm and all giggly together. They got into the car, and as the cab driver began to pull away from the parking spot and head on out, he turned to me and winked again and said, "I promised you no more than fifteen minutes." And off we zoomed to Lakeland, my workplace, as I sat in the backseat, feeling all sweaty, exasperated, and very wrinkled. Pulling up to the front of Lakeland, I quickly grabbed my purse and paid the driver, got out of the backseat, and started toward the front entrance of Lakeland. As the cab pulled away from me, I heard the girlfriend giggle and wave good-bye to me, and off they left in a dust cloud. Now I was dusty, disheveled, hot and sweaty, as well as in trouble for being late. I wanted to throttle that cab driver and his new little playmate.

Elinor was waiting at the front and hustled me into her office. She took one look at me and asked what had happened. I told her about my cab driver and his date, and she started laughing until she was crying. Soon, we were both laughing and trying to get me squared away to start working in the restaurant. Elinor told me, "From now on, just call me and I will send a car for you. No more bar stops for you!" To this day, I still remember sitting out in that cab waiting for the driver and his date. After that experience, when we called a cab, I would say, "Make sure the driver is not dating a new girl!" No one understood but I did. And now here I was, standing on the same spot, facing that same little dark bar.

Janice had earlier told me that the Gillioz Theater was gone; in fact, that whole block had changed. I would not have even known I was in Monett at that area if Janice had not confirmed it to me. I was really saddened to see that lovely old theater gone. I had worked there all though high school and attended movies there since I could walk in the door. That theater had been another home to me. My sister and my mother and my cousins, Betty and Janice, had all worked there. I loved that theater and its incredibly beautiful carpet, decorations, and colors. It was all gone now, just a memory also. I was so saddened by

Downtown Monett (second view)

This is a picture of Monett from my return visit in the late 1990s. On the left the old Monett Hotel had been torn down and replaced by a bank.

Also, the Gillioz Theater (further down the street) had been torn down. The loss of the theatre so changed the look of the whole street. On the right, at the front of the picture, on the first floor of the gray blue building, there was a book and magazine store (1960s) owned and managed by the Fleming sisters. Momma worked there during the day and it was a much easier job than her days in the Best Cleaners. I first met the Fleming sisters when they had their shop up across the street from the Post Office. Anytime I got a nickel I would walk down to their shop to get long, black licorice whips. We used them to play Lash LaRue cowboy games. (Lash never carried a gun, just a long black whip.) The candies were usually too old and tough to eat.

I don't think the ladies ever lost one penny on any item in the store. If the candy bar got old, they cut it up in pieces and sold each piece for a penny to customers. Usually children with a penny to spend bought the candy pieces.

I swear, in their old shop, the ladies only had one light bulb that hung from the center of the room and it was so dark in there. The sisters wore black dresses with black sweaters, winter or summer, with their hair up in a bun on their head.

Children were only allowed two minutes in the store to make a selection and then out. No hanging around there! The Fleming sisters were always good to Momma and she enjoyed working for them. The Sinclair Photography shop was next door. In 1967, I had my engagement picture made there.

the need to pull the whole building down and destroy it. It had been so incredibly beautiful in design and style. I remembered that when inside and I had entered the lobby or the women's lounge upstairs, I always felt I had arrived in some fancy ornate castle. It was so incredibly beautiful. I loved to go upstairs to the women's lounge and just sit and watch the lovely ladies come in to adjust their hats or hair and apply new lipstick. Everything was so glamorous and beautiful. And now it was only memories. Nothing to remind a person it had even been there at one time. It made that corner of the block look so empty and desolate.

I stood and looked down the block to the other corner. At the other end of the block had been the fine old Monett Hotel. I never was too sure who had stayed in the hotel as I don't think we had many business conferences or tourists. But all the same there it was, a large two- or three-floor building that housed hotel rooms and a large fine dining room where the finest always ate their Sunday lunch or dinner. I had never eaten there. I am not too sure that I had ever been in the hotel. An older girl in high school would always talk about the hotel as her parents owned the building. She could often be seen going in at dinnertime to eat her dinner.

Later when I was in high school, I noticed that on the side of this large building, the Monett Hotel, there was an annex off the side. It looked like it had been built as an afterthought. Actually, unless you walked around to the side of the building and looked for it, one could pass by and not even notice that the annex was there. The small attached building had a door leading into what looked like a small café. It could hold a few people in the shop while the waitress stood behind the counter.

At the time I noticed this annex, I was in high school and working in the small ice cream shop there across the street from the Monett Hotel. I was working there during the summer days and enjoying serving the hamburgers and ice cream treats to our customers. Business was often slow, and one day in particular, I happened to notice a black man walking up the street from the railroad station down the street from where I was in the ice cream shop. I stared as I had not ever seen a black person in my town or any of the stores. Certainly, there had never been a "colored" person in one of our restaurants. On this day, I observed a tall, dignified-looking black man dressed as a conductor in a black suit and maroon-trimmed hat that was often known as required for wear by

AREA RESIDENTS HAVE watched with sorrow as the once grand Gillioz Theatre has been razed to make way for an expansion by its neighbor to the west, United Savings and Loan. Constructed in 1931 at a cost of $100,000, the exterior of the Georgian Colonial structure featured intricately carved Carthage stone trim. Urns of the stone, which had graced the corners of the central area and both annex areas, were not salvaged, but much of the other stone work, representing what is now nearly a lost art, was removed intact by the members of Danny Vaughn's crew, contractors for the razing.

Gillioz Theatre Torn Down

My mother sent me this newspaper clipping from The Monett Times denoting the tearing down of the Gillioz Theatre in 1987.

Built in 1931 at the cost of $100,000, this beautiful theatre had been a large part of my early years. My sister Betty, two cousins, Betty and Janice, Momma and myself had all worked at this theater at one time in our lives.

The insides were beautifully decorated with plush carpets and drapes, vivid colors and ornate grillwork. It seemed that I spent most of my early life sitting in that darkened theatre watching those delightful old movies of yesteryear - cowboy movies with singing cowboys and their comedy sidekicks, or magnificent epics of Ben Hur or Ten Commandments.

It filled me with great sadness to see that lovely old theater gone forever. It had been my magic carpet to other countries and other lands.

the railroad. When I saw the man, he was walking up the street from the railroad station down at end of Fifth Street, at the end of Monett. Slowly, with determined steps, he whistled softly to himself, traveling up from the Railroad Station toward the Monett Hotel. I watched him as he crossed the street and entered the door to that annex. I could see him sit down. Immediately the waitress appeared and gave him a menu and a cup of coffee. He read through the menu and then placed it back on the counter and gave his order to the woman. A few minutes later, I saw him served a plate of food, and he began to eat, slowly, sitting there alone. After he had finished, he stood up, and the waitress appeared. He paid her, placed his hat back on his head, and came out of the door to the annex. The waitress had gone back into the other side of the hotel after she had cleaned his dishes up from the counter and cleaned where he had eaten.

Still standing inside the ice cream shop where I worked, I watched the man as he walked across the street and started heading back down to the railroad station. There the train was parked for the night. He would probably sleep the night in the train and leave with it as it pulled out early in the morning with customers and baggage being shipped. I looked over at the clock and noticed that it was just five o'clock, an hour or so before beginning sunset. It was the first time I had seen a black man in Monett, and it had roused my curiosity. Why I had not ever seen such a thing? Actually, I realized, I had not really ever seen a black man or woman in this area. It's not something one thinks about if one is not aware of it. I was not. I had never given it a thought as to why all the townspeople were white. They just all were. That was the way Monett was. I had never thought of other people of color or nationality. Of course, when we went to Springfield or Joplin, there were different people. But it wasn't so in Monett. That was just the way it was. No one striving to get in and no one striving to get out. It was just settled and that was life in Monett.

Thinking back, I remembered from what I had heard whispered in town when I was a teenager: "colored" people were not allowed in Monett after sunset. Of course, there were no written signs posted anywhere in the town nor any particular notation anywhere that would be a bearer of this news. There was no person walking through the town admonishing all "coloreds" to be out of town and gone. There were no "colored" people to admonish. I had just never seen any black people during my life in town. I think this notice of information was just known, by all people, black or white. I was surprised I had not found out about this matter until I was in my early teens. I had never noticed that people in our town were all white. Why would I notice? I had never known anything else and never really thought about it. And then one day, I did see a person of color in town, and he was walking on our street and entered the Monett Hotel. It had certainly struck me with surprise. I wondered why no one ever talked about this matter or remarked about it. It was as if the town had just been completely whitewashed, and that was the end of the matter.

Around this time in my life, I learned further as to why there were no black people in town and about what had occurred in the past years of Monett. A classmate in my grade was talking in history class and related what she knew about the reason there were no black people in Monett. She was talking to a few of us before the teacher had started the class. She said she knew it for a fact because her family had told her. We all shared disbelief, but we listened to what she had to say. She said that in the late 1800s, early 1900s, the victim, a young girl, had been on her way, walking to her church. She was walking from her parents' home in the country, down an old dirt road, and traveling to her beloved church that she devoutly attended each Sunday. On the way, she was attacked and killed. When she was found, her throat had been slit. The townspeople of Monett and surrounding towns were in shock. Who among them could have done such a horrible thing? She said that a newspaper added that she had fought valiantly to preserve her maidenly honor and had died chaste. The fact that she had not been sexually assaulted had caused the local women to gasp in thankfulness and to gossip among themselves. Suddenly, the townswomen were frightened at nighttime in a town that had not even locked their front doors. Once close and friendly, now neighbors were watching each other with questioning thoughts. Murder was spreading its evilness where once it had been thought to be incomprehensible.

Then began the rumbling whisper that the killer of this young woman had been a black man. Who he was, that wasn't brought up, just that the killer had been "colored." Surrounding community townspeople became riled up. People became angry. The men were fearful for their women and children. Who might be the next victim? Common sense and town law were not being looked at sensibly in any

HOME AGAIN, HOME AGAIN, JIGGITY, JIG   19

near town or the surrounding communities. Emotions were taking over the situation, and tempers were reaching the high point of boiling over the pot of racism and bigotry.

Blood boiled and the finger of guilt needed to point to someone. The unknown killer must be found and incarcerated to protect the honest, hardworking neighbors in the communities. And so, as a result, there were people riding through the countryside and rounding up "colored people" and their families. There were a few actual lynchings and much in the way of burning of homes. Local "colored people" were driven from their homes, and many barely escaped with their lives. Running with only their clothes on their backs, they left the lands surrounding the community. The "colored people" who survived this large uprising by the local white people had escaped into Joplin, Missouri, and over the borders into Oklahoma and Arkansas. When tempers had settled down and the "blood" had cooled, so to speak, there were no more "colored people" left in the surrounding communities. And so it had stayed right up during the days I lived in Monett in the 1950s. It was highly suggested that there be no colored people allowed in Monett after sunset.

With the railroad going right by Monett and our large station located at the side of Monett, there was one problem. Many of the people working the railroads were black people. Crewmembers on these passenger trains normally remained on duty for the entire run, including assigned meal and sleep breaks. When the train stopped in Monet overnight for repairs or routing, black people were on those trains. It was then settled that the black people could come up to Monett to eat from two establishments: the Monett Hotel and the ice cream shop where I worked. They were allowed to walk up and get their food and then to go back to the train they were working in. And they had better accomplish this movement before sunset. After sunset, no "colored people" were allowed. It was plain and simple. That was the way it was in Monett. Nothing written, just understood. Some people didn't know about it. It was not talked about. I had just heard it from a few people.

Now I stood there on Main Street looking at where that fine old building, the Monett Hotel, had been located, and it was gone. Just like the ruling that there could be no "coloreds" in Monett after sunset. Ironically it wasn't so much that the population had been changed with the addition of black people but the arrival of Mexicans up over the borders of Arkansas and into Monett to work in the chicken and turkey plant.

I took another look at the old ice cream shop where I had worked those summer days at the end of my high school years. That building was still standing in the same spot. I laughed how I was never able to accomplish making that little swirl on top of the ice cream.

While working in that ice cream shop those two summers, I became aware of a middle-aged man so named "Whistling Jeff." When the man was born, there were some problems in his birth that led him to grow up as a man-child. He was a grown man yet had the mind of a small boy. He was seldom seen except on Sundays when he attended his church with his mother. I was soon to learn that there were certain things that were very important to Whistling Jeff and that was his Bible, his church, his suit/tie, and paper cups.

So on Sunday afternoons, after church, his mother or uncles would drive him down to Broadway and let him walk the street by himself where he could look in the window shops and enjoy "peeks into our lives" in the downtown of Monett. He would be dressed in his suit and tie, usually from another era, given to him or donated by a used clothing shop. He took great pride in his striped tie and white shirt with his suit. With his hair slicked back, and dressed in his finest Sunday suit, while carrying his large family Bible, he would walk down the street stopping only to look in store windows. Often, passing people out on a stroll themselves would greet him and ask how he was doing. Shy in nature, he ignored them most of the time and just walked along quietly, whistling and peeking into the store windows. That was actually how he had gotten his nickname Whistling Jeff. You see, he loved to whistle. No particular tune, just various melodies of his own liking. Walking, whistling, and smiling, he enjoyed his Sunday outings. But then he would spy a paper cup lying there by the curb or in the street. He would quickly become so excited. Standing for a few minutes as if to judge this little cup, he would slowly walk over and place the cup there by the curb upright. Taking a step back, he would give a boisterous step forward and loudly jump on the paper cup. The now-flattened cup would make a large sound of "whoosh" with escaping air and explode in sound. Whistling Jeff would laugh with delight and then continue his own gait down the street until he spied another cup to jump on. The sound of the smashed cup gave him such a delight. It made one almost in the mood to try it oneself. Why not? He made it look like such fun. His excursion would be usually the two blocks down the main street, until he reached the ice cream store where I worked. Then his mother or uncle would be waiting for him. He would laugh and get into the car and go back home to have Sunday lunch. The Sundays were happy days for this man. I do have to add at this time that I never saw any youth or person taunt "Whistling Jeff" or tease him. Bystanders just enjoyed watching him jump on his paper cups. He had enjoyed his Sunday walk another day.

We then drove up the block to where my two-story home had stood all those many years. It hurt me to see that the building was completely gone. After Dad died, the house had been sold, and they had torn it down and built two small office buildings. I stood there looking at the two small buildings, and it was as if I had never even existed. There was no sign that I had ever lived there with my family. My name was not written into the sidewalk by the side of the house. In fact, there was no sidewalk. There was just gravel for cars to park by the buildings. No old oak trees in the backyard or the big rock fence at the end of our property. Nothing was there. It was as if I had never been there at 508 Bond Street. I had left no evidence that I had ever been there. It took a few minutes for the realization to really sink into my brain and to accept that there was no longer a building where I had lived. The home would just have to live on in my heart and the old memories. Past pictures jotted through my memories and my mind, of course, but no tangent object to reach out and touch. Where I stood, we had always parked our car or cars in front of the building which was Dad's clock shop and in back, our family home. I stood looking at the parking area and remembered when Momma and I would return from some trip or errand in our old Caddy. I was riding with Momma as we would pull up and park in front of the building, Dad's clock shop and our home, facing the building. As Momma turned off the car engine, she would always take a moment, turn to me, and say in a singing voice, "Home again, home again, jiggity-jig!" Well, here I was, jiggity-jig, but certainly not home again. The home was gone.

After some very sad moments of realization that my home truly was gone, we packed back into the car and I asked Janice to take us up to the house where we had first lived in Monett. There on the corner of Fifth

Picture of my home after remodeling and refurbishing

When I was living in St. Louis and teaching, 1980s, Momma wrote me that she and Dad had finally been able to start refinishing the outside of the house with new siding and paint. Momma and Dad were so proud of being able to refresh the house and make it more attractive.

I was so pleased the first time I was able to come home and could see all the improvements in person. It had taken many years of saving to accomplish these updatings.

Today, it is so easy for young people with their credit cards - but at this time, people used layaways or paid by cash. If one did not have the money, then one could not get the item. It was as simple as that. You just had to wait until you could afford something. With this matter, a person certainly knew the value of each little penny.

Momma had also been able to wallpaper and paint the rooms inside the house. Momma always loved having new wallpaper on the walls in each room.

Street and Cale Street, I saw our old house. It was the white two-story home where my family had first lived in the upper street apartment. I got out of the car and stood there looking at the white house where I had lived my early seven years or so. The house looked so much smaller now than I had remembered and was greatly in need of some fresh white paint. Looking up at the window on the side facing Cale Street, I could almost hear Momma hollering out my name, "Susie!" while telling me to be sure and stay where she could see me. That was a good memory. I sighed and then looked across the street ahead at the Beeler home and next to their home, my dear Presbyterian Church where I had attended Sunday School and church. A beloved location full of memories to me. Ironically the Beeler house was just how I had left it except it was very quiet now. No opening of the screen doors or Viola singing her church songs as the sounds wafted through the front windows. Looking closer at the church I saw that my old church had been modified and now welcomed a congregation of a different choice.

Slowly I turned to my right, and there, in the middle of the lot, across the street from my old childhood residence stood the large, two-story home where the Evans family had lived. How I loved that home, and I loved to visit all the people there; Mrs. Evans, Priscilla, Jimmy, Roberta, and little Joey. The memories came flooding back over me, and I could feel the early beginnings of my life surrounding me with such a magnanimous force. Suddenly I was right there again, aged four, sitting on the curb, waiting for Priscilla to come home from school. I stood quietly there by the curb and looked down. I could see myself, sitting there all young and eager, waiting and feeling surrounded by loved ones of my family and friends. I was sitting there on the curb waiting and hugging my precious cigar box close to me as I awaited Priscilla to come and get me.

Then I realized something. As if by magic, I suddenly knew why I was being called back to my childhood locations. I had to go back to the very beginning of my life or my family's lives. I had to understand who had come before me and why. What their story had been. This had to happen before I could truly begin these memories and follow my wandering thoughts of yesteryear. I had to begin with all the wonderful stories of days long before I was even born or thought about, of my family's families and how their lives had led through the years to my life. Then maybe I could better understand today and how my life had all come to this point.

You see, when I started to write this story, I didn't even know the name of my grandparents on my father's side or any of my great-grandparents. I knew nothing of where they came from or where the lives of these families had all started. How could I write about myself unless I knew where I had come from and who had proceeded me? I needed to know about them before I could tell the story of myself.

I became determined to learn about my family history as I set down early stories of my life. There was much to learn about during the days I was to visit Monett again. I thought of this matter as we journeyed on to Pierce City to begin our visit.

Photo of Monett taken during my return visit in the 1990s

A different view of Monett shown in a photo we took when we were on our return visit in the 1990s. It all seemed so different to me to return and look at.

So much growth and change. I still felt welcome and comfortable in my hometown Monett but I missed seeing the old familiar faces. I always liked walking into the stores and being spoken to by name from the clerks. The work staff would ask about my mother or how I was doing in school. I liked the closeness felt from a small community and the local people that I knew. Of course, everyone remembered that I wanted to be a school teacher and they would congratulate me on such a fine choice of a vocation. This would make me feel all the more determined that I had to succeed in attaining a college education to go and teach.

Chapter 2

I Have Ancestors?

To begin my life story, I believe Christmas is my favorite holiday in the world. Even when, as a child, my parents had few dollars for presents, I didn't really care. I just loved the whole season. I loved the music, the snow, the decorations, church celebrations, and most of all, the stories. There were stories from the Bible and a lot of stories in the books that were read to me each night. I must admit, now, that among these Christmas stories told to me, my favorite was the one about my birthday. My birthday story always made me feel very special and loved. It was a happening, a celebration, all to be just before Christmas arrived.

I was born in an old stone farmhouse that stood silently and gray beneath an early morning Christmas star. A light dusting of white snow lay on the ground. It was Sunday, December 20, 1942.

My mother, Lela, was the daughter of a Missouri-bred man and woman who had lived and worked small farms in the Ozark's land of hills and rocks. This had been their married life: long days of hard work with a small sense of accomplishment. I had been told stories that my grandmother, Ethel, had been from a wealthy family and had grown up in a fine large house with maids and servants. Her great-grandfather O.P. Johnson had owned and profited from his own local Johnson's Mill near the town of Spencer, Missouri. It was always said that grandmother Ethel had married beneath her when she married her husband, Marion Clayton, the son of local dirt farmers. My great-uncle often explained that his sister Ethel had married my grandfather Marion because she was enticed by what she had witnessed on her visits to his family farm. She liked the comradeship of his large family gathered all together at meals. It was pleasant to join Marion's nine brothers and sisters, with parents, John William Clayton and Martha Ellen Cantrell, sitting round the large kitchen table talking together and eating, loud and boisterous and filled with laughter. This was all opposite Ethel's own strict, quiet, formal upbringing where a "child was to be seen and not heard."

Once, when I was little, I remember Momma taking me to visit the woman who I was told was my great-grandmother, Priscilla. I was informed to sit quietly in the parlor and to not move or speak or even make one single little noise. I was as quiet as a mouse. While the house was sparkling clean in color and style and filled with colorful paintings, furniture, rugs, and knickknacks, I was instructed strongly that I was not to look up or touch anything in the house. I was so nervous during the whole visit I breathed a large sigh of relief when Momma and I were once again in our family car and heading home.

Many years later, I learned of another side of this ancestor, my grandmother's mother Priscilla Johnson (for whom my Momma had been named) and her husband John Gist, through a newspaper clipping. I recently found that my grandmother Ethel had very romantic parents, as evidenced by a poem John had published in a newspaper two years after Priscilla had died.

"Two long years, the fourth of March have dragged their weary way. Each day I think of you, My Dear, and the pleasant life we lived.

It won't be long, Priscilla Jane, to resume our happy Earthly life In our Heavenly Home Above.

The hours and days that drag so long Since you have gone away. Will seem but the length of a Robin's song

When I am with you again to stay. Sadly missed by John Gist."

I also found a snapshot of John taken at the time the poem was written. The picture shows John standing beside Priscilla's tombstone that listed her name with date of birth and death. Beside her grave is John's tombstone with his name, awaiting the later inscription upon the time of his death.

Photo of O.P. Johnson and wife, The couple pictured on the right are O.P. Johnson and Mary Ann P. Johnson

I do not know the couple pictured on the left side. On the right, O.P. Johnson was the early generation leader on my mother's side of the family.

O.P. and Mary Ann had sixteen children with two dying in childhood. O.P. made his early fortune in his mills on the land he acquired. O.P. and Mary Ann deeded two acres of property for the burial of Johnson family near his general store and the Antioch Church at the Antioch Cemetery. He accumulated considerable property and built large meal, flouring, and carding machine mills on Turnback Creek run by waterpower. This was later called the O.P. Johnson Saw and Woolen Mills in Paris Springs.

In 1869, O.P. Johnson discovered lead ore northeast of Mt. Vernon and did some prospecting.

I think the two men made a stately presence with their long beards, fashionable in those days. When O.P. died, he left no monies to his children. He figured they had gotten all they needed.

HOME AGAIN, HOME AGAIN, JIGGITY, JIG 29

After more readings, I loved that I found the story of my early family member, O.P. Johnson. First of all, to bear pride in his name and later to name his son O.P. Jr. also interested me. I confess, the name O.P. tickled me. Later, I actually found a picture of O.P. and his wife Mary Ann. He looked to be of strong fortitude and small humors. To reiterate the side of my mother's family, descending from farm laborers, millers, and shopkeepers were my mother's great-great-grandfather, Oliver Perry Johnson, known all his life as O.P. Johnson, and his son William Perry Johnson, later known as O.P. Johnson Jr. I continued to read that Johnson Sr. married Mary Ann Pilkerton in Tennessee, and at around 1849 he moved to Washington County, Arkansas, and remained there about a year and came to Lawrence County, Missouri, and settled near where Summit Church now is. Then he came to Mt. Vernon and established a carding machine on the public square, by permission of the authorities of the town. His carding machine was considered a public necessity as the wives, mothers, and sisters spun, reeled, warped, wove, and made all clothing worn by men, women, and children. The propeller of this carding machine was a large milch cow, which was led and tied on an incline wheel. When the rotation of the wheel began, the cow was compelled to keep stepping, which kept the machine in motion. Mr. Johnson continued his work here about seven years and left for the place where he remained the balance of his life. When he went to Turnback Creek some nine or ten miles northeast, he built a little corn mill, covered it with a shed, a sawmill, and carding machine. Johnson's mills were known for miles and miles and patronized by farmers near and far. He accumulated considerable property and built large meal, flouring, and carding machine mills on Turnback Creek run by waterpower. This was later called the O.P. Johnson Saw and Woolen Mills in Paris Springs. O.P. and Mary Ann had sixteen children, two dying when children. In 1869, O.P. Johnson discovered lead ore northeast of Mt. Vernon and did some prospecting.

The area near Turnback and Johnson Creek was called Johnson Mills for the five mills and businesses owned and operated by O.P. Johnson and family. Later, a resort hotel was built at the chalybeate springs and managed by Eli Paris, and the town was organized and platted as Paris Springs. The post office from Ozark Prairie was moved to Oliver Johnson's store, and that area became known as Spencer. In 1858, O.P. Johnson was a witness in *State v. James Price* for the murder of Edward Yancey Kimmons on the public square in Mt. Vernon.

Photo are daughters of O.P. and Mary Ann Johnson with granddaughter Gertrude

Back Row: Belle Johnson Clark, Mattie Ann Johnson Colley, Maggie Johnson Marrick, Elizabeth Johnson Welaford. Front row: Gertrude Johnson Merrick, Mary Ann P. Johnson (mother of daughters and wife of O.P.) with Gertrude Welaford, granddaughter.

Elizabeth J. Johnson   **Jacob L. Johnson**

Pictured is Elizabeth J. Johnson Welsford (1863-1932) with husband C.M. Welsford (1863-1900) The photo was taken in Mt. Vernon, Missouri.

Jacob L. Johnson is son of O.P. and Mary Johnson. Shown in picture with wife Lillian Gertrude Johnson. Photo was taken in Fresno, California.

Antioch Cemetery

O.P. Johnson deeded 2 acres of his land for a cemetery where the Johnson family may be buried.

On Decoration Day my family would drive down and spend the day cleaning the graves of our family members and decorating with flowers from our gardens. Grandma Ethel Clayton would always regale us with stories and tales of her family that were buried in the cemetery.

Around 1923, the old Highway 66 took part of the property, and the old church was torn down.

The graves of O.P. Johnson and his wife were moved to Rock Prairie Cemetery in Halltown.

A town truck was brought in to lift the caskets. O.P.'s casket was full of water, and they hoisted it on end to drain it before loading it onto the truck.

His wife Mary Ann's casket was completely dry. The lid fell off during the process, and a perfectly preserved flower was found in her hands which were folded across her chest.

Antioch Church

The Antioch Church or the Little Brick Church is on the land deeded by O.P. Johnson for the cemetery.

When we arrived at the old cemetery, Grandma would point out the old brick church (as it was called) that her grandparents had built and that she had attended as a child. Then we would go inside the large entrance and begin to clean and rake the leaves from the old graves to ready them for the flowers. We would all spread out and work in areas. By noon, all the graves would be clean once again and decorated with all the flowers we had brought along. Then we would spread out a large blanket on the ground under a shady tree to enjoy all the good food Momma and Aunt Rena had prepared for us.

Today, I am happy to say that my cousin, Janice and family, still continue this family tradition and visit the graves to clean and decorate.

My mother, Lela, in younger years

My mother, Lela, is shown holding a neighbor child in front of farm where my grandparents lived at that time.

No electric lights or indoor plumbing, it was early to bed and early to rise every day with hard work on the farm. If they didn't raise it or make it, they didn't have it!

With no indoor plumbing, I always made Betty, my cousin, escort me to the outhouse, a toilet located in a small shed outside the house. This one was located behind the house. Betty had to stand outside the door to make sure no snakes were around. And then I kept a large stick to take with me inside the privy to protect me from spiders. It was a scary endeavor to go to the bathroom in those days!

In 1885, O.P. Johnson and his wife deeded two acres of property for the burial of the Johnson family and the Missionary Baptist Church, known as the Antioch Church, near Johnson's store.

At the age of eighty-one, O.P. Johnson (born September 5, 1826, in Tennessee) died March 29, 1908, and was buried at the Antioch Cemetery, on his own land and near his residence. In his will and last testament, O.P. Johnson gave nothing to his children. He said he had already done for each and every one of them all he had desired and intended but that the payment of debts and funeral expenses were to be equally shared among his children. He did leave his grandson, Walter Clark, fifty dollars. Truthfully, I don't think the children were surprised and did not really expected to inherit from O.P. What happened to his fortunes were not further noted. I'm hoping his widow, Mary Ann, was well tended.

At around 1923, the old Highway 66 took part of the property, and the old church was torn down. The graves of O.P. Johnson and his wife were moved to Rock Prairie Cemetery in Halltown. A town truck was brought in to lift the caskets. O.P.'s casket was full of water, and they hoisted it on end to drain it before loading it onto the truck. His wife Mary Ann's casket was completely dry. The lid fell off during the process, and a perfectly preserved flower was found in her hands which were folded across her chest.

After all these thoughts of old family ancestors, my thoughts now turned to memories of our Decoration Day. For this particular time, we were on the way to clean and decorate the graves of all the Johnson family buried at the Brick Church Cemetery. One of the traditions of yesteryear that we have lost with our continued rush through the day and loss of family traditions is a day chosen from the Memorial Day weekend. When I was young, we called it Decoration Day. The Friday or Saturday chosen for our travel would be in May, after the spring flowers had bloomed so you could gather flowers to take to the graves. My mother and Aunt Rena would decide what day we would drive to the Rock Prairie Cemetery, Spencer, Missouri, where my grandmother's family was buried on the land her grandfather O.P. Johnson had donated for all Johnson family to be buried. This was a big family day and took days of preparation. First, Momma and Aunt Rena would determine what flowers to pick and take. They both had grown rows of lovely flowers: peonies, roses, daisies, lilacs, ferns, and

Queen Anne lace. For several days, to prepare, we had begun to collect the flowers, wrap the ends in wet newspaper, and place them in canning jars of cold water. All these bouquets of flowers were placed in the trunk of the car. That morning, early, Momma and Aunt Rena prepared the day's picnic lunch of fried chicken (Momma killed and plucked the chickens from our backyard), an enormous bowl of homemade potato salad, jars of pickles, olives, carrots and celery, dozens of cookies and a large double-layered chocolate cake (baked from scratch and frosted early that morning), homemade loaves of bread, and a chest filled with chipped ice. Mason jars were also packed to drink cold, icy springwater from the well near the cemetery. We would load the food into the car and pack in Momma (who drove), Aunt Rena, Grandma Ethel, Betty and Maureece (Aunt Rena's children and my cousins), and myself, and off we drove in our old Ford jalopy to make the two-hour drive down to Spencer, set back in the Ozarks down dusty roads to arrive at the cemetery about 9:00 a.m. It was an excursion not soon to be forgotten each year. All of us packed together in the old car with food, flowers, and Grandma Ethel continually talking about everything in the world that made absolutely no sense to any of us. It was a family event.

Along the way, Grandma Ethel regaled us with stories of her family and ancestors who had lived on farms in the area. She always loved to tell the story of her husband's grandfather, who was sitting at Sunday supper with his family. Disturbed by sounds of a ruckus, he had gone to his front door because of shouting and shooting and a lot of yelling. When he opened the door, he was to face a group of men from a battered and ragged guerrilla Yankee troop of men who were passing by the farm and were hungry. As the gentleman being discussed stepped through the door to shout at the men to get off his land, one of the Yankee men shot him dead right through his forehead. The gentleman fell dead right on his own front steps. The soldiers grabbed various chickens and a pig and rode off.

This gentleman was buried on his farmland. Years later when the state, while building highways, came through the area and purchased this ancestral farm, they made ready to move the graves on to the Brick Church Cemetery, where members of the Johnson family were buried.

Ethel and Marion Clayton with you children

Pictured are my grandparents as a younger Marion and Ethel Clayton. My mother (Lela Priscilla) is shown sitting on her father's knee and there are the two brothers Roy and John shown. Note the boy's dress with the shirts and large bows. This was popular in those days for young boys dressed in fashion popularized from the novel, Little Lord Faulteroy, by Frances Burnett. Grandma Ethel was very proud of her small waist, as can be seen in the picture. Sorry to say, the small waist disappeared after the birth of six children. Five of those children survived. The last child, Muriel, lived one day, 1936. Later, I was born on this farm delivered by Grandma Ethel with Grandpa Marion holding the kerosene lamp.

Ethel and Marion Clayton (later years) with family on farm

Photo of Clayton family on porch of farm house - First row shows Ethel Clayton, with Rena and Raymond (nicknamed Dinky later shortened to Dink) in center and Marion Clayton on end. Back row are John, Lela (my mother) and Roy Clayton. Hard work and low economy tells on the faces of Ethel and Marion. Always renting the property and many moves, Grandpa Marion was never able to earn enough monies to buy his own farm.

Family members said Marion died because he was just "plumb worn out!" Momma explained to me that the farms where they had lived had always been rented property. Grandpa never could amass enough money to buy a farm or property of his own. Grandpa Marion was slim with brown eyes and dark brown hair. During his lifetime, he worked as a farm laborer for Frank Cherry in Mt. Vernon, Missouri. He was a simple man. Grandpa was registered for the World War I draft, 1917-1918.

It was recorded that when he signed the census, September 12, 1918, he signed it with an "X."

At the time of this particular gentleman's opening of his grave, the old wooden casket was accidentally dropped by the crane workers when they tried to lift the casket and move it. The old wooden coffin fell open to reveal the elderly gentleman in death repose. Much to the surprise of the present workers and present family members, the collapsed coffin revealed the corpse to be in excellent shape as if he had been buried only the day before rather than so many years earlier. In fact, the family members swore that you could still see the musket hole straight there in the middle of the forehead of the dead ancestor as when he had been shot that fateful day. We would all squeal with delight at the story, and Grandma would laugh.

When we arrived at the old cemetery, Grandma would point out the old brick church (as it was called) that her grandparents had built and that she had attended as a child. Then we would go inside the large entrance and begin to clean and rake the old graves to ready them for the flowers. We would all spread out and work in areas. By noon, all the graves would be clean once again and decorated with all the flowers we had brought along. It was a joyous sight to behold to see the graves looking loved and revered again. We were establishing spiritual connection between the present and earlier generations through the cleaning and decoration, or so it seemed to me. I just know it made me feel proud of our accomplishments.

Then Momma and Aunt Rena would spread the large blanket they had brought out on the ground, and we would all dig into the packed food and drink gallons of cold springwater from the mason jars. It was a wonderful day together filled with memories and a day of reverence. Later, we would pack everything back up and begin our journey back home. Betty, Maureece, and I would often nod off to nap, tumbled together as little tired puppies. Sometimes we would awaken to hear Grandma Ethel continuing in her patter of talk while Momma drove home talking and laughing with Aunt Rena. It was a gentle remembrance of a loving day.

As I look back upon these childhood trips and visits, I can understand how Grandpa Marion's family gave Grandma Ethel a sense of belonging and love. Studying the photo taken on the day of my grandparents' marriage, I see a young and hopeful bride standing by a man whom she has chosen to fulfill her life with purpose and love. Romantic also, they had chosen to be married on Valentine's Day, February 14, 1914.

Aunt Rena in her early years

On the right is pictured my Aunt Rena, Momma's sister, in her early years before her marriage and going to California to live. She is pictured with some friend, probably out on a Sunday journey.

Aunt Rena was always a part of our family and she and Momma were very close as sisters. I would hear them talking in low voices and then just giggling as young teenagers when they got together. I liked that for Momma. I honestly believe they saw each other almost every day. They always had something to talk about to each other. One could hear Aunt Rena say, "Now, Lela, do you really think…. or did you know…." Aunt Rena always had a specific way that she stood, arms folded in front and she would shake her head while talking. Often, on Sunday afternoons, Momma and I would drive out to Rena's home and join all the family for a home cooked dinner. It would be a nice visit.

But I also recognized a face on my grandfather that had already begun to show signs of weariness from endless tasks of life to accomplish. He was seemingly already worn by the cares and times of his earlier life with his family as a dirt farmer. I wondered if perhaps he also knew that he would never be able to fulfill his new wife's yearnings and quest for life. Perhaps it was too daunting a task for him to carry on his shoulders. In later pictures, I see that I was right in my early supposition of my grandfather. Both grandparents, Ethel and Marion, are posed in front of their small and rented country home and farm, looking worn and wrinkled, frazzled with a visual loss of her hopefulness and his energy. For whatever reason, over the years, the marriage of my mother's parents had proven to be physically hard and often unsuccessful. Life had not chosen to be kind to my grandparents.

Momma explained to me that the farms where they had lived had always been rented property. Grandpa never could amass enough money to buy a farm or property of his own. Grandpa Marion was slim with brown eyes and dark brown hair. During his lifetime, he worked as a farm laborer for Frank Cherry in Mt. Vernon, Missouri. He was a simple man. Grandpa was registered for the World War I draft, 1917–1918. It was recorded that when he signed the census, September 12, 1918, he signed it with an "X."

Coming from a more genteel family, raised with maids and expensive surroundings, Grandma always seemed to be looking for a better place, a greener pasture, so to say. Each time when they seemed to be just struggling to their feet, Grandma would begin to pack their meager belongings in boxes and make them move to another farm, another location. This made it even harder for Momma's family to ever succeed because they never stayed long enough at any one farm for Grandpa Marion to see a profit. The family always said that Grandma's constant moving and fretting wore my grandfather "plum" down. In 1951, at the age of sixty, Grandpa collapsed while outside at the farm. He died in the hospital in Monett. They said he was just worn out.

Momma was born in 1919 and lived through economically hard times, including the Depression. Born to Ethel and Marion Clayton, she had two older brothers, John and Roy; one younger brother, Raymond; and one younger sister, Rena. Actually, Raymond was always known as "Dinky" so nicknamed by his older brothers because he was so small. Soon the name Dinky was shortened to Dink, and that was his name for the rest of his life. No one seemed to know him by any other name except Dink.

Momma once sadly told me about how one brother had died shortly after birth when she was just a young girl. She, and my aunt Rena, always talked with great sadness about the passing of this tiny infant boy. Momma said she was holding him in her arms when he stopped breathing and his little soul passed on. She felt so sad that such a small little baby never even had a chance for life. The baby was named Muriell and lived January 24, 1936, to the next day, January 25. The baby was buried in the Johnson graveyard on a parcel of land that had been set aside by Ethel's Johnson family, O.P. Johnson, so that any person in the Johnson family may be buried there at no cost.

Following the death of the infant, Momma's sister Rena said that she and her father, Marion, drove the horse and wagon down the country road that day to the Johnson gravesite where the newly buried infant lay. In the back of the wagon was a granite tombstone that the father, Marion, had purchased to place on top of the baby's grave. When they arrived at the site, Rena and her father Marion, they could not find the man who was to carve the baby's name and life date on the tombstone. So Rena said that she and her father Marion carried the tombstone over to the grave. There, on that cold wintry day in January, they both worked and struggled to carve the infant's name and date of birth on the tombstone. They used what tools they had in the wagon. It took hours in the wintry wind, but Rena said that her father was determined that the tombstone would be carved that day. He was so worried that the baby would be forgotten. Today, you can still see the small tombstone with the hand-carved lettering, crudely chiseled in the stone, denoting the infant's name and small life on this earth. This was to be the last child for my grandparents.

The three boys in the family learned young in life about chores and working a farm. From their early years, they were busy from sunrise to late evening working beside their father. Momma and her sister were inside helping their mother to clean, cook, preserve, and prepare food. They sewed and made all their clothes. Their blankets were quilted in evenings from squares of material that had previously been their clothes and were now worn out. Nothing was thrown away or wasted in this household or during those times. They were taught frugality as a matter of survival. Years later, when I was a young child, Grandpa's mother came

Momma and friends on the farm

Momma is shown in picture on the far right in polka dot dress. I believe she is shown with a couple girl friends who lived nearby on the farms. This looks like a relaxed summer day, outside enjoying the weather and friendship. Probably a Sunday, free from daily chores, and a more relaxing day. I think Momma always had the happiest smile when she was pleased about something or found something to be humorous. Momma always loved a good chuckle or story and being with friends.

to live with Grandma and my aunt Rena, who was divorced with two children and living back on the farm. I remember my great-grandmother, my grandfather's mother, as a very old woman dressed in old-fashion black clothes. She wore only black, and she sat in the parlor all day in an old wooden chair by the wood stove, spitting tobacco occasionally into a large aluminum can that had once contained some vegetable. If the can wasn't there, she would spit on the floor. To keep the area more tidy, the floor was in linoleum, and a hole had been cut for the can to sit in, eliminating areas where she might miss the can when spitting the chewed tobacco. I can remember her when I visited the farm with my mother during holidays and summer. The elderly lady would not come to the table to eat any of the prepared food unless she had had a hand in the preparation. So I remember Grandma or Rena always making sure that the old woman had peeled some potatoes or in some way had contributed to the preparation. I really don't remember ever having spoken with her. I called her the "black old crow," much to my embarrassment today. But as a small child, I didn't know better or understood all her happenstance.

Everyone in Momma's family worked hard each day to keep food on the table. There were no days of leisure or relaxation. If the family members didn't grow or make something, then it wasn't there to eat or to have. As far as education, Momma finished the fifth grade. She told me that it just wasn't possible for her to go to school. She was needed to be home to help with the farm chores and work inside the house to prepare the food, canning, cooking, or cleaning. When she had gone to school, Momma said that she only had a piece of homemade bread to eat with bacon grease smeared on it each day for lunch. When I would make a face about the thought of eating bacon grease, she would just hug me and explain, "Many another child was envious that I had this to eat. They had nothing."

My mother's siblings, John, Roy, Dink, and Rena, all had had to leave schooling early in their lives also. Again, they were all needed to work on the farm and just couldn't be spared the day away from their chores. Their lives were to be joined around these small farms in their "growing up" years. Quietly and simply, they had small amounts of excitement in their days or nights. "Early to bed and early to rise" was their motto during those years.

-Uncle John and Aunt Geneva

Uncle John was Momma's oldest brother. He was the one who was the popular car mechanic and worked in Cassville at an auto repair shop. Well known in the area, people would come in asking for John to work on their auto. John married Geneva early in years and they were married all their lives together. They never had children and mainly stayed in Cassville.

Once in a while they came to Monett to visit the family but mainly stayed within themselves and their own lives.

Later Years - Ethel and Marion Clayton

Ethel and Marion Clayton on their farm. Grandma Ethel in daily dress with Grandpa Clayton, always in overalls and hat, enjoying a puff on his pipe. Yard looks bleak but I always remembered it in spring and summer filled with flowers, blooming trees and lots of tall grass to run and play in.

I can just barely remember being with Grandpa Clayton in his garden by the side of the house. He loved to work out in the garden and grow the vegetables they would be eating during the winters. Grandma Clayton always seemed to be cold or chilled. Even though Momma and Aunt Rena would buy her nice dresses Grandma would add material to the arms or hem to make the dress longer. It did not matter if the material was the same or not. She might sew plaid to stripes or such. Sometimes the dresses would appear quite comical with their many different patterns and colors. Her legs would get cold also so I can remember her in five to six pairs of hose on each leg. Of course, all five or so pairs would not stay up evenly so there was always a pair or two that were falling down around her legs.

**This is a picture of Ethel and Marion Clayton as
I knew them in their later years of life**

I loved to visit my grandparents on their farm in Cassville. Grandma was an excellent cook and there was always smells of food cooking and baking in the old fashioned kitchen. With no electricity and a water pump at the sink, all kitchen work was hard and tiring. The old black iron stove was daunting to see with a small stack of wood nearby to keep it lit and cooking. Momma and Aunt Rena would pitch right in and help with the meal as there were many there to eat. An elderly relative sat in the parlor in front of the old wood stove. Dressed entirely in black, she would never partake in the meal unless she had set the table or peeled some potatoes.

Momma (Lela) and Uncle John shown on the farm

Interestingly enough, this is the only hat I ever saw Momma dressed in. This picture shows Momma with her brother John (wearing mechanic uniform from his job in the Cassville Auto Repair Shop.) in the yard of their farm.

On the other hand, my father, Glenn, was born in 1908 and was raised in the prospering, Midwestern town of Joplin, Missouri. Born to parents with a reasonable amount of education, the family was large. Dad had four brothers and two sisters: (James) Jim, (Harry) June, (Pershing) Rube, Shadrach (Shade), Erma (Iris), and Doris. In retrospect, I don't think any of Dad's family was called by their given names. Actually, I was always fascinated by Dad's brothers' names, yet, once you got to know them, the names seemed to fit each of them. They were loud and boisterous and filled with earnest mischievousness of the times. In regards to education, Dad bragged that he had completed the seventh grade before he was forced to quit to help support his family. You see, my Dad's father, Perry James Stone, at the age of fifty, died of intestinal cancer in 1935 in Joplin, Missouri.

When I began to write this book, I didn't know too much about Dad's family. His mother, Mittie Ellen Thurman, born 1889, quoted from the Bible and portrayed a very pious woman. She dressed simply in black with no jewelry or embellishments. Her home was strict and quiet. She prayed often and loudly and quoted much from her Bible. I only met her one time when I was around eight years old. At this time, it was a family reunion, and my dad's brothers and sisters enthralled me. They told such marvelous jokes and stories. I could have listened to them for hours. When we gathered around the two long tables outside in the backyard to eat on that warm summer day, Dad's mother began a long droning prayer for the blessing. All stood with their head bowed and hands folded in submission. And then, one of the sons, my uncle, loudly exclaimed, "Halleluiah, the food is blessed, we are all blessed. Amen." Everyone laughed except Grandma as she frowned and laid her Bible beside her on the table. But I truly believe that I saw a small smile just beginning to unfold as she bent her head to look at her plate of food. And with that, we all sat down and began to eat. Loud talking filled the summer air with laughter, smiles and stories for all to hear. I loved to be a part of life with my father's brothers. I seldom ever saw them again during my life, but I always remembered that family reunion and all the wonderful humorous stories and loud, boisterous laughter.

Grandma Mittie lived to be 78 years old. She died in a rest home January 11, 1967, in Joplin, Missouri. Mittie lived 32 more years after her husband, Perry.

On the far left is my father, Glenn E. Stone, with his brothers

On the far left is my Dad, Glenn E. Stone, along with his brothers pictured together at their mother's home in Joplin, Missouri for a family reunion.

That would be the only time I met all of the Stone boys and visited my Grandmother Mittie Stone's home. I hope I get this order (right of the brothers), starting with my Dad on the left; Glenn, James (Jim), Harry (June), Pershing (Rube), and Shadrach (Shade). The sisters Iris and Doris are not pictured. Eating in the yard with tables filled with food, I remember a day of boisterous laughter and storytelling at the reunion. I always wished I could see Dad's brothers again and get to know my cousins and members of the family.

But, Dad kept a separation from his family and I never really got to visit with them. I always knew that Dad loved his family, but for some reason, did not want to communicate with them.

As a result I just knew their names but nothing about their children or grandchildren. When Dad's mother died, we did not go to the funeral. Dad went alone.

Grandpa Perry at graduation

Perry Stone (my grandfather) is shown in the last row, on the right, in front of wall. Graduation Day with his classmates pictured and school proudly decorated with the American flag on display. He was my dad's father, Perry James Stone, who died at an early age of fifty in 1935 in Joplin, Missouri of cancer and was buried in Joplin, Missouri.

Dad never talked about his father. In fact, I don't remember ever hearing stories from Dad about his parents or his family. I knew that his Dad, Perry, had died early in life as I never had met him. I remember when Dad's mother had a heart attack and he rushed up to see her in Joplin, but that is all I know. I have always wondered why Dad chose to not spend time with them. They all seemed to be so interesting and funny to me.

Grandpa Perry Stone with his mother, LeAnna Crenshaw Stone

LeAnna Crenshaw was the daughter of Alvira (Little Chaney), a Cherokee Indian, and John Crenshaw. LeAnna gathered roots and leaves to make medicinal remedies for the family. One family member recalled how potent LeAnna's remedies were and that one "could not stay in the house when the roots were boiling." LeAnna Crenshaw Stone spent her later years with her daughter Nell in Oklahoma. She died in 1934 and was buried in Joplin, Missouri. She was eighty-five years old, approximately.

When I was a small child, Dad would speak of his family, and he would often tell of his grandmother who was a full-blooded Indian. He would recall how beautiful she was with long black hair down her back and bright brown eyes. He said that she never used a toothbrush but a small twig found in the backyard, yet she had firm and white teeth. Determined to find out more about my ancestors while I was writing this book, I contacted a friend of mine, Barbra Hathcock, in Columbus, Ohio, and asked if she could find more information on my family. The results were incredulous. My father had been right; my family descended from Native Americans on his side. I was fascinated as I read about these earlier ancestors.

My great-great-grandfather was (Shadrach) Solomon Westley Stone and was born in 1836 in Terre Haute, Indiana. He came to Kansas, Indian Territory, at an early age with his parents and settled on a black dirt farm on the Little Osage River near the present town of Fulton, Kansas. In 1886, Solomon Stone was married to Minerva Jane Graves. His father, William Stone, performed the ceremony as justice of the peace of Bourbon County, Kansas.

Solomon and Minerva settled on a small farm next to his father's farm. Soon after the marriage, Solomon and his brothers James and Cord were called into the Union Army. Solomon served as a sergeant in the Twelfth Kansas Calvary. He was wounded in the leg and came home wrapped in a flag in 1863. And that is where the story becomes even more interesting, sort of playing out like a Hallmark story on television of the early pioneer days.

While returning home, Solomon, outside of Fort Scott, Kansas, came across two half-breed Indian children, a boy about eight and a girl between eleven and thirteen years old who were members of the Cherokee Indian Nation. Dreadfully sick, the two children were sleeping under an army wagon because they had been quarantined outside Fort Scott as the two children had the measles. Solomon Stone took the two gravely ill children on the road to his home with him. Walter, the young boy, died of pneumonia and complications on the road while traveling to Solomon's home. LeAnna, the sick girl, continued the journey home with him.

Arriving home, Solomon found his wife, Minerva, entertaining a neighbor by "sitting on his lap, hugging, and kissing." Being informed that this was a common occurrence during his absence, Solomon "put away his wife and refused to live with her." Continuing this unfolding drama, several years passed, and in 1865, LeAnna Crenshaw and Solomon Stone were married. Couldn't write a better love story than this one. I was fascinated with how this whole story played out, Solomon finding the two sick children, arriving to find a cheating wife, and, two years later, marrying his young ward, LeAnna. At this time, Solomon's brother James returned home from the war and worked in the drug business with pharmacies and doctors. He made an entry to *Capper's Farm Magazine* and won a money prize and gold watch. Solomon's brother Cord died after the Civil War as the result of starvation and other privations suffered as a prisoner in the Andersonville prison.

Adding to this intriguing story of my early ancestors, I have to add the story of how William and LeAnna had arrived with measles at the Fort Scott in Kansas.

In my readings of my ancestors, LeAnna related the story of her parents. Her mother was called Alvira (Little Chaney) and was a Cherokee Indian. In her youth, John Crenshaw gave an army sergeant a five-dollar gold piece to release Little Chaney to him. When John Crenshaw took Little Chaney home with him, his parents didn't approve, so they went to Arkansas.

During the Civil War, John left to fight for the Confederate side, leaving Little Chaney on the farm with their children Walter and LeAnna. At this time, LeAnna spoke through the ancestral findings of how beautiful her mother, Little Chaney, was. Continuing, it was said that Little Chaney was a full-blooded Cherokee Indian and was very hardworking. She never quit working. They had a large farm with livestock and a new barn the husband/father built before he went off to war for the South. And then a group of renegades came. They took Little Chaney, the mother, into the barn and abused her very badly. Luckily some Union soldiers came along, and the renegades ran away. The soldiers then took the horses and butchered the cattle for food. The soldiers put Walter and LeAnna in a wagon with their mother on a mattress filled with corn shucks. The soldiers gave them a team wagon with high sideboards covered with army canvas and they told the children to get out of Arkansas. They were to go to Fort Scott, Kansas. The mother died on the second day on the road. She bled to death. The children, Walter and LeAnna, "took their mother and drug her to a wash-out in the side of a hill. They put her on the mattress and pulled the sideboards off the wagon and put them over her. Then they carried rocks all day and stacked them on her so nothing could get to her like wolves and other animals."

LeAnna related that her momma had foreseen trouble when her daddy left to go fight for the South. Little Chaney had gone up the road from the house for several days to bury eggs. She had told the two children where the eggs were buried. For many days, they had eggs to eat, and they let the horses graze at night. After several weeks, the two children made it to Fort Scott, near Pittsburg, Kansas, where they then became sick with the measles, and that was where Solomon came along into the story.

Continuing, around 1894, Solomon and LeAnna, with their children, all moved by train from Kansas to Joplin, Missouri, bringing furniture, bags, and baggage. When they first arrived, they had to stay several days on the dock at the train depot until they found a place to live. According to statements made by LeAnna, she said that the mud surrounding the depot was so thick that if men stepped off the board sidewalk or store porches, they could become hip-deep in the mud. The Stone family soon learned the truth of the old Missouri warning—stay out of Missouri and stay out of the mud!

The story is told how Ruben, my grandfather's brother, split his pants and the mother, LeAnna, made him pants out of a green cover from their family organ, but the material wasn't enough for long legs, so his pants only came to his knees or so. And he had no shoes. Being resourceful, Great-Uncle Ruben set himself up there on the docks, and he began to play the family organ entertaining arriving travelers and those waiting for a train. Soon, Ruben received enough monies to buy a new pair of pants and shoes at the general store named Yellowhammers.

Some days after their arrival and Ruben's entertainment of the locals, the Stone family, Solomon and LeAnna, with their children, moved about two miles down from the depot and set up housekeeping in their large two-story home. The depot personnel were greatly relieved upon their moving because Ruben's music was gathering bunches of people to listen to his music. The personnel wanted Ruben to quit playing so they could get the people away from the depot.

About this time, when Ruben was fourteen years old, Mr. J. Frank Walker came by their residence to sell a piano or organ to the household. LeAnna Stone, in response to his sales pitch, replied that she did not want to purchase an organ but that she was offering her son Ruben to work for Mr. Walker. Looking over the young man, Mr. Walker agreed because he could see Ruben was strong as well as stout. And so Great-Uncle Ruben went to work for Mr. Walker in his music store and stayed there for the next fifty years. During his early days, Ruben rode his bicycle around the township for sales work and used a horse-drawn wagon for deliveries. Ruben could place a piano on a strip of carpet and carry it into the house. If there were steep stairs, he needed some help. In fact, the story is told that he would claim to people watching or passing by that he could carry the piano on his back some ten steps or so. People would bet and then to their dismay find they had lost their bet as they watched Ruben carry the piano as he had promised. Often, Great-Uncle Ruben bragged that this was how he kept himself in free cigars. My grandfather Perry, brother to Ruben, also had a musical side to him and worked some in the store too. I might add that the store also stocked sewing machines and phonographs.

Adding to Ruben's skill in piano selling and delivery, he could play by ear. He could hear a tune and sit right down to play it. In fact, he became a popular entertainer in the mining district in Ornogo and near Joplin, playing nightly in the old Club Theatre in Joplin. The story is added that Ruben and his friend, Percy Wenrich, were very interested in piano playing in Joplin and often frequented Walker's music store to play on a piano or down on the other end of the street at the local saloon. There many famous Negro performers entertained the nightly crowds with their expertise on the piano playing ragtime. Later, Percy went on to New York to Tin Pan Alley and became famous in his own right with his own famous songs "On Moonlight Bay," "When You Wore a Tulip" and "Put On Your Old Gray Bonnet," to name a few.

I loved that information I discovered, as I read about this Stone family, my grandfather, and his parents. Ruben and Percy, living in Joplin, loving to play music so much, and so hungry to learn new skills, frequented the saloon and whorehouse at the other end of the town, listening to highly skilled Negro ragtime piano players such as John W. Boone, "Blind Boone," who composed "I'm Alabamy Bound." And sometimes Scott Joplin, living in Sedalia, Missouri, would come into the saloon to play with the other famous pianists. Sometimes the saloon proprietor, Lionel "Babe" Latour, would hide Ruben and Percy behind a screen so they could listen to Scott Joplin and other favorites play during the night.

S. Solomon W. Stone lived off his pension from the Civil War, and his family was active in civic and church affairs. As a couple, Solomon and Leanna had six boys and four girls. A relative, Paul Stone, recalls that he had seen a tintype of Shadrach Solomon Wesley Stone and that he wore a felt hat, a three-fourth-length coat, a sword, a braid, and a full beard. He was handsome, and he was a very religious person. Other relatives praised him and always referred to him as "Father Stone."

S.S.W. Stone, in 1912, while visiting a daughter in Mena, Arkansas, died at the age of seventy-three of a heart attack on the steps of a church. He was buried in the Old Baptist Quarter of Forrest Park Cemetery, Joplin, Missouri. His tombstone reads "Solomon Westly Stone 1836–1912." Grandfather Perry, Grand-Uncles Ruben and Paul, with my great-grandmother, Leanna, went by train to Carthage, Missouri, to pick a tombstone for the grave. It was a one-day trip, eighteen miles.

LeAnna Crenshaw Stone survived on until 1934. In the information I found from my ancestry, one grandchild, Jimmie, recalled how his grandmother LeAnna would tell him stories from the war years (Civil War). He continued, "I have a list of remedies that Grandma put up through the summer and fall for winter months. She believed to always put up enough for one's family and used pure grain alcohol for a preservative." Once, the grandchild recalled how Grandma LeAnna gave him a laxative in the fall, and it kept him in the outdoor toilet all winter. Her medicines were potent and effective, using roots, berries, leaves, and flowers. The grandchildren helped her gather these needed items. It was noted that one could not stay in the house while some of those medicinal pots boiled. The fumes from the liquids were toxic. Leanna boiled enough cough medicine down and made square chunks of candy like fudge. I read that the cough drops never lasted the winter if the kids found them. And her laxatives were as a hard candy and a person sucked on them. Adults were one size of a marble, and children had one the size of a pea.

LeAnna Crenshaw Stone spent her later years with her daughter Nell in Oklahoma. She died in 1934 and was buried in Forrest Park Cemetery in Joplin, Missouri, beside her husband. She was eighty-five years old, approximately.

Among Solomon and LeAnna's seven children was William Osmer Stone. He had red hair, played the fiddle and violin, and worked the mines in Joplin, Missouri. He died when he was eighty-three years old. He had dementia in his later years and would wander off and be confused. In 1950, he wandered off and was missing. When they found him, he had drowned in the Powder River.

The other children were Lewis, Annie, J.W., Bertha, and my great-uncle Reuben and my grandfather Perry.

As a child, I heard my father recalling his early life living with his father Perry and mother Mittie and siblings. Dad had been, and still was, fascinated by fast living, alcohol, and women. It was the days of the flappers, bee's knees, "hootch," dancing the Charleston, and "Oh, you kid!" The life was exciting, and Dad was a good candidate for it. He told of how, in his teenage years, he was a driver for delivery of illegal "moonshine" to various speakeasies in Joplin and the surrounding areas. This was a good living for him until one night a sheriff and three deputies chased him in their police cars. He related how they were hot in pursuit, chasing him in his Model T Ford and shooting their guns at his car. He managed to evade them and hid out in an area of trees and grown grass. But the next morning, when he surveyed his car for damages, he found three bullet holes in the back of the car, and that was enough for him. He handed down his driving gloves and let someone else deliver the goods!

Following that endeavor, he said he had a short stint as an ambulance driver until he came upon a five-car accident where blood ran down the street. Again, he handed in his driving gloves for another pursuit in life.

At this time, he married a young woman. He was hired in what he called a "slaughterhouse" where they made dog meat and glue out of horses. On Sunday afternoons when we took drives up to Joplin to see a John Wayne or Audie Murphy movie playing in town, he would often drive us by the location to see all the horses that were going to be slaughtered in the next few days. That had been where he worked. I would always sit in the backseat and cry silently as I looked at all the hundreds of beautiful horses that were soon going to be dog meat and glue. I hated those trips to the slaughterhouse and where he had worked. I often wondered how he had been able to face such a job each day, morning to night, with the killing of the horses.

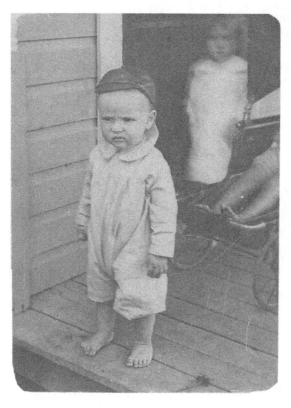

"Buttons" Stone

This is a picture of my Dad, Glenn Stone, when he was a young boy. I don't know what age but one can clearly say that he was not happy in this picture.

At this time he had the nickname of "Buttons" - for two reasons. One - he was as small as a button, and two - he had big, deep brown eyes, like a button! Thus, he was often called Buttons until he was a young man. Then, his nickname became Stonie and stayed with him the rest of his life. I think he was called Stonie more than Glenn during his lifetime.

Glenn Stone, my father, in younger days

My father, Glenn E. Stone, is pictured at work in his early employment. Married and with children, he had to find gameful employment to support his family.

He told me that, in his early years, he was employed in Joplin working in the slaughterhouse where they killed horses to make glue and dog food. Several times when we had taken a trip to Joplin, Dad drove us over to the factory and showed us all the beautiful horses in fenced areas that were going to be killed. I remember sitting in the back seat crying as I looked at all these beautiful horses. Dad told me that there just wasn't a use for the horses anymore.

Dad had previously tried "bootlegging" and being an ambulance driver in his younger years.

Now that he was gainfully employed, despite his love for the daily shots of whiskey, he married a young lady while they were very young. Family members did not approve of the woman marrying my father, Glenn, and would not have anything to do with him. It seemed that Dad would never fit into his wife's family. The marriage soon did fall to sad times. Two children, Glenn and Roberta Ruth (nicknamed Betty all her life), were born quickly. Life was a hard burden for Dad to bear— married, two children, working daily in a "slaughterhouse," and living on a meager income. Alcohol became a salvation to Dad's inner urgings and quieted his own unhappiness. Then came the third pregnancy, and another daughter was born in 1937. This birth did not go well, and the mother, Dad's wife, died in childbirth at a young age. He always told the story of her death with tears streaming down his face. He said that she just "bled to death" right before his eyes. There was nothing the doctors could do. Years later when I watched the movie *The Eddie Duchin Story* starring Tyrone Power and Kim Novak, I matched it in my mind to my father's plight with his first wife. In the movie, Novak, as Duchin's first wife, dies in childbirth and "bleeds to death." I saw my father in the role of Eddie Duchin sitting by the hospital bed of his wife, begging her to live. Of course, in reality, it was not this romantic. Whatever was the scene of the young wife's death in the hospital, Dad lost the custody of his two older children and small infant to his wife's sister. He was not even allowed visiting privileges. He was always blamed for his wife's early demise. The family of his wife did not forgive him or accept him. He was a lonely person adrift without his wife and children.

Following his wife's death, Dad became a bus driver for the Ozarks Trailway, locating himself to Monett, Missouri, and driving routes through areas of Missouri and into Tennessee. This was when Dad met my mother.

In the late 1930s, my mother moved to Monett to work in the local bus station as a cook. She had learned old-fashioned stomach-filling cooking skills growing up on the farm and was thus employed at the bus station. Dad had headquarters for his routes in Monett at this small station on Main Street. He would come into the bus station to set up his passenger lists and have a bite to eat. He began to talk to Lela, my mother, and romance blossomed.

I never knew anything about their early courtship or their beginning a life together. As I watched my parents, around my teenager years, I always felt that they could not have been more mismatched. Grandma Ethel always said "a pot for every lid." Perhaps so, but something was wrong in this "pot and lid." He was loud, boisterous, and loved the fast lane. He was very bored with the life he had. Momma was quiet, shy, and content with a simple home life filled with warmth and security. Once Dad told me that he used to shower his wife Lela with gifts—he would always bring home candies and flowers to surprise her. But one day, as he presented a flower bouquet to Lela, she turned and retorted, "Who died?" Dad said he threw the flowers in the wastebasket and never bought her a gift again. I don't know how much of that was true. It seemed a rather small and short summing up of lost affections. Momma never talked about it. I just know that I was born in 1942 on my grandparents' farm.

Momma, (Lela Priscilla Stone), me, (Glenda Sue (Susie) Stone) and Dad (Glenn E. Stone)

My hair was in long curls for this picture. I am in the middle of Momma and Dad. It seemed that many of my dresses were in pink with always a big bow in my hair.

Because Momma and Dad both had black hair, people would often stop me and ask me where I got my lovely, auburn hair. One time, remembering a joke I had overheard, I politely answered "from the milkman". I certainly shocked that lady. Momma quickly admonished me that I should never say that again! But, I have to admit, she did have a small chuckle in her voice when she said that.

Chapter 3

My Life Begins

And so we reach the time of my soon-to-be arrival. The year 1942 was a struggle for many people. Pearl Harbor had taken place just the previous year, and our men and women were dying overseas in a war that few of the townspeople even understood. We had been attacked in our own home grounds in Hawaii, and that was too close for America. Every person was pulling with all their strength to help in this war at any method they could. President F.D. Roosevelt called for the nation's determination and strength, and it was given to him. Full force. Democracy and pride in our country was strong despite the hard economy at home and deaths of our fighting soldiers overseas.

At that time, few births happened in hospitals. Few people could afford to go to a hospital. My mother had planned to go to her parents' farm in Cassville for my arrival. Her mother, Ethel, would help with the delivery. They both had experience with birthing a child in their own lives. If problems arose, a doctor could be brought in. Momma and Dad had planned to drive down to Cassville that following week for her to stay until the baby arrived. Dad had to finish his route and would be returning to Monett Sunday early evening.

But for some reason, Momma woke up that early morning, Saturday, December 19, and decided she wanted to go home now, that day, as soon as possible. So she got her small suitcase packed with the baby items and some clothes for herself and began a slow journey several blocks down the street to Broadway where the bus station was located.

Clayton Farm - 1940s

John Clayton, Momma's older brother, was a well known auto mechanic in the area and often on call for special repairs in an auto shop in Cassville.

One of his cars is parked in front of the old farmhouse where the Clayton family lived at the time I was born, 1942. This picture with the old car reminds me me of a scene from John Steinbeck's "Grapes of Wrath", with the words, "our people are good people; our people are kind people. Pray God some day kind people won't all be poor."

Because Dad was a bus driver, Momma had a free pass to ride the Ozarks Trailway bus to any location at any time. So she got her ticket and waited to get on the bus to leave for Cassville and her family. When the bus driver, a friend of my parents', came into the station to gather his passengers, he was surprised to see my mother when she stood up. She was definitely huge in pregnancy and, as he later recalled, "looked like she was going to pop at any minute." He wasn't too sure about this trip and told Momma of his worries that he might have to birth the baby right there on the bus. And he continued, "Just like the maid in *Gone with the Wind*, he didn't know nothin' about birthing no babies." Momma laughed and told him to just get her safely and quickly to her mother's home, and the women there would take care of the "birthing."

A few soldiers and several farmers with their families boarded the bus, and soon Sam, our driver, was heading down the highway with Momma and me on board.

After riding in the bus an hour on the road, Momma went into labor, just like Sam the driver had predicted. Watching Momma out of the corner of his eye, Sam began to drive a little faster to get Momma to her family on their farm in time. Driving the bus into the Cassville Bus Station, Sam opened the bus doors for passengers to leave the bus and then announced that this bus was heading straight to Momma's family farmhouse with no time to spare. He said that he would not be stopping at any of the outer Cassville stops but would be heading straight to the home of the pregnant woman's family.

And that's how the bus arrived at the doorstep of the old farmhouse that late Saturday afternoon with several passengers still on the bus and Momma in labor with me. Sam promised to drive the remaining passengers to their own destinations at a later time. He wanted to be present for my arrival. Amazingly, the several passengers agreed. They seemed to be in no hurry to their own destinations that Saturday evening.

You can imagine my grandparents' surprise when they stepped off their old farmhouse cement porch and saw their daughter, Lela, being escorted by the bus driver with several strangers who were getting off the bus also. Sizing up the situation quickly, my grandmother, Ethel, escorted my mother and the bus driver to the smaller stone farmhouse across the yard. Momma was made comfortable in the large iron bed while my grandmother gathered her necessary equipment to get ready for my birth.

In the larger farmhouse, Grandpa Marion escorted the passengers from the bus and offered them chairs to sit in by the fireplace in the parlor. He then proceeded to place prepared food out on the old wooden kitchen table. My two uncles, Roy and Dink, had just finished their chores and were cleaning up to eat some supper. They were surprised to see the strangers, the bus, the bus driver, and Momma. Visitors were seldom to this farmhouse. Grandpa and my uncles rooted out several bottles of homemade wine and passed them around to the waiting. Grandma became furious at the menfolk for drinking the wine and becoming boisterous in the parlor. She did not tolerate "imbibing alcoholic spirits" nor thought it seemly to be so noisy while a child was being born.

And that was how I entered the world. Delivered by my grandmother while my grandfather held the kerosene lamp overhead. I was cleaned, wrapped in a warm blanket, and placed next to my mother under the heavy quilts that had been sewn by generations of women in my family. An hour or so later, my father arrived at the farmhouse and quickly joined the celebration of the arrival of his daughter, Susie. The bus driver, Sam, was named my godfather. He took this appointment very seriously until his early death from cancer. He loved to tell the story of my arrival, almost on his bus, to whoever would be listening.

That following Christmas Eve, Thursday, December 24, 1942, my parents took me to the doctor. At the same time, I received an examination, and the doctor on duty filled out my birth certificate. Legally I was named Glenda Sue Stone, but that name never seemed to stick. I always was called Susie. When I was older, people often asked me if my mother had been a fan of the movie *Wizard of Oz* and had named me after the good witch Glynda. I would always smile and say, "No, her name was spelled different than mine. I was named after my father, Glenn."

While reading my birth certificate, I had to laugh over the occupation section filled in by my parents. My dad had written that he had been a bus driver for the past three years and still was. My mother marked that she was a housewife, but she had marked the last day of her being a housewife as December 19, the day before I was born. I guess she didn't count the following day giving birth to me, December 20, as being a housewife also.

My early years were spent contently in a rented apartment in a two-family house on Fifth Street, back in Monett. We lived on the second floor, and the owners lived on the first floor with their two sons. When I was around two years old or so, Dad had a nervous breakdown or a small heart attack. I have never been completely knowledgeable about this matter. I only know that he quit driving the bus and stayed home, often in bed for days at a time. Momma continued working at the bus station as a cook. She was home during the day with me and then worked the evening shift from 5:00 p.m. to midnight. My father took care of me at night. I can remember Momma calling me before I went to bed to talk to me and hear about what I had been doing. I would be sitting on the bed in my nightgown ready for sleep when Momma would call me, and I listened to her on the phone telling me that she would be home soon and instructing me to go to sleep right away.

After about a year, my father became more outgoing in life again. He had gathered some strength and seemed to feel more normal. He wasn't working yet and often spent a lot of time in bed sleeping, but at nighttime, while Momma was at work, he would visit his favorite place, the local bar on Broadway, with me in tow.

Dad was a gambler. He had a great skill at the cards—they seemed to just "jump into his hands." He never won large stakes, but he won enough to keep himself in whiskey and would often buy drinks for his friends in the bar. During these several years, Dad would dress me up and bring me along to his gambling sites. There I sat late in the night, next to Dad at the gaming table. When I fell asleep, Dad would just lay me on a booth near the table and cover me with a coat or tablecloth. Dad would continue playing his cards and drinking his whiskey. Actually, I became a good luck charm. I had been born with auburn hair. Not the bright, carroty red hue but the golden red auburn color that was not very common in that day and age. In fact, Dad used to always tell me that I was named after my great-aunt Sue. It seems that she had auburn hair, the same color as mine, except that she was ashamed of her hair color. She felt that the auburn color was a sinful color and unbecoming to a genteel woman. Thus, she shaved it all off and wore a stocking cap all her life. Needless to say, I never felt such a desire to follow in my namesake's footsteps and repeat such an abandoned solution as to shave off all my hair. Might add that she never married, either. I could see why not. But whatever, during my early years, men in the bar that

Here I am as Daddy's lucky charm

Shortly after I was born Dad had a physical problem where he stayed home and rested a lot. I never really knew what happened but either it was his heart or he had a mental breakdown.

He just seemed to shut down and wanted to sleep much of the time. Dad quit driving the bus and stopped working. As a result, Momma worked nights as a cook in a cafe and Dad would take care of me during the night.

Often Dad would take me with him to his favorite bar downtown in the evenings and join in some poker game.

Because of my bald head with a fuzz of red hair, I was considered a "good luck" charm and patrons of the bar and friends of Dad would often rub my head for good luck in their poker game or just for general good feelings.

It's lucky I grew up with hair and not have a bald spot on my head from the many rubbings!

my father frequented saw me as a "good luck charm" and would often rub my head of auburn curls for good luck when they joined the card games. To this day, I marvel at the fact that I did not grow a bald spot on the top of my head from the many "lucky" rubbings. During these early years, I was my father's delight—his companion, his princess, his little darling dumplin'. He used to sing an old Gene Autry song to me titled "Roly-Poly, Daddy's Little Darlin'." I loved that song. Dad would croon the song to me as I fell asleep in my bed at night. I felt a special attachment to my father. After all, I was his little darlin'.

Dad loved to show me off to everyone he would meet. Friends or new acquaintances, they would all listen as he recited how intelligent and talented I was. There is a picture taken of my father and me at this time. I am standing on a small cement bench in a photographer's studio next to my father. I have my pudgy left little arm placed around my father's shoulders. He is sitting next to me on the bench wearing one of his favorite two-piece suits, probably brown in color, with his silk tan or brown shirt, and wearing round spectacles fashionable of the day with his white Stetson hat sitting atop his head. There is a slight smile on his face that, if in color, would show three gold caps he had placed on his teeth on the right side of his mouth. This had been done during his younger years. Three whole teeth on his right side were solid gold and seemed to glisten with a Midas glint of brightness when he smiled his lopsided smile or when he talked. My father loved gold. He always wore his Masonic ring on his right hand and a gold ring with a large diamond on his left hand. His shirts always sported golden cufflinks with the Masonic symbols, and his tie tack was a Masonic symbol placed on a bar with a gold chain hanging down. Although we, as a family, were always lacking in spendable money, Dad was flamboyant in his dress and fashion. Only the best would do for him; silks, gold, tailor-made suits to his style, white Stetson hats. He stepped out in style.

He was short in stature, around five foot five, and displayed coal-black hair parted in the middle and combed smoothly back. His face betrayed his American Indian heritage with high cheekbones, large "tomahawk" nose, and brightly lit mischievous black-brown eyes. When he was a child, his siblings called him "buttons" because of his own smallness in stature and those enormous brown eyes.

And there we are in the picture together. I am standing there with my arm around his shoulder while he slightly holds my right hand at my fingertips. We are both staring seriously into the camera, posed for eternity. I love that picture. Sad to say, this picture denotes the soon-to-be ending days of our companionship, at least on my father's side.

But at that time, I was the good luck charm, and people rubbed my head for their fortunes. Of course, often when Momma got off work at midnight and she headed home, she found our apartment empty. She knew immediately where to find us. She would enter the bar and bear right to our table furiously and loudly berating Dad for exposing me to such a life of gamblers and low-life drunkards. At this time, she would claim me and take me home to be placed in my own bed to sleep the rest of the night. Dad would sneak home later after he had lost his entire stake or had drunk up all his winnings.

When I was about four years old, Dad's son and daughter from his first marriage, Glenn and Betty, came to live with us. I never knew why they suddenly arrived and moved into our apartment in Monett. I just knew that they were now a part of our family. As they were so much older than I was, I rarely saw them or spent much time with them. I have several pictures today of me outside standing beside Betty, my sister. Those are really my only reminiscences of that time and our new larger family. It was amazing to me that they were living with us because Dad had been denied them after his wife had died. But for whatever reason, they were with us to live and go to high school.

One Saturday morning in December 1946, my father awoke us with a new special gift he had borrowed for a few days. It was a "magic" machine that would record our voices onto small 45-rpm-size records of various colors; red, orange, and yellow. Dad gathered us together at the early hours that particular Saturday morning to show us how the machine worked. At this point, I might explain further that during the war years, these machines had been used to make recordings on records that could be mailed overseas to soldiers to hear their family and loved ones speak to them. Each record held about twenty minutes of recording and had served well for the soldiers overseas in the war as they listened to their loved ones back home. The records were thin waxy vinyl with large labels on them for identification.

Now my father had the idea that we could record us those few days we had the machine. He predicted that we would be able to record our voices for destiny and listen to them someday in the future. It was so exciting.

Daddy's Little Darling

Often Dad would croon Gene Autry's old favorite "Daddy's Little Darlin'- bet you're gonna be a cowboy someday!"
This picture happily depicts the two of us - buddies and pals! Daddy and his buddy - me, Susie!

HOME AGAIN, HOME AGAIN, JIGGITY, JIG

Dad quickly put the machine together with the microphone in place. He then called me over and held the microphone out to me. There was never a need to invite me twice to sing or tell a story.

Even then I was a regular hambone. I could perform for everyone at the drop of a hat—I loved to sing and dance or tell my version of nursery rhymes. When one listens to these records today, I have a very distinct pronunciation of words in my stories—such as *breakfast* as "break-fast" or *wolves* as "woofs." Dad always said it was the "Dutch" in me.

Each start of the record opens with Dad saying, "And now, little Susie Stone is going to sing you a song (or tell a story). What are you going to sing for us, little Susie?" At this time, I proudly regaled everyone with my telling of the "Three Little Pigs" and huffed and puffed for about three minutes for all the little pigs, as I exclaimed, "Not by the hairs of my chinny chin chin." I also sang from "Sioux City Sue" a few verses I knew, and was definitely off-key. I talked with Momma about what she had been doing and what she was going to do. Momma shyly told me she was going to go do the wash and make me breakfast. I agreed that I could eat all her pancakes.

Glenn came on one of the records to croon his favorite song, also "Sioux City Sue," but I soon broke in and stole the microphone. As I had previously said, I was used to being the main person in the spotlight, and I had no tolerance that someone else might be the star of the show. Our neighbor boy, Joey, came over and recorded himself singing "Silent Night" on one side of the record. I am sure that if a dog were present when listening to this recording, the dog would begin to howl from the sharp high notes Joey presented in his rendition of "Silent Night." It almost made me howl when I listened to those recordings again recently.

Along with my stories and songs, Dad recorded a reading on one record. They were words he had written. It seemed he had planned to make copies of that record and send to his friends for Christmas. I don't think he accomplished this matter, but the recording is very mellow and kind as he speaks of his philosophical musings regarding life in general. His voice was kind-sounding as he spoke. It would have been a kind Christmas greeting to send to friends. He speaks of living a good life, being kind to one another, friendship and kindness for one's neighbor. He refers to the Bible while speaking: "I will lift up mine eyes unto the hills from hence cometh my help." Today, as I listen once again to his recording, I am touched by the gentleness in his voice. I am also moved by the expression of his writings. Years later, I found a box full of newspaper articles Dad had clipped and saved from the Joplin newspaper. He wrote often to the editor, and his writings were printed in the Letters to the Editor section. They were musings with political tones, philosophical tones, and general words of authoritative advice. He was very proud of those printings of his written words. He often mused that he would have liked to be a journalist.

But on that specific Saturday morning, we spent the early hours laughing and recording our voices, stories, songs, and musings for our own sentimentality. Dad later returned the machine to the shop where he had rented it, and we stored the seven records away to listen to someday. Ironically, despite many, many moves on my part, I came across those same seven records several years ago. Unable to play them, as I did not have a 78-rpm record player, my daughter took them to see what she could do. That Christmas, she surprised me with copies she had made of the records onto CDs. Not all the records could be saved. In fact, originally these records were only designed to last a month or so to be played by their recipient while away from home. To my amazement, these little records had lasted some sixty years and, as Dad had predicted, were listened to by a whole new generation of people, including my cousins, husband, and daughter. I had copies made and sent them to family members including my brother Glenn so he could hear his recording of singing "Sioux City Sue" so long ago.

During these recordings, it seemed to be happier times for my parents. My father cajoled Momma gently to speak into the microphone and tried to wean her from her shyness and to be more outspoken. They laughed together at my silliness and showed parental pride in all my verbal storytelling and singing. Years later I listened to these records with a sadness brought by the realization of the record's contributions to my memories. Rather than a recording of family love and the gentleness of being together it posed a memory of what should have been and never was to be in later life. Rather than becoming a memory of what was, the records became a memory of what might have been.

The next few years were happy and kind years. Dad had returned to driving the bus on his routes during the day. Momma was home all day and worked evenings at the bus station diner. Betty and Glenn lived with us also, but we didn't see much of them. They worked or attended high school during the day and were out in the evenings. I was busy with my own little world of dolls, my dollhouse, and all its furnishings and books. I loved to read books with my Momma and for her to read them to me also. Our days were busy but gentle in retrospect. Summer days brought Momma's attention to putting up fresh fruit and vegetables for the coming winters, along with her other many, many household jobs. During these summer days, Momma would get me up early, just at sunrise, and we would drive out to a neighboring farm where we could pick all the strawberries we wanted. Sometimes we would wander from the plowed fields and gather some blackberries or gooseberries in the surrounding woods for jams and pies also.

Often, as we picked the rich, red strawberries from the rows, I would eat some as we moved along down the aisles filling our basket. Momma would often laugh at me and say that the farmer should weigh me when I arrived and then weigh me when we left to see how many strawberries were in my tummy. She would laugh and say that the farmer was surely losing money as she was sure I was eating more strawberries than I picked. I didn't care. They just tasted so good!

As I had said, we would leave for the farms early in the June mornings before the sun became too hot. Momma would pack a basket for us filled with two mason jars of water cooled by chunks of ice from an ice block. She would wrap the mason jar in a cold rag and place it in the basket where it would stay cool to the taste most of the planned trip.

She also packed a few snacks of fruit in case we became hungry. Sometimes we also found a mess of collard greens growing in the woods. Momma would pick the greens and wrap it to take home to clean and cook with fatback chunks or lard for dinner that evening. We were delighted to find the greens, as they would taste so good that evening with fresh, hot cornbread for supper.

To this day, I don't believe I have ever drunk water as cool and sweet as that water in those old glass mason jars where chunks of ice floated.

When we came home from our trips to the farm, Momma would wash and prepare the fruit. Usually we had enough for supper's dessert that evening. Large blackberries covered with fresh cream tasted awfully well. I would nearly fall asleep at the table because I was so tired from the trip to the farm and being outside most of the day. They always say that fresh air makes one sleep a good night's rest. And that was so on those summer days.

The next weeks would entail busy days in the kitchen where Momma was boiling the glass jars and cooking the various fruit for canning. These processed jars of fruit promised winter pies and breakfast preserves on the kitchen table for later. In July, we began the work of canning and preserving vegetables for various uses in the winter. Momma loved to make stuffed green peppers, stored tomato, corn, succotash, green beans, and large green pickles of all sizes and tastes—some sweet and some not. Bread and butter slices were my favorite. They were crisp and sharp to the taste. We had a huge walk-in closet, and Dad had added shelves for Momma to place her canned goods on for storage when she was done. All the finished products added to our shelves of food for the coming winter and provided our family with good homemade foods. It was just the way things were done. Momma seldom went to the grocery store. She didn't need to. She made everything herself. Momma could just walk into the closet and choose some canned article of food for that meal and serve it. They all tasted wonderful. During these years, *cocooning*, a term used by retail analysts to describe the phenomenon in which people actively avoid straying from their houses, was the life we lived. Everything that we needed was right there in the house.

Because I had red, auburn hair, my skin was pale and subject to harsh sunburns and freckles. To protect my face, Momma always had me wear a sunbonnet. I hated to wear those things. When we went to the farms to pick the fruit, I had to wear the hated sunbonnet all morning while in the sun. Everyone seemed to be staring at me. No one else wore them. I begged with Momma to not make me wear the sunbonnets to the farms. But it was of no use.

My grandmother Ethel made my sunbonnets from old scraps of material from previous sewings or sackcloth from feed sacks. Dating back to the 1920's to 1930s, feed and flour manufacturers sold their products in cotton bags. Because of economic hardships and WWII, women used the unbleached cotton to make underwear, clothes, quilts—the cotton bags were for whatever their needs were. And that was where my sunbonnets came from. The cotton sacks had become so popular that the manufacturers added color and prints. Flour, sugar, beans, rice, cornmeal, feed, and fertilizer came in these cotton sacks. All these products were used, and the sacks were saved for making various items for the home and family. I remember our kitchen curtains were made from this sackcloth, and Momma made lovely pillowcases for our beds. And the hated sunbonnets too. Grandma Ethel would always have two or three she had just made for me whenever we would go visit her on the farm. It was hard for me to be polite in accepting them to wear. Grandma couldn't understand why I didn't want to wear them. She had worn them most of her life when she was working outdoors or in the fields. And she had not had such pretty designs or material with trim for her sunbonnets then. The sunbonnet was part of her everyday wardrobe. It felt natural to her.

I did agree that the sunbonnets were lovely to look at and that they certainly did do their job in protecting my face from the hot sun and the sporting of freckles, but the sunbonnet was so hot to wear. My hair and face would get all wet and sweaty under the tied bonnets, and I felt like a grandmother myself. I would look in the mirror when I had on the sunbonnet and see only my grandmother's face looking back at me. I wasn't ready to be a grandmother yet. I wanted to be a young girl and feel the sun in my face and the soft breezes when I was playing. I had to devise a way to not have to wear the hated sunbonnets.

Whining and pleading worked to no charm. Momma was determined that I was to continue wearing the sunbonnets because her mother had told her it was important for me to wear them to protect myself from having a sunstroke.

One summer day, feeling completely at war with these hated sunbonnets, I gathered them up and poked them all into an old pillowcase and secretly carried them outside while Momma was busy on the back porch making butter in the old wooden churn. Quietly I carried the pillow sack out behind the large garage in the back and over to the woodpile behind the house. There I found a small garden shovel and began to earnestly dig a large, deep hole. After I had determined I had dug a large enough hole, I placed the old pillowcase full of the hated sunbonnets into the hole and proceeded to cover up the hidden articles. I then carefully placed rocks and piles of old sections of wood on top of the newly dug hole. And then I quietly slipped back inside the house to help Momma with the making of the butter for dinner that night.

For days Momma hunted and hunted for the sunbonnets to no avail. One day she stopped and turned to me and gave me a long hard look. I lowered my eyes because I felt that if I looked into her eyes I would confess everything to her about the hiding of the sunbonnets. Standing there with my head lowered, I suddenly heard a small chuckle and she said, "All right. You win. You don't have to wear the sunbonnets anymore. And I shall tell your grandmother that she is not to make any more of them for you to replace the ones gone." I pretended to not be concerned, but later, when I was in my room alone, I grabbed one of my dolls and danced a small little jig of absolute joy that I would now be free of the sunbonnets—yellow gingham and all.

As I had mentioned earlier, Momma did not go to the grocery store often. We had all we needed at home. Momma preserved and canned for the winter, churned our own butter, and baked our own bread, cakes, pies, cookies, and cinnamon rolls. We also grew most of our own vegetables in the yard garden: green beans, peas, carrots, lettuce, cucumbers, and more. They were always fresh on our table for our meals.

As for meat, we always had plenty. We had cages in the backyard where the chickens could roost and we could collect the fresh eggs each day. Dad would purchase half of a cow from the local butcher. Then the sides of beef would be cut into sections Momma listed and frozen in the large locker for us to pick up, as we needed. We obtained our hams and bacon from the pigs that we raised.

Dad would rent a small area of fenced land from a local farmer and buy a small set of piglets, maybe six to eight. He would keep them on the rented land and raise them until it was time to have them slaughtered. Each night, we would drive over to the land section outside of town and feed, water, and check on the pigs. I remember one of the first nights when the little piglets were all running around squealing and looking so cute, and I began to talk to Dad about names I had given to them. Dad stopped and looked at me and said, "Never give a name to your dinner," and walked away. I thought for a few minutes and realized what he meant. If I named the little piglets and made them my pets, it would be sad to see them sold as adults for our meals. It was good advice. Yet Dad developed a soft place each year. I could hear him laughing and joking with the little "squeakers" when we went out in the evenings to feed them. I know he wanted to name them also.

Summer days also brought the iceman. At this time, our icebox, as it was called, was made of two wooden boxes. The larger box was on the bottom and was where you kept the food. The top box was where the large cube of ice was placed. Often made of oak or walnut, the large box that stored the food had to be kept cold, though it did not run on coolant. The icebox was so named because it required blocks of ice, just like today's camping coolers.

The typical icebox was roughly the size of modern refrigerators, though somewhat shorter. The face had three to five hinged doors, one smaller and designated for the ice block. Interiors were lined with material such as tin and for insulation there was cork, or straw, among other popular choices. Internal wired shelves held the food. We did not keep a lot of food in the refrigerator because the coldness could only last as long as the block of ice lasted. A tray that was placed between the small block of wood holding the ice, and the large block of wood holding the food would have to be emptied often. The ice would melt during the day and drip onto the tray, soon filling it with water to be emptied, or else it would overflow onto the floor. We were taught not to open the door to the icebox often as it would let out any cold air that would be in there. Actually we didn't eat a lot of food that needed to be refrigerated because we could not always guarantee having a cold place for it. Leftovers were often covered with cheesecloth and set on the side of the old wooden shelf in the kitchen. The icebox often kept the milk, cream, butter, cheese, and salad dressings cool. We had ice cream only if we churned it ourselves and we would eat all of it at the time. There was no place to keep it cold and solid.

When we would make the ice cream, once or twice a year, it would be a complete day of work to hand-turn the handle while churning the cream and fruit to make the treat. It would also depend if we were able to obtain the needed ice chunks and salt. Fourth of July was usually one of the special days for ice cream.

But also adding to the treat of ice cream was a more obtainable cooling object during those summer days. We loved to chomp on those cool pieces of ice. We knew the schedule of the iceman, and when Momma would tell me that the day was Tuesday or such and that the iceman would be arriving soon, my friends and I would go and sit on the curb in front of the house and anticipate the arrival of the iceman. He would pull up in his old truck with the flat bed in the back filled with straw and blocks and blocks piled high of cold ice. It was wonderful to see and stand near it. We marveled at the iceman, who would step out of his truck and walk around to the back. He would say hello to the gathered children and ask me to tell my mother that the iceman was here. I would run up to the porch and holler up the stairs to my Momma that the iceman was here and ask her how many blocks of ice she wanted. Then I would tell the iceman. The iceman used tongs to grab the block and typically carried it over his shoulder, covered by a leather sheath. He would enter our house and walk up the stairs with the leather sheath holding the large block of cold ice over his shoulder. Then he would place it directly in the icebox. When he came back downstairs, he would laugh to see us waiting there patiently by the truck watching the constant dripping of water from the blocks of ice sitting on the straw in the summer heat of the truck.

Then he would ask if we wanted a chunk of ice. Of course, we all hollered "Yes!" to which he would smile and chunk large pieces of ice for each of us. And then he would drive off to the next delivery point. We would sit on the step of our front porch and patiently lick our summer treat—a cold piece of ice. It was a great treat to all of us and so appreciated on those hot summer days.

Along with the weekly visits from the iceman, we also had the milkman arrive each morning. He would pull up in his small van and open the side doors to display rows and rows of glass bottles holding milk, cream, or other dairy products. We always tried to get a peek inside of the cold van and ogle the rows of yummy dairy products. I would run upstairs and get my mother's order for the day of what she needed from the milkman. We didn't get a lot of things in the early days because of lack of monies. Once in a while, Momma would treat Dad to his favorite: a bottle of buttermilk that he loved in the evening. He would pour a glass of cold buttermilk and sit down at the table and dunk chunks of cold cornbread into the buttermilk and eat it. That was his favorite meal. I tried it several times but decided it must be an acquired taste. It was also a treat if Momma ordered any cottage cheese. We loved to eat that with some of our canned fruit or as a side dish with dinner. Cheese was very expensive, and we usually only ordered it during the holidays. Our glass bottles of milk always had a layer of thick cream on top for Dad to enjoy in his morning coffee. We couldn't have the cream, as it was his treat for his coffee before starting the day. The milkman would then collect the empty milk bottles, have a small chat with my mother about the neighborhood or some latest news, and on he would go to the next delivery stop. It was a socialization time for

Home Again, Home Again, Jiggity, Jig 81

my mother and a treat to all of us with the arrival of the dairy treats we might be able to get that day.

I remember once when I was walking home from downtown with my Momma, a woman whom we did not know well came up to us and was talking to my mother about some matter. She turned to me and remarked upon the loveliness of my red hair. Looking at my mother's own black hair, the woman then turned to me. Bending down to look me in the eye, the woman would smile and say, "And where did you get your lovely red hair?" Remembering something I had heard my mother laughing about one time, I quickly replied, "From the milkman." The woman stood up and gave Momma a frown and walked quickly away.

My mother started laughing and made me promise to never, ever say such a thing again. It wasn't until many years later that I realized how much harm I could have accomplished with that silly answer. But at the time, I wasn't worried because as I remembered, our milkman didn't even have much hair, so the joke was really on the woman.

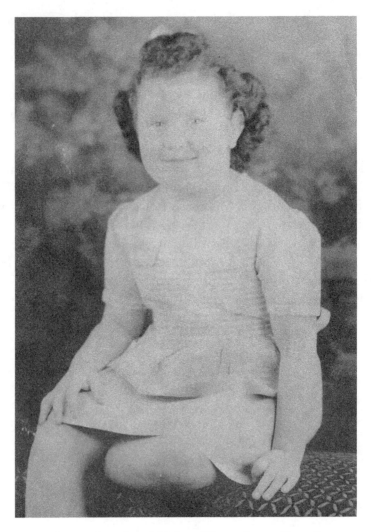

Remember the old joke - "from the mailman"

Momma would spend time brushing my long hair with all the curls. My hair was always naturally curly. Sometimes she would brush my hair up into a net to keep it all in place when I was out playing. The net was much like a snood from years past hair fashion. The net would be of a light fabric and not easily seen over my hair but kept the hair in place and fashionable. The top was bobby pinned to my head. I was an active child with running, riding my bike and various outside games. This net kept my hair in place and not all over my face. Momma didn't mind that I was active and busy all day but I should still always look neat and ladylike.

Chapter 4

Meet Viola and E.P.

I remember our neighbors across the street from our home, Viola and E.P. Beeler. I never knew what E.P. stood for—I guess now it doesn't really matter. No matter what his name was, he would always just be E.P. As I remember, Viola and E.P. were older than my parents, or at least they seemed to be to me. Viola was a tall woman, strong and large in a matronly sort of way. She had a broad face and teeth that seemed to fill every spare place in her mouth, and you could always see the teeth because she always seemed to be smiling. Even though she was tall, she always was able to bend down and give little ones a huge hug and smile into their face. She always smelled like violets to me when she gave me one of those large hugs. Her real beauty lay in her hair. Coal black with some white strands in the front sides, her hair hung almost to her waist. Of course, we never saw her long hair during the day. She always wore it up, with the braids wrapped around her head. Her hair was just beautiful, and she took great pride in her hair always being smooth and with all hairs in place. She was a lovely woman with her braided hair and soft flowery dresses that she wore each day. Simple in style, the dresses seemed to just flow as she moved across the room, and her feet were placed solidly in women's fashionable shoes of the day, solid-heeled and the top at the ankles. Viola was comfortable and stylish with her chosen soft dresses.

As for her husband, E.P., well, he was shorter than Viola and small in stature. As best I remember, E.P. always had a big smile on his face. He

83

seemed pleased in his life. And where Viola had so much hair, E.P. had none. His head was bald and shiny. His head always seemed to be red from too much sun where he worked all day outside as a house painter. He wore white coveralls over a short-sleeved shirt. The coveralls were often splattered with some color, whatever paint he had been painting that day. His feet were always shod in round-toed work boots always splattered with colors of paint. But on Sunday morning, in preparation of church, E.P. would be all polish and shine. He would wear his best Sunday suit, shirt, and tie, and his shoes would be shiny and styled with his sparse hair wet and smoothed back. They made a lovely couple as they headed out each Sunday morning for Sunday school and church. They attended an evangelistic Baptist church outside of Monett in the countryside, and this small church filled each Sunday with happy and joyful participants, led in voice by Viola and E.P. They truly enjoyed gathering together with others and voicing loudly in song their love of Jesus. Sunday was their favorite day of the week.

Sometimes, I would go to church with Viola and E.P. and listen to them sing and rejoice. I enjoyed those Sunday visits with them and felt privileged that they had invited me. After church, when we returned to their home, they would often invite me to stay for Bible reading and later an early supper. We would sit together in the dining room where a soft, cool breeze blew through the room, lazily moving the lace curtains at the window. We sipped iced tea with lemons floating in the green iced glass pitcher on the table. Sometimes, Viola or E.P. would read softly together from the Bible and offer small prayers of comfort to each other. I enjoyed sitting and listening as I shared Viola's freshly baked cookies and later her fried chicken for supper. They were special days of comfort to me.

For some reason, Viola and E.P. had not been blessed with their own children. So they often took in other children who needed a safe home for a time when their life had been overturned in some manner. At this time in my life, they had brought home a young boy, Johnny, who was the same age as me. I think I fell in love with him the first moment I saw him. He was smaller than me and seemed frail in stature. He had soft blond hair and the most beautiful smile I had ever seen on another child. His blue eyes just sparkled when he talked and laughed. From the moment he came to live with E.P. and Viola, he became my best friend, and we played together every single day we could. I have

Johnny and Me

Johnny came to live with Viola and E.P. Beeler, across the street from our house, while Johnny's mother was in the T.B. Sanitorium in Mt. Vernon, Missouri.

Johnny and I were "buddies" during that year he was there visiting. We played all day, running, riding our bikes and swinging in the tire swings that hung in the backyard off an old oak tree. In the background you can see Momma's vegetable garden with tomatoes and other good vegetables for Momma to can and preserve for the winter days. The clothesline is also there where our newly washed clothes usually hung. We shared the clothesline with the owners of the house where we lived. They were our landlords and always very kind to me and Momma.

a picture of Johnny and me with his tricycle, and I love to look at the sweet smile on Johnny's face. He was to stay with the Beeler family for that summer while his mother got well. She was in the tuberculosis sanitarium during those months and was unable to care for Johnny. He loved and missed his mother very much. Once, Viola and E.P. drove Johnny to Mt. Vernon to visit his mother. Johnny was happy for days, and I believe it helped his mother improve her health.

During the summer, Viola and E.P.'s church would invite a traveling minister in to preach to their own congregation.

On those hot summery nights in July and August, their church would secure a local farmer's cow pasture where they would set up a large tent for the evening revival meetings. It was a cooler place with the light summer breezes blowing softly through the sides of the open tent. In preparation, the farmer would mow the adjoining grassy areas so we could sit on large wooden benches placed in many rows side by side under the large tent.

My mother, Lela, was a people watcher. She could sit for hours watching people and be totally entertained. These evenings were the highest moments of her enjoyment. She loved to see all the local people who had walked or driven from all around the countryside to attend. Dressed in their Sunday finery, the women arrived wearing light summer dresses as they gathered together with the sunburned, balding farmers wearing their cleanest overalls. Children danced in jubilation within their own clusters of families and friends. Mothers brought baskets of fried chicken with fruit and vegetables to enjoy as a picnic dinner they spread on blankets near the tent before the revival meetings. Clear, refreshing ice water was served in old mason jars.

It actually was a festive night with all the local people gathered together to share in their celebration of the Lord. The minister read from the Bible in loud, disparaging words that threatened "hell and damnation" for all attending that were not "walking in the ways of the Lord." The choir and congregation members sang joyfully to the twinkling keys of the old upright piano located at the front of the tent by the pulpit. It was a loud and joyful sound in the night with the lifting of songs and prayers to the heavens above.

My mother and I sat together in the back of the tent on those old benches, surveying the large, colorful scenes. We joined together in the singing of those wonderful old hymns that joyfully announced the wonderment of "walking with the Lord" and how "blessed it was to be saved." We weren't members of the church. We didn't go to the pulpit and confess our sins. We didn't speak in tongues or roll on the grounds in joyous jubilation of "witnessing." What we did feel was the glorious sharing of a great religious love from the many people attending. Our hearts were filled with those wondrous and joyous sounds as we spent hours together in that lowly cow pasture, on those old wooden benches, in that large old revival tent.

The Fourth of July arrived with gusts of hot summer winds. The day promised to be hot and hotter. Momma was busy in the kitchen cooking chicken and baking bread in preparation of our picnic that evening in our backyard. We planned to eat our picnic in the yard and enjoy our own fireworks that Dad had purchased downtown at the stalls set up in front of the stores on Main Street. Fireworks were easy to obtain in those days, and everyone had their own show planned for the evening. I had my snakes to light and watch as they wriggled on the sidewalks, and later I would be able to enjoy my sparklers while I ran around in the yard writing my name in the air with the glowing sparklers and pretending to be a princess with a magic wand.

That evening, after our picnic supper, my family was gathered on the grass of our backyard with the family who lived on the first floor of the house. Out came all the fireworks, and the evening show of bangs and bright lights began. Dad had been shooting Roman candles when he gave one to Momma and told her to light it and shoot one. It would be fun, he told her. Momma wasn't too certain of this manner, and after we all assured her it would be fine, she timidly hit the end of the Roman candle and it began to shoot out the bright colors into the air. Suddenly, the candle kind of sputtered and burst the balls of fire out of the rear end, hitting Momma full in the stomach with such a force that she screamed in pain and doubled over, clutching her stomach. Dad ran to her and stamped out the Roman candle that was still sparking and sizzling on the ground beside her. He then grabbed Momma up in his arms and carried her upstairs into their bedroom and placed her on the bed. She was moaning in pain and had her eyes tightly shut with tears rolling down the sides of her face. Dad told me to go outside and sit on the front porch and then he called Dr. Kerr and told him to come immediately to see about Momma.

I walked slowly back downstairs and sat down on the front stairs. I was so scared that Momma was going to die. Our landlords sat with me until the doctor arrived and went upstairs. And then Dad came down to sit with me. He sat down and pulled me over to hug me and assure me that Momma was going to be just fine. After all, Dr. Kerr was with her now, and he could cure anything and anyone. I laughed a small laugh at the thought of Dr. Kerr and how safe he made a person feel.

While we sat there in the evening on that front porch, the stars began to appear in the dark evening sky. Dad told me to look up at one of the stars that was especially bright in that night sky and to say a special prayer for Momma to get well. Tears were falling down his face as he talked to me about a special little baby that would be living in the sky now with God and perhaps would often play on that special star we saw up in the sky. I looked at that star and wished for the baby to be happy in the sky with God.

Later, Dr. Kerr came down to tell us that Momma was going to be just fine but that she needed lots of sleep and care. We could go see her but not to disturb her. Dr. Kerr left, and we walked quietly upstairs to see Momma sleep. Dad kissed her on her forehead and walked to where I stood in the hall outside of the room. He closed the bedroom door and told me to go get ready for bed.

I could hear Dad sitting in the living room in the dark, softly crying as I fell asleep.

The next day, Viola and E.P. came over and sat and talked with Momma and Dad and read the Bible to them. I think they gave them comfort at this time and helped Momma heal. Viola gave me a chalk ceramic dog to place in my bedroom by my bed. I named it Sunny and kept him in my bedroom for many years.

Momma and Dad never talked about that day to me. I guess that they figured I would have been too small and would not have remembered the event. But I had remembered, and for so many years of my young life, I would often look up at the stars and wonder how my little baby brother liked living there and being with God.

Fall arrived, and the evenings had grown cooler in the late hours. I didn't want to go to bed that night because I was worried about little Johnny, my friend. He had felt sick that day, and Viola had brought him inside and placed him in bed because he had a fever and was coughing. Dr. Kerr was called.

After Dr. Kerr had looked in on Johnny, he came over and spoke to Dad. He told him that I was not to go over to the Beeler house until he told me that I could because Johnny had whooping cough. Momma gasped in alarm when Dr. Kerr said that word because at that time children were dying from this illness, and there seemed to be no cure. Dr. Kerr looked at me and checked my temperature. He assured my parents that I seemed healthy and to keep an eye on me for a few days.

I was worried about Johnny. I didn't really understand what whooping cough meant, but it sounded very serious, and I was worried that Johnny might die in the night. Dad let me go down and sit with him on the front porch for a few minutes. We could look across the street at the Beeler house, and I could see the lights on in the house, especially the light in Johnny's bedroom window. We could hear his loud barking cough as the spasm of coughing fluttered through the front screen door and outside into the yard. The cough sounded awful, and I was so afraid that Johnny would just cough himself to death.

Dad asked me to look up into the sky and find a special star to say my prayer for Johnny to get well. I looked up into the sky and prayed that night for special angels to surround Johnny with health. I told them how much I loved Johnny and that he had to stay here to be my friend.

And then I went to bed. I didn't sleep much that night. Johnny's bedroom window was dark, but I could imagine Johnny lying in bed sick. That morning, I awoke early, dressed, and rushed down the stairs to sit on the stairs and wait for word of Johnny. Dr. Kerr soon arrived and went into the house through the front door opened by Viola. She looked like she had been up all night. Probably she and E.P. had been sitting outside Johnny's room praying for him to be well. Later, Dr. Kerr came out of the house and walked over to me sitting on the porch. He patted me on the head and told me that Johnny was doing very well and that he believed that soon he would be feeling better. But he warned me—I still couldn't go visit him yet. That was good news. I could wait until Johnny was feeling better, and we could once again resume playing our many games together.

Johnny did get well, and so did his mother. Shortly after Christmas, right after the New Year, Johnny left the Beeler home to return to his mother. They moved to California where it would be warmer and she could heal better. I greatly missed my friend that winter but liked to think of him in sunny California enjoying days at the beach with his mother. I know that Viola and E.P. were sad to see him leave their home. Shortly after Johnny left, they adopted a teenage girl. She arrived at their home carrying more than her baggage. She had with her a burden of years past of neglect and abuse received in various foster homes where she had lived. She always seemed to feel anger and resentment toward all who tried to extend her comfort or safety. As a result, the few years that she lived with E.P. and Viola were tumultuous and often violent. She refused to abide by their home rules of no smoking, no alcohol consumption, or curfew hours. She especially refused to participate in any form of religious life in their house or church. After several years, she just packed her limited belongings in a suitcase and walked out the house and traveled on to her own disheartened destiny.

During the following years, Viola and E.P. opened their homes to children who needed a home for an undetermined time while their parents were arranging themselves to be able to take care of them. It was like a foster home where children could be placed while they waited for their parents to gain the ability to care for them again.

Janice, my cousin, is enjoying her birthday party

A birthday party at Viola and E.P. Beeler's house for baby Janice who is sitting in the center of the table with her many gifts. Pictured: first person in line (I do not know), Viola Beeler, with Aunt Rena, Maureece, Betty, Momma, E. P. Beeler, Naomi, and me. I don't know the other children behind Janice.

When looking through these pictures, in the book, I laughed to my cousin, Janice, that she was in more of the pictures of my family than I was. I laughed that at every picture taken Janice just popped up. My mother and Rena, Momma's sister, were very close in the family. They saw each other almost every day and always took care of each other. Janice and I are cousins and an age difference, but I feel as if she and I were sisters and not cousins. This is also confusing because we have seldom lived in the same vicinity. I believe it is because we are like our mothers and thus we are like sisters. We talk often long distance and it is as if we have always been next door to each other. That's nice!

Chapter 5

The House Across the Street

Summertime was filled with active play outside. My neighbor was my staunch cohort in all our Indian romps around our homemade tepee in the large side yard. We were both fascinated with the lives of Indians of yesteryear and their existence in our early America nation. As a result, we created life games as we imagined how Indians must have lived and spoke at that time. Not really having much to base our games on, we just used our imagination and what we had heard on the popular radio show "The Lone Ranger." Although we loved the Lone Ranger, we were always interested in his companion, Tonto, as the duo fought injustice in the American Old West.

The landlord helped us drape an old blanket over two tied poles and make a rough Indian gathering of sorts like a tepee. Inside this tepee, we placed various pillows to sit on and homemade articles we had created to look like Indian ware: a peace pipe made from tied sticks with a chicken feather hanging from it, or a store-bought Indian chief war bonnet that we took turns wearing according to who was the Indian chief. The other would wear a headband with a feather in it, also bought at the local dime store. We would build a pretend fire from a pile of sticks to make it look like we were sitting around a burning fire inside the tepee. There we would cook our Indian dinners or smoke the peace pipe while discussing what we were going to do about the approaching "white men" or settlers.

Playing Indians was a great pastime for us each day. Of course, we had pretend bows and arrows that we made from sticks and strings. But to us, they were real. We even invented our own Indian language, spoken and in sign, and often dance an Indian dance around the campfire of our own creation. We whooped like demented Indians dancing around the campfires while there was always a pretend white man or an Indian from another tribe sitting as hostage. Playing outdoors was so much fun in those days creative with usage of surrounding items. With a small need to buy anything, we created everything in our own imagination.

An old enormous oak tree in the middle of the back portion of land was our favorite spot for hot summer days as we swung in the old tire swing hanging from the oak tree. We also had thick ropes hanging from the tree branches. Large knots at various lengths were tied in the thick ropes so we could jump and grab the rope and swing in a loop under the tree. Grass could not grow in that area because of our active feet, so we always stirred up the dust while playing on the swing or the ropes. Great memories come to mind of lying face down on our stomach and swinging softly around and around on that large tire swing. It was so cool in the shade of that large oak tree swinging endlessly on this tire swing. We would spend hours and hours there under that old oak tree swinging, laughing, and talking. A simple way to pass time outside—no need for any expensive toy or game. All that was needed was a strong tree branch, a rope, and an old tire.

Summer ended, and early September arrived with school days. Because I was born in December, I was just a few months short of the age of five when school started, so my mother opted to keep me home from kindergarten and promised me that I would start school in the first grade. Momma said she was just not ready to let me go yet. She wanted to keep me at home for one more year.

I always regretted Momma's decision. I was very lonesome that year while the neighbor children attended kindergarten. I lost that year of meeting other classmates, establishing friendships, and learning the preschool curriculum. It left me behind in school when I started the first grade, and I had no friends. Friendships had already been made, and there seemed to be no opening for a new student.

But at this time, I stayed home, slept late, and played around the house waiting for Hubert to return home from school so we could play our outside games of cowboys and Indians. I would also sit upstairs on the living room floor and play with my dolls or paper dolls. I loved to dress my paper dolls and create stories for them to act out. I also read a lot—I loved books. Momma read to me at night, and during the day, I reread the books she had read. I was a good reader! Of course, I was fascinated with stories and loved to create my own stories to tell Momma as she worked in the house at some household task. She loved to hear me talk and sometimes would sit down with me and give me her full attention while we talked about some story or book.

And then it happened. A family moved into the big white house across the street from my house. I was sitting on the porch playing with my paper dolls when a car and an old truck pulled up on the other side of our house and parked. I put down my paper dolls and stepped off the porch to walk over to the curbing on my side of the street. To my amazement, I watched as an entire family folded out of the car and went to stand in the yard looking at the empty house. Now the house had been empty for some months now, and I had been secretly wishing that a family of children would move in so I would have new friends to visit with. And there they were. I saw two boys and two girls, a mother, and a father. They were all talking loudly and excitedly and reaching back into their car to pull out boxes and various packages. They began to walk up to the door that led into the kitchen, and soon they all disappeared into the house. Windows began to be opened, and I could practically hear the family moving throughout the house as they looked at rooms and exclaimed back and forth to each other about the things they liked or did not like in the rooms. I could hear them shouting out what room they wanted for their bedrooms, the voices seemed to float out to where I stood as they opened the windows in the room where they journeyed to. My ears seemed to burst with all the pandemonium of shouts and laughter that now filled a once-empty house. I practically hugged myself and giggled out loud at the excitement I felt with this large family moving next door to me. As I watched and listened, I visualized all the fun things we would do in play. I just knew it was going to be wonderful, and I would lose my lonely days at home alone.

As an only child, I had always felt so lonesome with a lack of brothers and sisters near my age. Yes, Betty and Glenn were my family from Dad's first marriage, but they were so much older than me. They never had time for me. They were always going to work or to school.

The Evans family move in!

This picture is from my revisit to Monett in the 1990's. The houses have changed some from when I had lived here as a child.

The house on the left had been white and later blue and filled with all of the Evans family - Mr. and Mrs. Evans, Roberta, Priscilla, Jimmy and Joey.

Momma, Dad and I had lived across the street in the white house on the second floor. Our landlords, the Jones family, lived on the first floor.

You can see the curb where I would sit and wait for Priscilla to come out and see me. Also, on the second floor, the small kitchen window was where I would eat breakfast and watch to see Priscilla and the others come out to go to school. I always loved to wave to them. The front porch of their house was where we spent many summer days when it was raining.

We would sit and read or plays games until the sun came back out. Then always hopscotch and jump rope.

Now here was a house full of people across the street. I felt certain at least one would want to be my friend. I sat down quietly on the curbing by my yard and waited to see what would happen next. The mother had driven the old car to the house, and it had been filled with the children and various boxes and packages. The father had driven the old truck that contained suitcases, boxes, and various pieces of furniture. Soon, various members of the family began to come back out of the house and go to the car or truck to carry items into the house. Within a few minutes, an energetic line of busy feet and loud voices were seen carrying their belongings into the house, back and forth, kitchen screen door slamming and opening, reminding me of a line of busy ants carrying their found food into their nest.

At this time, my mother heard all the commotion and came downstairs to see what was happening. She walked over to where I was sitting on the curbing, and I jumped up quickly to announce to her that a family was moving in next door, right across the street. Momma laughed at how excited I was with the new family. She expressed hope the mother of the household would be a friend she could get to know and chat with at times. She stood and watched as the children were carrying items into the home. I asked if I could sit on the curbing and watch the moving in, and she told me I could as long as I promised that I would not cross the street by myself. I agreed and sat back down to continue watching. Momma told me that she would go over with a casserole or pie later to welcome the new family, and I could meet everyone then because she was going to take me with her. And with that promise, she went back upstairs to continue her busy tasks in our apartment. I was filled with anticipation of being allowed to go over and meet the new neighbors later.

Soon, the car and truck had been cleared out of items, and the house seemed to settle down as rooms were set up for living in. Bedrooms had been chosen, clothes were being placed in closets, and soon, I could smell food being cooked. The mother was preparing a lunch for everyone to eat. I was certain they would be hungry after all that work. At this time, Momma called me up for my lunch and an afternoon nap. My cheese sandwich with an apple tasted so good in anticipation of the afternoon events. I quietly went into my room to read a book and take a nap with my favorite doll.

HOME AGAIN, HOME AGAIN, JIGGITY, JIG   97

When I awoke, I quickly flew to the window in our kitchen to look over at the neighbor's home to see if they were still there and not just something I had dreamed about. Yes, the car and truck were still there, and I could still hear noises coming from inside the house. Momma combed my hair and said we would now go over to visit our new neighbors. In anticipation of our visit, Momma had prepared a macaroni-and-cheese casserole. We always had a large loaf of American cheese as it was a commodity and lay available in our fridge. The elbow macaroni cost only ten cents a box, so Momma felt she could afford to share this particular dish. Besides, Momma reasoned to me, every family member always enjoys a good hot macaroni-and-cheese casserole. Momma winked at me and said that maybe later we would take over one of her fresh apple cobblers. I smiled because I knew that everyone loved Momma's fruit cobblers.

Momma and I walked over to the house across the street. She carried the large Pyrex dish filled with the still-hot casserole wrapped in one of her fluffy kitchen towels made from sack cloth and two hot pads to help carry the dish. We crossed the street and walked up the steps to the kitchen screen door. Momma knocked on the screen, and I stooped forward to try to see into the room. The screen quickly swung open, and we were greeted by a short plump woman with white hair pulled back into a bun at the back of her head. As I looked up to the woman, I noticed how short she was, but mainly I noticed how beautiful her blue eyes were as they looked down at me and twinkled when she spoke. Welcoming Momma and me into the kitchen, she took the hot casserole dish that we offered to her. She placed it on the kitchen table and offered us chairs to sit upon. She replied that things were basically in an uproar with their just arriving, but they were busy working at getting all set comfortably. Momma and I sat down at the table and smiled. The woman introduced herself as Jesse Evans, and Momma replied with our names and that we lived just across the street. Mrs. Evans chuckled and said that she had seen me sitting on the curbing watching as they had moved in. She was sure I would soon be over to meet her children.

When Momma told her she had brought her a macaroni-and-cheese casserole, Mrs. Evans laughed and expressed her satisfaction and thanks for such a nice gesture. I gathered a quick peek into the other two rooms and couldn't help but notice the sparse furniture in the rooms. Mrs. Evans saw me looking and explained that more furniture would be arriving in the next days. She told Momma that with four children it was hard to keep chairs and tables in one solid piece as each child was boisterous and tumbling and wrestling often happened in the rooms as the children played. But as I looked around, I just saw a house that was already beginning to be filled with love and comfort. It all looked just fine to me.

Mrs. Evans then served cold sweet iced tea to us, and we sat and sipped the tea while talking to her at the kitchen table. That was when I began to meet the other members of the family. First appeared the oldest daughter, Ruth. She was in high school, and Momma spoke that she was about the same age of my half sister, Betty, who was presently living with me. Ruth was glad to hear this, and she said she hoped they would be friends. Then the oldest son, Jimmy, ran in. He was a charmer. Short in height, he had a huge open grin and the biggest ears I thought I had ever seen on any one person. Mrs. Evans laughed and introduced Jimmy to us as he ran out the kitchen screen door. It was explained that he was on his way to work at the local grocery store. Although young, the grocer let Jimmy work in the back of the grocery store as a box boy for a few hours a week. He would open boxes of newly arrived goods and place the cans on the shelves.

And then I heard a cheerful hello and looked over into the living room to see a young girl walking into the kitchen. She introduced herself to us and said her name was Priscilla. Momma laughed because her middle name was Priscilla. I think an instant friendship formed there in that one small moment between Priscilla and my momma and me. She just seemed like the nicest person I had ever known.

Looking back, I remember Priscilla to be all legs, knobby knees, and a funny face. She was rather skinny and somewhat tall for her age. She was three years older than me but already seemed older to me than her years. She pulled up a chair and sat down next to me and poured herself a glass of sweet iced tea from the glass pitcher sitting on the table. Sipping the tea, she wiped her brow and explained she had been busy upstairs setting up her bedroom with all her favorite items. Taking the last sip, she asked me if I would like to go up and see her room. I replied a quick yes, and up we went to her room on the second floor. She had a large window in her room that actually faced our house across the street. I laughed and told her we could wave to each other from our facing windows. Priscilla smiled and agreed with me that it sounded like a nice idea. I loved Priscilla right then when she smiled her smile. I felt like I had found a sister that I had always dreamed about. We looked at her record collection. Priscilla was very proud of the few record albums she owned and loved to play them on her used portable record player. She opened what she said was one of her favorite records from the RCA album of Vaughn Monroe and his orchestra. I didn't know the music and had never seen a record player like this one. My parents had an old wooden upright gramophone in the living room that Betty and Glenn listened to their records on. But now, I had never seen a record player this small. Placing the 78-rpm record on the player and pushing the button to start the machine, I was amazed to watch the record drop smoothly down and the record's arm to swing over and start playing the music. It was like magic to me. Priscilla laughed to see my face as I watched the record begin to play. And then I heard Vaughn Monroe sing. I loved his voice and the music. I was so excited I could barely sit still. But we sat down on the floor and listened to the whole album. Much to my regret, we soon heard Mrs. Evans calling me back downstairs, as my mother was ready to leave for home. Priscilla promised me that I could come over again and listen to her music with her. I ran downstairs so happy and left the house with my mother. I waved good-bye to Mrs. Evans and thanked her for the visit, and Momma and I walked across the street and back to our home. When we were upstairs to our apartment, I told Momma all about Priscilla's record player and listening to the music. Momma just smiled and said that maybe someday we could afford to get such a smaller record player. It would be nice to own.

I didn't meet Joey, the youngest member of the family, until days later. He had been with his father watching him load a few more things on their truck to bring over to the house. Joey was a few years younger than me.

Days passed. I could see Priscilla, Ruth, and Jimmy leave each morning for school. Sometimes they walked and sometimes they rode their bikes. I watched them from the kitchen window while I ate my breakfast of milk and cereal. Priscilla always looked over and waved a big cheery wave to me as she left. It made me feel so happy that she remembered our promise to wave to each other from the windows. She always knew that I would be there looking for them as they left for school.

It was that winter that Dad brought home the rented record machine to record our voices on the records as we sang or talked. Little Joey was recorded singing "Silent Night."

The days passed, and soon it was summer again. The holidays had been joyful. I had enjoyed visiting the Evans family at their home for the holidays. They had a huge Christmas tree and made all the ornaments that they hung on the tree. That one Saturday afternoon, when they were putting up their tree and decorating, Priscilla invited me over to watch and help. Early that afternoon, she came over to our apartment and asked Momma if I could come over to visit and help. Momma said yes, and Priscilla walked me across the street to her home. Of course, as Priscilla had promised to my Momma, she held my hand as we crossed the street to their house. And I made sure to look both ways before we crossed. I almost ran along beside Priscilla because I was so excited. I couldn't wait to get over to her home and start the Christmas decorations. Together we made paper chains of all colors and Mrs. Evans popped some popcorn to string, and eat, for the tree. After it was all decorated and the lights were turned on, I believed it was the best Christmas tree I had seen. Jimmy, Priscilla, Joey, and me, with Mrs. Evans, had all decorated the tree. Of course, my own Christmas tree at home was beautiful, but this tree had been decorated with all of our own artwork and laughter. I just felt all warm and friendly when I looked at the Evans's Christmas tree. It may have hurt Momma sometimes because I wanted to be at their home all the time. But I think she understood how I longed to be with a large family and share in laughter and games with them.

Chapter 6

Et tu, Brute?

It was early spring, probably April, of that year, 1948, when an accident happened to E.P. Beeler across the street. He was a painter by profession. He painted houses inside and out. He always seemed to smell of fresh paint. One could tell what hue of color he had recently painted because splotches of green or blue or pink or such would be on the white coveralls he always wore over his shirts. And his large work shoes had splotches of paint on the toes of them. He kept all his supplies in a small garage he had in the back behind his house. I always loved to go in the garage and smell all the different fumes and smells from the various paints and supplies he had stored. It just seemed that everything E.P. touched had splotches of different color—his ladder, the cement floor of the garage, the tops of the closed paint cans. It was a rainbow room of sorts with E.P. always busy there cleaning brushes and putting away paint cans on the various shelves.

This particular afternoon, E.P. had been painting a house on a job. He was at the top of the ladder when he leaned one way and the ladder fell another way. As a result, E.P. fell to the ground and was knocked unconscious for a few minutes. Upon regaining consciousness, E.P. began to sit up, but he screamed in pain when he tried to move his legs. Upon hearing this noise, the house owner had come running out to see what the disturbance was and found E.P. on the grassy ground. He bent down to examine E.P.'s legs, and to his consternation, he found that the left leg had a break, and the bone was showing through the skin. This

101

was a serious injury. The bone was actually extending through E.P.'s leg. The owner wanted to call an ambulance immediately and take E.P. to the hospital. But E.P. would have nothing of that. He absolutely refused to go in an ambulance and told the owner to call his wife Viola to come get him.

Now remember E.P. was not a young man. I believe he would have been in his middle fifties at this time, and injuries do take their toll more so as one ages. Bones become more brittle and harder to heal.

Well, as I heard from Momma talking to Dad, Viola arrived with some friends of theirs from their church group. They placed E.P. on several boards that were in the back of E.P.'s truck and carried him from the backyard where he had been painting and placed him carefully on the back of the truck. But I was told later that E.P. was screaming loudly during this venture and crying with pain. Viola was also crying at the sight of her husband. The parishioners then drove E.P. slowly back a few blocks to his own home. There they carried him as carefully as they could into the inside of his house and placed him on large comfortable couch in E.P.'s own parlor.

Momma and I watched them carrying E.P. into the house. Dad was standing with us, and then Mrs. Evans from across the street came over and joined us. She had brought little Joey with her to see what was happening at the Beeler house. They both came to stand by Momma and me. We stood and watched.

My father walked quickly across the street, walked up the front steps, and entered the Beeler's house to see what had happened. Later he told us that when he arrived in the parlor he found various men and women sitting in the parlor and standing together praying, singing, and reading loudly from the various sections of the Bible. He looked over to the couch and found E.P. writhing in pain while Viola stood beside him crying. Then Dad saw E.P.'s leg with the bone extending out of the skin. Wasting no time, Dad told Viola that they had to get E.P. to the hospital immediately or he just was going to lose that leg or maybe even die.

Upon Dad's words, the various parishioners began to pray and sing even louder and close tightly around E.P. on the couch. Viola vehemently told my Dad that he was to leave their home immediately. She continued that they were all praying for E.P. to be healed from his pain and for their prayers to repair his broken leg. Dad replied to Viola that prayers were good, but E.P. still needed to go to the hospital

HOME AGAIN, HOME AGAIN, JIGGITY, JIG   103

and repair his leg. Viola demanded that Dad should leave, and one of the parishioners escorted Dad from the premises. All the years we had known E.P. and Viola, we knew of their strong religious beliefs through their evangelical church. They had always been active in the church on Sundays and attended Bible studies in the evenings. But we were not aware of their strong belief of healing of the body through prayer and Bible readings until this moment. This had never really come up in discussion. And now it had. E.P., Viola, and their church members were there to spend the night in prayer and wait for E.P.'s healing through their prayers and singing. It was a test for faith and belief. Literally. With all previous words in exchange and promises, both E.P. and Viola had stood strong behind their acceptance of faith healing through spiritual means. The church followers were present for the ritualism of "laying on of hands" and lay claim to solicit divine intervention in initiating spiritual and literal healing. It was a moment of truth to E.P. and Viola despite the pain and threat of further complications. They felt they had to maintain honest belief and strength through the Bible reading and their fellow parishioners.

We saw Dad come out of the Beelers' house and knew he was mad as he strode across the street toward us. Dad was really mad as he told Momma what he had seen and heard. He told Momma to call Dr. Kerr, the police, and an ambulance. E.P. had to be taken to the hospital. Momma was afraid to make the calls and told Dad maybe they had better not get involved. At that time, Mrs. Evans wished us the best but felt she should go back home with little Joey. She felt it might all get to be a little too exciting for Joey to watch at his young age. She waved good-bye and headed back home across the street on our right side.

With that, Dad stomped into the house and up the stairs into the apartment. He walked down the hall to the closet, and after bringing out a large tin box, he walked back out into the living room and reiterated to Momma to please make the phone calls. To our surprise, Dad was carrying the tin box that held his two six-guns from the top shelf in the closet. He began to strap on his two gun holsters onto his hips and placed the two six-guns into the hip holsters. He then placed his Stetson hat onto his head. For all five feet six inches of his body, Dad meant business. Dad stated to Momma that E.P. was going to be taken to the hospital even if he had to pull a gun on Viola or one of those parishioners. Fearing for Dad's safety and maybe Viola also, Momma placed the three calls. Almost immediately, we heard the ambulance's sirens with the policemen in their cars traveling through the streets of Monett to the Beeler home. This was certainly not an everyday occurrence for our household. I couldn't decide to be proud of Dad as he stood there in his holsters and guns or to be very afraid for him. Also, I had to fight from giggling at the sight of my Dad dressed like one of the cowboy heroes in our favorite Saturday evening movies. He definitely had the look of our favorite cowboy, Audie Murphy, at this moment.

Dad straightened his guns in their holsters on his hips, tilted his hat a touch on his head, and walked down the stairs and across the street. I could tell that Dad was determined he was going to get his way in this matter or else. Momma was certain also. We both ran down the stairs and out onto the front of the yard so we could see and hear better what was happening. Just as Dad was ready to step up on the curb across the street, Dr. Kerr, Monett's family doctor, pulled up in his car. Pulling the brake, he quickly stepped out of the car and slammed the door. Striding over to Dad, he bellowed, "Stonie, what the hell do you think you are doing?"

Now I have to add that Dr. Kerr stood well over six feet tall, large in body frame, and completely bald. He was an imposing person and contained a large bellowing voice that simply added to his physical force. As he stood looking down at Dad with a somewhat quizzical, if not smiling, face, he asked Dad. It was rather like the meeting of David and Goliath.

Looking up at Dr. Kerr, Dad quickly assessed him of the situation in the Beeler household, gesturing wildly yet keeping his hands near to his six-gun holsters. After listening to Dad, Dr. Kerr nodded his head, and in unison, they both bounded up the front steps and into the house. At this point, the parlor had reached a fever point of emotions with the parishioners praying, reading, and singing. E.P. screaming in pain while Viola sobbed hysterically. She was also attempting to join in the singing with the other parishioners.

Dr. Kerr strode over to the center of the room, held up one of his large hands, and quickly hushed the whole room with one huge bellow—"Shut up!"—while he told Dad to keep his guns in their holsters and to stay out of his way.

Moving over to the couch, he placed his big medicine bag on the floor and knelt on one knee to look at E.P., who had suddenly shut up also. Deftly examining the broken leg and extruding bone, Dr. Kerr stood up just as the three policemen arrived in the room. Turning to the surprised policemen at the sight they were beholding, Dr. Kerr ordered the policemen to assist the arriving ambulance drivers so that they could load E.P. into the ambulance and take him to the hospital. The policemen were alternating staring over at Dad, not quite certain what the situation called for, and looking at Dr. Kerr. It was rather a humorous situation. The quandary of those policemen had to bring a smile to one's face. They did not want to tangle with Stonie or confront him for his guns as they were not quite certain what his intentions were. Obeying Dr. Kerr definitely seemed to be their first train of thought. Dr. Kerr won out, and they walked over to ascertain the situation with the man on the couch.

Dr. Kerr then turned to calm Viola. He told Viola to go find her hat and purse so that she could go in the ambulance with E.P. Viola did just that and was soon ready to leave with E.P. No one questioned Dr. Kerr. Everyone just obeyed, just as he knew that they would.

Attaining his own way, Dr. Kerr courteously thanked the present parishioners for their strong and steady prayers and singing and suggested that they might want to go home now and have dinner. Then they could come back later to further help the Beeler family. He was certain that the Beelers would be needing their continued support and prayers. The parishioners agreed and began to gather their own things to leave and go to their own respective homes. The thought of dinner prepared had a comforting appeal. Dr. Kerr then informed my Dad, Stonie, to go home and put up those guns before he shot someone and got himself arrested.

The attendants carried E.P. out to the waiting ambulance. I can tell you this: E.P. and Viola were strongly still fighting the "devils" of their own belief, only now silently. They honestly wanted to be strong and stay and pray and sing, but also, they both wanted E.P. to be taken care of and mend his leg. It was a dilemma of many sorts. One could hear E.P.'s screams of denial even as they drove him off to the hospital. It seemed his screams were louder even than the siren of the ambulance. Viola had demurely climbed into the back of the ambulance to leave but not before she had turned to my father and informed him that neither E.P. nor she would ever forgive him for calling the ambulance. Dad just shrugged and replied that they would appreciate his efforts later.

Viola and E.P. Beeler with Janice

This picture was taken later in years with Viola and E.P. Beeler. Janice had grown up a lot since her previous picture at her birthday party.

Growing up, Janice would often visit the Beeler's house and enjoy being with them. I often visited them at their home also.

Since my family did not have a television at this time, I worked out a deal on Sunday evenings to watch the "Oral Robert's Show" with the Beelers and then they would let me watch "The Loretta Young Show". Pretty soon they found they liked the show as much as I did and would join me in watching.

Once in a while, Momma would come with me and enjoy the television. We enjoyed watching the beautiful Loretta Young make her grand entrance on her show.

Loretta Young would enter the door and into the room with a large swirl of her dress and we just thought she looked so very lovely. She had such a style about herself.

We watched Sunday night "The Loretta Young Show" together on their television until Dad got Momma and me a television for our own home. We enjoyed having our own television, but you know, we missed sharing the television with the Beelers sometimes.

For years, E.P. and Viola would not speak to either of my parents. They would just turn away and pretend that they did not hear either of my parents speak. They still accepted me and did not blame me, but they couldn't forgive Dad for causing them to weaken, or so they said.

I believe that Dad actually saved E.P.'s leg that afternoon, or at most, his life. And I believed that E.P. and Viola realized that also, but their pride would not allow them to acknowledge the fact. Both of them were shamefaced that they could not have held out for the prayers and belief of their own faith and the belief that they could be cured through their own faith. It made them feel as if they had lost or shunned their faith. None of this would be later realized. The situation had been a moment of truth, and E.P. and Viola felt they had failed the "test."

E.P. walked with a limp for the rest of his life. Together, Viola and E.P. lived a comfortably long life together in peace and kindness. They remained faithful to their church and the parishioners who never seemed to hold any recriminations against them. Momma and Dad always felt bad that they had to force the situation but also were thankful that E.P.'s life or leg had been spared. As for me, I was just amazed to have seen all this drama in one episode: E.P. on the couch surrounded by praying people, Viola wailing and crying, my father striding across the street with his six-guns strapped on his hips while wearing his noted Stetson hat and tall Dr. Kerr taking charge of the whole situation. It was certainly a "happening" in our daily life. Mrs. Evans later told Momma that she was sorry she had left and not stayed to support Momma, but truthfully she added, "It was a little too much excitement for her to watch!" Momma just smiled and winked at me. It had been a little too much excitement for us also!

Chapter 7

School Days

That summer was a busy summer for my neighboring friends and me with our toy two-way wrist radios that we were able to get in the mail. Avid readers of *Dick Tracy* each and every Sunday morning in the newspaper's comic strips, we had been able to save up enough to order these super wrist radios to wear. They were just like the one that Dick Tracy wore. Of course, they were plastic toys, but they looked official on our wrists, and we had great times running around our yard playing like we were with Dick Tracy as policemen. A few years later, when Dick Tracy finally married Tess Trueheart after an eighteen-year courtship or so, I had to have the baby doll, Bonnie Braids. She was just like Dick and Tess's baby in the comic strip. You see, Bonnie Braids was born with braids on her head, and my doll had braids also. I could pull them out to be longer or push them back in to be shorter. I loved my Bonnie Braids, but I don't think she proved to be too popular with other children. And I have to add, along with our comic strips in the newspaper, we loved our summer radio programs. So many exciting shows to listen to—"Sergeant Preston of the Yukon" was probably our favorite until later when "The Lone Ranger and Tonto" arrived.

Priscilla, my neighbor, came over often and would stay inside with me and play paper dolls or enjoy my dollhouse with me. I had a wonderful playhouse. There were two stories filled with furniture and a family of five with a dog. I was very proud of this dollhouse and often enjoyed playing on the floor in front of the toy house. One day, Priscilla asked me if I would like tiny dishes and goblets for my dolls to have on the dining room table to eat from. I was excited at the thought. So Priscilla told me to have some aluminum foil the next time she saw me, and she would make me some dishes and goblets for the dolls. I was excited.

When I approached Momma for the needed pieces of tin foil to make the toy dishes, she told me that I should look for another item. She felt the tin foil would be too thick for Priscilla to manipulate into such small items, so she suggested that I acquire the foil wrappings off gum and use that item. She gave me one of Dad's cigar boxes and told me to start hunting for gum wrappers. Luckily, everyone in my family liked to chew gum, so all I had to do was convince them to give me the wrappers and not throw them away. Over time, I became pretty adept at peeling the foil from the waxed paper that wrapped around the gum. I could even pull the foil off in a full small sheet without a tear. Then I would smooth out the sheet and place it into my treasured cigar box to await the next meeting with Priscilla.

I would gather my cigar box with the foil treasures and ask Momma permission to sit on the curb and wait for Priscilla to come over. She agreed as she could see me out of the kitchen window. There I would sit on the curb, holding my cigar box filled with the small sheets of foil, and wait for Priscilla to see me and come over. Soon, she would appear at her kitchen screen, wave, and come over to sit with me on the curb. Then she would ask for my cigar box, and she would begin her crafty magic. I would sit and marvel at how her fingers so deftly twisted and turned the small sheets of foil until she held a small goblet for wine or milk, just perfect to sit on the dining room table. She made plates and small silverware and goblets. Each were evenly proportioned and perfect in size. I kept them safely in my cigar box for the time when I could take them out and set them on the dining room table in the dollhouse. Sometimes, Priscilla would come upstairs to play with me, and we would use the silver dishes in play.

I so loved having the Evans family across the street from our house. I liked to sit on the curb and listen to all the noise and laughter I could hear through the open windows during the day or early evening. It seemed that the house just burst with happy sounds: screen doors opening and shutting, a wave of hello to me, someone laughing, or strains of music coming from the record player or radio. It was special times to me when I was invited over to play with Priscilla and Joey. Ruth was too old to play but would often sit and talk to me. Jimmy was busy with his job and his friends. He was looking forward to getting a driver's license someday.

The Evans house had a porch in front, and we liked to sit there on summer days reading comic books or library books. Whenever we found a piece of chalk, Priscilla and I would draw a hopscotch game on the sidewalk and spend hours hopping back and forth tossing our favorite rock. They were happy summer days. Also, Priscilla was able to use her mother's sewing machine in the dining room. She was making most of her own clothes, and she would often let me sit and watch her sewing. Once or twice she made some clothes with me for some of my special dolls from scraps of her own clothes she was sewing. I really liked that. Sometimes, Mrs. Evans would invite me to stay for supper. I was often a visitor to the large blue house across the street from me. I liked to be there.

Then came the fall and time to go to school. I would be entering school for the first time. All six years of my life, so far, I had worn my hair in long curls. They hung long on my shoulders and a little down the back. My hair was a dark auburn and thick in growth with lots of curl. Momma had to brush it often to keep it neat and ladylike. She always tied a pretty ribbon with a bow on top of my head to hold the hair back out of my face. I was proud of my hair. People stopped me and Momma to remark how beautiful my hair was. How lovely the hair color was. They added that red hair is not always popular to have but that my auburn hair color was "just perfect" and lovely to see. I wore lots of pink clothes and hair ribbons. Often just to prove that pink and red did go together. I have to admit it—I did love my hair. One might even add that my hair made be feel much prettier than I would have felt if it had been another color. My hair was my pride.

Dad was proud of my hair also. Members of his family had had auburn hair like mine, and he liked me to wear it long and in curls. He often remarked upon how pretty I looked with my long hair and ribbons. He complimented my mother about how nicely she kept my hair, even when I had been outside running and playing. I know it added more work for Momma, but I always thought that she also took pride in my hair. All the other school girls that were going to be in my grade also wore their hair the same way with long curls and ribbons.

I thought I would be starting school with my long hair and wearing matching ribbons.

About two weeks before school started, Momma took me to the beauty shop downtown on Main Street. It was the shop that Momma always went to when she needed a haircut. I had never been there as a customer. I had just gone to watch Momma get her haircut. And now, Momma was taking me to the shop for a haircut. We went there on a Saturday afternoon while Dad was asleep and I was told to sit down in the salon chair. They put a cushion on the seat to make me taller in the chair and then the woman put a round plastic cape around my shoulders and asked Momma how much to cut of my hair. To my surprise, Momma told her to cut it short. She told her to cut off all my long curls. I sat there silently watching my long curls fall slowly to the floor where they lay as dead leaves on the ground in the fall. My hair was falling from my head to the cement floor, and all I could do was sit silently in disbelief that I was getting a haircut. I really didn't know how to act or what to say.

When finished, my hair was short and bobbed with front bangs. I sat looking into the mirror. I didn't even recognize myself. This was not Susie sitting in the chair with the short hair curled around her face. This was not the pretty girl with the long hair and colorful ribbons. This was just a girl with short curly hair. It was not Susie.

Momma paid, and we left and walked back home in silence. I had no words to say. What could I say? It was too late. My hair all lay back in that salon on the floor. I saw the worker sweeping up the long curls. I heard some of the women ask if they could have one of the curls to keep as the hair was so pretty. I was silent as Momma smiled and told them they could have the curls. My heart seemed to shrivel up even more knowing that strangers would now have my lovely auburn curls.

When we returned home, Dad had just gotten up from his afternoon nap. He was in the kitchen getting a sandwich to eat when I walked into the room. He turned with a smile for me, which slowly turned to a frown of disbelief. He stared at me and called out to my mother. "Lela," he called, as he twirled me around by the shoulders to look at the back of my head. "Where is Susie's hair?" Momma walked into the kitchen and told Dad that she had cut off my hair to get ready for school. She continued that she did not have time to brush and curl my hair each morning before I went to school, so she had decided to cut the hair. Besides, she added, it would be cooler and more comfortable for me.

Dad took a long angry look first at Momma and then at me. He walked out of the kitchen, down the stairs, and drove off in the car. He was gone for several hours. He didn't even invite me to go with him as he usually did. He just left. Not knowing what to do or say, I walked down the hall and went into my bedroom and sat down on my bed. I sat there, hands folded neatly in my lap and stared at the wall trying so hard not to cry. Momma began to fix supper. When Dad came back, he didn't say anything to Momma or to me about my haircut. In fact, he never said anything about the haircut. But from that moment on, my life changed with my Dad. Before he had always treated me as his "little darling," called me "Daddy's little dumpling." He laughed with me and talked to me. He loved to read to me and take me with him everywhere. He would hold my hand and brag to everyone to come see his beautiful daughter with the lovely long auburn hair. I was no longer that girl. Of course, you can laugh and say, "But hair grows back. You would soon have long pretty curls again if you wanted them again." That's true and I understand that today, but at the time that it happened, I did not understand that fact in my head. That was the day that I became the "ugly child." I was never to feel pretty again. Not the same pretty as the days with my long pretty curls. I was now the plain child with short hair.

I entered the first grade that year. Miss Smith was my teacher, and I loved her dearly. She loved how I said the word *breakfast*—seeming to say "break-fast." Dad always said it was the Dutch in me.

Miss Smith would often have me get up in front of the class and recite what I had eaten for "break-fast" that morning! And I loved it! I have always been a showman—I love to be in front and speak. I loved to talk. So often I would entertain my fellow students as I related my daily "break-fast."

But sorry to say, I was not a popular child. Maybe it was entering a year after all the other children had started school in kindergarten . . . the fact I was actually shy . . . felt like the ugly duckling . . . not really for sure. But I do remember that I spent most of the school year alone or standing with teachers on the playground and talking to them. Years later, when I was a school teacher, I remembered my early years and always made sure to be accessible to the students who weren't the most popular or seemed shy and alone. I knew how it had felt when I was their age.

I did love ball and jacks at that time and could sit on the sidewalk by the school building for the whole recess, playing jacks by myself or sometime with a few other girls. And of course, we had the playground equipment. At one time the teeter-totter was all the rage, and I would force myself to go down and ride. But the games had become a little rough, and there were some children who liked to get on the teeter-totter and try to bump you off. They would wait until you were up in the air on your side of the teeter and then they would bounce hard on the ground. Several times I was almost knocked off when I was in the air. After that, I decided I liked it better playing jacks on the sidewalk.

Of course, I never told Momma that I was unhappy at school. I just did the best I could and was excited to be back home each day. Priscilla was often with me to play and talk to and her family, also. My sister Betty was still living with us but my brother Glenn had moved back to Joplin to live and work. He had dropped out of high school and felt he could find better jobs in Joplin.

Dad was beginning to be more full of energy and seemed ready to go back to work. He was concerned that he could not maintain his strength while driving a bus. So he began to look around for other ways to earn a living. Things were changing, and he said there were many opportunities if one just figured out the best thing to do. He seriously looked into being trained in repairing refrigerators. About this time, we had purchased a used electric refrigerator. Momma loved it because she didn't have to empty the water collected in the tray from the dripping ice block, and she could keep more food cold. I have to admit we missed our visits from the iceman and the cold chipped ice we would receive from the deliveryman. So Dad had figured that with more and more housewives purchasing the refrigerators for their kitchen, it would be a great business to repair them. He took some classes in how to repair but soon decided it was not the job for him. He didn't want to have to lift the refrigerators. Dad noted that this was sometimes required. So he looked into other ideas. Without telling Momma or any members of the family, Dad began looking into clock and watch repair. No one else was repairing clocks in Monett, and Dad felt he had a real knack for this job. He loved to just sit and tinker, and he never became impatient with the smallest detail. He would also be able to sit quietly and relax. He just didn't have the strength at this time to lift or move heavy objects or drive a big bus.

Dad sitting in front of shop

Dad is sitting on small step in front of the building shortly after we had bought it and moved in.

The sidewalk shown leads up to the kitchen entrance at the side of the house. This picture was taken before Dad had the signs painted by James, nextdoor, and hung up in front of the shop.

The small step where Dad is sitting leads upstairs into the two apartments and two sleeping rooms. The renting of the apartments gave us extra cash and were usually steadily rented.

Dad often kept summer chairs out in front to sit in and watch people go by. He liked to chat with everyone. I loved to sit in them and read, especially on rainy, summer days.

Chapter 8

A Change in Residence

So Dad had settled himself into the idea of becoming a clock and watch repairman. Anything he could read about for the repairing, Dad became an avid reader. And then Dad found a large building on Bond Street that was perfect for his idea. Located just one-half block down from where we lived, Dad found a second-story building that was available for sale. And without any words to Momma, he bought the building. That evening he came home and told his wife what he had done and his ideas for our new home. Momma was in shock. At first, she would not even listen to Dad. She shut herself up in the bedroom and would not come out. Finally, she allowed Dad to come into the room and talk to her. They kept the door shut while they talked, and I could not even hear about this new move. I waited in suspense.

When Momma and Dad came out of the bedroom, she announced to me that we were going to walk down to the building Dad had bought and look it over. Betty came with us. We cut through our backyard and walked down the small alley to our newly acquired property. Momma was still sniffling and was not really happy as we walked along. Dad was talking as fast as he could with ideas he had for the building. I was upset to move from my friends, the Evans family, and the Beelers.

Upon arrival from the back view, Momma gave a loud gasp and just stood there silently as she took in the backyard and large two-story building. Even today, I find it hard to completely describe. The building was a second-story square building with a second-floor deck and steps

115

coming down from the deck. A small building, like a storage space, stood by the stairs. Walking on down the alley, we kept staring at this strange boxlike building, all two stories of it. The tarpaper siding was worn, and some parts hung from the sides. The building was sorely in the need of painting. And then we entered the building, on the side, through the kitchen. That's when Momma really began to cry. The walls were like cardboard; old, dirty and broken linoleum on the floor; and some parts were just old wood floors with holes in them. There were two bedrooms, living room, and kitchen on one side of the building. Then you entered a hall that would lead to the front or to the other side of the building that had two more bedrooms. The only problem was the hall was filled to the top with coal. I can't even begin to tell you how dirty and sad the whole building was and how dismayed we were at the thought that we were going to living there. And all the time, Dad was talking on and on about what a great investment the building was going to be and how cheap he had bought the building. Momma was not listening to anyone; she was just standing and crying. I stood next to her and looked around in dismay also. Betty, my half sister, who was always cheerful, laughed and said, "Come on, Lela, some paint and wallpaper, new linoleum, and the house will be just great." Momma tried to smile. Dad laughed and agreed with Betty nervously.

Then Dad told us to step back outside and walk to the front of the building to see where he planned to have his clock and watch repair shop. We walked around the corner, and there was the front of our building, all square two stories, bleak and dark and greatly in need of paint. On the right was a torn screen door and solid door that led upstairs. Dad was quick to point out that the upstairs contained two lovely apartments with four rooms each including a kitchen. And then down from there were two sitting rooms with beds. The large bathroom was shared by the tenants. Dad was quickly explaining how the rooms could be rented for extra income.

I don't think Momma was really listening as we then walked up the two large steps leading into the front of the building. Two large screened and solid doors greeted us. On either side of the doors were two large windows displayed inside the building. We walked in and found a large room the whole front of the building, a bathroom down from the room, and a side storage room. The whole front was available for Dad's shop.

Dad explained with all the monies saved in the purchase of the one acre of land and large building he would be able to hire workmen to clean up the building and make it livable for us. He also showed us how we were located right across the street from the town hall, town library, and fire station. We were exactly one block up from Main Street. It was the perfect location for Dad's clock repair shop. People would be able to walk up to the shop or park their cars right in front of the shop in the five slots available.

At this point, there was not much one could do except to accept the situation and make the best of what was there. Without a lot of detail, during the next few months, the coal was hauled out in trucks and sold, which gave Dad some more monies for the repairs of the house. Momma hired a woman to come in and wallpaper all the rooms. Betty and I painted the woodwork, trims, and windows. Dad installed new linoleum in all the rooms. The bathroom was cleaned up, and the front area was made usable with paint, wallpaper, linoleum, a workbench for Dad set over in one corner of the shop and four large glass showcases to be filled with things for Dad to sell. It took many years to repaint the outside and do repairs and even more years before new siding in soft green to be put in place. Actually, that house took the rest of my parent's life to continuously be working on, but it soon became home for us. Strange, shabby, and definitely unique, but it became a home for us.

One of the first things Dad had done, also, was to commission our neighbor James to paint shingle signs to hang in the front. Large black letters announced Glenn Stone's Clock and Watch Repair Shop, 508 Bond Street. Musical supplies were available. Later in years, Dad also carried some musical instruments: guitars, a few violins, and an accordion. I might add, Dad always had supplies in catgut string for the instruments and picks. They were on display in the glass cases. Actually, it would take a whole book just to talk about the shop. I often have dreams today, after all these years, of being in the front shop and watching the two tall front screens banging open and shut in the wind.

Once we had the back part of the house available for us to move in, we moved our furniture. I had the far backroom, Betty had the center room, and there was the living room and kitchen. Across from the hall that ran right down the middle of the house, Momma and Dad had their room and a storage room. Up the hall was the bathroom, and then one walked through the hanging curtain Momma had made, and there was the front shop. My half brother Glenn had moved back to Joplin with his aunt at this time. We had little gas heaters in the living room and my parent's bedroom. There was a heater in the bathroom and one in the front shop. To my amazement, the house was always warm and comfy even in the coldest of winters. I had read once that our house had been the very first post office in Monett. From the age of the building I could believe it. Once you recognized that it had been a post office, you could better figure out the shape of the building and how it had worked. In the kitchen, over the area where the stove stood, the wall jutted out. This area looked to have been the chute where they would shoot mail down to sort from upstairs. Now it was covered by wallpaper and had become part of the wall. We got a cat to chase away the mice that had previously lived there. Soon we had settled in to live and work in the house.

Dad set up his shop and opened for repairs. He placed several old comfortable chairs over on one side near the large gas heater and offered a sitting space for visitors who liked to chat with Dad. And of course, Dad was in his element. He loved to talk and to be considered an authority on all he discussed. Dad was well read. He enjoyed the classics and had a small collection of fine books in a bookcase by his side of the bed. Men, often farmers, would drop by in the afternoon or Saturdays and sit. Dad would work on his clocks or watches, smoking his continual cigarette, and expound on his theories and thoughts. He became the all-knowing and omnipotent clock repairer, eager to exchange views with all who entered. Of course, the occasional bottle was passed around for a sip or two, adding fuel to even more discussions.

Once the house had been cleaned up and repaired we all seemed to be settled into the house, tall thin walls, clock shop in front and all. An elderly deaf and dumb woman named Cora moved upstairs in the side apartment. She had few visitors, and I soon discovered she was often lonesome. One day I went upstairs and offered to sit and play a game of Chinese checkers with her. It was a fun event, and soon we were able to communicate to each other by hand symbols and pointing. Before long I often went upstairs and sat and played cards or board games with Cora. We would sit and laugh and laugh while playing the silly games. I often let her win, and sometimes she honestly did win. She was rather like a grandmother to me and often surprised me with edible treats she had baked.

HOME AGAIN, HOME AGAIN, JIGGITY, JIG   119

My sister Betty worked at the local shoe factory down past Main Street. She was a secretary and enjoyed dressing up in fine dresses and expensive shoes. She did love her shoes and had quite a collection of them. With her curly red hair and spontaneous laughter, she was a popular young woman and often went out on dates in the evening. I loved to sit and watch her finish her toiletries, applying makeup and lipstick and perfume. She had excellent taste in clothes and colors to go well with her auburn hair.

My father loved to trade. He existed completely by the barter system. If he saw something that he wanted, he always found a way to trade something he had for the item. It never failed. About that time Dad came home one day with a large machine gun and three or four army blankets from World War II. It seems that he had traded some guns or such for the machine gun that had been used in the war by the Germans. It had actually been a Nazi machine gun and it also had a belt of bullets that had not been fired. Soon after Dad placed the machine gun in the side front window on display. He dressed up the bottom of the window bench with blue material and placed the machine gun there pointing on the left with the whole belt of bullets placed in the gun as if it were ready to fire. People would come into the shop for weeks to get a look at the real Germany "Nazi" war machine gun and how it was all fitted with the bullets. Of course, Dad had many a story to tell about action in the war with the "Nazi" army. Not that he had fought in the war, but he was well read about history and liked to enthrall who listened about stories of various known battle spots and war strategy— expounding loudly about many of the well-known generals and Army leaders; McArthur, Patton and Eisenhower. Dad even had large books with map of the various war locations and would show the gathered men where the battles had taken place. As I had said earlier, Dad had truly found his realm—a ready-made audience all eager to listen to him and have no expertise or knowledge to ever question what he told them. They were there, in the shop, daily, enthralled with all the knowledge Dad could expound upon them.

And the whole time that Dad talked, he continued to fiddle with broken clocks and watches working toward finding the secret move that would repair and complete the time measurers back to working condition. I might add, at this time, because so many of the clocks bought in for repair, were owned by farmers who had owned these clocks for generations of their family. When they left the clock for repair, they would explain to Dad that they had no monies to pay when the clock had been repaired but that they could not bear to keep the clock on the mantle or wall and see it not ticking and keeping time. Dad would always just cluck softly at them and, with soothing words, say, "Don't worry. I shall just get this lovely old clock back to where it can chime and tell the time and it will sit here and wait for you to find the few dollars you would need to pay for the repair. When you do, come by and the clock will be ready for you." And with that, he would tie a small white tag to the side with the name of the owner and the date it had been left for repair. I can truthfully say that during my lifetime of growing up in this house behind the clock shop, I grew up listening to some twenty to forty clocks all ticking and chiming in accordance, all day and all night. Every room in our house, in the front shop and down the corridor, had clocks hanging on the wall or placed on a shelf or mantle or dresser top. I can also truthfully say that I never once heard a clock chime or tick out of time to all the other clocks. When the time approached, all clocks would chime at once, and completely in time and tune, with each other. I never, ever heard one separate chime from all the others. Each approaching hour or half-hour was much like a practiced orchestra, leader with bow in hand raised high and upon movement, all clocks chimed in time. The clocks were large ones and very small ones. Some twinkled, and some loudly chimed the total day. And each day, Dad would walk around slowly and methodically winding each clock and adjusting it's time of sorts, listening and looking, listening and touching, acknowledging each clock to its own fine tuning and mechanical workings. My father truly loved those clocks. And when the farmer or person would one day return to hand over the few dollars they had accumulated to pay for the repair of the clock, I know that my father was sad to hand it back over to the owner. He had become attached to the sound and tick of that particular clock. And before the clock would leave his shop, he would always place a small sticky label to the back of the clock that declared his name, shop, and phone number, in case the owner needed to bring it back. But you know, I don't ever remember anyone ever bringing back a clock. When they left my father's shop, they were ready to chime and tick to tell the time for the rest of the owner's life. Soon, another clock would be in place of the empty spot on my father's shop wall. The clocks arrived and they left.

Glenn Stone Clock Shop signs appear

Dad had James, our neighbor, paint the hanging signs and the shop information on the windows. I think the painted windows and banners helped to spruce up the building. The library was right across the street and I loved to go in there and sit and look at books. It was air conditioned and filled with so many books to read and learn from. I was absolutely spoiled by the different librarians who were always willing to show me new accesses of books or the section of all the classics. There I learned to visit with Charles Dickens and meet all the many characters in his stories or sail across the seas with Robert Stevenson in "Treasure Island." And when I read "Jane Eyre" nothing could stop me further from dwelving into all the wonderful reading delights held on those shelves in that library. It was my home away from home!

Betty, sister, and I Christmas Shopping

Betty, my sister, and I are all dressed warm to walk downtown and do some Christmas shopping. We found a lovely star shaped rhinestone pin to give to Momma for her Christmas present to wear with her favorite black suit. It made a lovely gift. Momma never let me put my hands in my pockets because it ripped the material. So, if you notice, I have just the tip of my fingers in my pocket!

There were no other people, it seemed at that time, repairing clocks or watches, so Dad soon became the clock repair wizard of the surrounding counties. One would think that this would have made us rich but to the contrary. Dad did not charge much expense for repairing—there was little expense accorded. Dad would mainly take the clock apart, oil and clean each little part, sometimes replace some small clog or wheel, and slowly and methodically place all the parts back together again to make a whole clock. And then he would listen and look. Soon he would figure out the mysterious ache in each clock and set it all to right again. Dad looked at it as rather a large picture puzzle in dimensions. It was fascinating to watch.

So with the small amount of monies coming into the shop through clock repairs, my family had to look to other methods of maintaining a bank balance. As I said, my sister worked in the shoe factory, but she did not contribute much of her salary to our own budget. Momma had begun a job at the local dry cleaners and worked there five days a week steaming and pressing people's clothes. It was a hard job for Momma standing on her feet all day and pushing the presses. When she came home at night, she was always so tired.

Chapter 9

Nein on the Coat

At this time, I needed a new coat. I had outgrown my old coat. But we really didn't have the needed monies to pay for a new coat for me. And then Dad got the bright idea of making me a coat out of the army blankets he had gotten with his machine gun trade. Dad told Momma to take me and the two blankets to the woman who lived at Marshall's Hill, across the railroad tracks. She took in sewing and was very skilled in her labors. Dad said the material of the blankets were very warm and would make me a very good, warm coat. So Momma took me and the blankets to the woman to have a coat made for me. When she finished, it truly was a very warm coat. It had a warm lining, round collar, buttons down the front and side pockets. It actually was very stylish and the color of the army brown was actually a good match with my long auburn hair. When I put on the coat, Momma inspected it and said to me, "It's a lovely coat. The material is warm and heavy, makes an excellent, warm coat. Just don't tell anyone it was made from a Nazi army blanket. They might not understand."

I wanted to take the coat off and throw it away. But necessity made me wear it. Every time I wore it to school or downtown, I was always afraid that someone would stop me and begin to shout and point at me that I was wearing a coat made from a German Nazi Army blanket. I was sure that everyone could spot it immediately. Of course, at that time and age, I wasn't really sure what a German Nazi Army was or who they were. I just knew that we had fought the Nazis in the war, so

124

I was sure it would not be good for me to be wearing a coat made from their blankets. I actually had nightmares about that coat where people would begin to scream at me that I was a Nazi. It was a warm coat, but it caused me a lot of mental anguish at that time.

Heim's Hatchery had their office in the building next door to our home. The front was where they took orders for seeds and supplies for the farm animals. In the back, they stored the various bags of items and supplies. One day, they had placed a baby calf in a pen in the front of the building near the front large paned glass. As soon as I saw the calf, I fell in love with the little animal and would go in after school to spend an hour or so sitting and talking to the calf. Although the calf had a salt lick in the pen with him, he took a real liking to my coat and loved to lick it. I guess the coarseness of the coat's material reminded him of the mother's side. But without me really noticing it, as I stood talking to the calf and petting it, the calf had licked a discernable spot on the left side of my new army blanket coat. Momma noticed it first. She stopped me as I walked by her and said, "What happened to your coat?" When I looked down at the left side of my coat, I saw the rubbed part of the coat where the calf had been licking it. Immediately realizing that was where the calf had been licking when I was petting him, I denied all knowledge of what had happened to my new coat.

Now Momma had always been very stern about wear and care of my clothes. We did not have much money and were thus very frugal. I was always warned not to place my hands in any pockets on my clothes or coats because it would pull the pockets loose from the material. Although I loved to put my hands in my pockets, I knew never to do so. And now, I had this worn spot on the side of my coat. Momma was very angry at me for being so careless with my new coat. Personally, I had high hopes that I might not have to wear it anymore. I had often hidden the coat and pretended I could not find it when it was time for me to go outside. I did not want to wear this dreadful coat anymore. It made me feel so un-American, and I had so begun to hate the coat and what it had been. Nothing could change that feeling in my mind and heart.

At that moment, I felt very confident and determined. I raised my eyes to my Dad and spoke very determinedly that I did not like to wear the coat. I explained that it had been made from a German Nazi blanket, and I felt disloyal to my country when I wore the coat. I told

Dad how I especially felt very sad in the coat when I stood to say the Pledge of Allegiance or placed my hand over my heart as the flag passed by me at the Christmas Parade. I told Dad that I felt I was being not loyal to my country that I loved. My teacher, Miss Smith, had told the class that whenever we heard the "Star Spangled Banner," we stood stand at attention, no matter what we were doing or where we were. I added that the wearing of the coat made me feel wrong to salute the flag or sing a patriotic song. At the end of my speech, I was amazed. I had never dared to go against my father or tell him that I did not like something that he had given to me. I was sure that I was going to get a whipping for what I had just said. Although I had never received a whipping from my father in all my eight years, I was sure that this was going to be the day.

I stood and waited, looking at the floor beneath my feet, as Dad stood and looked at me. He stood for a few minutes just looking at me and then he turned to my mother and said, "Lela, she is right. Let's give this warm coat to someone else that needs it and let's go see if we can find a lovely used coat for Susie to wear. A coat that Susie can wear proudly when she sings the 'Star Spangled Banner' or when she salutes the flag marching by at the Christmas Parade." I knew Dad had finally understood how I felt about the coat. Dad loved the American flag. He was always proud to salute the flag when it was in a parade. He honored our armed forces and veterans. Dad now understood what I felt when I wore this coat.

And to my amazement, that is just what we did. Momma found me a warm, lovely brown checkered coat at the used clothing store and bought it for only a few dollars. I was warm and happy. I felt like an American again. And the fine coat with the licked splotch went to another child who would never know what it was made from. Thanks to that little calf, I felt just as warm while happy again to feel patriotic love for my country. You just never know how things may come to be.

Although we had moved, I still often went up to my old neighborhood to play with my friends Priscilla, James, and Joey in the Evans family, and a few other neighbors. I would often see the Beelers, E.P. and Viola, outside working in the yard. Often, they would invite my mother and me to go with them to Springfield and do some shopping. We loved to join them on those special excursions. Today, one can drive from Monett to Springfield in twenty to thirty minutes, easily with the highways. At that time, we traveled on old country roads, and it would often take two hours to travel to Springfield. Of course, we always made it a day. We would leave at eight o'clock in the morning, E.P. would be driving with Viola sitting on his right. Momma and I would be in the backseat. We would always get dressed up in our good clothes and be prepared for a day's venture. Now I have to remind, we didn't have any monies, but in those days, it did not matter. Momma and I loved to do what is called "window shopping." We could go to Springfield and walk through all the fancy new stores and look at all the lovely dresses and shoes for hours and never purchase an item. Momma also loved to find a comfortable place to sit, out of the way, and watch the people walk by. Often she would lean over to me and make some comment, mostly funny. We were never making fun of the people rushing past us, just enjoying some of the quirks or dressings of some of them. Momma also loved to make up stories about the people passing by—where they were going, what they were doing, or where they lived. I would often chime in some added part or description. It was a gentle entertainment. Didn't cost us a penny and gave us a relaxed atmosphere of interest. After E.P. and Viola had accomplished what they had come to Springfield to do, we would drive over to our favorite restaurant *Cat and the Fiddle*. All of our family loved to go to this restaurant whenever we were in Springfield. I seem to remember they had an all you could eat buffet daily, and that always pleased us. A lot of good food and prepared for a good, reasonable price. Everyone paid the same amount of monies for their meal.

Chapter 10

Traveling With The Beelers

But I forgot one of the reasons we loved to travel with the Beeler family to Springfield. E.P. loved to speed through the yellow light. We could never figure out what it was, but when he was approaching a four-corner light or such, and if the light turned yellow, E.P. would gun the motor as fast as he could and just speed right through that crossing as if there were no signal lights at all. Of course, the whole time E.P. was giving the hard hit on the gas pedal, Viola was screaming at E.P., "Now, E.P., don't you dare go through that light . . . E.P. I can tell you are going to run those lights . . . E.P. Don't you dare speed up that car!" And then whoosh . . . we would speed through the four-corner stop and be to the other side as the signal light overhead turned to red.

E.P. would then just slow back down to normal speed and drive slowly along the road, minding all postings and signals. Viola would adjust herself back into her seat and give her braids and hat a gentle tug to put all in place until the next signal light or crossing area. And so it would go, all through the trip, with E.P. gunning the car through the yellow light to the other side and Viola screaming right along. Momma and I would always be laughing in the backseat. Soon, whenever we saw the approaching yellow light and knew that E.P. was going to be racing through that corner section, Momma would whisper to me, "Give it that old E.P. Beeler!" and off we would go through the section, E.P. driving as fast as he could and Viola bellowing at the top of her lungs for him not to do it. "Give it that old E.P. Beeler!" became our battle cry whenever we would see a four-corner section and to this day, my husband and I will still shout it out whenever we see a four-corner stop. We don't zip through the intersection, but we do roar out the "E.P. Beeler" at the top of our lungs and then laugh and laugh at my memories of E.P. and Viola in our drive to Springfield. To my continued amazement, E.P. never received a speeding ticket on his car or was ever involved in a car wreck.

Chapter 11

What Dreams Are Made Of...

I practically grew up in our local theater house, the Gillioz Theater, just a block down the street from our house. Located on the corner, on Main Street, the Gillioz was a large two-story theater that had been built in 1931. It was like "what dreams are made of"! I always felt like I was entering some magic castle or magic land when I pushed open the large glass entrance doors and walked into the tiled and ornate lobby. On your left would be large posters of coming attractions, on the right was the concession stand. Usually the large copper popcorn popper would be sending forth wafts of butter and popcorn while hot kernels jumped and dove out of the popper into the pile of popped delight inside the large glass cage that housed the popper. And there also was the glass floor cabinet displays of various candies and gums. To the left was the stack of paper cups, various sizes, and the soda machines with the ice. The concession stand was a delicious greeter, and if you were lucky enough to be the bearer of a quarter or dollar, you owned the keys to the castle. As I always arrived early to the movies, I would stand gazing over each item for sale in that glasses cage. "What item would I purchase to eat during the movie today?" I asked myself. It all depended on the amount of monies I had been granted. Most usually it was a quarter. The perfect decision had to be reached as to what candy would last the longest for the amount of monies I could spend. I never purchased a soda because I knew that if I got thirsty I could get a drink from the ice-cold water fountain located in the inside lobby to the left.

The Gillioz Theatre

This was my home away from home - The Gillioz Theatre. Built in the 1930s, the theatre was so architecturally beautiful.

Vivid in color and design, one could just sit upstairs in the lounge for hours and enjoy the view inside and outside through the balcony.

My sister, Betty, was the first one to work there. Then, Betty, my cousin, me, Janice, my cousin, and finally Momma.

It became a regular family tradition, in some ways. But, before I worked there, I spent many hours sitting in the darkened theatre watching all the movies, cartoons, and weekly serials.

One Saturday afternoon, when I was very small, Momma decided she wanted to go see a movie matinee. It was really raining that day and had been for some days. There was water everywhere. Momma got an umbrella and we walked down the block to the movie house and entered. Dad was home working in the clock shop.

While watching the movie, unbeknown to us, the rain kept pouring and soon, Kelly Creek overflowed and water was pouring down the main street. To our dismay, water began to pour into the theater and down the aisles in the house of the theater. Momma and I became very scared. We went into the lobby and stood while waiting to see what to do. Other people were there also getting worried and scared. Then, to our surprise and relief, up drove Dad in his Greyhound bus. He parked the bus in front of the theater and came in to get Momma and me. He also took some of the theater customers with us and delivered them at their home also.

It took him several trips before he got everyone home safe to their homes. The bus could easily drive through the water where a car could not go as it would become flooded.

Dad also drove up and down the main street and rescued people on the sidewalks. Dad became quite the hero that day and a picture of him in his bus was on the front cover of The Monett Times that week!

The water fountain had a small set of steps in front so that kids, like me, could step up to get their own drink of water at any time. I loved to get a drink from that fountain as the water was always so clear and cool.

Most of the time I purchased candy wafers because they had the most pieces to eat for the price of one thin dime. And there were many flavors. The licorice flavor was my favorite one, and I would always save it for the very last candy to eat. If one properly sucked on each wafer during the movie one had to be sure not to start on the wrapped candy during the cartoons, advertisements and news. One had to wait until just as the movie started so the candies would last one throughout the whole movie. Or pretty near the end of the movie. Because my sister worked at the theater, I was able to attend free so I was pretty much the expert on attending the theater. I was there every Saturday, sometimes twice, and every Sunday afternoon and night and sometimes a couple of nights during the week, although not as much because I had homework and school the next day.

My sister worked in the Gillioz Theater as an usher or ticket taker. When you arrived in the lobby to enter the movie house, she stood to the side of the main door to go in by the small ticket box. She wore an adorable uniform of slacks, jacket, and small hat on her head. She looked just like all the uniformed ushers in movie advertisements. She would smile and welcome the incoming patrons of the theater, take the ticket, and invite them to enjoy the movie! She was smiling and pleasant to all and laughed with many people who were her friends. The populace enjoyed being greeted by Betty with her winning smile and lovely auburn curls that she wore long to her shoulders. The uniform was a brown hue with gold braiding on the shoulders of the jacket. The slacks had a pleat down the front and were loose fitting. The jacket was fitted at the waist and had large gold buttons down the front with gold epaulets on the shoulders. The small box hat fit sidewise on Betty's head with a small band of gold ribbon that tied beneath her chin. I was always so proud when I walked into the lobby and greeted my sister. I felt such pride that I knew the ticket lady at our theater and the other staff members of the theater. I felt very special when I went to a movie those years.

Once the movie had started, Betty would close the ticket box and turn in her tickets to the box office for verification. Then my sister would pick up her steady flashlight to begin her duties as a walking usher. She would stand at the two entrances of the movie house, left and right, and watch that the audience members behaved themselves. Periodically, Betty would walk down each side of the theater to observe all seated members. If Betty spotted someone with feet reclining on the seat top before them, she would quickly walk over and shine the flashlight on the feet and remind the patron that they were to keep their feet on the floor at all times. No one was ever to lean back in the seat and place their feet on the seat in front of them. And no one was to talk loudly. If so, Betty would shine her flashlight on them and shush them quietly. If she would have to reprimand a theater audience member three times, she would then ask the person to leave the theater. Their ticket monies would be refunded. Of course, it would have to be a pretty bad situation before this matter happened.

Betty was a very authoritative person in this position and seldom faced disturbances. Theater audiences, at this time, were polite and obeyed proper etiquette. But there was one problem that was often faced by Betty in her job. Betty loved to laugh. And when she did laugh, everyone within earshot and sometimes beyond, knew that Betty was laughing. Her laughter was infectious and loud. If a comedy was showing that particular evening, sometimes the manager had to order Betty to not watch the movie through the curtained area in the back. But if Betty already knew the movie, just hearing the dialogue in the movie would set her off, and the audience could hear Betty all over the house. She had a terrible time keeping her mouth shut and not laughing during the funny movies.

Betty had a particular fondness for Bob Hope and his comedic performances. Well, when the movie *Son of Paleface* starring Bob Hope, Jane Russell, and Roy Rogers, arrived in 1952 to our theater house, Betty almost lost her job. She could not stop laughing at the movie. Even when she couldn't watch the movie, she would start laughing and laughing at just hearing the dialogue. Pretty soon she would get the audience members laughing just at Betty's laughter, and people would complain because they couldn't hear the movie over the laughing of Betty. I would just shake my head, as I sat in the movie house, and smile. Actually, I wanted to laugh just like Betty someday when I grew up.

Every once in a while, when a comedy movie did not catch on to the audience, the manager would tell Betty to go sit in the backseats to get people stirred up and laughing. Sometimes it worked, and sometimes it did not. There were movies that Betty couldn't even get laughter started. But for the most part, I was thrilled to see my sister worked in the theater. It made me feel special to know the other members in the theater also and speak to them by name as I entered the theater. I was always greeted with kindness and courtesy. Actually, I was spoiled during those years. I fairly had the run of the theater, sitting anywhere I liked, attending by myself, and sometimes being snuck a small soda or box of butter popcorn. Those days are special memories to me.

I was also very proud to be in this beautiful and ornate theater house. The entrance carpet was bright red with black scrolled designs running through it. Upstairs, the women's lounge was like a Spanish castle sitting high in the clouds. It was styled with 1930s décor of Spanish grilled designs, painted murals, and thick aqua blue carpets. I loved to sit there reclined on the sofa dreaming of magic carpet days and flying escapades to foreign lands. I had only to rub some ornate lamp to be granted my three wishes by the theater genie. Sometimes, I would sneak up into the lounge and sit back off in a corner unnoticed as women came in to smoke a cigarette, powder their nose or chat among themselves regarding their date or husband. I loved to listen to the gossip and watch the women in their evening ensembles. During those days, men and women dressed neatly and fashionable to attend a movie on Sunday evenings and during the weeks. Lovely dresses or suits, hats on coiffured hair, matching purses and shoes were the call of the times. Men often wore suit and ties. Not to say that the audience members were wealthy, but there was a dress code that was adhered to by all attending. People enjoyed getting dressed up in their finest and attending the movies in those days.

Of course, during family night or Disney movies, people were more relaxed in their dress code, but it still was maintained. No casual or frumpy clothes.

I was a lone person. I didn't attend the movies with friends. I didn't really have a lot of friends. I was more of a loner alone in my own thoughts. And I was an observer. I loved to watch people. I didn't go to movies to just watch the movies. I enjoyed watching people. How they talked, walked, or dressed. What they said and how they laughed when it was funny. Girls who were with their boyfriends. Wives and husbands. I enjoyed watching people and listening to them. I formed my own ideas about life from what I watched and listened during those evenings

Smiley Burnett at The Gillioz Theatre

I loved western movies and when I found out Smiley Burnett, famous comedy sidekick of many western stars, would be appearing at the Gillioz Saturday afternoon I had to be there! Finally Saturday arrived, and as I am getting ready to go to the theatre and meet him, Momma asked me if I felt okay - she told me that I look rather pale and sickly. I tell a small fib and tell her I am just fine! I so want to meet Smiley. So I go to the matinee program and sit and watch the movie. After the show, we are told that as we walk out the door, Smiley will be waiting there and we will get our pictures taken with him! Wow! I can't wait. Finally comes my turn and I step out and "bang" our picture is taken and he moved on for the next child as hundreds are lined up to see Smiley. I give them my address and walk on home. I have such a bad headache now and feel so awful. When I walk into the kitchen, Momma takes one look at me and says, "Susie, let me see your tummy!" Yep - I had the measles. I have always wondered about that and hoped Smiley didn't get sick with the measles from me!

spent in the theater. I can honestly say that the Gillioz Theater was my home away from home. I had found my own area of recognition—the magic of celluloid. The land of make believe. To this day, I still have dreams where I am entering that grand old theater and walking through the lobby into the house. I can still stand at the back of the house and see audience members sitting in their chairs while they watch some movie on our large back screen. The memories still linger in my mind, and I can visit that lovely place once again, after all these years.

The theater had its own style of how the movies were to be shown. During the summers, Saturday morning, once a month or so, special children shows would be presented. Children of all ages could attend the movie for an admittance price of a label or lid from our local dairy products. For a carton of cottage cheese, usually my admission price, I could enter the movies and spend two hours of Saturday morning in the darkened theater digesting cartoons and usually a Western movie or a sports movie. Baseball was a popular show.

Saturday matinees were from two to five. I would eat lunch and rest or read a book, and then off I went to enjoy the matinee that Saturday. Cartoons opened the afternoon, followed by a serial showing of *Flash Gordon* or *Hopalong Cassidy* in some gun-shooting, horse-riding Western. Hopalong was our hero, and we worried each week as the short serial section ended with him tied up in some chair with tarantulas crawling slowing toward him or some other such villain to battle. We would worry all week about the fate of Hopalong and could not wait until the next Saturday to see what further adventure awaited. Then the movie of the afternoon would appear. Lash Larue, Kit Carson, Gene Autry, Roy Rogers, among many, would ride across the screen shooting at the ornery horse thieves. And in the end, the hero would kiss the girl and ride off into the sunset. It was too wonderful to behold. During the week, I would enact these same movie scenes I had witnessed from the past Saturday, for my friends Priscilla and her brother James. They loved to see and hear me tell them of these cowboys and their adventures as they did not have the necessary monies to attend the movies like I could.

Saturday evening, the movies were more for adults. John Wayne would entertain, comedies with the Marx Brothers, the Three Stooges and Bob Hope with his Road Movies, Tarzan in his jungle movies, and sometimes there were murder mysteries. I was there, Saturday evenings, 8:00 p.m. to 10:00 p.m. I would have gone home from the matinee to eat some supper, rest, and go back to the movie house. Many times, my father came to the movies also. He loved the Western movies, and of course, John Wayne was his idol.

Sunday matinee was the premiere of the week's show. First shown for the matinee and then slated for Sunday evening, the chosen popular movie would show each night Monday through Friday night. These were the more popular movies and were usually large box office draw. These were the movies that the audience members dressed up for. It was like premiere night on Broadway. It was the festive night of the week for entertainment following Sunday church and dinner.

Actually, the theater manager had a most entertaining way of presenting the week's choice of movie.

When I was in high school, I learned more about how the theater manager had set up the Sunday matinee showing for the week's show. He had met with the Catholic Church and agreed with the priest that he and two nuns may attend the afternoon matinee of the Sunday show for approval. This memory was recently invoked when I watched a delightful foreign film titled *Cinema Paradiso* released in 1988. The film took place in a small town in Italy and was a remembrance piece by a young boy growing up. He had become a friend of the local projectionist in the movie house. This friendship gave the boy privileged information about the films shown and the workings of the theater. In the film, prior to the viewing by the public, the projectionist would show a newly arrived film to the local priest for his perusal and judgment regarding the merit or adult rating of the movie.

During the premier showing of the film, the priest would ring a small bell to signal to the projectionist that a part or section of the movie was too racy or of some "forbidden material" to be shown to the viewing public. The projectionist would stop the film and, at that time, abide with the priest's ruling and snip out that section of the film. It didn't matter if the film continued in correct sequence. The movie was now ruled acceptable for the parishioners of that church to watch in the theater. The priest had made it so.

My story shows a different slant to the *Cinema Paradiso* theme but in many ways the same. While I was working at the local movie theater, I would always get excited about the Sunday-Friday movie. This was the "big" Hollywood hit movie which had just been released and would be the latest of interest to movie fans. An avid reader of magazines about

Hollywood stars and movies, I was always updated on the latest releases of movies to the theater and eagerly bided my time for them to arrive for the Sunday-Friday schedule.

Sometimes the really big epic movies would stay to show in our theater for an extra week or more. *Anastasia, The King and I, Giant,* and *Around the World in 80 Days* all warranted an extra week of showing for our patrons. Our two biggest blockbusters were *The Ten Commandments* in 1956 and *Ben Hur* in 1960. Both movies ran a full month in our theater. The audience came more than once and just kept coming.

Now comes the theme of this story. Many of the locals were not even aware what happened each Sunday afternoon in our local theater. Each Sunday matinee, prior to the evening night performance, the big movie chosen to run Sunday through Friday of the week would be shown at 2:00 p.m. The audience was usually small, but the main members in the theater would be a priest and several attending nuns. Since I worked in the theater I had now become aware of the practice of the priest previewing the "big" movie of the week to make his judgment for his later announcement in church.

I became very interested in the viewing by the priest and nuns of the movies that would be showing. I even began to make bets with Pop as to what the priest would determine about the film that would be shown that Sunday.

One slow Saturday afternoon, I was in the concession stand working with Pop who was the ticket taker. Mr. Bourne had come down to the lobby to smoke a cigarette, and we were just doing some small talk. I then consulted Mr. Bourne on a matter that had been bothering me. I asked him about the allowance of the priest to attend the Sunday matinee where he could make his decision about the movie and announce to his parishioners. I wanted to know how he could be so nonchalant about the whole matter. Wasn't he concerned about how this affected the audiences of the theater? If the priest did not approve the movie, he would leave and go back for an early dinner and then to the church for the Sunday evening worship. At this time, the priest would announce his approval or disapproval of the film that would be showing in our theater. I continued to Mr. Bourne that it didn't seem fair that a movie would be shown to small audiences because a priest had determined the movie was not suitable for the parishioners to attend. It was a loss of money to me, as far as I could see. I wanted to know why Mr. Bourne was always so courteous to the priest when he actually brought a loss of revenue to the theater.

Mr. Bourne listened to me courteously, and then he laughed while he snubbed out his cigarette in the large silver ash stand filled with sand in the lobby. He looked over to me and responded, "Well, you see, it actually is a benefit to me and the business of the theater."

He continued, "Well, I discovered that when the priest comes in to watch a movie and he disapproves the choice, he will go back to his parishioners and during the evening Sunday mass, he will announce that the week's movie had been deemed unsuitable for viewing. He will tell them that they should not attend that movie. Now, I might add, human nature is interesting. I have found through the years that if a person is told he must not do something, without a really logical explanation as to the harm of the action, that person is going to want to do it, no matter the consequences."

"And that is what happens here. If the priest bans the show, that movie will be a sellout during the week and be packed with most of the people he told not to watch it. Why? Because they want to see what has been forbidden to them and why it was forbidden to them." Mr. Bourne smiled and began to walk out of the lobby and back upstairs to his office. As he left, he turned back to me and said, "Watch the movie this Sunday afternoon and see what I mean."

I looked at Pop, who nodded his head in agreement.

That Sunday matinee we had only a few patrons in attendance. The local priest had arrived early and had sat in his usual place in the last row, middle section, back against the wall, with the three attending nuns next to him.

I was able to close the concession stand early because it was so slow. I resolved to go into the movie house and watch the movie and keep the priest in purveyance for his decision.

And this is where it gets interesting. Billed as "the Mighty Spectacle that Stunned the World," the movie for this week was to be *The Miracle* released 1959. The movie starred two new stars, Carroll Baker and Roger Moore. The film was set during the Napoleonic era, in Spain, where a young postulant falls in love with a handsome British soldier who is recovering with others of his regiment after being wounded. Before leaving, he asks her to leave the convent and marry him. The postulant, devoted to the statue of the Virgin Mary, asks her for a heavenly sign and leaves when nothing happens. Then the statue of the virgin descends from its pedestal and takes her place while she is out in the world searching for her lover, Roger Moore.

Now that right there would be a suit for an instant disapproval. But it continues. The young postulant (Carroll Baker) goes about the world and has many lovers who die until she finds her young soldier again.

I had been watching the movie with one eye and keeping the other eye on the priest and nuns to the left of me. I had purposely sat near the priest so I could watch him during the movie. So far, they had sat as rigid as statues. I couldn't really determine any thoughts they might be having about the movie yet.

And then, right at the romantic moment when the young postulant finally finds her young lover and they are embracing, I see the priest suddenly arise and begin to walk out of the aisle and out of the theater followed by the three nuns. Well, I could tell what his announcement was going to be in the church that night. It was definitely not going to be a good review or one that would recommend the movie to his parishioners. I sighed and turned back to the movie to enjoy the end of it.

Later, after watching the end, I was sorry the priest had not stayed. It might have changed his mind about determining the eligibility of the film for viewing. After the postulant reunites with her first lover, the army officer, she realizes that her real place is back in the convent where she must quickly return. She leaves him, returns to the church, and, as she kneels to pray in the chapel, the statue of Mary, which had been covering the postulant's place as a nun, steps back on the altar. A rainstorm begins outside with torrents of rain falling on the drought-ridden grounds and saves the life of the townspeople. To me, this was a pretty good ending and certainly an endorsement of the choice to be a servant of God. But the priest didn't know this. He left too early.

That evening, as I stood in the concession stands, I was eager to see what the audience number would be. Sure enough. Just as Mr. Bourne had predicted, we had a sold-out audience. The priest had returned to his parish and announced from the pulpit that *The Miracle* was not of a rating suitable for viewing. Just like human nature, it only whetted the interest of the parishioners, and there they were, sneaking into the theater, quietly. Many, upon seeing their friends, other parishioners, would laugh and respond to each other with a denial of "Don't you dare

HOME AGAIN, HOME AGAIN, JIGGITY, JIG   141

tell that you saw us here at this movie." Of course, the others couldn't tell because they were attending the theater themselves.

Just like Mr. Bourne had predicted. He couldn't have asked for a better promotion for the movie *The Miracle*. We had large audiences all that week to see the movie.

In *Cinema Paradiso*, the priest had a bell to ring to signal the removal of sections of the film. And yet, years later, the young boy returns as an adult and edits all the many cuts pieces of film and shows them on the screen. The audience views them. I was moved by the loss of it all. The first priest had signaled to cut out parts of the film that showed any kissing or emotional love. When pieced together, the edited film showed an incredible sequence of love and happiness to the audience members. They were not damaging scenes or hurtful episodes but only expressions of love for one another.

In my movie theater, a priest sat in judgment of the film and signaled later to adults that they could not attend that movie. And yet the parishioners still attended the movie.

Movies have been called the magical gift of life. Each of us must make our own decision to enjoy that gift as we see fit.

I think I can truthfully say that I grew up in that little Gillioz Theater. First I attended and then later worked there all through high school. The movies taught me many things through the years, e.g., how to dress like Audrey Hepburn and how to walk like Susan Hayward. I wanted to cry like Ingrid Bergman and get mad like Bette Davis. The female stars were my mentors, my leaders in life. The movies taught me lessons about life. I learned daily at the feet of these great stars on the wide screen while I was sitting in the dark house seats.

One Saturday afternoon, after Dad had been out to talk to Mr. Gunn and do some trading, I was surprised with a gift of a white-and-black spotted terrier. I loved him instantly and named him Friskie because he could not stand still. He was my puppy, and we had a great friendship. Everywhere that I went, Friskie had to be with me. Dad had traded something with Mr. Gunn for the puppy for me. Mr. Gunn bred various types of dogs and would sell or trade them to interested people.

In retrospect, Mr. Gunn was an older gentleman who lived with a large junkyard behind his house in the country. Dad loved to spend Saturday afternoons with Mr. Gunn as they looked over recent accumulation of guns, television and radio parts, breeding dogs, and used cars. Mr. Gunn had just about anything in his house or yard that a person could look for. He was a large boisterous person, always dressed in old coveralls, boots, plaid shirt and wearing a battered hat. Mr. Gunn had a sympatico friendship with my dad. They enjoyed Saturday afternoons looking, bragging, and exchanging sips from the shared whiskey bottle. I often joined Dad on these visits because I loved to hear the tales and stories Dad and Mr. Gunn would exchange. I would sit, quiet as a mouse, over in a corner and just listen to the two of them. Sometimes on sunny days, I walked around the junkyard in the back, peering into old cars and looking at piles of iron or copper. One time, as I was walking around, I saw something slithering along in the weeds right toward me. I screamed for Dad that there was a snake by my feet. He came running toward me telling me to stand still and not to move. As he was carrying a crowbar in his uplifted hand, I figured he planned to hit the snake and kill it. Those few seconds it took for Dad to reach my side seemed like eternity as I watched the snake crawling closer to me. When Dad reached my side, he gave some loud shouts and stomped his feet, and the snake took off quickly in another direction. I gave a huge sigh of relief. Dad laughed and said, "That snake was probably as scared of you as you were scared of him. He was just an old rat snake looking for his dinner. Out here there are plenty of rats."

With that, I went quietly back to the car to sit and await Dad's return. I didn't enjoy visiting the old junkyard as much from that day on. Or at least I tended to stay closer to Dad when we were there. No more venturing out on my own, you might say.

One Saturday morning, I was getting dressed and had gone back to my room to sit and read a book when I noticed that Friskie was not with me. I asked Betty if she had seen Friskie around. She looked at me and said, "Oh no, I thought you were up at the old house playing baseball. I heard the kids hollering, and Friskie wanted to go and play. I let him out to go be with you." And then the phone rang. A neighbor had seen little Friskie get run over and killed by a car. He had been running up to join me with the other kids. I was heartbroken at the loss of my little friend. Dad walked up to the neighbor's home and brought back Friskie to bury in our backyard. He wrapped him up in a small blanket and placed him in a box and buried him in the backyard right under my bedroom window.

To this day, as much as I loved my various pets and dead animals that Dad buried over the years, I never got over the fact that he always buried them in the ground under my bedroom window. In some ways, it was a nice thought that they were still with me. But it also bothered me that they were still with me. They were buried right under my bedroom window. Sometimes I would be afraid to go to sleep for fear I would wake up and Friskie or other pets would be standing there looking in my window, begging to come in. I never said anything to Dad because it might make him mad. But it did bother me for years. After my parents died, the house was sold and torn down to rebuild office buildings. I always wondered if they unearthed all the little bones there by my old bedroom window. I know at least seven dogs that were buried there. Also, there was buried a couple of cats, two birds, and a few goldfish. That area had become a small little cemetery.

It's no wonder that I sometimes have a dream today, after all those years, where my various pets come to me in the dream. When I ask them where they have been and tell them I was sorry I had not been feeding them, they always reply that all was fine. I laughed about the reminiscence of this dream and my little dead pets talking to me.

When I tell these stories, no one thinks of me as a crazy person, but one could become a little warped from these experiences. Or so I believe.

Chapter 12

King Kong Lives!

As I had mentioned earlier, Betty worked in the theater where I often attended.

My own continued nightmare of a gorilla chasing me down the street probably surfaced in the 1950s when I was around eight or nine years old. This nightmare was created following a very traumatic happening to me in our own little Gillioz Theater.

My sister, Betty, was in high school and worked in our local movie house in the concession stand. Her boyfriend, Jimmy, just happened to work there also as the ticket taker and usher. Together, despite working in the theater, they were also often full of high pranks and silly tricks. On just such a Saturday afternoon, I arrived shortly before one o'clock as I always did just before the afternoon's matinee. I loved these Saturday afternoons. The theater was filled with loud boisterous children and a few brave parents sitting in the darkened auditorium to thrill at the adventures and challenges met by our star cowboys of the day.

Right on schedule each Saturday afternoon, the matinee would open with several funny cartoons, and then we would be treated to the latest serial adventure stories of Flash Gordon or Hopalong Cassidy. These cliffhanger serial shorts ran thirty minutes and were always thrilling and challenging to us.

We loudly cheered our heroes as they faced life-threatening tasks each Saturday and hurrahed as they were saved. We knew they would be presented with new adventures for the next weekend and daydreamed

HOME AGAIN, HOME AGAIN, JIGGITY, JIG 145

of what adventures would be faced by these stars. We loved these serial stories and screamed loudly when our hero appeared on screen to face yet another villain.

Flash Gordon jettisoned us to another planet far away in outer space to fight Ming the Emperor and giant soldiers that could fly. Hopalong Cassidy made sure that "Hoppy" didn't smoke, drink, chew tobacco or swear, rarely kissed a girl, and let the bad guy draw first. What heroes!

One of the scariest serial I had ever watched was showing that afternoon matinee with Hopalong Cassidy. The adventure had been set in a deserted shack where the hero cowboy was tied up. The villain then proceeded to place huge, crawling tarantulas on Hoppy. This all was terrifying to me because I hated spiders, and here I was watching enormous spiders crawl all over my hero! Of course, later Hopalong got loose in time and was saved by his partner, Gabby Hayes. But during the time while the tarantulas crawled loosely around on screen, I ran outside to the lobby to visit with Betty so I wouldn't have to watch the spiders. She laughed and said she didn't want to see the spiders either. She shared my same fear of the creepy crawlers.

As I got ready to walk back into the auditorium, I passed from the lighted lobby into the darkened alcove that led into the seated area. And there to my surprise was a new exhibit for a coming attraction. I stared in disbelief. There was a large billboard of an island with natives fighting with sailors, and right there, as part of the display, was a giant gorilla standing in the darkened area by the billboard. I jumped and ran back out into the lighted lobby. Upon seeing my sister Betty, I ran over and told her that I had seen a gorilla in the theater.

Betty started laughing and turning to Jimmy, who stood in the lobby by the concession stand, told him about my seeing the large gorilla. They both laughed and told me that it was only a gorilla suit that had been propped up next to the billboard to advertise the coming attraction, *King Kong*. They explained that RKO Radio Pictures had released the movie, filmed in 1933, and audiences were going to be treated once again to the magic adventure of the beautiful woman and the gorilla who invaded New York City. In fact, *King Kong* would be showing in our little theater in a week. Everyone was excited to see the film. I expressed my doubt that everyone would want to be seeing that movie and began to cautiously walk back into the alcove to go back and sit in the darkened theater to watch the movie now that the spiders were all gone. I told Betty and Jimmy that the gorilla was no friend of mine no matter if he was called King Kong. I could hear them laughing as I left.

As I walked silently by the gorilla, I kept a cautious eye on this new object of my fear. It stood there, taller than me, and snarling, as if all its anger was focused completely on me. I wanted no part of this fellow or the movie he was to star in. As I walked through the arch to enter the auditorium to find my seat, I turned once more and cast a furtive glance at the gorilla to make sure it was still standing there. I wanted to know where that fellow was and what it was doing. Actually, my thoughts seemed to keep returning to this giant gorilla during the cowboy movie that followed, and I wasn't as interested in the plight of the singing cowboy as I usually was. I kept remembering the look of that gorilla as his eyes seemed to follow me through the darkened alcove. No matter that Betty and Jimmy had told me it was only a gorilla suit, it looked real enough to me. It gave me the shivers to even think about it.

I walked down the aisle and sat down in my seat to watch the beginning of the latest cowboy show. The movie starred Lash La Rue and his famous curled whip that he wore hanging from his gun belt. He was famous for his lightning strikes and flashes with the whip as he struck the villainous cowboy right on his hand and knocked the smoking gun out of his grasp. We loved Lash and his whip. But my concentration on the movie was being broken by my thoughts as they flashed back to that large gorilla standing in the alcove. King Kong sure seemed determined to cause terror in my heart.

Slowly, I became more engulfed in the thrilling movie and watched Lash win the battle on the range with his funny sidekick by his side. At the end of the movie, I sat and watched until the last credit had flashed on the screen. I loved to listen to the singing of the cowboys as they rode off into the sunset. I got up from my seat and began the journey outside into the still-darkened alcove.

And then I remembered the gorilla standing there.

I peered cautiously around the corner and looked at the display by the water station in the darkened alcove. I curled back in terror. The gorilla wasn't standing there. Nothing was there except the large pictures on display. I looked around for Jimmy or Betty. No one was in sight. I seemed to be the only person in the whole theater.

HOME AGAIN, HOME AGAIN, JIGGITY, JIG 147

I stepped out into the alcove with shaking legs. I had decided that I could run quickly through the alcove and be out in the lobby before the gorilla in hiding would even notice I had passed through. I laughed to myself about how silly I was being—after all, the other children had passed through and nothing had happened. Why did I feel the gorilla was only interested in me?

I summoned up all my courage and quickly ran through the alcove to the waiting doors with my eyes tightly shut. I actually ran into the closed door with a loud bang in my haste to get through to the alcove.

Opening my eyes, I pushed open the closed door and ran quickly out into the lobby filled with bright lights and sunshine. I took a deep breath of air with relief. I was safe—I was in the bright light away from that gorilla. I stood there and tried to gather my frazzled nerves and calm myself.

And that was when I heard the mighty roar. I turned quickly back to face that darkened alcove hardly daring to believe what I had heard. And then I saw it. The gorilla was standing there, as tall as I could imagine, and he was beating his chest in savage rhythm. He was staring straight at me.

I quickly looked around the lobby. There was no one there. The concession stand was closed and Betty was gone. Jimmy, the usher, wasn't even there. It was only the gorilla, King Kong, and me.

I was too scared to even scream. I don't think I could have even uttered a small scream my mouth was so dry with terror. What was I going to do? There was a giant gorilla, and he was staring right at me.

And then he began to move. He sort of leaned down and loped through the door entrance and came out into the lighted lobby. He then stood back up, full and tall, and beat his chest while he gave out a thunderous roar. It made the hairs on the back of my neck stand straight up into the air.

And with that loud roar from the gorilla, I turned and ran right through the opened front doors and outside into the bright sunshine. I ran down the street and turned right up the small hill into the alley that led up to my house. I could see the house up ahead of me, about a half-block away. I didn't dare look back behind me. I was too afraid. I knew that if I saw that gorilla loping along after me, I would just faint away right there on the pavement. So I ran. I ran as fast as I had ever run, and as I neared the corner across the street from my home, I began to holler for my father.

I guess Dad heard me coming up the alley from the theater as I was running toward the clock shop in front of my home. He heard me screaming and shouting for him to help me. With that, he had grabbed the nearest thing, a broom, and had headed out the door followed by several men who had been sitting in the shop exchanging gossip and war stories with him. I saw Dad and the men standing there as I ran screaming toward them.

Dad ran over to me and grabbed me by the arms and yelled the question of what was going on. What was I running from?

I screamed, "The gorilla . . . there is a gorilla chasing me."

And with that, we all turned to look behind me. There wasn't a gorilla running after me. In fact, there wasn't anyone. Not even a passing pedestrian or a car. No one. It was just me running and screaming that a gorilla was chasing me.

I stood there looking all around. I didn't understand. I knew I had seen a gorilla in the lobby. I turned to Dad and told him about how King Kong had roared at me and beat his chest and then had begun to run after me. Dad looked around in questioning searches.

The men with Dad began to laugh. "Well, Stonie, next thing you know, your daughter Susie will be running home and telling you that a spaceship had chased her."

And with that, they walked off nudging each other and laughing.

Dad was furious. I had embarrassed him in front of his friends. I had scared him in concern for my safety and for what—no one was in sight. He asked me angrily if this was a trick I was playing on him.

I started crying and stated emphatically that a gorilla had been chasing me, but I didn't know where he was. I shrugged my shoulders and waited for Dad to speak.

He turned to me and told me very sternly that I was to go straight to my room and stay there. No supper that night, and I was not to leave my room or play with any toys. I couldn't even read a book. I could only lie on my bed and think about what a silly thing I had done and how much trouble I had caused. Dad was mad.

With one last look around for the roaring gorilla, I walked sullenly into my dad's clock shop and down the hall to my bedroom. I shut the door to my room and threw myself down on the bed. Tears washed into my pillow as I lay there feeling very sorry for myself. I couldn't figure it out. I had seen a gorilla. It had chased me home, and now I was in a lot of trouble. The world was not fair.

And then, as I flopped over on the bed and turned toward my large dollhouse sitting on the table by my bed, I saw a very large spider silently weaving a web right there in the living room of the dollhouse. That was the topping on the sundae.

I covered my head with my pillow and let loose with the tears and sobs. It wasn't fair. I had seen a gorilla, and it had chased me home. And now a spider was in my dollhouse, and all I could do was watch it weave its web. I couldn't even call my father to come and kill the spider and get rid of it. It had complete control of my dollhouse. I was so angry.

I guess I fell asleep then. I was so worn out from all the excitement. I was awakened by a knock on my bedroom door as it opened, and Dad stood there with Betty, my sister, by his side.

To my amazement, Dad explained to me that Betty and Jimmy had come home laughing about the joke they had played on me. As part of the publicity for the coming attraction *King Kong*, the manager had told Jimmy to dress up in the gorilla suit and hand out flyers to come see the movie next week. But Betty and Jimmy thought it would be funny to scare me with the gorilla suit and make me think it was alive and chasing me. They had laughed and laughed at how scared I had looked and how fast I had run home.

I sat up and stared at Betty through my red and swollen eyes. She was very apologetic and sorry that she had scared me. She also apologized to Dad for causing him trouble in front of his friends. She promised that she would never pull such a silly trick on me again. And then, before he left, Dad told Betty that perhaps she should do a favor for me to make up for how she had treated me with the joke. Betty hung her head and agreed.

I sat and took all this information in. It was only a trick. There was no live gorilla. It had only been a funny joke to them.

And then I heard Betty ask me if there was something I needed that she could get for me. I thought quietly for a moment.

Betty threw away the spider after she killed it in my dollhouse.

It was shortly after my "King Kong" incident that Betty moved out of our house, out of town, and back to Joplin, Missouri, where her aunt lived. You see, Betty dearly loved pretty clothes, perfume, cosmetics, but, most of all, her shoes. Actually, it was a pair of shoes that set Betty's fate.

Betty Graduates and Moves On

Glenn, my brother, had already moved on to Joplin to get a job. Betty had just graduated from High School and was working in the Brown's Shoe Company in Monett. (Notice in picture on the left you can see my church, The Presbyterian Church, that I attended regularly until I left for college.) Shortly thereafter, that summer, Betty moved on to Joplin where she met her future husband, Bob. The house was quiet after Betty and Glenn moved out. After that I never really saw either one nor talked much with them. There was such an age difference and they were living their own lives now.

Betty had quit working at the Gillioz Theater after graduation from high school and had been hired at the local shoe factory, downtown Monett, the Brown Shoe Company. She worked in the office in some capacity as a secretary or an assistant. I don't remember at this time. But I do remember that the job changed Betty. She became involved in an even more busy social life. Each morning she left the house in a beautifully organized outfit: dress or suit, purse with matching shoes. She was beautiful to behold. Her face would be beautifully embellished with her choice of hues in cosmetics, all designed to enhance the face, not cover the face. And her auburn hair was worn long and curled to perfection. She was a fashion plate to behold. She also smelled extra nice. Sometimes she would puff a whiff of her perfume on my hand to sniff. It always smelled so good!

As a result of working in the shoe factory, she began to meet even more eligible young men. Men, Betty would add, that had potential because they had responsible jobs and were striving to better themselves. That was important to Betty.

After several months of working in the Brown Shoe Factory, Betty went on a large shopping spree in Monett, downtown. That evening she arrived home with packages and boxes of new clothes, and new shoes. One pair of new heels she was especially proud to wear and show to anyone that asked. Dad noticed her arrival home with all the packages. Betty had been sneaking in her shopping ventures silently and hiding them in the closet or dresser from Momma or Dad's view. And I was sworn to secrecy.

But that particular evening, Dad caught Betty arriving with the shopping packages. When he saw all the new items arriving with Betty, he asked how much money she had just spent on her new clothes and shoes. Betty crossed her fingers behind her back and replied, "All clothes had been on sale and had barely cost anything!" Dad was no fool, and he quickly began to inspect the clothes. I guess the real bone cruncher came when he found the box with the new shoes and the price of fifty dollars was still showing on the label. At that time, fifty dollars was way beyond our monies, our budget, and our ideas of spending monies. The idea of fifty dollars for a pair of shoes were way beyond any thought Momma or Dad would ever have had. I gasped with amazement.

Dad then told Betty he wanted to have a little "heart to heart" discussion with her in the living room. We all knew what that meant.

Betty put her packages in her bedroom and came back to talk to Dad. He looked at Betty and expressed his pride that she had gotten such a fine job, but he explained to her that times were particularly tough, and any extra dollar in the household was greatly appreciated. Of course, he did not add that because of his drinking we had even extra costs to be met each week. He always seemed to skip that matter when he was talking about each of our contributions to our home.

One could see that Betty was starting to get her Irish temper riled. She was angry that Dad would ask for any of her hard-earned monies that she made working all day. She didn't pour her monies down the drain with liquor, and she wasn't going to contribute any monies to Dad to help pay for his bourbon.

And that was what broke the camel's back. Dad informed Betty that she would have to move out of the house by the end of the week if she did not determine an amount of her paycheck she would pay to the household each week.

It was a no-win situation. Dad was determined Betty would pay or move. Betty was determined she would not pay and was mad that he would throw her out of her home. The next couple of days were noisy with door slamming and loud exchanges of words. That Friday, when Betty came home from work, she began to pack her belongings. She informed Dad that she was moving back to Joplin to live with her aunt. She said that she would be appreciated there as her aunt did not want any of her monies—she would be entitled to spend her own monies as she saw fit.

I helped her pack her clothes and personal items. Betty gave me a few pieces of jewelry and a pretty blouse to keep as my own. She then called a cab to drive her to the bus station where she would get a bus to travel back to Joplin.

You know, that pair of highly priced shoes, which were the main cause for Betty moving out of our house, turned out to be the turning point for her fate—her life changed from that move. While in Joplin, a few weeks later, Betty was working in an expensive clothing store as an elevator operator. She wore a cute outfit and stood at the elevator door and pushed the buttons to travel to different floors for the customers. She even wore white gloves. She loved her job.

Anyway, one day, a tall, husky man with light hair and a sweet grin got on the elevator, and Betty said it was "love at first sight." They

HOME AGAIN, HOME AGAIN, JIGGITY, JIG 153

talked as he traveled up and down the elevator floors, he asked her for a few dates and within a month, they were married and traveling to South Dakota to live on farmland near his Swedish farmer parents. And that was where Betty lived her continued years, still married to Bob, the young soldier just home on leave and visiting Joplin, Missouri, on his way back to South Dakota. They had three husky sons and one daughter, who was born late in their married life. It has been a good life for Betty. Makes one wonder what might have been Betty's life if she had not bought those shoes and was forced to go live in Joplin. Ah love. Betty met her fate, riding up and down those floors in that elevator on that very special day. Oh yes, she had on those new pair of shoes that day when she met Bob. It must have been fate.

Chapter 13

Arrival of Mr. Big Man

So now, it was just me at home. Glenn had left earlier to go live in Joplin. Betty had now left and was married. I felt very lonesome. One Saturday, Dad was going out to talk to Mr. Gunn and perhaps do some gun trading. I begged to go along and was allowed to go visit also. The real reason I wanted to go see Mr. Gunn was because I had heard Dad talking about the puppies there. He told Momma that they had just been born and were Toy Manchesters. Well, as one might guess, I got out of the car and walked over to the dog shelter and fell instantly in love with one particular small puppy there. He was all white and had the most adorable flop of his ears I had ever seen. Tiny little tail that was always wagging, and how he loved to run and bark. I just had to have that little puppy.

That evening when we were back home, I told Dad how much I loved that little dog. I started to cry and beg for this puppy as I promised how I would always take care of him and walk him and feed him. He would never be a problem in the home, and I just had to have him. Friskie had died, and I missed having my own dog.

Finally, after listening to me for two days and two nights, Dad relented. Mr. Gunn wanted two hundred dollars for the puppy as he was a purebred Toy Manchester. Of course, Dad did not have the two hundred dollars, but he did have a rifle that Mr. Gunn had been looking at and asking if Glenn would ever sell it to him. So to my great amazement, Dad went to meet with Mr. Gunn to do some bartering

154

and trading. That evening, Mr. Gunn had his new rifle for his collection, and I had my puppy. I proudly named him Mr. Big Man because he was so small and he was a Manchester. It made sense to me.

I loved that puppy. I loved to have him near me at all times, playing and running together. I had big plans for him. In my imagination, because Mr. Big Man was a purebred dog, I saw him performing someday in a circus or in a famous dog show. We would be famous. I worked with Mr. Big Man every day on his doggie skills. We practiced sit, roll over, jump, walk on the fallen tree limb, and many other special skills I was going to impart to him. Sorry to say Mr. Big Man was not too fast on the learning of the skills, but he was just always so happy, jumping and running with me, I could not get mad. I would just laugh and hug him in a special way because he was all mine.

A week later, I noticed that Mr. Big Man did not have as much energy as usual. He didn't eat his dinner, and he seemed to act like he was cold and shaking. Later that afternoon when he was napping, I noticed that his legs were moving very stiffly and not in the usual energetic moves of a dog chasing a rabbit in his dreams. I was getting worried about my little puppy. I told Momma about this, and she assured me that he was just probably tired from all our scampering and playing that day. I went to bed and left Mr. Big Man asleep on a rug in front of the heater in the living room.

During the night, I woke up suddenly sure that something was wrong. And then I heard Mr. Big Man whimpering as if he was having a bad dream. I got up from bed and walked in to find Mr. Big Man lying on the rug in an unusual way. His body seemed all stiff and his hind legs were drawn to his stomach. I ran through the kitchen to Momma and Dad's bedroom and hollered for them to please wake up. I told them that Mr. Big Man was sick and to please come look at him. Dad walked into the living room and took one look at my puppy and told me to wrap him up warm and to carry him to the car. We were taking him to the vet's place to be examined.

I tried to be brave and not start to cry because I was so worried about my puppy. He looked at me with such sad eyes, and I could tell he was in pain. Even though it was late in the evening, the vet met us at the door and led us into one of the exam rooms. He examined Mr. Big Man thoroughly and shook his head. He turned to Dad and asked, "Did you have this puppy vaccinated for distemper. My Dad shook his head and told the veterinarian that he had been assured that Mr. Gunn had given the puppies all their shots so they would not get sick.

The veterinarian shook his head and said, "Well, I don't think this puppy had any shots because it looks like he has distemper." At that time, I did not know what distemper was, but I could tell it was serious by the way the vet was talking. I began to cry and pet my little puppy on his head.

The veterinarian continued to talk to Dad about distemper and what it does to dogs that are not vaccinated. He told us that Mr. Big Man would never walk again, that he would be paralyzed all his life, and that he would be in a lot of pain. He told Dad that we should put Mr. Big Man to sleep. It would be kinder to do so.

When I heard the veterinarian say this, I began to cry loudly and protest. They couldn't put Mr. Big Man to sleep. He was my puppy, and he was going to be a famous star in the circus. I loved him with all my heart, and I could not bear to put him to sleep. I begged and begged my father to please let me keep Mr. Big Man and not put him to sleep. I promised I would do whatever was necessary to keep him alive and well.

Dad shook his head and patted Mr. Big Man on the head. "I am sorry, Susie, but I think it would be kinder to put this little puppy to sleep. You would not want to watch him living in pain each day, would you?"

I thought on this for a few minutes and got down closely to look into Mr. Big Man's face. "Dad," I said, "when I stood back and raised my head up, Mr. Big Man wants very much to live. He told me in his eyes to not give up on him yet. Can we please take him home and I will care for him every day, and if I do see him in constant pain, I promise we will bring him back to the vet to put him to sleep."

Dad looked at me, he looked at the veterinarian, and he looked at Mr. Big Man. And then he reached down and lifted the puppy up in his arms, wrapped in the old towel, and said, "Okay, we are going to take him home for a week. But you have to promise me that you will stand by your word."

I cried and cried and replied that I promised. We carried Mr. Big Man back to the car and took him home.

Momma helped me to find a box that would suit as a bed and Dad cut the side down. She placed newspapers on the bottom of the box and an old towel on top. And then we laid Mr. Big Man in the box, placing him in the front of the heater in the living room so he would stay toasty warm all night. Dad prepared half of an aspirin in some water and fed it to Mr. Big Man. I gathered an old blanket and laid down on the floor next to Mr. Big Man and told my parents I wanted to sleep there so I could be close to my puppy. I knew that he was scared and I wanted to be near to assure him that I loved him so much.

We slept the night and that morning I fed him some food and cleaned him up from his accidents. I had to go to school, and it was hard for me to be attentive in my classes. All I could think of was Mr. Big Man at home needing my help.

When I arrived back home, my little dog tried to wag his tail and raise his body to greet me. It just broke my heart to see him so fragile and broken. I honestly did not want to see him in pain, but I also honestly believed that he was determined to live, and I could not ever take that from him. Later that evening, Dad came into the living room and sat on the floor with Mr. Big Man and me. He told me that he had been reading in his large medical book that he had. He felt that the muscles were still alive. We just had to find a way to bring them back to his past strength so Mr. Big Man could walk again. He looked at me and winked and said, "I believe Mr. Big Man wants to live also."

So we began our nightly ritual with Mr. Big Man. We kept him in the little box, lined with papers and clean towels or old shirts. He could raise his head and eat or drink water. It was just that his hind legs did not work. Dad got a jar of our Vicks Vaporub, and every night, he would place some of that Vicks on his hands and then he would massage Mr. Big Man's legs. He would rub them and move them. Dad did small bicycle circles with his legs, pulling and stretching them, slowly working more tolerance to the movement by Mr. Big Man. Sometimes we would place a heating pad on his legs, and this would warm his legs after they had been massaged. Between Dad and me, we kept up a nightly routine with Mr. Big Man. We messaged, rubbed, cycled, and rolled his little thin legs for twenty minutes every single night. And then he was given half of a small aspirin to help him sleep. He seemed a little stronger each day. Maybe we were fooling ourselves. I don't know. I just honestly believed Mr. Big Man understood and believed with us that he could walk again.

When we told the vet what we were doing, he just shook his head and told Dad that he would be there should we decide to place Mr.

Big Man to sleep. Next, Dad went out to Mr. Gunn's residence, and I understand that he pretty much read him the riot act. He bawled out Mr. Gunn that he had been too cheap to give those little puppies their needed shots. He got even madder at Mr. Gunn when he learned that so far only Mr. Big Man had survived from the litter of six. The other puppies had died. Dad also told Mr. Gunn that he had better not ever see another dog or puppy there unless he had proof that all those dogs had been given their needed vaccinations. He further told Mr. Gunn that if he did not take care of these matters, he was going to take back his rifle he had traded with Mr. Gunn for Mr. Big Man. I guess Mr. Gunn listened to Dad because he never bred any dogs again. He for sure did not want to give up his rifle to Dad.

The days continued. Thanksgiving passed and we still worked with Mr. Big Man each evening. Sometimes I would tell Dad that I could honestly feel some strength back in Mr. Big Man's little skinny legs, but Dad just always laughed and told me it was wishful thinking.

Christmas Day arrived, and we had plans to go to Grandma Clayton's farm in Cassville. Aunt Rena with her children Betty and Maurice would be there. I was looking forward to spending the holiday there on the farm with everyone. Dad stayed home as he always did. He never liked to go visiting. So Momma and I loaded up food, our presents, and, of course, Mr. Big Man, into the car that Christmas morning early to go spend Christmas Day with our family.

When we arrived, we placed Mr. Big Man in his little box in front of the old wood burning stove in the living room. Meanwhile, the women were getting Christmas Dinner ready. Momma's brothers and their wives had arrived so the house was full of people with lots of noise, food, and merriment. When it was time to eat, we all went into the dining room to sit at the large old oak table. I left Mr. Big Man in front of the heat in the parlor figuring it would be best for him there. He was lying in his box asleep when I left him to go into the dining area to eat.

There was so much food to eat and we were all busy eating when I suddenly heard a loud yipping. It was as if Mr. Big Man was in pain. I jumped up from the table and ran into the parlor where I spied the most wonderful Christmas gift I could have ever received.

As I stared in disbelief, there was Mr. Big Man, slowly moving across the linoleum floor, dragging his little legs behind him. He was panting and yipping some, but when he saw me his little tail began to wag in a

Mr. Big Man and me

I love this picture. There stands with me my Mr. Big Man; friend, pal, confidant, teacher - all in this little white Toy Manchester. Even though he was a dog, he taught me about strength, patience and love, as few humans can do. Sick and paralyzed, Mr. Big Man had the courage and strength to walk again and live a generous span of a lifetime.

sort of jerky motion, back and forth. And I swear there was a smile on his face. I started blubbering as loud as could be and knelt on the floor to catch Mr. Big Man in my arms. I hugged him and hugged him. We had a real Christmas miracle right there in a small little white furry bundle. Mr. Big Man had walked.

Of course, it still took more months of continued muscle massaging and exercise, but Mr. Big Man was getting there. He was learning how to stand on all four legs. He could slowly move his hind legs as he walked. He was no longer dragging his back legs. He ate well and put on some weight and even became muscular in a rather scrawny rooster sort of way. I can tell you he fell a lot of times. He fell many times right on his little nose. Later in years I used to swear that his nose was a little crooked in front from all the falls. But Mr. Big Man walked again. He ran again. He played and played with me. We never became a famous circus act, but I didn't care. He was my puppy again, and I loved him so much. I was so proud of my father for helping me to save Mr. Big Man and to bring him back to a life of moving and walking. As for the veterinarian, he just shook his head and told Dad that love always worked wonderful miracles.

I can tell you today that Mr. Big Man went on to live in our home with us as an honored and loved dog for eight more years. One day, while I was at high school, Mr. Big Man quietly passed on in his sleep. I was so sad to have lost him, but I was also so proud for all the happiness and the lessons he had taught me. I thought I was teaching him how to do dog tricks when all the while he was teaching me about being strong in life. I have a picture of Mr. Big Man and me standing in our yard together. To this day, I still love to look at that picture.

Chapter 14

Doctor! He's Not Even A Nurse

I had previously mentioned that my dad had an enormous medical book by his bedside that he referred to for any illnesses that I had. He also would give medical advice to various customers who were in the shop to ask him about coming surgeries. And of course, he had his *Farmer's Almanac* copy that hung diligently on the kitchen wall with a pencil on a string next to it. We had strict advice to never touch the almanac or the pencil. Never. In some ways, my Dad had medical thoughts far in advance of the day—some that I have now seen come to fruition, in a different medical happenstance but along the general idea. For instance, my father believed in monthly colonics or colon cleansing. In this aspect, he would call me into the kitchen along with my mother and inform me that it was time for my monthly enema. At this time, no matter how much I pleaded against the matter, I would go to the bathroom with my mother and be given an enema. After my bowels had settled back to normal, I would be given a bottle of 7-Up and crackers. Sometimes I received a Hershey's candy bar. But each month, I knew that the matter would be remembered, and I would receive the cleansing.

I grew to accept these cleansings as a matter of fact. I was later surprised to find that it was not the norm for other children. And that was when, at the age of ten, I informed my father that I would no longer do the enemas. At this time, it was determined that I would continue in the cleansing, but I would receive a square of a laxative bar. Also, to sweeten the deal, once again, I was given a 7-Up drink and crackers for after the laxative had worked. I can say now that this matter continued until I was in the seventh grade. At this time, I informed my father that if he believed so much in the colon cleansing, he could take the enema or laxative. I would no longer do so. To my amazement, Dad relinquished his monthly demand, and I no longer had to take the laxatives for colon cleansing. Later I would wish I had stood up to this matter sooner. Perhaps it would have ended the matter.

My father also predicted at this time that someday there would be a red light that would be able to shine on an organ or such and remove it. This was when I was in the seventh grade also. So Dad told me that each evening when I came home from school I was to lie down on the couch and he would place a sun lamp that we had so that it would shine on my throat. The idea was to dissolve my tonsils by the heat and not by surgery.

So each evening, when I arrived home from school, Dad would get out the sun lamp and place it to shine on my throat for twenty minutes. Then he would examine my throat to see if my tonsils had shrunk in size. I remember hearing him bragging up in the shop to various members of his daily visitors about how he was going to remove my tonsils by heat. About the same time as when I put my foot down on taking the laxatives, I also said a determined no to using the sun lamp on my tonsils. Dad, to my surprise, again agreed to the matter and put the sun lamp away in the closet.

I will add that today, after all those many years, I still have my tonsils. But I often have to wonder if Dad was thinking ahead to what we now have with the use of laser light. Actually, I have added these parts about Dad and his medical ideas to explain that I really never thought anything about Dad and me massaging Mr. Big Man's legs each evening with Vicks Vaporub. Through the years, my mother and I had just accepted medical ideas that Dad might have and allow him to try them.

Actually, thinking back to those days when I was a child, people did not speak much about their illnesses. Most did not have the monies to go to hospitals and died at home with their family taking care of them. Cancer was not spoken about and one seldom heard about neighbors or family members who were sick with cancer. It was kept a secret. Truthfully, I have always believed that John Wayne helped to open the ability to speak the word *cancer* out loud in the 1970s. Mr. Wayne called it the "Big C" and made it a little less scary to talk about. He took the word *cancer* out of the dark basement corner and made it a word a person could talk about in public with other people. He also made people more aware of going to their doctor to have physicals to check for any possible cancer.

Well, that Saturday morning, I had gone out the front door of the shop, and to my surprise, when I looked down the block and across the street, I saw a very surprising sight. There were lines of people standing there on the sidewalk leading up to the little house there and onto the porch. The back of the line of people stretched back down the whole block. There must have been over fifty people standing there in line. They were people of all ages, young and old. People wearing their work clothes of overall and shirts, mainly farmers. Most of the people seemed to be older in years with sad, extended faces and postures. I called Dad out to see what was happening. He took one look and shook his head and said, "Well, I will be danged."

And with that he began to walk down the block and across the street over to the line of people to see what was happening. I waited back in front of the shop to see what he would determine. I could see Dad walking along the line talking to some of the people that he knew. After a short time, Dad came walking down the block and back to the shop where he sat down next to me on the front steps. I waited a few moments and then asked Dad what was going on with all the people waiting in line to see the elderly woman in the house.

Dad shook his head and looked over at the line of people. Then he said, "People always hope for a miracle. Those people are standing in line hoping for a miracle—that's why there are so many sad looking people standing there." And he continued explaining to me. It seemed that the elderly lady who lived in the little house had posted advertisement that she offered the cure for cancer. Despite the years of research and endeavors of doctors and scientists, this little woman had found the solution and cure for all. All they had to do was come to her home, pay her five dollars, and drink her miraculous cure. And that was why the people were standing there. Each person had a reason to be afraid of cancer and had brought their five dollars to be released from that fear.

Today we would laugh at such a venture or thought by these people or the old woman who was selling the "miraculous cure." We know there is no miraculous cure for cancer today. But at this time, she was like the Medicine Man of olden days selling a bottle of "cure all" for one silver dollar. As in the olden days when the Medicine Man offered all cures for what "ails one" in a bottle for one dollar, she offered all present the cure for cancer for five green bills. This woman was playing on the fear of death by cancer. Of course, I would remind that at that time, five dollars was a lot of money to a family, a farmer, or anyone. People didn't earn a lot of monies and certainly did not have a five-dollar bill to just throw away. This amount of money might be the monies for a month of groceries or other needed items. And yet these people had gathered the amount of monies to give to the woman for her cure. They believed this woman and believed that if they went into her home, paid her the monies, and drank the cure, they would no longer be faced with the ravages of cancer. Many of these people in line could not afford to go to a doctor or hospital for any treatment. In many homes, the word *cancer* was said only in secret or whispered about. People died from cancer. Cancer was the secret killer. It could attack anyone, young or old, rich or poor. Cancer knew no particulars.

Today, as I watched, desperation lined the faces of these singular people standing there in line on the sidewalk and eventually entering her home. After a few minutes as I watched, these same people walked out of her home, speaking to others as they passed by, and headed quietly back to their homes and cars. The line continued to grow.

Shortly after Dad returned to the shop, he went inside. Before long, the local police arrived and began talking to the customers waiting in line for their cures. Two policemen stayed at the front of the line while another policeman entered the home. Shortly thereafter, I saw the police escorting the woman out of the house and into the waiting police car. One policeman stayed at the home and motioned to all to go home as the other policeman began to board and lock the front door.

People slowly began to break away from the line and return home. Many were angry, and some cried in aggravation or desperation.

I was saddened to watch these people. Dad patted me on the head and told me that she was breaking the law. She had no permission to sell her cure, nor did she have any cure to offer to the sick people. She had taken the idea upon herself that she could make monies quickly from these desperate people. She was robbing hard-earned monies from people that were looking for miracles in their own lives. She was also offering false promises to people who had lost hope for life. Dad said that it was not right to hurt people like that.

Dad and Janice front of Shop

Aunt Rena would often drive by and go into the kitchen and visit Momma, her sister, where they caught up on daily news. They enjoyed a cold glass of sweetened iced tea and chatting and laughing together. I would often be at work at the Presbyterian Church or the Tastee Freeze downtown from our house. It always seemed that if I wasn't in school I was at work. Janice would often go up front and talk to Dad. Janice liked to tell Dad some joke she had just heard or show Dad some acrobatic trick she had learned to do. Adding to this story, I recall that Mr. Big Man was getting older now.

During the night he might sometimes have a little "puddle" somewhere as an accident. He had gotten more careless in his old age. On this particular night that I am remembering, Mr. Big Man had decided to "pee" under the two legged table that sat in the living room. This time he accidentally sprayed right on the wall plug there that had the cord to the living room lamp in it. The wire may have been a little splayed as it was old and the pee landed right on the wire sparking a few sparks which may have shocked Mr. Big Man who then yelped and gave a big bark. Awakening me, I soon saw the sparks and the smoke arising from under the table. Hollering help, Dad ran into the room and quickly unplugged the sparking wire, stopping the possibility of a potential fire. I hugged my dog and hollered, "Hooray! Mr. Big Man is a hero!" Dad looked down at my little dog in my arms and said, "In this case, I think Mr. Big Man was the hero and the villain!", and he gave me a wink!

Later, I learned that she had been selling small cups of her cure to each person. When the miraculous cure was later inspected by the police, they had discovered the presence of grape juice. The cure was just plain purple grape juice. In the back of the kitchen, they had found empty bottles of grape juice and more empties that the woman had placed in boxes of trash. There was no cure.

She did go to jail for a short term. She was elderly and not of a strong constitution herself. Interestingly enough, when I think back to this incident, I remark how people were afraid of the word *cancer*. People just didn't talk about it, and in fact, many elderly people died of cancer without their family even knowing they had the disease.

Chapter 15

A Christmas Story

The Christmas holidays were always a lonely time for me. As an only child at home, I mostly relied on my own interests and hobbies to entertain myself. I loved to play with dolls and paper dolls. I was an avid drawing and coloring person. I loved to keep myself entertained with my drawing interests and fashion design for my paper dolls. My father never participated with Momma and me for the holidays as long as I remembered. Dad would get up on Christmas morning and go work in the shop, keeping to himself. Momma and I would sit in front of our decorated Christmas tree, in the living room, back behind the shop and exchange gifts and I opened my Santa Claus gifts, knowing they were really from Momma. There were not a lot of gifts because Momma did not have a lot of monies, but she did her very best to find me lovely and fun gifts that I enjoyed receiving. She always addressed them from Momma and Dad, but I knew better. I don't think Dad ever knew what I had even gotten for Christmas. I had stopped showing him a long time ago because he never seemed interested. Years later, when I was working and had monies to buy presents, Momma and I would always stack Dad's gifts on his chair and leave them for him. Later, when no one was around, Dad would come in and open the gifts, throw away the cartons and wrapping paper, and put his gifts away in the bedroom. He never mentioned the gifts to either of us, but deep down I knew that he appreciated the gifts and that Momma and I still remembered him at the holidays. I have always been so sorry that he missed these

167

holidays with Momma and me. He seemed to just hurt himself mainly by his own inability to share love and special care at any time. He always seemed to be his own worst enemy.

This year, when I was around eight years old, I found a secret that Dad had been holding in his heart; this Christmas would turn out to be a little different. As a child, I would often stand quietly in the hall corridor behind the front clock shop and listen to Dad talking to whomever might be in the front shop with him. I was sort of a spy during those years, trying to understand Dad through the words he shared with other people. I was always trying to find out why Dad did not love me or want me around him. I thought that maybe listening to him talking might give me some clues. Also, I was always just plain snoopy and wanted to hear what Dad was talking about. I liked to hear his stories.

On this Saturday afternoon, Dad was talking to his friend John. The man lived in an old rundown house out along a dusty, country road, with his mother, wife, and children. At this time, to my amazement, he was speaking about Christmas and was telling Dad that his kids were going to be very upset because he was not planning any Christmas for them. He just didn't have any monies no matter how he tried. He was feeling downhearted and sad and looking for some way to be a better parent. Dad was smoking his cigarettes and listening as he took another swig from his bottle of whiskey. Then he tapped his cigarette on his large ashtray and leaned over the counter in front of him and said, "Listen, every kid needs a Santa Claus and I am going to make sure that those kids of yours have Christmas presents this year."

"*What?*" I leaned closer to the doorsill to listen to Dad. He was concerned that those children have a Santa Claus and Christmas presents? I asked, *What about me?* When had Dad made sure I had a Santa Claus or Christmas presents? I didn't resent the children getting presents, but I would have liked to also been thought of in the same regard by my dad. I was jealous of Dad's concern for other children and not for me. I turned and walked back down the hall and on through to my own bedroom. I sat down on my bed while my mind whirled with questions and images. Of course, I wanted the man's kids to have a Christmas. That wasn't what I was upset about. I was mad because my dad was going to make sure they had a Christmas when he didn't even care if I had one. Dad didn't even care that I wanted this wonderful doll in Main Variety's shop window downtown. How I wanted that doll. It was a large doll with the most beautiful face and braided hair. It would stand upright and you could take the hand and it could walk along your side and say, "Mama." How I wanted that doll so that I could walk it around the house with me and talk to it and I could dress it in pretty little dresses. All the other girls in my classroom were asking Santa Claus for this doll, and I really wanted the doll also. Whenever I could, I loved to walk downtown and stand in front of the Main Variety store and look at the doll on display there. I never tired of just standing there and looking at the doll and imagining how fun it would be to play with the doll. Whenever Momma saw me staring at the doll in the window, she would always come over and say to me that Santa might not be able to bring this doll to our house. It was very expensive. I would just smile at Momma and try not to think about that. I really wanted that doll. With these thoughts, I flounced around on my bed and hid my face in my pillow. I felt such pain and hurt in my heart it caused some tears to fall silently on my bedspread. Dad thought more of other children than he thought of me. Those were hurting thoughts in my mind.

The next few days I watched Dad in action. Christmas Day was drawing near, and Dad was busy with his plans for those children. He put out the word to his cronies that they could contribute to his efforts with used toys and some monies. Bicycles and tricycles began to appear in our shop. They were placed over on the right side of the large shop area awaiting some care and fixing up. Some bags of children's warm clothes and some boxes of toys began to appear in the shop also. Momma sorted through the clothes and repaired and laundered the clothes that had seen harder wear. Most of them were all acceptable clothes for the children and would prove to be good additions to their wardrobe this cold winter. I liked knowing they would be warmer. There were many scarves, hats, and pairs of gloves to wear with the collected warm coats and sweaters. It seemed to make me feel a little kinder in Christmas thoughts for the children as I saw how needed these clothes were for them.

I helped Momma and Dad clean up the assortment of toys and even contributed some of my own puzzles and games. Dad painted and varnished various items, and soon there was a large gathering of cheerful toys and warm clothes. Momma and I began to wrap various toys and clothing in bright Christmas paper and place them in boxes for delivery. Dad and a couple of his friends were busy repairing and painting bicycles of all sizes and shapes and scooters. One little rusted wagon soon became a bright and shiny red wagon to be placed under the Christmas tree for a child to enjoy. To my amazement, the front shop began to look something like Santa's workshop and we were all the little elves under Dad's guidance preparing a special Christmas for the children.

Christmas Eve arrived, and Momma and I went to church to enjoy the evening's festivities. I was an angel in the nativity pageant and even had a line to recite, "Let your light shine in the darkness," as I lit the large candle on the podium. I always loved our church Christmas pageant and being a part of the Christmas activities. After the evening service, we went back into the meeting room and joined the others by the decorated Christmas tree for refreshments. Each child was given a small box of candies and a book about Jesus. It was a special evening for us as we visited with friends and neighbors together in our church.

When Momma and I arrived back home, I went right to bed to await Christmas morning. I was curious to know when Dad was leaving to take the gifts to the little house, and I wanted to see them all packed in the car. That Christmas morning, I awoke early at 5:00 a.m. as I heard someone walking through the house. It was Dad, and he was starting to pack up the toys in our car parked in front of the shop. I jumped out of bed and threw on some clothes and went up to the front of the shop. I watched as Dad started to pick up a box to carry to the car and load it up. To my surprise, Dad turned to me and said, "Susie, grab a box and help me carry these packages to the car for delivery." I began to help as much as I could in carrying out the gifts. When the car was all packed and the last item carried out, I jumped in the front seat because I wanted to go with Dad to deliver the gifts. Dad climbed into the driver's side of the car and started up the motor. He never said a word. I settled back in the front car seat and relished in the warm heat from the car vent. It was a cold Christmas morning, and the wind was blowing cold air all around us.

Dad drove out of Monett and headed out into the country area. Turning off the main road, Dad pulled onto a side country lane, and down we went on a dirt road lined with large, tall trees. I was amazed looking around me from the car window at how dark was outside in this country area with no streetlights or lights from passing cars. It was pitch dark except for our car lights dancing before us on the dusty, windblown road. We turned right off the road onto an even dustier road that led up to a junkyard. Their home was behind the piled junk and sat off to the right surrounded by tall weeds and a few trees. There seemed to be an open area in front of the home, dusty and filled with broken furniture and trash. A large porch was in front of the house with a few steps leading up to the front door.

The house was dark and quiet. No one was up yet. It was early, nearly 6:00 a.m. and with the overhead clouds presenting the possibility of the arrival of snow, the yard looked large, luminous, and just a tiny bit scary. If it hadn't been for the reason of our arrival at the house, I might have been nervous about going into the yard filled with a large area of overgrown weeds and scattered junk, tires, and broken furniture.

Dad got out of the car and began to unload the boxes and bikes. I helped. No one ever locked their homes in those days, and certainly, I thought, they didn't have much worry about anyone trying to break into his house to steal anything. There was doubtfully much value in those belongings in such a small, shattered building. I could see the old jalopy truck parked near the side of his house. The front door opened silently for Dad, and he motioned for me to start bringing in the packages. I got out of the car and carried a box up on the front porch and into the darkened front room where a small, shapeless Christmas tree had been placed. Small handmade ornaments hung silently from the branches. I figured the children had probably made the ornaments the night before and hung them carefully on the tree with hopes that Santa would soon be there to see their efforts. Looking around the dismal room, I placed the box quietly on the floor by the tree. I quickly headed back to the car to bring in more boxes. Dad was busy bringing in the bicycles and red wagon to place in the room. He never looked around the room but just quickly and quietly went about the business of placing all the Christmas items in the room by the tree. Momma had also baked some Christmas cookies and purchased some little candies. I placed these items on the tables in the room.

We completed our tasks quickly and quietly with never a word or a glance at each other. I was in complete amazement to see my dad in this role. Dad seemed sort of shy to exhibit this caring and concern for another person. Neither of us looked at each other or said anything about the occasion but continued to work. We were both shyly embarrassed.

Waiting for the Christmas Parade

We loved our Christmas parades down the main street. Everyone would come into town and wait to see all the floats, the marching bands and Santa Claus, of course!

Excitement for the Christmas Parade coming

The excitement would build each minute while all waited for the Christmas Parade to arrive!

Soon, the music from the marching bands could be heard and everyone knew the parade had started.

Arriving with the music and sound were the many floats and of course, Santa Claus.

Christmas Parade arrives downtown Monett

Marching bands, colorful floats, beauty queens in modern cars, and lots of color, joy and sound arrive for all to enjoy! The Christmas parade was always a favorite each year.

Home Again, Home Again, Jiggity, Jig

Just as we completed the last task, we heard someone stirring in one of the rooms off from the front room. Dad motioned for me to quietly head back out of the house and go to the car. I ran quickly through the front door and out onto the porch and then headed out to get into the car. Dad followed me and closed the front door as he left. We both climbed back into the waiting car and sat for a few minutes, watching the dark house. Snow was just beginning to fall with large snowflakes that promised to cover the countryside fully with the clear beauty of a white Christmas morning. Dad turned on the car's windshield wipers, and they began to swish back and forth across the front window of the car removing the landing snowflakes. We sat and stared at the darkened house. I used my imagination to create a forthcoming scene of happy children, of many ages, racing around the front room and their Christmas tree. Bright tissue paper would be flying into the air with the child tearing into their chosen gift. It warmed me inside to think about such a scene. I hoped it would be happening just that way soon. I wanted the children to be hurrying out soon to see what Santa Claus had brought them and all the Christmas presents there under their decorated tree.

Dad put the car into gear and slowly pulled back away from the house and turned to go down the dark country road. Feeling the warm air circling around me from the car's heater, I settled back comfortably down into the front seat and looked ahead of me at the roadside illuminated by our car's front lights. Snow was falling gently on the car's front window and the wipers swished back and forth wiping the glass clean. I sat silently with my own thoughts. As we neared home, I smiled to myself. It was going to be a nice Christmas that year for Momma and me even if I didn't get the doll that could hold my hand and walk beside me. It would be just fine.

Chapter 16

War Comes To Town

As you may remember, we used to live across the street from the Evans family on the corner. Although we had moved a block down from their home, I still was allowed to walk up to their home and play with the children, Priscilla and Joey. Sometimes James, or Jimmy as we knew him, would join us in board games or reading comic books. The older sister had married and moved out to be with her husband and baby.

Jimmy had turned eighteen in February of that year, 1952, and he was all excited to join the navy. The Korean War was going on, and Jimmy said he wanted to see some action with the navy. He wanted to be an airman and fly in the airplanes. Jimmy was short in stature and wiry in his build. Everyone teased Jimmy that he was perfect for the airman apprentice program because of his easygoing personality. Jimmy knew no strangers. He was always able to face life with a grin and a hand out to help. Jimmy had signed up for the navy and had received his assignment. He was all set to leave and on this special day for Jimmy, I had gone up to visit the Evans' home. Jimmy was leaving home to complete his recruit training and begin his basic theory training in aviation fundamental skills with the airman apprenticeship training program. When I arrived at the house, everyone was in the kitchen finishing a large dinner. The table had been filled with many of Jimmy's favorite dishes to eat. I walked into the house just in time for a big piece of coconut cake. Jimmy was all dressed in his navy uniform and seemed a little nervous and yet very excited.

176

I could tell that Mrs. Evans was not at all excited and often turned her head to hide her tears. But everyone acted excited for Jimmy and pleased of what he had accomplished. After finishing the cake and milk, we all gathered in the living room to wish him a safe journey. After many hugs and kisses and noisy well wishes, Jimmy put on this hat and gathered his suitcase for departure. His father drove him down to the bus station for his travels to report for duty.

The house suddenly became very quiet after Jimmy left. Priscilla and I helped clean up the table and wash the dishes. Mrs. Evans went upstairs to lie down for a while and rest. I felt so sad to see everyone. This home that had always been filled with such loud boisterous laughter and joy was quiet and empty. After I finished the dishes with Priscilla, I decided it would be best to go home and leave them all to deal with Jimmy's absence the best way they knew.

I walked home and told Momma how sad the visit had been. She told me that she would go visit Mrs. Evans the next day and see how everything was. At that time, I didn't really know much about the Korean War, but I knew there was fighting and people were killed. I saw that on the newsreels at the theater. Later when I watched a newsreel and it showed soldiers fighting, I felt afraid for Jimmy and worried about how he was doing.

Often, when I was at the Evan's home, Priscilla would get out a letter they had received recently from Jimmy and share it with me. It was interesting to hear about his daily training and duties. Mrs. Evans would often exclaim how she worried about him because he was so young and away from home. He had just turned eighteen.

It was shortly after Jimmy's own departure to be in the navy that our own family became more involved in the Korean War. It was a Sunday afternoon, and I was in the kitchen setting the table for an early supper. Momma was at the stove frying chicken. Loaves of freshly made bread sat cooling on a rack at the cupboard with a two-layered chocolate cake, just iced, sitting on the side also. Potatoes were boiling on the stove to be mashed later. As I was at the table, I looked up and out the kitchen window to see my brother strolling up the sidewalk to our house. A young woman was walking with him.

I hollered to Dad and Momma and went to open the kitchen door screen to let in my brother Glenn and the woman. After greetings and a few hugs with Dad and Momma, Glenn introduced us to Thelma, his

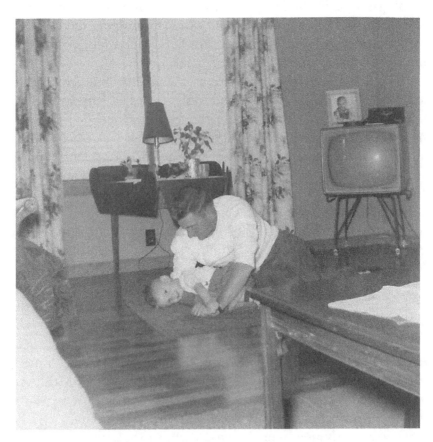

Glenn Returns Home from Korean War

After Glenn returned home from his service in the Korean War, he and Thelma settled into their home and began their family. Here Glenn is shown playing with his first born son, Scott.

I think this is such a cute picture of Glenn and Scott enjoying play together. It was good to have the soldiers home from the Korean War, those who had lived through the battles, and time to rebuild lives and families.

new wife. They had just been married and had traveled down to see us and tell us the good news. After well wishes and greetings, Momma invited them to have supper with us. She assured them that there was plenty for all.

Momma continued to cook while Dad and Glenn went up to the front of the shop to visit. I sat and talked to Thelma. She was so pretty in her outfit and had such a nice laugh. I wanted her to stay and talk to me more. Momma told me, "They will be visiting us for a few hours before they have to leave. Glenn has to report for duty soon. He is leaving to fight in the Korean War."

When I heard the words *Korean War*, I shut up immediately. Another person I knew was leaving for the fighting. That really scared me. How sad, I thought, that Glenn and Thelma had just been married, and he had to leave right away.

Later, when supper was all ready and placed on the table, Glenn and Thelma came to eat dinner and joined us for the delicious food. Fried chicken, mashed potatoes, creamed cauliflower, green beans, fresh baked bread, and, later, a chocolate two-layered cake with icing. Of course, a large pitcher of sweetened iced tea sat on the table for all to drink. Later, Glenn was amazed with Momma's creamed cauliflower. He told Momma that he had never eaten cauliflower in all his life, but tonight he just could not stop eating her cauliflower. Thelma laughed and asked Momma for her recipe. Of course, there were plenty of praises for the rest of Momma's cooking, but I just always remembered how amazed Glenn was as he ate another helping of the cauliflower. Glenn asked Momma for the recipe so his wife Thelma could make it for him someday when he returned home.

After cake, Glenn and Thelma left to go back to her home. It all seemed so sad to me. I helped Momma clean up the kitchen while they were gone, and I thought about how I knew two men now who were fighting in the Korean War. I would have to say a special prayer for each of them at night.

As I connected with the thoughts of wartime regarding the Korean War, it was now springtime, and carnivals or fairs often arrived downtown for a week or so. This time, the fair was held on the main street with a wonderful old carousel right in front of the Gillioz Theater. I wanted to spend hours riding my favorite horse in the musical circles. As long as I had a dime, I could be found riding and riding in a circle on that beautiful carousel. On the Saturday afternoon, they had bingo games. Momma really loved that, and we would sit and play games in the afternoon while drinking our favorite soda pop. With Main Street, lower part, filled with carnival rides and such, some of the special exhibits were placed right in front of the Monett Library. There was one large trailer with paintings all over the trailer depicting a woman sleeping in a glass coffin, and she had long hair to the floor and long fingernails. It cost twenty-five cents to go in and look at her. I didn't have that much money, so I stood outside and watched other people going up the steps into the trailer to get a "gander" at the dead woman. I really didn't see the reason to pay money to go into the trailer and look at a dead woman. I could stand right there on the street curb and look at all the paintings on the trailer and see as much of her that I wanted to see. When some of the people I knew came out from looking at the woman, they told me that she must have been buried alive because her hair had kept growing, and it was all over her and was lying on the bottom of the coffin. And they could see her really long fingernails on her hands preserved in the glass coffin.

I just shook my head and told them that I would rather not have bad dreams from looking at the dead woman. Truth be told, my monies were spent more enjoyable riding my favorite carousel again and again.

One of the reasons I now bring up the exhibit of the dead woman with long hair was that several years earlier I had gone to see another tent exhibit at a fair held outside of Monett on some farmer's acreage rented by the fair's owners. Dad and I had driven out to look at the rides and enjoy the atmosphere. There were several tents that had been placed for a quarter admission to see their wonderments. Dad was busy talking to some friends and neighbors while passing around a flask of whiskey, so I passed the time watching people enter the tents with exhibits. There was one tent that promised a look at a pony with two heads. I had decided I did not want to see that exhibit because I would feel so sorry for the pony. But a little later on, I heard a passing farmer angrily announce to all that wanted to listen not to waste their monies to see the two-headed pony because it was dead and stuffed. That made me feel even worse and glad I had not gone into the exhibit. But I had to admit, one particular exhibit had caught my attention. The sign at the front read "Captured Jap head on display." I wasn't too sure what that would be, so I kind of hung around listening to the speaker talk about what could be seen for one quarter in the exhibit. He promised that one could gaze upon the head of a dead Japanese soldier killed in World War II and preserved for all to look upon. Many men standing there just growled and spit on the ground while walking away with disgust. One farmer replied, "Why would I want to spend my monies to go in and look at a dead Jap?"

A few minutes later, the speaker was busy, and I saw my opportunity. I snuck into the tent bearing the dead Japanese head. Another farmer had walked in, and I just walked along with him as if he was my father. And there it was. The tent had been placed on an area of ground with grass and dirt. Right in the middle of the tent was a long bare table made from two sawhorses and a door. When one walked over to the table they were looking right into the closed eyes of a man's head floating in a large jar with yellow liquid in it. The head looked young, black hair floating in the liquid, and the eyes were closed as was the mouth. It just floated there in the yellow liquid seeming to question why and where he was. It made me very ill to look at it, and I began to back away to go back outside and get some fresh air. Suddenly the older farmer began to holler and move quickly to the table. He was mad at the Japanese head and obviously going to smash the jar open. The speaker ran quickly in and, with help, held the man back and led him from the tent. When they were outside, as I had followed the men, the farmer dropped his head into his hands and began to cry. It seems that his son had been killed in World War II fighting Japanese in the Pacific. Having never seen a Japanese man up close, the farmer had gone into the exhibit to see what a Japanese person looked like. Other men began to express their resentment that the dead Japanese man was floating in the jar and that the tent exhibit should be closed and then to get out of town. Several men voiced that the tent might just burst into flames one night if it didn't leave soon.

About that time, Dad came over to get me so we could head home. I heard later that the exhibit was closed and the tent was gone the next day. I was glad. The head of the Japanese man may have been our enemy during the war, but I didn't like that he was left there helplessly floating forever in the yellow liquid. It just further reminded me how much suffering was caused by a war, any war, on both sides, my neighbors or some Japanese man, far away in another country.

Chapter 17

Tickling Those Ivory Keys

About this time, somehow my father traded something for an old upright piano and had it transported into the storage room off Momma and Dad's bedroom. I fell in love with the piano immediately and begged to be able to take lessons to be able to play the piano. Although money was tight in those days, Momma and Dad relented and set up arrangements for me to take piano lessons once a week from Mrs. Rose. At that time, lessons were one dollar a week, and whenever possible, I could buy sheet music or piano books to play from.

Once a week, Momma gave me one dollar, and oftentimes it took a lot to spare that one dollar, and I would walk over to Mrs. Rose's home after school. I would take my piano lesson and then walk home afterward unless it was bad weather. Then I could call my parents to drive up and pick me up.

Mrs. Rose was a small, gentle woman at the age of sixty or so. Her hair was all white, and she wore it in a bun behind her hair. Straggles of white hair always poked out from the bun. Small in stature and weight, she seemed to always be dressed in a chiffon pale dress, often in a floral design. One of the things I like about Mrs. Rose the most was that she liked to talk and listen to me. Sometimes after the lesson, Mrs. Rose would serve me a cup of hot tea and a small sliver of cake or sandwich. We would sit and talk while sipping our tea together.

I think I was in awe of Mrs. Rose. Her home was a beautiful design, with a plush blue and pink decorated living room where we sat. She

182

always had a bouquet of flowers, usually roses, in a vase on the table by the piano. When she served tea, it was in a lovely floral china pot and matching cups and saucers. It was an elegant time for me, and I absorbed all the colors and style like a sponge. I wanted to live in such neatness surrounded by all the pretty china and flowers. I also might add that Mrs. Rose was very certain with me as a pianist and pushed at me to practice more and work on my piano scales. But although I loved the piano and loved to play it, I also loved to see Mrs. Rose and visit her in her living room drinking tea or playing my week's assignment; I was lazy in practice at home.

During this time, Mr. Big Man was frisky in life having been healed from his affliction. For some reason, as soon as I went into the room to practice my piano lessons, Mr. Big Man would run into the room and sit down on his haunches on the floor beside me. As soon as I began to play, no matter what tune, Mr. Big Man would throw back his head and howl loudly with all his strength.

Of course, I would get mad and holler at Momma to come get Mr. Big Man and take him out of the room and to shut the door. But Mr. Big Man would not have anything like that. No matter what I did, somehow he managed to get back into the room and to sit and howl, or "sing" as my Dad said, with all his might! I couldn't hear what I was playing for the constant howl of Mr. Big Man.

At first it was funny and I would sing along with Mr. Big Man as I played the piano. But soon it became tiresome.

And then one day, Mr. Big Man stopped rushing in to sing as I played the piano. He just wasn't interested anymore. Maybe I had become more accomplished in my skills or I was finally hitting the right notes. For whatever reason, Mr. Big Man became a stranger to my piano-playing hours and slept peacefully by the fire as if he had never been a howling dervish before.

A few years later, Mrs. Rose retired from teaching. She had become too frail and ill. I missed visiting her home and sharing our talks and teatimes.

Dad then placed me with Mrs. Phillips to continue my piano lessons. I could still walk to her home for my lessons, and if there was bad weather, Momma would give me a ride. I enjoyed the thirty-minute lessons on the piano with Mrs. Phillips. She was more flamboyant than Mrs. Rose had been. Mrs. Phillips was younger, perhaps in her late forties or so at the time. She had dark black hair and wore bright and colorful clothes. She played the piano loud and with classical style and filled one with energy and strength. I wanted to imitate her in being flamboyant. Mrs. Phillips also played the accordion. She could really make the instrument play. Her fingers seemed to fly over the keyboards as she moved the accordion open and closed with her arms. Her accordion was black and red with silver trim, and it was beautiful to watch as she stood there, one foot tapping, dressed in colorful dresses with petticoats under the skirts. She looked like a gypsy would look in my imagination. She just vibrated with music and strength at these times.

To my amazement, Dad came in the back one day with an accordion he had traded for and gave it to me. He wanted me to learn how to play it. Now this accordion was smaller than the one Mrs. Phillips played. I was thankful for that matter as her accordion seemed like it weighed a ton, and I was not sure I would be able to move it open and shut and play the keyboard. At least this accordion was smaller and easier to hold and maneuver. It was pretty with brown and beige colors showing acorns and leaves carved all over it. So to my surprise, I began to take piano and accordion lessons with Mrs. Philips. I tell you, when I left her home after an hour of lessons, I was exhausted. Thirty minutes of piano and thirty minutes of accordion was a lot to work through. And it was work, pumping that accordion with air to make it play. It was really hard work also. It took a lot of concentration to move your arms in rhythm while also playing the two keyboards with your hands, all in time with the music. I was often afraid that my arms would look like those of a body builder. But when I looked at Mrs. Phillips, her arms looked normal, and she had been playing the accordion most of her life.

So the months continued with my progress on the piano and somewhat with the accordion. Now, each year, Mrs. Phillips held a recital, and all her pupils had to play a selection in the recital whether they wanted to or not. I did not want to. It was all too scary for me. But each year, I would start to practice extra heavy on the piece I wanted to play, piano and accordion, and start to gear myself up for the heart-pounding occasion.

And to add to all this nervousness, for some unknown reason, Mrs. Phillips would always choose me to play a duet, also on the piano with her and later a duet on the accordion with her. I never knew why and would often suggest others who might also play a duet with her, but she would just shake her head and add that I would be the one she had selected this year. Dreading the occasion in my sleep and each day of counting off to the calendar, soon it would be the night of the recital. No matter how I tried, I could not hold back the march of time.

Usually the recital would be held in an auditorium in a church or school. Mrs. Phillips had a lot of students and all their parents would attend.

Following the occasion, a light serving of sandwiches and dessert would be served for all who attended. It was a beautiful occasion, and if I had not been so nervous, I would have enjoyed sitting in the soft candlelit and decorated room to listen to the various students play. Also, Mrs. Philips treated us to her musical displays. But then it would come the dreaded time for my own recital for the solo on the piano and accordion and then the dreaded duet on the piano and accordion with Mrs. Philips.

I once found a picture of me all dressed up in my cousin Betty's long blue satin dress and sitting at the piano the night of the recital. Flower displays and candles adorn the piano where I sit. I am barely looking at the camera for the picture because I am sure I am going to vomit at any moment. You can tell from my face that I am positive that I am about to embarrass myself and the whole family with a sudden dash out of the room. But I prevail and each time managed to put on a fairly good musical selection as solo and then as duet. Somehow, I survive to greet another day and breathe a sigh of a prayer of thanks that once again I have made it through to another year of a recital.

I only played the accordion for one more year, and then I told Mrs. Phillips that I no longer wanted to play the accordion. I then gave it to Dad and told him he could sell it, trade it, or learn to play it himself but that I had had enough with hauling the instrument around and trying to pump enough air into it to play. I think Dad understood, despite his wanting me to play the accordion really well, like one would see on television. He quickly sold it to another person who greatly wanted to learn to play the accordion. I hoped the accordion had gone to a happier home. A few years later, around seventh grade, I discontinued piano lessons altogether. I was just too busy with school to be able to rehearse enough for lessons. I could play most of the music I had and to my own enjoyment. I wasn't a superb player, just a comfortable, enjoyable

Family Visit

Aunt Rena was now home from the T.B. Sanatorium, married to Paul Essary and had baby Janice. Betty and Maureece were back with all of them and lived in a little house in the country they just bought. Pictured, left to right, Betty, Susie, Janice, Grandma Ethel, Aunt Rena and Maureece.

Town Hall

Town Hall sat right across the street from us. The side facing us was the Public Library.

I loved that building and was in there almost every day, when I could. Around the corner was the Town Hall, Police Station and the Fire Station.

Election days took place in the Library. As I remember, Dr. Kerr, our family doctor, was also in the building. Dr. Kerr was a large, tall, bald headed man with a voice that boomed like Goliath in the Bible. He could make me tremble and shake just saying hello to me! But, he was a good man and always busy taking care of the townspeople who were sick. I remember once that I was sitting in the waiting room to see him and he walked into the room and asked how I was. When I said that I was just fine, his voice boomed out at me questioning why I was in there then! I wanted to run right home. Dad and Dr. Kerr were good friends. Dad read many medical journals so that when he called the doctor he would tell him all my symptoms and what he thought was the matter with me. Dr. Kerr would then bellow the question of why Dad had called him if he knew already what was the matter with me. Dad would always retort to Dr. Kerr, "because you can write the prescription and I can't." That would always set Dr. Kerr into laughing!

piano player. During the years, I often played the piano at church for the youth services or at school gatherings when I was teaching. The ability to play the piano always came in handy for teaching and other times of joining together with friends.

I do have to add one of my fancies during this time. The room where I played the piano had a door opening to the outside, and during the warmer days, I would have the door open with just the screen door closed. Our home was located across the street from the Monett Library, town hall, police department, and fire department, all housed in one large building. Of course, there was a lot of people going in and out of these buildings at all times of the day. In my fancies, or imagination, I would open the door and play my piano loudly, sometimes singing along, with the image of being heard by a famous person or agent. I would often pretend that as I was playing the piano during those days, some famous person or such, would be leaving the town hall and hear me playing the piano or singing. Continuing to my fantasies, I would pretend that the famous person would cross the street and walk into Dad's shop and ask where the lovely piano music was coming from. In my dream, Dad would then walk them down the corridor and into the room where I was playing. Often I would dream that Rock Hudson or Mitch Miller would hear me and quickly sign me up to become a famous star or piano player. Funny. I have no idea why I included Rock Hudson in this fantasy. I guess I chose Rock because he was just so handsome. Needless to say, no one ever came to knock at my door to sign me for a contract or whisk me off to Hollywood Land.

Chapter 18

Oh, Dem Golden Slippers

As I had mentioned before, my father sold and traded musical instruments in his shop. There might be a banjo or guitar hanging on the wall or a violin placed in a glass case on display. Dad also sold supplies for the musical instruments as picks and strings. In the summer, he always had a supply of grass harps on hand and some sets of bones. I was always interested in these wooden musical instruments. They were 5–7 inches in length and curved resembling small barrel staves. When a person held the two bones, or wooden sticks, between one's fingers and moved your wrist, they would knock together. An experience player of the bones could get a rhythm going much like someone tapping on the floor with their feet. I liked to watch a talented person playing the bones, oftentimes playing them on their chest or arms also.

The reason I mention the bones is that it was now time for the annual spring minstrel show that was annually presented in our town hall auditorium. Along with the minstrel show presented was the beauty contest sponsored by local businesses showcasing our own Monett lovelies. I remembered my sister, Betty, had entered several years earlier and had placed second in the competition. We had all been very proud of her.

This year, my friend Priscilla had decided she really wanted to enter the beauty contest. The problem was that she had no one to sponsor her for the contest. A fee had to be paid by the sponsor, and she had not been able to find anyone to pay the fee. When my father heard about

189

Priscilla's plight, he offered to sponsor her in the contest. Although the fee was very expensive to us, twenty-five dollars at the time, Dad felt it would be good for his business to have the name of his clock shop and musical instruments listed on the program.

So Priscilla began to make a lovely pink long gown to wear in the contest. She was very talented on the sewing machine, and with help from her mother, she was able to create a very lovely pink, strapless gown to wear for the evening's performance in the contest. Dad loaned her a rhinestone necklace and earrings from his store to wear with her gown that evening. Priscilla glowed like a regular princess when she had finished getting all dressed in her gown and jewelry. I was so excited to see her looking so lovely. We were certain she was going to win in the beauty contest that evening. We could not imagine a lovelier girl than Priscilla with her light blond curly hair, clear complexion, and lovely ensemble. She was an absolute knockout! Also, one had to add that Priscilla always had such a sweet demeanor about her. The way that she talked and acted, her concern for everyone, and gentleness she presented to each person made her an absolute winner to me. How could the judges not immediately recognize her beauty and manners when they saw her presented on the stage?

That evening, Momma and I were all eager to attend the minstrel show and see the beauty pageant. We had walked up to Priscilla's home earlier and seen her all dressed up in her pink gown and jewelry and she looked so pretty. Mrs. Evans was just beaming with smiles when she looked at her daughter. Mr. Evans then drove Priscilla and Mrs. Evans down the two blocks to the town hall auditorium so Priscilla would arrive all cool and calm. Momma and I walked back down.

When we arrived at the auditorium we found the seats almost all filled. The local people enjoyed these spring festivities, and the gentlemen from the local civic organizations enjoyed performing in the show. They had rehearsed the three-act minstrel show and presented themselves in rare form, strutting and dancing and singing on the stage. Banjos strumming and singing was very popular with the songs of yesteryear to the audience. And of course, after the minstrel show would be the beauty pageant which many parents and friends had come in support of their family member or friend.

When they announced that they would now have the parade of participants in the beauty pageants, Momma and I were so excited. Mrs.

Evans was sitting with us also with little Joey. I could see Dad standing in the back. He had come over later to watch for Priscilla in the pageant. He was not much for watching the minstrel show but wanted to see Priscilla and hear the announcement of his sponsorship.

When Priscilla walked out on the stage, we were so proud of her. Although she was only sixteen years old at that time, she looked so ladylike and lovely there on the stage in all her pink lace and finery. We clapped loudly and cheered for her as they announced her name and that she was sponsored that night by Glenn Stone's Clock Shop and Watches, Musical Supplies on Bond Street. Priscilla stood smiling sweetly and then walked across the large stage graceful and with great charm. She gave a small bow and then walked back off the stage. I was sad to see her leave the stage. She just looked so very beautiful to me standing there under the bright lights.

After all twenty-five contestants had had their moment on stage, the judges sitting in the front rows turned and put their heads together to make a decision. To our sadness, Priscilla did not win, nor did she even place. We were so disappointed. We were just certain that Priscilla would win. But many women told us that she would have a better chance next year when she would be a little older. We agreed that, yes, there was always next year, but we were silently wishing that she could have won that year, right then. Later, when we waited downstairs, outside in the cooling evening, Priscilla and Mrs. Evans came down to meet us. We all hugged her and gushed about how pretty she had been on the stage. You could tell Priscilla had a few tears of disappointment in her eyes as she nodded bravely that next year would be a good time to try again.

Priscilla handed the rhinestones to Momma and we waved good-bye. Mr. Evans had the car to drive Priscilla and family back to their home. Momma and I crossed the street and walked over to our home. When we entered the house through the alley side into the kitchen, we could hear Dad up in the front of the shop already back to working on his clocks and watches. Momma took the jewelry back up to place in the glass cases for sale. I got ready for bed and fell asleep dreaming of lovely pink gowns and how pretty Priscilla had looked that evening.

Chapter 19

Meeting the Mick

Sundays, at this time, had become a day for trips, or day trips, as we called them. Dad and Momma would decide where we would be going that day, and Saturday night we often went to bed earlier so we could be up and about early on Sunday. Momma was always the most energetic one, and I still marvel at her energy. She would arise early, set the loaves of bread to rising, put the two layers of chocolate cake in the old oven to bake, and step outside in the backyard where she would catch a chicken, wring its neck, and pluck off its feathers. She would then come in and cut it up into preferred pieces and start frying it in her big iron skillet. By then, I was up and helping her with various chores to prepare for the trip. Dad would wander up into the shop and work with some broken clock or watch, smoking his daily Camel cigarettes and humming to his music playing on the radio.

Momma and I put together the makings of a large bowl of potato salad, and I was allowed to frost the two-layer cake. My favorite job as I was allowed to lick the bowl for remaining icing.

We then packed up the salad into the large ice chest filled with chipped ice that Dad had gotten. Loaded up several large mason jars of water and packed the chicken in the large picnic basket Momma had along with a large tablecloth, napkins, salt, and pepper. I always believed it was a banquet fit for a king!

And off we took in our old Ford driving to the favored city of Joplin, Missouri. All the way on the trip, I sat in the backseat and smelled the

192

aroma of hot fresh bread, fried chicken, and chocolate cake. It made me giddy with the thought of all that good food to eat soon at a chosen picnic area. I am not sure why we always drove particularly to Joplin. Perhaps because it was the city Dad had grown up in or he just liked to go there. But off we traveled to Joplin, driving along the one lane of highway, with curves and hills and farmers in the road with their tractor or cattle crossing. The drive usually took two hours with driving through each small town on the way. Later, the highway with four lanes would make a drive to Joplin a twenty-minute venture, but not in my days. I loved to sit in the backseat and sing to myself with my dolls. I enjoyed the different scenes we passed through, and I often imagined previous pioneers walking over the lands with their own wagon of children and food. I was always an imaginative child.

Sometimes we drove to Joplin simply because the theater there was showing a new Audie Murphy or John Wayne movie. Dad could not wait until these movies would travel on down to Monett to our theater, so we drove up to Joplin to see the movie. After we arrived in Joplin, and the weather was nice, we would find a picnic area and set the table there to eat. Following our banquet, we would clean the mess, load up the car again, and head to the matinee of the chosen movie.

My father loved the movies and thought nothing of driving to Joplin just so he could see the movie before it arrived. Impatience. Of course, once it arrived in Monett, he would go to see it again.

About once a month, Dad loved to drive down to the Will Rogers Memorial in Claremore, Oklahoma. He never grew tired of walking through the museum while looking at the pictures, saddles, and various items of interest that Mr. Rogers had collected. It was a very beautiful memorial and museum, and I enjoyed learning about the history of Will Rogers. Momma, who always wore her two-piece black suit, silk blouse, and strand of pearls, would often just sit in the lobby and enjoy watching the people walking by. She was a people watcher and loved to talk to them while learning about where they lived. Dad would always take me over to one particular silver saddle that he claimed was given to Will Rogers by a famous movie star in Hollywood who was kin to us. I don't remember the name of the famous person, but I liked the idea of one of our family members being rich and famous. It was during these days that I became very interested in the plight of the American Indians and living on the reservation.

One bright summer Sunday, Dad decided we would go fishing in Joplin. He was longing to visit an old fishing spot of his younger days. So we just drove up to Joplin without any food packed. It was a nice excursion for Momma as she was able to just relax and enjoy the trip. When we arrived in Joplin, Dad drove off to a side of the area we had never been to before and down an old dusty country road. He then drove the car off to the side of the road and parked it under a cooling shade of trees. He then told us to grab the poles and follow him down to the small creek set back into the wooded area a small distance. We followed him down, and there was a most lovely shaded area, with warm large rocks to sit on and a lazy creek meandering by filled with fish to catch and enjoy for Sunday dinner. Momma sat under the tree on a large rock in her pretty gingham dress and sandals and enjoy the cool breeze. She wasn't really interested in fishing. Dad and I sat down on the bank of the creek while he put the worm on my fishing hook for me. We had purchased the bait on the way to the fishing place. Then Dad and I sat back to let the fishing pole do the work.

About that time, we heard someone walking over to our selected area of fishing. Upon turning to look, Dad and I were surprised to see a young man standing there who was no other than Mickey Mantle. Born in Oklahoma, Mantle had begun his minor league baseball career when we met him. He had been promoted to the Class-C Joplin Miners of the Western Association in 1950 and had recently won the Western Association batting title with a 0.383 average. And there he stood with fishing rod in hand looking for a place to sit down and fish on that warm summer day. Dad was so excited at seeing Mickey Mantle and couldn't wait until he could brag about this venture back to all his cronies back in the shop Monday. Mr. Mantle was most kind and rather homespun, just like any normal person, and enjoyed some baseball talk with Dad as he sat and fished. I believe Mickey Mantle had hoped for some quiet time to sit and fish and so he explained that he was going to move down a little further and see how the fish were biting. Dad shook his hand and thanked him for the visit time. Mickey Mantle then surprised us with an invitation to his newly built restaurant in Joplin. He wrote a small note and gave it to Dad and told him that we would be guests at his restaurant to enjoy some country fried chicken. All Dad had to do was give the manager the handwritten note. He then waved good-bye and left to try his hand elsewhere with the fish.

I believe it was that moment that Dad had lost his hunger for fresh fish for supper, and we loaded up our equipment in the car and drove back in to Joplin to locate the Mickey Mantle restaurant or what was known as the Mickey Mantle Holiday Inn. The baseball hero to millions was part owner. "See the Dugout and Mickey's Trophies" is what it said on the marquee. The Dugout was the name of the cocktail lounge. Besides lending his name to the monumental motel sign, and receiving a share of the profits, Mantle also contributed to the business by coming up with the slogan for the fried chicken served there in the restaurant: "To get a better piece of chicken, you'd have to be a rooster." Today I still find it hard to believe but they actually used that slogan. I remember Dad laughing and Momma rather shocked when she read it. I didn't understand what the slogan meant until many years later.

Well, we found that fried chicken to be almost as good as Momma's fried chicken, and she didn't have to cook it. So that day, we feasted on plates of fried chicken with the compliments of Mickey Mantle. Over the years, we often returned there to enjoy the chicken during the colder days we traveled there. We never saw Mickey Mantle again, but Dad enjoyed telling his fishing story of the day!

Now, in telling of those traveling day trips in the car, I have remembered the good times of the trip. Gathering the food and packing it all into the car. Traveling with Momma and Dad in the front seat. Sharing the adventure of the drive and seeing movies or museums. Dad loved to visit another museum in Joplin in an old hotel with the most enormous gun collection one can imagine. Every crook and cranny of that old hotel had guns placed on the wall or placed in glass cabinets. It was most interesting. These were all wonderful museums and places of adventure and travels.

It was the drive back home that always ended my enjoyment of the day. Dad always kept a pint of whiskey in the glove compartment, and as we took off on the trip home, Dad would start taking longer and bigger sips of his whiskey. Of course, this brought worry and anger from Momma, who would ask him to not drive while he was drinking. She would also offer to drive home, and he could just sit there on the passenger side and drink. But Dad would have no part of this. He drove drinking and erratically. Over the lane onto the other side, around the cars if going too slow, at a fast speed, Momma would start to cry. I would curl up in the corner of the backseat with my dolls and often

Football Game on the farm

When Momma and I would go visit the farm in Cassville, I enjoyed getting to play with Maureece and Betty, my cousins. I guess we had been playing football because Maureece is wearing a football helmet. Left to right - Maureece, Ronnie, Betty and me. I don't remember the little boy in front.

cry from worry of us being killed in a car crash. Often I would just cry myself to sleep only to be awaken by Momma when we pulled up in front of our home.

I have always believed an angel rode with us during those Sunday drives back home and protected us from harm. I have often asked myself why Momma and I would look forward to the day trips knowing how they would end with Dad drunk and driving erratically and arguing with Momma. I guess we always hoped it would be a good trip one day, and we would be able to enjoy the ride back home.

Chapter 20

I Don't Think We're In Kansas

Summertime and we often were looking to the skies—tornado weather. When the early summer days approached and the weather station began talking about storm clouds and appearing storms, the townsfolk often would shake their heads wisely and remind each other that tornadoes do not follow water, and they do not jump over lakes or large bodies of ponds. After all, they would remind each other, we had Kelly Creek, less than a mile from Monett. No tornado was going to hit Monett—no, sir, they argued. That creek there would keep out the tornado.

Each summer, as the sky would darken and lightning flashed across the large billowing sky, I would remind myself what I overheard those farmers say. "No, sir, no tornado was going to hit Monett." But when I looked out the window on the darkening sky and could hear the intensity of winds grow, I found it hard to believe the wise stories of these seasoned farmers.

As a small child, around eight years old, I can remember my father coming to tell me that the skies were darkening up and he wanted to show me where to go in case we needed to shelter from a tornado. Momma was at work at the cleaners, and I had been reading a book on my bed in front of a fan because it had been a hot and humid day. Dad came to my bedroom and told me to follow him outside. He walked me to the backyard and over to the large rock wall that ended our property. The wall itself was around 5–6 feet tall and thick with mixed cement and large rocks. On the top of the wall were pieces of broken glass

HOME AGAIN, HOME AGAIN, JIGGITY, JIG   199

embedded into the cement because the neighbor woman who had built the wall did not want any children sitting on top of the wall.

Dad walked me over to a corner of the wall that had been zigzagged around an old tall oak tree. In that corner, Dad told me that if he hollered "tornado" to me, I was to run outside to this corner and crouch down for protection. He spoke very sternly to me and said it was very important for me to remember his instructions . . . "Run to this wall and crouch down on the ground and wait, back against the wall," in case Dad should spot a tornado heading to our town. I agreed to the instructions and told Dad most fervently that I would follow his directions.

Living in Missouri, I had grown up knowing the terror and dread of approaching tornado season. I always dreaded those afternoons where the sky would begin to darken and the temperature would drop quickly from a hot smoldering day to a cool, wind-blowing afternoon. One could feel the electricity in the air—it seemed that the hair could just stand up on your arms and the back of your neck from the intensity building in the weather and air. Dad would always turn on our local radio station to listen for any forecast of approaching storms. He would keep the radio on in the store, listening as he worked. People would often stop in the store to spend a few minutes of conversation with Dad, talking about the weather and listening in solemn quiet to the weatherman. "Yessiree," the visitors would often comment, "there was an old Indian legend that reportedly foretold the fact that Monett and some of the surrounding areas would be kept safe from impending tornadoes because we were in a valley and between two waterways. A tornado would not jump a waterway. Thus, we were safe here in Monett from tornados. Kelly Creek would keep us safe." Dad would just listen and shake his head. He wasn't too sure if Kelly Creek was the way to keep Monett safe from any approaching tornados. So far, Monett had been kept safe from these approaching storms of wind and hail, but a person just never knew. The spinning tornado was just like the child's toy, a spinning top. Let it loose, and one could never foretell where it would spin!

It seemed the storms likened to appear mostly in the afternoons. I would often go out and sit on the front steps to our shop and watch the skies for any darkened clouds. When the winds began to blow and the clouds let loose the rain, I would especially begin to get nervous.

One could feel the changing in the weathers. Something was building in the airs. Often Dad would come out and sit with me as we watched the skies. We could still hear the radio in case some storm warning would be given.

One afternoon, as we sat on the porch following a sudden down pouring of hail, we saw two little white tornadoes swirl around the lawn behind the Monett Library. Just two small white tornadoes, not much taller than me, dancing across the lawn, darting across the driveway and on into the gravel parking lot where they skipped lightly into the air, disappearing as if they had never been there. We sat there with gaping mouths, neither saying a word until they had disappeared, and then we laughed at the marvel of seeing such small tornados dance away in front of our eyes.

I might add one feature of living across the street from the Monett town hall, library, and fire station, we had the outdoor warning siren stationed less than a block from our home. If that siren went off, we heard it. That was for sure. And if that siren did go off, we knew to be aware of the possibility of approaching tornado and to get to shelter. As I had told before, since we did not have a basement, Dad wanted me to go to the outside wall, but as I was often home alone when possible tornado alarms would go off, I wanted to stay inside and use our walk-in closet as a hiding place of shelter. It was a large walk-in closet with my clothes hanging on one side and my parent's clothes hanging on the other side. At the end of the closet were shelves of stored objects and Momma's canned products. I liked the comfort of the closet and the light I could turn on when I entered the closet. I felt I would be more comfortable and safe there rather than outside alone in the storm against the wall. Dad later relented and let me use the closet as a shelter in case we had an approaching storm.

I don't remember that I ever had to actually go into the closet to hide from an approaching tornado, but there were many, many warnings and many sightings in the dark, rumbling skies. Then, I would hear the all clear warning sound, two loud beeps, and I knew that the storm had relaxed and cooling rain was present. That always felt so good to have arrived. Another storm would have passed us by, and we were safe, once again. The old farmers would just nod sagely and agree it was because we had Kelly Creek.

Also, when Momma and I were visiting Aunt Rena's home, we had her old root cellar in the backyard where we could take shelter. Aunt Rena was deathly afraid of storms and especially tornados, so she had had this old root cellar cleaned up and reinforced to be used by the family in case of bad storm warnings.

Aunt Rena was prepared. She kept her newly canned vegetables and canned fruits on the shelves at the end of the cellar along with blankets and pillows. This was in case they had to spend the night in the cellar. She had kerosene lamps, flashlights, a radio, water, and food. There was room enough in the cellar for Aunt Rena and Uncle Paul, along with Betty and Janice. If Momma and I were there at the time of the storm, we were welcomed there also. Sometimes, if a storm had been predicted at night, Aunt Rena would drive by and tell Momma and me to come on out to stay the night in the cellar. There was plenty of room. That way we could sleep safely through the night.

Momma and I would decline. One afternoon, we had stayed in the cellar with the family during a storm. Neither of us liked being down in the cellar, no matter what the prediction, and not all being so enclosed. So we would say that we would come out if it really got bad. We were going to just stay home and see how the night goes. Rena would go home, shaking her head, saying that she was surprised we would want to stay in the house. Aunt Rena would then go home and round up the family to get everyone ready and in the cellar for the night or the all-clear alarm to be heard.

As for myself, I always had to be up pacing the floor and looking out the windows to see what was happening. Often, I would just sit up on the front steps to watch the skies to see what was approaching. When I felt things calm down, I would then go inside and go to bed.

Later, when I was older, Momma and I would often joke together when the skies would darken with possible rain or winds. We would look at each other and say, "Better to not go out to Aunt Rena's house today or she will make us stay the night in the root cellar." Honestly, it was only in fun, and we sometimes envied her that safe warm root cellar for protection from the storms. But even today, living in New England, I am taken back to those afternoon darkening skies and approaching storms and will go out on our front porch to watch the skies and the rain.

I must add also, on May 4, 2003, a tornado roared through the little town of Pierce City, Missouri, and laid it all to waste. Pierce City, being just a road piece down from Monett, one wondered about the old safety notion of Kelly Creek's protection. I myself could not help feeling disbelief at the wonderment of the tornado striking little Pierce City with such vengeance. After all my years of sky watching during the nights and afternoons while living in Monett, I had begun to agree with all those old farmers and believe that my hometown was immune from the swirling strength of tornadoes and storms. In 2011, the month of May brought devastation from a tornado to Joplin, Missouri, where my father loved to drive us to visit for the day. Many townspeople expressed regret that the old Indian legend had not held up to truth and saved the land and homes from the tornado.

It was the summer of 1952. I was to be ten years old that year in December, and the summer days were busy and fulfilling. Dad had added more business variety to his clock shop and watch repair through his repairing of lawn mower machines. People would stop by and drop off their lawn mowers for Dad to look at. He would sharpen the blade under the machine and neighbors would then drive by and pick up their lawn mowers again. Sometimes, the people would wait while Dad sharpened the blades. This kept Dad in front busy repairing the arriving lawn mowers. He also took in bicycles to repair and repaint. Most of the time, the bicycles just needed new chains or wheels. In fact, that was when and how I got my lovely red bicycle. In one of Dad's trades, he was able to collect a girl's bicycle that needed some new wheels and brakes. After he had repaired the bike, he painted it a bright red and surprised me with my very first bike.

I loved that bike. I had red vinyl tassels attached to the end of my handlebars so that they flew out behind me as I rode the bicycle as fast as the wind. Or at least in my mind, it seemed to be as fast at the wind. One time, Hubert and I put a playing card on the wheel spokes and secured it with a clothespin so that, as we sped down the street or sidewalk in Monett, we made the sound of cardboard flapping in the wind—or some such sound. Sort of like a motorboat chugging along the river or maybe the sound of one walking down the block holding a stick and sliding it along against a fence. "Pickity, pickity, pickity." Maybe that is a better description of the sound the playing card made flapping on the spinning spokes of the wheel. It was a thrilling sound, and Hubert and I would laugh when we got our bikes going fast and the card hit the spokes. "Pickity, pickity, pick."

I had a radius of two blocks I could ride the bike in during the day. I was not to ever go beyond that radius. And I obeyed that ruling until I tried riding my bike down Catholic Hill. First, I should clarify, it was not actually Catholic Hill. I had dubbed the large hill that name because it was in front of the Catholic Church.

I loved to ride my bicycle up the hill and turn it around, at the top, square my bike up so that it faced down the hill to the bottom, lift my feet off the pedals, and zoom down the hill; hair flying, arms spread akimbo, and feet splayed out and away from the pedals/brakes. The ride was incredible. It was honestly like flying. One felt like any minute the bicycle would become a small one passenger airplane and just zoom off into the blue sky and fly around Monett for about two minutes. It was incredible to experience. Naturally, each day, I spent most of the morning pedaling up to the top of the hill, panting and sweating as it was a long hill. Turning my bike around so that I faced down the hill, I squared myself on the bike, and at the count of three, off I would zoom, back down that hill, arms and feet extended and riding the wind. And then it happened. Just as I reached near the bottom of the hill, which was a four-way stop, I saw a car moving from the left side of the street, and it was coming through the intersection. I knew better than to go through the intersection, but I was going too fast to stop the bike. I had already put my feet back on the brakes, and I was exerting all my strength to get the bike to stop, but I was going too fast. So I leaned myself to the right and forced myself to fall off the bike to get myself stopped and/or hit the oncoming car. I was lucky. I was only bruised and scared—no broken bones. At least not from the fall.

In that one brief second, I realized my error—my Dad was driving the car that almost hit me as I zoomed down the hill and into the intersection. As I looked up into Dad's face while he helped me up from the fall, I heard him screaming at me, "Are you okay? Susie?" I could only nod my yes and try to get my bearings so I could stand back up. He then looked around to make sure no other cars were coming, and then he shook me ever so slightly and told me firmly to get back to the house "immediately." And with that, he let my arms go and turned back to the car. Walking over to the car, he turned once again to look at me, shook his head, and got into the car where he drove slowly down the street to our home, about two blocks down. I gathered myself, checked my knees and hands for scrapes, and hopped back on my bike to hightail it home, immediately.

Dad was waiting by the front of the shop when I arrived. As I pulled up in front of the house, Dad motioned me to get off the bike, and then he took my bike by the handlebars and walked it over to the steps and, lifting it, carried it up the two steps and into the front shop. There he placed a chain and lock on it. When I had entered the shop, Dad turned to me and informed me that I could not ride my bike for a month as punishment for riding the bike down that huge hill. He also told me how close he had come to spanking me right there, but he had saved his temper and would just offer me this punishment. With that, he tugged on the chain and lock to make sure it was solid and set the bike over in the corner of the shop. He told me that I could come back for the bike in one month to ride it again and that I was never to go up that hill again *or* I would lose my bike forever.

I agreed most hastily. I would never have wanted to lose my bike. I loved to ride it so much, so I quickly agreed to never go up Catholic Hill again and to be more cautious when out riding my bike. He reminded me that rules were important to obey, especially when it could mean losing my life or becoming seriously hurt.

So for a month I watched my bike longingly, and I never rode up Catholic Hill again. Dad was right. I had been foolish with my own life and perhaps endangering some other person's life if I should hit them with my bike as I zoomed down that hill. And I could also have caused an automobile wreck. I really realized how stupid I had been that day riding my bike so carelessly and never strayed from the rules of the road again. It had been a good lesson for me to learn and may have saved my life from a future wreck or injury.

School was out now, and we were going full-fledged into those noted hot summer days.

Chapter 21

Polio

I was an active child. I loved to run and play, to ride my bicycle, and to walk. As soon as I was up each morning early and finished with breakfast and my chores, I would be outside and playing, weather permitting. If it rained, I would often sit outside on our front porch and watch the rain with my dolls and toys. I was never bored and had a very active imagination. I was alone almost all those days, but I didn't really seem to miss other children. I kept myself busy with my own interests. I loved to read and listen to the radio. I was fascinated to just sit and watch people walk by or stop and talk. I was inquisitive and eager to learn about new things at all times.

It was the summer of 1952, and I was ten years old. We had begun to hear about a new threat—polio. Dad read in the paper that the polio epidemic was rising faster than the population, and this was the height of the baby boom. This news of the polio epidemic seemed even more notable because serious outbreaks had occurred in all the forty-eight states and in the territories of Alaska, Hawaii, and Puerto Rico. This epidemic was really becoming frightening to each household because no one knew how to protect oneself. The doctors were not quite sure how it was infecting the adults and children. No one could tell us what to do to protect ourselves. We didn't know how it traveled to cause infection. Did it blow in the wind, transfer as germs on the hands or when one sneezed? Was it in the food or on our clothes? What made one family become ill with polio while no one else did on the block? Or why did

205

one child in the family become ill when no one else did in the family? How were the patients picked to become ill? It was a quandary and no one found a solution.

As I heard more about this new growing epidemic and increasingly troubled news as it hit our small town in Midwestern Missouri, I became afraid. What should I do to not become ill? It was scary—one got a headache, a stiff neck, and then *wham!* The sick person was placed in an iron lung not capable of breathing on their own. And pictures of an iron lung were terrifying. I saw several in magazines at the doctor's office. Sometimes, during an afternoon I would walk across the street and down one-half of a block to Dr. Kerr's office and go in to the waiting room to sit and read their magazines. The nurses and receptionist all knew me and told me it was okay to sit there *if* the room was not crowded with patients. Then I could not stay. But if the waiting room was not busy, I could sit there and read the many magazines. And that was where I saw pictures of the iron lung and people were inside them, fighting for air as the machine forced their lungs to continue moving up and down, pulling in air and pushing it out. Also, the magazines described it as an airtight metal tank that enclosed the entire body except the head and forced the lungs to inhale and exhale through regulated changes in air pressure. However described, the iron lung looked terrifying to me, and I sure was hoping I would never have to be placed into it. I carried one of the magazines up to a nurse and asked her if their office had an iron lung. The nurse told me that the closest hospital to have an iron lung was in Springfield. She also explained that luckily we had not had to have one yet in Monett and winked at me as she told me to go back and sit down out of the way.

I was still worried about this iron lung and the polio that one could catch. A wink from a nurse was not going to calm my fears.

In fact, each night, as I prepared to fall asleep, I would first say a nightly prayer asking that God would please not give me polio while I slept and to please keep me safe from it. Then I would begin my nightly inspection as I lay very motionless and felt my body lying on the bed, arms lying flat and legs and feet lying straight out flat on the bed before me. Then I could take in account of each part of my body. Did I have a headache? No. Did I have a sore throat? No. Did my arms hurt and could I move them? At this time, I would raise each arm, one at a time, and move it up and down to make sure that they were able to be moved.

HOME AGAIN, HOME AGAIN, JIGGITY, JIG   207

Then I would do the same with my legs as I determined that neither leg was stiff or paralyzed. Then I would take large breaths of air into my lungs to make sure they were indeed working well.

Each night, I went through the same procedure even when I was so tired I could barely keep my eyes open from my day's excursions. I did not want to be caught unprepared. If I were to contact polio, I wanted to make sure right away so I would have a better chance to fight the illness. Each morning as I awoke, this was the first thing I would do also. First, before I could get up, I had to ascertain how my body was and to make sure that I had not suffered any paralytic illness during the night. Then, as all was found in fine condition, I would breathe a small prayer of thanks to God, hop out of bed, and be about with my daily plans.

As more news came to our little town about the polio epidemic, Springfield and Joplin, being larger cities, became more filled with polio victims, Dad began to study how this polio was transmitted. After a week of reading and such, Dad determined that flies must be the transmitters of polio. He added that as flies could be an easy transmitter for a disease with their flitting around trash and into the house to land on one's food or tableware. He made a good check that all windows had good strong screens on each window and checked the screen doors in front and back. He warned Momma and me that we were always to keep the screens closed and to go in quickly and sharply into the house, not allowing any flies into the house. He also placed flyswatters in available places so that one could easily swat any fly should they be seen buzzing around in our house.

At this time, each family unit was responsible for their own trash disposal. We had a huge cylinder barrel outside at the end of our yard by the old concrete wall where all our trash was burned. Every day or so, Momma or Dad would go out and set the trash on fire in the barrel and stand watch over the burning until the last of the flames were finished. All trash was burned in the barrel at that time. I was not allowed to man the trash burning as Dad felt it should be the responsibility of an adult.

At this time, Dad also decided that I was not to play out in the backyard near the trash barrel those hot summer days because there were flies in and near the barrel, and I would be accessible to any flies to land on me.

So Dad made up a new ruling for me to obey each day. I could get up early, and after my chores and breakfast, I could go out and play, only more simple games, not with so much running and sweating. Then, when I came in to eat lunch, I was to stay inside and go take a cooling bath and change into clean clothes and go to take a nap or rest during the hot afternoon. I could lie on my bed and read comic books or library books. Dad had placed a small fan by my bed to keep me cool as I read and rested. It was a rule. Sometimes it angered me because I liked to keep active outside and not be lying around inside. And to have to take a bath and change clothes really was not of my interest. But Dad was very firm, and soon I became used to the schedule and began to look forward to reading and resting in the hot afternoon on my bed with the small cooling fan. I also felt more safe from the threatening polio illness somewhere out in the hot summer days ready to pounce on me and put me in an iron lung.

So continued the summer days.

You may remember my talking earlier about Johnny Heims, a young man who worked next door at the Heim's Hatchery that his father and uncle owned. He would often spend the day in the store helping with book accounting and recordkeeping for his father. I had gotten to know him through my visits to his store to pet the farm animals they often brought in. That summer, Johnny was often in the store as he had just graduated from high school and was planning on leaving for college that fall. He was finished with high school and looking forward to college soon and ready to face the world. Life was looking good for him. I loved to visit with him and listen to him tell me of his plans for college study and how excited it was to get out into the world. I liked my visits with Johnny, and even though I was eight years younger than he was, I always felt that he regarded me as an older person and respected my thoughts and interests.

That particular night was the last baseball game of the summer, and it was with our old rival Aurora. Spirits were high and everyone was pulling for Monett to win the game. Momma and I went to the game up at the baseball field and watch as Monett did surely win that night. To our own thrill, Johnny Heims proved to be the hero of the night. He had hit the winning home run that had given them their needed score to beat Aurora. He was the champion as he was carried around the field on the shoulders of his comrades in baseball. He left to go celebrate with friends and was eagerly cheered on by parents and neighbors leaving the field that night. Momma and I walked back home after the game and talked about how nice a young man he was and that we were so happy that he had such a great future planned out for him.

That next morning, I was awakened earlier than usual by Momma, who was standing there crying lightly. She told me to wake up that she had sad news to tell me. After I had set up in bed, Momma told me that Johnny had been rushed to Springfield during the night and placed into an iron lung. They were not sure if he would live. He had polio.

That dreaded word. Johnny had polio. I shook my head in wonder. How could Johnny have polio? He had been the baseball hero last night. He had been the champion. He had won the game as he ran around the baseball bases while the crowd stood and cheered. He had been with his friends and fellow comrades and celebrating with his girlfriend. How did he get polio? What had happened?

No one knew. And polio had struck our small Midwestern town of Monett. Polio was among us. We knew someone fighting for life in an iron lung. It was too close to home. People became afraid. Parents were afraid for their children.

We all hoped Johnny would become well, but now we had to worry that polio might seek out one of us to attack. People thought, *Better not to go to the movies and be exposed to someone that might be coming down with polio. Or go to a restaurant for that matter. Probably not safe in the grocery store.* And each person thought about that night at the baseball game—had anyone else come down sick with polio and been placed in an iron lung.

For a few short days, the town was silent and still. People did not go out and shop or seek entertainment. It was better to stay inside and be safe. Slowly as no one else became ill with polio or have had to be rushed to Springfield for placement in the iron lung, people became less afraid to go back outside and participate in the outer world. People began to shop again, go to movies or the outdoor theater, and to restaurants. People, took a deep breath of "thank goodness" and went back to their life. But Johnny was still in the iron lung fighting each day for his life with his family gathered near and praying for his return to health.

Weeks passed, and word came back that Johnny may spend years in the iron lung until he had recovered full lung capacity again and able to breathe on his own. In a few hours, Johnny had gone from a strong athletic champion to a weakened and very sick young man. They were not sure if Johnny was going to live. There were many months of waiting as Johnny slowly fought his battle to regain his own life again.

There would be no plans. Five years later, Johnny was finally able to come back home and live a normal life again. Of course, it was not a normal life in all aspects. He was left forever in a wheelchair as he had lost the strength in his arms and legs to be able to have support. He was paralyzed from the waist down, and one arm no longer functioned. He still had his inner beauty and sweet smile, but his life beyond Monett would no longer be a plan. It was not to happen.

To this day, I still ponder that evening of that infamous baseball game. Out of all the people gathered that starlit night at the baseball field, from Aurora and Monett and surrounding communities, all sitting outside and in their cars, walking and running, sitting and talking and eating, what made Johnny the victim of polio. Why just Johnny? Why not three more people or ten more people. But always to my amazement, there was just Johnny. Fate, it can be hard to hide from. But even with fate as the winner, what made polio to choose one person . . . just that one person and no one else?

Chapter 22

Houdini Who?

About this time, Dad met a person in Monett who loved to tinker with objects and fix them as much as Dad liked to. Only this person liked to fix electrical objects while Dad loved to tinker with clocks and watches. They made a perfect pair in the aspect of tinkering but not in looking at. Dad was short in stature, tending toward being plump and dark in hair, eyes, and skin tone (because of Native American ancestry) while Dad's new friend, Woody, was the complete opposite. Woody was tall and thin as a reed, light in skin and eye color, and the top of his head was bald with large masses of bright auburn hair shooting out in curls and curls around his ears and back of his neck. They made a strange-looking couple walking or sitting together—rather a Mutt and Jeff look from the old comics. But they were avid friends. They could sit and tinker, each on their favorite object, while expanding and expounding on all that the world could provide in knowledge and facts. Both loved philosophy, the classics, and religion. They could talk until blue in the face with each other's theory or idea, neither changing the other's opinion but having a great force of time in just the discussion. And to add to the differences, Dad was a firm Democrat while Woody was a never-to-be-changed Republican. For two men that seldom came eye to eye on one conversation, they still had a great time trying to meet that one idea of sameness.

Actually, as they got to know each better and loosened their own thoughts for each other, they did find one thing where they both shared the same interest and theory—dreams. Not dreams that foretold the future, or how to get rich, or who was going to become president. They were interested in communication, or let's say, communication through dreams.

They spoke of communication through the air, from a dream or a reading. They questioned the possibility of words spoken and heard by another without someone speaking. They spoke of communication through unspoken words, through the mind—across the world, through the night—without speaking. Much like the radio and television wires that Woody worked on each day. They looked at the electrical wires that transmitted words for others to hear. They asked, could the brain do such a thing? They read about other such thinkers. They spoke often of Harry Houdini.

To the occultist, occultism is conceived of as the study of the inner nature of things, as opposed to the outer characteristics that are studied by science; i.e., the relationship between one thing and another to explain the "inner nature" of the thing itself. By defining a thing solely in terms of its external relationships or effects do we only find its external or explicit nature. Occultism, on the other hand, is concerned with the nature of the thing-in-itself. It all fascinated Dad and Woody.

Then, they began to read about Harry Houdini, who had died on October 31, 1926. He was known for his own "magic," tricks, cards, and various effects he had created to astound the attending public. They both were fascinated with the reported news from an interview with Houdini after he had been saved from a near-death act in frozen waters of New York; his mother had appeared to show him the way to be saved from the frozen death. And yet, after Houdini had been saved, he found that his mother had indeed been dead at the moment that she had appeared in his sight to lead him to safety. Communication in dreams. It fascinated my father and Houdini. Was this true? Dad explained how his mother had appeared in a dream to him once when she was ill. Woody nodded sagely and agreed that perhaps Dad had had the same dream as Houdini had experienced. What caused this ability to communicate with others through dreams?

Then, adding to this discussion, Dad added that when Houdini had died, he had made a pact with his wife, Bess. They would communicate through death by a noted word or such to send a message from beyond. They were fascinated with the idea of Bess continuing to hold séances for years following Houdini's death until she gave up on the communication from death. And with that they made their own pact. Dad and Woody had concocted their own communication with each other should one of them die. Only they would know what the communication would be so that no one could pretend or make mockery of the communication. So together, much like two small boys, they swore to secrecy what the agreed form would be to communicate when one had passed on to their "great reward." And then they went on together as friends, talking and laughing together about other thoughts and problems. Sitting together tinkering with whatever they would have to solve. There was Dad in Woody's little fix-it shop behind his home in his garage where he sat among discarded radios and televisions that he had gathered to repair. Or one would see Woody visiting Dad in his own shop, in front of our house, while Dad tinkered with his clocks. They had a warm and funny relationship.

Later, the late evening was shattered by the telephone ringing. Momma answered the phone and called to Dad to come quickly. The phone call was for him. When Dad rushed down the hallway to the kitchen, he grabbed the phone quickly from Momma and said, "Hello." Momma stood by and looked worried.

Dad listened on the phone for a few minutes and then hung up. He turned to Momma and said very simply, "Woody is dead." And then he walked up to the shop and sat down to tinker on his clocks and smoke on his cigarettes in the half-light of the shop up front.

Momma sat down and stared quietly out the window. I went back to bed to read. I figured I would find out more the next day.

It seemed that although Woody was a young man, he did have heart problems. That evening, Woody had eaten supper with his wife and children, gotten up from the table, and said he was going back out to the shop to work for a while and left the house. He walked out to the shop, turned on the light, and walked into the shop and just dropped dead. Instantly dead. His heart had just stopped. The wife came out and found him in the shop when he had not come in to go to bed later. She then called Dad to tell him.

Dad went up to see Woody's wife the next day, and Momma took some baked food for the family. Together they made arrangements for Woody's burial to take place in a few days.

After the burial, Dad would sit late up in his shop and smoke his cigarettes and tinker with some clock he had to fix. He didn't really talk about Woody, but you could tell he was missing him. Several months later I heard Dad crying up in the shop that night while sitting alone and staring out through the shop windows. He smoked his cigarettes and had a record playing on his old player. But you could hear him crying softly and talking to himself. Days later, I was sitting on the front porch, and I heard Dad talking to an old customer who had stopped by to sit and talk to Dad for a spell. The man had expressed his sympathies to Dad about the death of Woody and what a shame to die so young. Dad nodded in agreement and smoked his cigarettes. And then, the man sat up quickly and said, "Wait a minute, didn't you and Woody have an agreement that whoever died the first, you would contact each other?"

Dad agreed that Woody and he had come to that agreement. Then the man said, "Well? What has happened? Have you heard from Woody or has he come in a dream to you?"

Dad said, "No, I have not heard from Woody and I don't think I am going to be hearing from him." Then he told the visitor, "I think God just has too many radios and televisions to fix for Woody and I don't think Woody will have the time to communicate with me." The visitor just nodded and sat there quietly until he left. I don't remember ever hearing about Woody or his name again. I think Dad was right. Woody was just too busy up in heaven.

Friday, early morning, Momma answered the telephone and received a surprise invitation. Mrs. Evans, mother to Priscilla and Jimmy, had called to invite Momma and me up to their home on Fifth Street to enjoy a going-away party for Jimmy, who was leaving for the navy. Momma told Mrs. Evans we would be there and thanked her for the invitation. Momma planned to take her favorite devil's food cake with luscious homemade chocolate icing. It was the best ever, and Jimmy always said it was his favorite so Momma thought he would enjoy the cake for his party. I asked Momma where Jimmy was going, and she told me he had joined the navy. I was surprised because I knew at this time we were involved in the Korean War. After all, my half brother, Glenn, was stationed over there and was fighting in the Korean War in the army. I could not imagine that anyone would want to go there to fight, especially someone so young as Jimmy was. I had seen the news movie reels at the theater and saw the battles and killings. It looked awful.

I asked Momma again why Jimmy was going there and how Mrs. Evans felt about this. Momma explained that now Jimmy was eighteen years old and had graduated from high school, so there was not much Mrs. Evans could do. Jimmy could make up his own mind and do what he wanted to do. I could tell that Momma was worried about Jimmy leaving so young, and I knew that Mrs. Evans must be even more upset. I was sure it would be a hard party Sunday to keep a happy attitude as nobody seemed to want Jimmy to leave, except Jimmy.

Sunday afternoon arrived, and Momma and I walked up to the Evans home on Fifth Street with the prized homemade devil's food cake, just iced. It smelled so good. When we arrived at the house, Priscilla opened the kitchen door for us to go in and joined the other guests sitting in the living room and the parlor. There were other neighbors and friends sitting around on chairs and the couch talking to each other. Priscilla showed us all the food that was sitting out on the table and invited us to enjoy. She also asked us what we wanted to drink. Momma and I each asked for cold water, and we went inside to join the others. Of course, Jimmy was enjoying being the center of the party with all attention on him. Questions of where he was going, what would he be doing in the navy, and other such were all keeping him busy talking to each person. He looked so handsome and proud in his navy uniform. Momma and I felt pride in knowing such a fine young man but felt sorry for his mother, Mrs. Evans, who was going to be worrying so much about her son.

Jimmy was good-looking in a small-town, homespun sort of way. Of course, I had known Jimmy since I was five years old or such. We had played hopscotch together and sat all day reading comic books on rainy days. I had known him most of his life, and now he was so grown-up and all funny-acting. His ears still stuck out on each side of his head, but I figured his navy hat would squelch those "Dumbo" ears back. Sorry, that was my nickname for Jimmy's ears. They weren't really so big, but he was thin and that seemed to make his ears more obtrusive. Jimmy was thrilled when he learned that Momma had brought the devil's food cake and promised to eat a big slice after he had finished the fried chicken and potato salad waiting on the kitchen table for all to eat and enjoy.

School Days - Fifth Grade

This is my fifth grade class. Truthfully I don't remember much about it. If you are looking for me - I am sitting in middle row, near the Christmas tree and have a scarf on my head. I must have been going somewhere that night to have my hair in curls. It could have been near my birthday because the room is all decorated for the holiday. It is nice to look back and see all of us, so young and energetic.

School Days - Sixth Grade

Mrs. Voght ran a tight ship in the classroom - or at least I always thought so. Again, Christmas time with all the decorations. Looking at the murals in the background - I have to laugh.

They are all drawn mainly by me. For some reason the class members didn't want to draw on the murals, so I ended up drawing most of it. I loved to draw and color the murals. Looking for me - I am in the last row in the striped dress with belt. Surprise, my hair is not up in pin curls and a scarf! Happy sixth grade - we are all growing up!

The afternoon passed quickly with everyone laughing and talking together. The food was soon mostly eaten, and Priscilla began to clean up in the kitchen, washing dishes, and I helped by drying. We talked together about how much she was going to miss Jimmy when he left for the navy Monday. She was worried about him being among the fighting and killing in Korea. I agreed. We promised we would each say special prayers for Jimmy each night and be especially attentive to good thoughts about him. I also promised to write Jimmy letters often and hoped to hear back from him.

Momma and I stayed later to help Mrs. Evans clean up after the guests and family members had left. Then Momma and I walked back home. We talked about the afternoon as we walked home, and both were feeling sad for Mrs. Evans. We also both expressed concern about Jimmy.

Jimmy left home that Monday and headed out to report to duty. The Evans family saw Jimmy off at the bus stop on Main Street. It was a quiet house that whole week with Jimmy gone now. Priscilla and I kept busy with a dress she was sewing, and we were always reading books. Of course, we were still listening to our local radio station and talking about our favorite movie stars. We often talked about the movie *The Quiet Man* with John Wayne. We could just swoon every time that we thought of John Wayne and when he kissed Maureen O'Hara. That was just so super to see. Our other favorite movie that we had enjoyed was Gary Cooper in *High Noon*. Even though it was a Western, we had so enjoyed the music and excitement of the movie. Of course, I had the record with Tex Ritter singing "High Noon," and we would often play it and sing along to the song. We missed Jimmy, but life seemed to go on with its regular days and nights.

Chapter 23

A Two-Legged Table

That month, Dad said to Momma that he wasn't making enough monies through the clock shop and her working at the cleaners each day so he was thinking about getting the bus route to Oklahoma City, Oklahoma, going again. He had driven it each day back when he was younger before he had gotten sick, and he had heard the contract was available again. Momma said she did not want Dad to drive at this point unless Dr. Kerr agreed it would be fine. Dad said that he had that all solved. He had hired a young man named Max who would drive the bus each day down to Oklahoma and back. He even said that he had already signed the contract and obtained a bus for Max to drive and that he was going to park it across the street for Momma and me to clean it up ready for customers. And sure enough, Dad did go get the bus and park it across the street. Momma set me to ironing the covers that went across the top of the bus seats while she went out and scrubbed out the floor and seats of the bus. It was in good shape so that when we added the seat covers, it was all ready for travel again and waiting for Max to arrive to take it on its journey. Max arrived two days later. He was a young man about twenty-four or so and had been driving a bus since he had turned eighteen. He had a good driving record and seemed pleasant enough. Dad had told him he could stay in one of our bedroom apartments upstairs, and Momma would make him a breakfast each morning except on weekends when there would be no trips to Oklahoma. He also received weekly pay from Dad. Max

219

seemed in agreement with it all and took his small belongings upstairs to get settled in with his apartment. He had the one bedroom and the bathroom was down the hall for all to share. Once a week, Momma went upstairs and changed his bedsheets and gave him clean towels, and then she cleaned the bathroom. We had placed a few pieces of used furniture in the room with the old comfortable bed. It made for a nice apartment for Max. I would often help Momma with the work of keeping up the apartment.

So Monday through Friday, Max would appear at our kitchen door for breakfast at six o'clock. He was a nice young man—tall, slim, sandy blond hair—and always courteous with an easy grin. My biggest complaint about Max, he liked to tell corny jokes. He thought the jokes were funny. I thought they were painful. The pain came when I had to listen to them. Max arrived and ate a hearty breakfast at our table with us, and then he would go over to get the bus parked across the street. Off Max would go to drive down to the Greyhound Bus Station on Main Street to pick up his passengers who would be traveling to Oklahoma City, Oklahoma. When he returned in the afternoon, usually around five, he would then go upstairs and relax or clean up. Most of the time, he then walked downtown to the local diner or Greyhound's diner and ate his dinner. He never really made an appearance other than for breakfast and just seemed to keep to himself. That was fine with me as I really was tired of his corny jokes.

At this time, we also had a larger one-bedroom apartment rented to an older woman. She had moved in about the time Max had come to live in our apartments. Her apartment had one bedroom, a large living room, and a small kitchen. She used the bathroom down the hall. One day, when I was upstairs with Momma to help her clean the bathroom, I met this older woman and asked Momma if I could go visit her for a little while. She seemed so lonesome.

The woman, Cora May, was most kind and happy to see me when I walked into her apartment. Her door was open, and she saw me when I appeared in the doorway. She motioned for me to come in and sit down. At that time, I realized what Momma had meant when she told me that Cora May was "deaf and dumb"—she could not hear or speak. That was why her apartment was so quiet when I had been with Momma cleaning. I signaled to Cora May that I loved to play cards and board games. I had brought my favorite Chinese checkers with me, and

I motioned that she might want to play the game with me. Cora May's face lit up with pure delight, and a large grin appeared on her face. She quickly placed a large table in the center of the room with two chairs on either side. Thus began our several years of friendship where I would go up and visit Cora May to play various board games or cards. She was a good player and won most of the games. When she did win, she would throw her head back and laugh her silent laugh loudly. Well, to me, it seemed like it would be loudly if she had had the ability to make sounds. But at this time, it served well. I knew that Cora May loved to play our games and enjoyed my company. Although no words were ever spoken, we spent many hours through the next couple of years enjoying our times together playing the games. During those visits, I learned about the joy of communication, no matter how it was done, by speaking or signing or just smiling and talking through happy eyes. I enjoyed my visits with Cora and our hours playing the games or cards. She was patient with me as a young child, and I enjoyed her company as an older woman who shared her love of life through her silent laugh.

When Cora May died in the hospital of heart failure, her family members arrived to decide what to do with what small belongings and furniture that she had left in the apartment. To my surprise, an argument had arisen over who should get the table that Cora and I had used all those times to play cards or games on. And now, they were fighting over who should get the table. It was a lovely old, round table of oak with four claw legs that rested on large glass balls. I am sure it was a valuable antique because of the claws on the glass balls. To Cora and me, it had simply been a table for us to enjoy our games on. But now there were two people in the middle of the living room arguing over the table. Unable to decide who should get the table, one of the persons took a saw and cut the table in half.

Of course, as you can imagine, the table no longer served its function because it could not stand up with only two legs on each part of the table to support it. It fell to the floor of the apartment and lay there with no further interest from anyone. At that time, Dad came up to see how things were going, and I told him about the table lying on the floor that they had cut up because no one could decide whom it belonged to. Dad looked at the two sides of the table and shook his head. I also told Dad that it had been sad to see them cut up this table because it was the table Cora May and I had played the cards and games on.

Two Legged Table

This little table has quite the story. As I told in my writing - the table was cut in two during an argument in Cora Mae's apartment. When it was cut in half, it collapsed because it could not stand on two legs.

My father took it downstairs and nailed it to the wall and that was where it stood all those years until after my parent's death.

When it was sold - I didn't know at the time it was being sold or I would have gotten it - but it was lost to me and I thought I would never be seeing it again.

Then last year, to my amazement, Janice called to tell me she had found it stored in a barn or such, after all these years and that she had bought it. We knew for sure it was the table because Dad's address label was on the bottom.

So, now it has been returned to the family and it sits happily in Janice's home, beneath some of her clocks. At this time in the picture, the little table was shown proudly bearing Christmas decorations. Good to see that little table again!

Two Legged Table with Momma and Dad

To further note the table, this picture was taken after high school graduation and there on the right of the picture you can see a part of the table nailed against the wall, with my high school graduation picture on it along with the green lamp, one of Momma's doily and Dad's ashtray. Right beside the table would be Dad's beige naughyde chair and hassock. Momma and Dad are shown standing in the doorway between the kitchen and the living room. Dad has on his sunglasses which he took to wearing the last part of his life, inside and outside.

Dad then asked one of the persons who had been fighting over the table if he could have one of the table parts. The person agreed to give it to him remarking, "It isn't of any use now!" Dad picked up the table half and carried it downstairs to our home.

Inside, Dad got his hammer and some nails, and he carried the table half into the living room. Placing the half table steadily against the wall by his chair, where he always sat to watch television or read the newspaper, Dad placed the table and nailed it to the wall. It stood perfectly straight and solid there. Momma then came in and placed a newly ironed lace doily that she had on the table, and Dad put an old large ceramic lamp on the table. The lamp was large and green with a crème beige lampshade on it. He then placed his favorite enormous ashtray on the side of the lamp on the top of the table. He then sat down in his favorite chair to survey his work. The table once again stood upright, strong and steady ready to facilitate Dad's lamp, ashtray, and, later, a high school graduation picture of me. That same table stood by Dad's chair with the huge ashtray brimming over with cigarettes, some lit and some as large lumps of ash. Shining on the table was the same lamp lit to brighten Dad as he read the newspapers or sometimes in the evening when Dad was watching television. He had an old beige leather foot hassock to rest his legs on when he was sitting in the chair. And there, night after night, for the rest of Dad's life, he sat in his chair, feet on the hassock, lamp turned on, next to that little two-legged table. The large ashtray would also be sitting on the table supporting the many cigarettes that Dad would smoke during the day and night. In the small shelf area between the two legs of the table, Momma placed a chalk dog figurine on a smaller doily. I loved that table just as much years and years later when I would go home to visit and there stood that small, two-legged table, proudly serving Dad as he watched his favorite television show.

I had mentioned before how much I loved to attend the local theater. That summer brought a new problem that changed how I attended the Gillioz Theater. It seemed that ringworm, not worms itself but a fungal skin infection, was on the rise for some reason, and all public locations were under strict new health rules. That is, all public locations where a patron might place their head, as on the headrest of a theater seat. So as a medical alert and under health standards, it was required that all patrons attending the theater could only be admitted if they wore something on their head to protect them from leaning their heads back on the seat. Women and girls had to wear headscarves and had to have them on when they walked into the theater. Men and boys had to wear hats on their heads.

So it became a common custom for me to wear a scarf on my head when I entered the theater. When I got home, my mother would always have me wash out the scarf to dry on the clothesline. She felt it was better that it be clean each time I wore it. I agreed. I was afraid of getting ringworms on my head and having to shave all my curly auburn hair off. In fact, the theater was so strict ushers walked up and down the aisle of the theater during a show making sure that the people had kept on their scarves or hats. If the usher saw that a person did not have their scarf or hat on, the usher would shine their flashlight on the hapless person and demand they place the hat or scarf back on. This ringworm scare lasted well into the early winter. Then one day, it was just announced that scarves and hats were no longer a requirement. I was glad. I like to wear scarves on windy days but felt uncomfortable wearing them while watching a movie.

And you know, to this day, I still get uncomfortable whenever I arrive at the theater and go in to sit down. Often, when I place my head back and settle comfortably into the theater chair, I still hold my head just a few notches above the headrest, at least for a few minutes.

The warm summer days passed quickly. I still worried about polio each day and did my daily checks that all my limbs were still moveable and made sure that I had no headache. I was busy in the summer days helping Momma with the laundry, washing and hanging out the clothes. I rode my bicycle and traveled about the areas of Monett near my home. I loved to visit people who lived nearby and stop for a small chat each day. Our neighbors were often kind and shared a few minutes of time with me. I remember we had a family move into a rental house down the alley from us. There was a mother and father and a young daughter, about my age. Her name was Rosa, and she was so pretty with dark hair and brown eyes. They talked a lot and noisily, and sometimes I could not understand what they were talking about. The language was foreign to me, but I loved the food I would smell cooking on the stove. Different smells from what I would smell on my mother's stove. I asked Rosa what they were eating that smelled so good, and she told me pasta and gravy. I had to think about that one. Our pasta was always macaroni, and I couldn't imagine eating gravy made from milk and flour with the macaroni. I shrugged and figured people like all sort of things. Maybe it was good. Rosa's mother was not always very happy sounding and seemed to be always talking loudly at her. But mainly, when I looked at Rosa's mother, I was so surprised at how big her bosom was. The woman seemed to have an enormous bosom. They looked very uncomfortable, and I had never seen a woman in Monett who had such an ample bosom. One day, I got up enough nerve to ask my mother a question about Rosa's mother. I asked Momma why Rosa's mother had such a big bosom. We were doing the laundry at the time, and Momma was busy wringing out the clothes. When I asked her the question about Rosa's mother, she stopped for a moment, looked at me and said, "Because she is Italian."

I accepted the answer not really understanding but figured Momma would tell me the truth about whatever I needed to know. Rosa and her family moved shortly after that, and I never got to find out if it was true that Rosa's mother had a large bosom because she was Italian. Later I figured Momma had told me this just to shut me up. She never liked to talk about such personal things as a part of a woman's body.

Chapter 24

Visiting Neighbors

Of course, my favorite neighbor to visit was Hazel, who lived across the alley from our house. We were facing her backyard, which had a large fence around it. Hazel would let me come inside the fence and sit in her yard during the day and visit with her dog, a large black mixed-breed female. We would often sit out under her shady trees and enjoy the many flowers that bloomed in her large yard. Hazel had a large two-story home with a big front porch and a lovely green yard in the back. Summer mornings were special to me when I went over to sit in Hazel's backyard and read one of my many books. It was cool and shaded there. Often Hazel would come out and sit with me while sharing an iced glass of sweetened tea and sometimes a cookie or two. Hazel liked to talk to me about the books I was reading and shared stories with me about when she had grown up. Sometimes, Hazel's sister with her husband would be visiting, and they would sit with us also. I enjoyed those simple days relaxing in the backyard.

Hazel was probably in her late fifties at this time. She was a large woman with long copper-colored hair that she always wore up on her head in a bun. She had a large face with a sharp nose and large teeth with the most wonderful smile that she seemed to share with everyone, me included. She loved a good hearty laugh. To earn a living, Hazel had a small seamstress shop down off Main Street where she had a woman sitting and repairing left objects for repair. Hazel also did taxes, and her shop would be very busy from fall until April where she would be doing everyone's taxes. That was why she would often have time to sit with me in the backyard and visit. During the summer, she spent a lot of time home with just the tailoring and repairs being handled in her shop.

Sometimes when I visited, Hazel and her sister would be busy in the kitchen cooking and baking. The kitchen smelled so lovely. Music would be playing on the radio, and Hazel would let me stay and often eat dinner with her and her guests. I loved all the talk and laughter complete with silliness and jokes. It made me feel comfortable and happy. As I was an only child and Dad was working up front in the shop and Momma worked or baked or cleaned, I was often alone. Sitting in Hazel's home filled with noises, music, laughter, cooking, and life, I was enthralled. It was the same as when I went to visit Priscilla and would sit in her home with her sister and brothers. It just felt so good to share in all the noises of life.

After dinner, Hazel would often go into the parlor and sit down to the piano and begin to play old time favorites like "Moonlight Bay," "I've Been Working on the Railroad" (always a favorite), or "Bicycle Built for Two." It was always understood that at this time I could stay for a few songs, and then Hazel would turn to me and wink and say, "Susie, I believe it is time for you to go home."

Hazel would always be one of my good friends until she died many years later at a later age from cancer. She was a good woman, and I loved her beautiful sense of humor. She enjoyed life to the fullest. I was always appreciative that she shared some of her life with me.

During the summer of 1949, my dad had a bright idea of setting up a movie theater outside in our side yard. Granted the yard was large enough and had a lot of gravel on it so the grass would not be a hindrance. There was a large white building at the end of our property that could be used as a movie screen. Dad figured that with the rental of a large movie projector and a movie each week, he could set up an outdoor movie theater in our yard and invite neighbors to come enjoy a movie. The people attending would be responsible to furnish their own chair but for a cheap price of attendance like one dollar, Dad figured the neighbors would not mind to carry their own lawn chair over to watch an entertaining popular movie under the bright evening lights. When Dad eagerly discussed all his plans with Momma and me, we both were sitting there with our mouths opened wide in disbelief. Momma was the first to ask, "Where did Dad figure the audience would go to the bathroom during the movie as she surely was not going to open her door to invite all these people to traipse through her home and use her bathroom. She added most emphatically, "We may have a simple life and home but no strangers will be invited to walk through our house."

Dad thought a minute and just replied, "I guess they had better not drink any water or such then!" Then he continued that Priscilla could come down and help me sell tickets and collect the monies and help people place their chairs to watch the movies. Dad then muttered something like, "And of course, Momma would fry up some hamburgers, cheeseburgers, and hot dogs to sell. Maybe some popcorn also!" And that was when Momma exclaimed that she was not going to have any part of this latest wild-flying scheme of Dad's and to just forget any part from her. And she knew Aunt Rena would not want to be a part also. I had to agree with Momma. The idea of having people sitting in our yard watching a movie that Dad was showing on the projector and Priscilla and I running around trying to help the people be comfortable did not sound too appealing to me. I could just tell that the people would be quick to anger and take their hostilities out on Priscilla and me. I also did not see how Dad could get any movies that they would want to see.

Of course, later I knew that Dad would probably only be showing westerns as those were his favorite movies.

Although Dad continued to argue his point of view regarding an outdoor theater out in our yard and how his friends, the cronies who came and sat in Dad's shop in the evening and shared a sip of his bourbon, had all agreed to the movie theater outside in the yard. Let me tell you, the thought of those guys sitting out in our yard watching some Western movie and passing a bottle of bourbon around among themselves made me even more certain that this was yet another "certain to fail project" of Dad's. Nothing looked promising about the idea. And I added when talking to Dad, what about when it rained and people were in our yard demanding a movie—how could you show a movie then? Dad was angry. He really had high hopes about making this work. He felt his family had let him down. We heard about this matter for several summers as he lamented how he could have been a millionaire from the selling of the shows in our side yard. Then the summer of 1952, I had to laugh. It was announced in the papers that the Gillioz Theater had built an outside theater on the outskirts of Monett where you could drive your car and sit in it and watch movies. There were restrooms, food, drinks, and speakers to make each movie heard. A drive-in theater. I was so relieved to hear about this happening. Now I thought Dad will be quiet about his idea and go to the local drive-in theater and enjoy their movies. But alas, Dad did not stop complaining; he just added more fuel to the matter as he said Gillioz had stolen the idea from him and had built the outdoor theater along with what he had wanted to do! Dad always lamented that he had not turned in a patent for his idea of an outdoor theater.

I was very much a loner as a child. There really were not any children in the neighborhood, or if they were living close, they were in a rental house and moved often. So I learned how to keep myself occupied and happy. I was naturally very snoopy and always interested in other people. I delighted in listening to other people talk, especially older people. I always felt they had much to teach and to share. Along with visiting Hazel next door, I also liked to visit Mrs. Mains, who lived in the very large ornate house on the corner of our street. Her son painted signs for a living and had, in fact, painted the signs Dad hung in front of our clock shop. James did an excellent job. He also was an incredible oil artist. His artwork looked just like paintings that had been painted by an English artist of the 1800s, William Turner. Although Turner painted in watercolor and James painted in oil, their landscapes were quite similar. Of course, I did not know that during the time I was visiting and looking at James's paintings but did recognize the fact later when in college studying art.

James was single and in his thirties when I first met him. There was a large cellar on the side of the house leading down to the studio James had created. Actually, James's father had originally created the studio, but he was dead now. So James spent most of his waking hours there in the cellar painting signs when he had a job, but mainly he painted landscapes in oil. He loved to paint, and his landscapes were incredible to see. His companion was his faithful dog, Wolf. I didn't really like Wolf that much because he was always wanting to fight my dog, Mr. Big Man, and because Wolf actually did look like a wolf and was as big as a wolf, I was afraid to let Mr. Big Man near him. That is, until one time. I was out walking Mr. Big Man in our alley and playing with him. He was on a lease at the time. Suddenly Wolf came running out of the cellar with James walking behind him. Pulling Mr. Big Man near to

HOME AGAIN, HOME AGAIN, JIGGITY, JIG   231

me, trying to protect him against this large running and snarling dog, I hollered at James to come get his dog. Before either James or I could do anything, Wolf had charged at Mr. Big Man, and the fight was on. I was afraid to even attempt to pull Mr. Big Man back to me because Wolf was literally drooling and attacking with all his strength at my small dog. I was terrified. Mr. Big Man was yelping and crying as Wolf rolled him around on the ground and snarled over his prone body. I was bawling and screaming for help. Then, suddenly, out of nowhere, Mr. Big Man jumped up from the ground and dove under Wolf and latched onto his stomach and all the hairs there growing from his stomach.

To my amazement, no matter how much Wolf turned and stepped, Mr. Big Man held on. Wolf could not shake my dog away from his stomach. Mr. Big Man had found the vulnerable spot of Wolf, and he was going to be the winner of the fight. Mr. Big Man was determined. I watched in amazement as Wolf stepped backward and forward, whirled around in circles, and still Mr. Big Man held on. I think Mr. Big Man knew that if he ever let loose of Wolf, he was a goner.

Just then, James arrived on the scene and quickly called Wolf to his side. Mr. Big Man dropped from where he had held Wolf in his stomach and crept over to my side. Wolf crept silently on his haunches to James and laid down on the grass near the feet of James. I had never seen Wolf so placid. James looked up at me in amazement.

Quickly I picked up Mr. Big Man and hugged him. I was so afraid that he had been hurt. James took him from me and looked him over. He then laughed and handed him back to me. No blood on Mr. Big Man, and he seemed to be just fine, no broken bones or injuries. I started crying and laughing and hugging Mr. Big Man with all my strength. I was so proud of him and so happy he had not been hurt. Me and Mr. Big Man, we were partners and companions. He was defending me from Wolf and had been so very brave for such a small little guy against such a large snarling dog as Wolf. James laughed with me and promised that he would never let Wolf get away from him like that again. But James added with a wink, after this little wrestling match, he didn't think that Wolf would want to tangle with Mr. Big Man again. Wolf had learned that strength could come in many sizes. I laughed. I was so proud of my dog, Mr. Big Man, and how he had strived to protect me. He was my friend and bosom buddy.

Sometimes on my visits to neighbors, I would go down into the cellar where James and Wolf were. Wolf now tended to stay over in the corner and away from me now. That was fine with me. James would be painting on his job appointments creating various signs for his customers. On special occasions, James would be painting a landscape. I loved those times. I could talk to him and sit on the cellar steps with Mr. Big Man. Mainly I just sat there and watched him paint. It was fascinating to watch him create these lovely landscapes on the canvas.

Sometimes the mother, Mrs. Main, would invite me inside to have a glass of lemonade with her. She liked to sit and chat with me for a few minutes. The first time she invited me into her home upstairs, over the cellar, I was very quiet and apprehensive. The house was so very beautiful and contained all these gorgeous antiques, carpets, large brocaded drapes, and large expensive-looking furniture. On the walls hung some beautiful landscapes painted by Mr. Main or James. I loved to look at them, and to my amazement, there were light fixtures that were placed over the paintings, just like in a museum. Mrs. Main would turn on the lights in the early evenings to better show the landscapes. Also, she kept the house very dark during the day. All blinds or shades were pulled down tightly to protect from the sun which might fade the expensive drapes or carpets. Mrs. Main was very explicit in this matter, especially to her maid. I couldn't help but stare at the woman who had been hired as the maid because she wore an outfit just like the maids in the movies. Her dress was black with a white apron and small white hat on her head. When I would go visit, the maid was always busy cleaning and dusting the house.

On one occasion, Mrs. Main's granddaughter, Joyce, came over to visit, and I was invited to the house to play with Joyce. When it came time for lunch, Mrs. Main invited me to stay for lunch and eat with Joyce in the kitchen. She told me that the maid would make the meal for us. We could have whatever we wanted. But first, I had to run home to ask my mother permission to stay.

When I ran into our kitchen at home, I quickly told Momma that Mrs. Main had invited me for lunch with Joyce and that the maid would be fixing it. Momma gave me a look of surprise and asked me what the maid would be preparing for lunch? I answered that I did not know, but we could ask for anything we wanted. I did say that the maid had told me she had made deviled eggs that day, and we might have one of those. Momma shook her head and reminded me that I only liked the way she made deviled eggs. She also reminded me that if I did not like it, I could not spit it out on the plate. That was very rude. I thought about the matter and told Momma I still wanted to have lunch with Joyce, even if I had to eat the deviled egg.

So I went over for lunch with Joyce. The maid had fixed us fresh, cold lemonade to drink, and there were carrot and celery strips to eat on a little plate on the table. She then served each of us a tuna fish sandwich on our own plate and a deviled egg half-snuggled near the sandwich. The sandwich was delicious, and then, with great trepidation, I bit into the deviled egg. It was perfect. I even asked for another half. After we ate lunch, Joyce and I played with our paper dolls a little longer, and then it was time to take a nap.

When I arrived home, Momma quickly asked me about my lunch. I told her I loved the deviled eggs.

The following Saturday I decided to ride my bicycle up the alley to Priscilla's home to visit and see how Jimmy was doing in the navy. When I entered the kitchen door after Priscilla had opened it, I was immediately struck by how silent the home was. No boisterous running and wrestling in the living room or doors being slammed as children ran in and out of the house. Priscilla, who was now thirteen and most certainly interested in boys, had been busy at her sewing machine making a new summer dress to wear to a birthday party at her friend's house. Priscilla was always very popular in school and often busy with her friends, sports (she loved to play basketball), or just reading and doing her schoolwork. Even in the summertime, she was busy and didn't always have as much time for me. She was kind and happy to see me, but our interests had changed in many ways. I found Mrs. Evans sitting at the kitchen table looking at *The Monett Times* as she drank a cup of coffee. I was surprised that there were no cookies baking in the oven or chicken frying on the stove. Also, the older sister had now married and was away living with her husband. The house was quiet. Mr. Evans was at work or off running some errand. Baby Joey was playing with his toys on the floor. I was taken aback at how much the house had changed since Jimmy had left for the navy a few months back. I sat down by Mrs. Evans at the kitchen table and was surprised to hear that Jimmy had not been writing many letters back home. Mrs. Evans figured he was probably so busy fighting in the Korean War and didn't have time to write. You could tell that she was very worried about how he was doing and scared he might get hurt or killed. Priscilla told me to come in with her and talk while she sewed on her dress. I reminded Mrs. Evans that my brother Glenn was in the army in Korea now, and we never heard from him, either. He was a cook for the army and probably very busy cooking lots of food for all the guys! I also told her about the recent picture his wife Thelma had showed to Dad where Glenn was standing in front of a cave with some other army guys. Glenn was holding a dead pheasant with the wings outspread, tip to tip. We guessed that the pheasant was going to be dinner for them that night. I stayed for a little while and then left. It just wasn't the same in the house with Jimmy away at war.

Dad Returns to Bus Route

It was at this time Dad decided to return to his bus driving. I think Dad loved to drive and he enjoyed being out on the road going through the country and meeting people. He actually proved to be a hero several times while on his route. Once he saw a car on fire after a wreck, and pulled over and helped the hurt driver. He also kept all passengers safe while a tornado passed right near the bus on the highway. He pulled over and stopped the bus and got all passengers into the ditch beside the road and kept them safe. He received an award for this deed from the Ozarks Trailways. He was very proud of his bus and kept it in good shape. During the summers I enjoyed traveling on the bus along his route to Oklahoma City, Oklahoma and back each day.

Chapter 25

Busy Days

That summer, Dad decided he was going to go back to driving his bus route from Monett to Oklahoma City, Oklahoma, each day, Monday through Friday. The young man that Dad had hired was talking about moving on to another bus route in Tennessee anyway, so this seemed perfect for Dad. Momma worked each day at the local cleaners, and I would be back in school in September. Meanwhile, as it was summertime, I could sit in the front shop and read my books or draw while tending the shop. It was pretty simple. People could leave their clocks or watches to be fixed. I knew how to mark them and place labels onto them for identification. If they wanted to see Dad, they would have to come back in the early evening or on a Saturday. We didn't keep any monies in the shop, and we seldom ever sold anything.

So my summer began that year of 1952. We arose each morning early, usually around 5:30 a.m. I would dress quickly and make my bed while Momma began to prepare breakfast in the kitchen. Dad would start getting dressed and getting his bus papers and notebooks prepared for the trip. After breakfast, Momma and I would go over and inspect the bus for cleanliness. I would often sweep out the bus while Momma placed newly laundered and ironed scarves to tie onto the headrest of the seats. Purely for hygienic effect, the small cotton covers at the top of the seats also made the bus look tidier and clean. Dad would head out to the bus depot by 7:00 a.m., Momma got dressed for work, and I cleaned up the kitchen, washing and drying the dishes and putting

236

them away. Momma usually helped me with the old iron skillets she used as they were heavy to lift.

By 8:00 a.m., Momma was on her way to work, and I set up my station in the front shop. If I needed to go to the bathroom, I locked the front door and placed a sign in the window reading "Back in five minutes." I also played the local radio station for music to entertain me as I read my many books. It was a simple life those days, but we all worked to make it complete. Each person knew their specific job and never slacked. I also loved to write letters. I had a pen pal at this time I had met through school. I had chosen her name, and she lived in Holland. We had great times writing to each other during these years and did continue rather spontaneously through high school. She married right after high school and began her family early. That was the last I heard from her. It had been interesting to listen to each other's lives as we grew up. Today I am sorry I no longer remember her name or have any of her letters. They would be interesting to look over and relive our early years together as friends.

Working in the shop each day, I did miss being outside and riding my bicycle, but I was getting older now, and Momma thought it best to stay around the home more. It was also about this time that I began to enjoy embroidery work. I never had the same, gentle hand that Momma did in her embroidery work, but I did have a certain flair for the sewing in detail the stamped pictures on material. I loved to use bright and colorful embroidery thread when sewing and only used the smaller needles to sew with so that I did not leave large holes in the material. Momma taught me many different sewing maneuvers, such as how many threads to use in various stitches or how to keep the back of the embroidery as neat as the front.

Saturdays would often find Momma and me at the Main Variety store, downtown. We would go back in the back of the store and look at all the lovely embroidery kits filled with large and small stamped pictures to embroidery. I would get to choose a small doily to embroider, and Momma would usually choose a pillowslip for a future gift or for our own home. Momma liked to have all our bed pillows covered with lovely hand-embroidered pillowcases. And all the tables in our home had lovely handsewn doilies placed on the table under lamps or such. Each laundry day, these pillow slips or doilies were washed and carefully starched. They were then hung on the lines so that they dried evenly. Later, I was taught how to iron carefully each embroidered piece, keeping out the wrinkles so the embroidered pictures seemed to shine as oil painting by foreign artists on our tables and beds. Momma took great pride in all her lovely embroidered linens. Her embroidered items were often wished for as gifts at Christmas, birthdays or wedding showers. Many brides were thrilled to receive a hand-embroidered pair of pillowslips from Momma for their linen hope chest.

It seemed Momma's hands were always busy, if she wasn't cleaning or cooking or at work, she always found embroidery in her hands when at rest in her favorite old platform rocker. I loved to sit beside her on the couch and sew on my own little embroideries. I did become quite talented in the chore and created some lovely pieces for my own home later. Neither Momma nor I developed skills with the cross-stitch or crochet. For some reason, neither appealed to us. Grandma Clayton loved to crochet and would often fill in the lovely lace pieces for the pillow slips after Momma created the stamped embroidery piece. Later, Momma began to love to make quilts. She had saved various articles of clothing, and she began to cut the necessary squares from the old pieces of clothing. The yellow quilt that lay each day on my own bed was made from cut squares of my old dresses. I loved to lie with the blanket on me and look at all the many sewn pieces in the design that came from my earlier clothes. Momma's baby quilts became all the rage for baby showers, and many mothers-to-be invited Momma to their baby shower in the hopes of receiving a baby quilt from her. They were seldom disappointed. A very nice touch today is that my daughter Melissa loves to quilt and makes lovely pieces as Momma once did. I am thrilled to see this artistic creating of quilts passed down the generations from my mother on to my daughter. Today, Melissa has the quilt Momma had started on as a gift for me, but she died before she could completely begin it. Melissa hopes to finish it someday.

Our car at this time was an older Nash. Dad had picked it up at one of his trading ventures. I think we got it mainly because Dad liked the fact that the car had a reclining front seatback that met the rear seat. Also, as I remember, it was easy to start up on cold days, but the heater did not always work, and many mornings I sat back in the backseat wishing for a warm heater to keep me warm when we were out running errands or out for a ride. As I had said before, Dad had gone back to driving his bus route to Oklahoma City, and Momma worked all day at the local cleaners. But still there just wasn't enough monies coming into the household to pay the bills, small as they were. Every penny counted in those days. So Dad had worked out a contract to deliver the Joplin newspaper every morning. There was a small route in Monett, and Dad had agreed to get the newspaper up and out to all subscribers bright and early of each morning including Sunday mornings.

Thus began our early morning adventures with the newspaper delivery system. Every morning, now, I was to get up by 5:30 a.m. and go up to the front of our shop to await the delivery of the Joplin papers to be rolled and delivered. Soon, as Dad and I sat in the front shop, a newspaper van or truck would pull up in front of our shop, and the man would flop down the newspapers on the sidewalk in front. Dad would go out to carry in the newspapers, and I would get ready to start rolling. Thus, we stood for a good thirty minutes rolling the newspapers and placing rubber bands around the rolled paper. Then Dad would load the papers up into the front passenger side of the old Nash, and off he would go to deliver the papers to all the subscribers. Sometimes I got to go back to bed for a few snuggly moments under the warm covers, but soon the morning would begin.

I think Dad really enjoyed driving around Monett during these early morning hours, with the front seat lying down and the newspapers rolled on the seat beside him. I was impressed with how quickly Dad learned the route to deliver and how adept he got at throwing the rolled papers out the left or right side windows. That took a good throwing arm to get the papers to fly speedily out the Nash window and land in the chosen front yard of the subscriber. Seldom did Dad miss and have to go back to place the newspaper in the rightful spot. Sometimes, if we had overslept or running late, I would hop in the backseat of the Nash and roll the papers as Dad delivered them. We would then return home in time for Momma to be cooking a warm, good-smelling breakfast for us.

I can understand why Dad enjoyed the early morning drive around town delivering the newspapers. All the streets were silent and often dark. Above in the sky, one could see the stars soon to fade away as the morning sun would appear. All was silent, even the birds. Dad said as he drove he could just see Monett and its residents coming to life each morning as lights began to come on in homes and stores downtown. I have to admit that I really enjoyed those early morning rides with

Dad. Sometimes, as we finished the delivery, Dad would stop at the local diner to get some cigarettes, and I would watch people arriving for coffee on their way to work. Everyone was talkative and cheerful to greet with a big hello. Also, the early morning train would be coming in and to this day, whenever I hear a train blow its early morning whistle as it pulls through town, I am reminded of those early rides around town delivering the newspapers.

Years later, in the late 1950s, as I had explained, Dad loved his Nash. But it was getting very old now and needing too much work done to it for us to afford. Dad had been talking about our need to get a newer car and had been looking around at the car lots. Then one hot summer day, Dad totally surprised us with our new car. Well, it was not a new car, but it sure seemed like one to us. That Saturday afternoon, Dad came in through the shop and hollered for Momma and me to come out in front and look at his surprise. Momma and I quickly walked outside, and to our amazement, we stood there looking at a powder-blue Cadillac. Now at that time, the Cadillac was not looked down upon as a gas guzzler but as a car of pure luxury. And that is what this beautiful powder-blue Cadillac was to my parents. The inside was soft and luxurious with big comfortable seats. But what really won Momma over was the incredibly cold air conditioning. With one push of a button, the car filled with luxuriating, cool air conditioning. And on that summer day, it felt wonderful. Dad had Momma get into the driver's side and start up the car. It started right up and just seemed to purr with delight. I know Momma was almost purring with delight at how cool the car quickly became. Then Dad had Momma start pushing buttons, and, just like magic, the windows began to go up and down in the front and in the back. The windshield wipers began their trip back and forth across the windshield. It was all push button! No more turning of the window handle to open the window and having to open all four windows to the fullest with the hopes of catching a cool breeze while driving. This car was luxury. And we couldn't wait until winter with the warm heater blowing through the vents. We were always freezing in the old Nash and wishing for a car heater that worked.

To my amazement, Dad wasn't even intimidated by the powder-blue color of the car. He just loved the car! It was his pride and joy. Momma just giggled like a teenager. She loved the car also!

HOME AGAIN, HOME AGAIN, JIGGITY, JIG   241

Through the years, the Cadillac was the only car that Momma and Dad would own. After the powder-blue Caddy came the soft pink. (Yes, soft pink, and again, to my amazement, Dad never felt embarrassment about owning the pink Cadillac. He only felt pride.) The last Cadillac would be a canary yellow. Dad always said he could throw the newspapers he delivered out of a Cadillac window just the same as he could out of a Nash.

October brought cooler weather and colored leaves. I enjoyed my walk home from school even more on the sunny fall days because of all the colorful trees and leaves swirling around my feet as I walked down the sidewalks toward home. I might add here that I was not a very popular child in school. I really had no friends. There were other children that would sometimes say hello to me and talk for a minute, but there were no real friends.

Not to sound whiny or complaining, but I went to school only because I was told I had to go to school. I rarely had any interest in school or what was happening. None of the teachers seemed to take any particular interest in me. Today I can understand things more clearly, and I can realize that much of this was because I was so apathetic in actions, working the level that would keep me in good standing. I seldom spoke or worked hard to achieve any matter until soon it was what was expected of me. No one looked at me to present a special report, recite some magnificent poem, or present a startling science paper. I was just quiet, shy, interested in myself and my own interests. I had no friends and did not exchange responses with them. I would say that I was probably very boring at that time. As a result, it was probably too much of a task to raise me to a higher level. The only teacher I remember who particularly enjoyed talking to me and working with me was Mrs. Smith, my first-grade teacher. This teacher found a small response in me and took it to develop it further. She loved the way I said breakfast. So each morning, she would have me report to her personally what I had eaten for breakfast each day. She said it made her day more enjoyable. It always made be happy also. It seemed that when I said "breakfast" at that time, I pronounced it as "break-fast." Dad said it was just the Dutch in me.

Through the school years, I sat alone in the corner of the room, at my desk, and kept busy with schoolwork or projects. For the most part, I was alone. Actually, I think I created most of my alone time. It was at home that I was in my best environment. I was happy and comfortable in my home surrounded by all the things I enjoyed doing. I rather enjoyed my own company as I read my books, listened to the radio or music, played the piano, walked, rode my bicycle. I drew, colored, painted, and loved my paper dolls. I spent hours designing and painting clothes for my paper dolls to wear. I kept all the dolls and clothes in a cigar box. My hours were busy before and after school and on weekends. For the most time, I did not really miss having friends. I was a loner, and I was very shy. I was also an observer. At recess time, in school, I would stand off to the side and watch all the other children play. I liked to do that and seldom ever wished I could join them in play. I had found that if I stayed quiet then I wasn't really noticed. I wasn't teased by the more popular children.

I was a plump, short little girl. My dresses were not very new or fashionable. My shoes were always solid and comfortable. I usually had my nose stuck in a book. When I went to the movie theater, I always sat on the right side while all the kids sat on the left side. I enjoyed the movies more when I sat alone so I could concentrate on the movies. On the side where the kids sat, they were always talking and running around acting silly. I wanted to see the movie and not be silly in the theater. So again, I was alone. Often at recess, I was busy jumping rope or playing jacks or hopscotch on the sidewalk. All these were one-person games, and I was happy just quietly playing them. Sometimes, a teacher would come over and urge me to join with the other kids, but I always just smiled and said, "No, thank you." Sometimes, when I walked home, a few kids would follow me and taunt me with silly sayings. But I just ignored them and soon they went away. Most of the time I just smiled and ignored the kids who teased me, and they looked for other children to taunt, growing tired of me. It seemed to work to my benefit. To show an example of what I had created about myself, I would refer to my spelling bee win in the sixth grade.

That Saturday morning, we were going to our local radio station KRMO as a class to participate in a spelling bee on the station. I was rather excited about going there but not particularly excited about winning or even participating. Everyone knew this one boy was the champion speller and always received A's on his spelling test. Everyone knew that he was going to win. I asked Momma to drive me to the station. Momma dropped me off on time, and I went inside the radio station. Soon, all the class and the teacher Mrs. Voght were present. We stood in a circle around the microphone, and the spelling bee began. Quickly some students lost, and they sat off to the side. The words kept coming from Mrs. Voght, and to my amazement, I was still part of the spelling bee. I was spelling all the words correctly. A few more words were spelled, and then it happened.

I was one of the final two contestants in the spelling bee. It was between me and the spelling champion in our class, and Mrs. Voght gave the winning word. The boy received the word first, and I stood silently expecting it to be announced that he was the winner and I was second place. That was okay with me. But then I realized that everyone was looking at me, and there was a stunned silence in the room. The spelling champion had misspelled "squirrel," and he had had to sit down. I was the only person standing, and the word had gone to me to spell. I could win the spelling bee with the correct spelling of "squirrel." I slowly spelled the word, and to my utter amazement, I won! I was the sixth-grade spelling champion. I don't think Mrs. Voght's face could have looked more surprised than my own. I won. When I was given the smiling congratulations and winning spelling certificate, I could feel Mrs. Voght's surprise. Ah well, I was growing used to that. I accepted the certificate and was feeling pretty good about myself about the win. Later when I got home and announced to Momma and Dad that I had won the sixth-grade spelling bee, I was met with surprise from my parents that there had been a contest. I was the winner.

That Halloween, we were allowed to bring a costume to school and change into it during lunchtime. I had brought some old, larger clothes, and had planned to dress as a hobo. But when it came time to change into the clothes I decided not to wear them. I enjoyed how the other children dressed up, but I felt better in my own clothes. When I got home that night, I decided I would like to go to a few homes dressed up and do some trick or treating. Momma was surprised as I had never gone trick-or-treating before. During those years in 1952, children didn't really go out at night and trick-or-treat for candies. This year, I decided I wanted to try it. Momma said I could go if I got home before dark and only went to certain homes. I agreed and began to put on my hobo outfit.

Momma gave me an old bag to carry, and off I went to the few homes I had decided to visit. I traveled up to see Viola and E.P. Beeler.

They did not really have any treats to hand out but promised me a cookie one day when visiting. Mrs. Evans and Priscilla gave me a popcorn ball they had made. Priscilla was getting dressed to go to a Halloween party at a friend's house. She had a date and was all excited. She had made herself an outfit dressed as a fairy princess and looked so very pretty. I wished her well for the party and told her how lovely she looked. I had then decided to walk up to the house where the nuns lived, next to the Catholic Church. I had often seen the nuns going inside their home and wondered what it looked like.

When I rang the doorbell to the house where the nuns lived, the porch was all quiet and rather dark. Suddenly, the front porch light came on and the door opened and there stood a nun who I knew and would often say hello to. She laughed and invited me inside. As we stepped into the front room, she turned and shouted laughingly, "Come, ladies, and see who is here to have a trick-or-treat." About five nuns came running into the front room and gathered around me asking many questions: "What was my name? "Was I Catholic?" "Why wasn't I Catholic?" and so on. I couldn't even get an answer in. I told them I was there as a hobo for trick-or-treats, and I showed them my bag I was carrying. The first nun shouted, "Hooray, we have a trick in need of a treat." And with that, she placed me in center of the room while the other nuns sat down in chairs and on the couch. "What was my trick?" she asked me.

Well, I had not thought of that. I had no idea what trick I could do for them. I thought and thought and then decided to sing my little nursery song for them. Setting down my bag of candies previously collected, I posed my arms as a little teapot and sang, "I'm a little teapot, short and stout, here is my handle, here is my spout. Just tip me over and I pour out." And I bent as if I was a teapot pouring out water. The nuns loved it and just laughed and clapped with delight. They gave me come cupcakes and a couple of cookies. I then told them that I had to leave and go home as it was beginning to get dark. I was so happy to get out of there before they made me sing or dance again for them. That was my last trick-or-treaters, and I headed home to tell Momma about my adventure and to go to sleep. Walking and trick-or-treating was a tiring task.

Chapter 26

Honor The Veterans

Previously I had mentioned that we had four apartments upstairs that we rented. It wasn't too often that we had any tenants, but at this occasion, Dad had rented the two one-room apartments to two older gentlemen. Each apartment was just a bedroom with a bed, dresser, chair, and small table. The bathroom was down the hall and shared. But to the two men, their small apartment was perfect. They each only seemed to have a small suitcase of their belongings. I soon found out why they didn't really seem to care about their belongings. Each payday, the two men would go get a bottle each and proceed to going back up to their separate apartments and get totally washed-out drunk. Usually, after a few days, Dad would go up and check on them and make sure they were still alive. During this time, they had mainly drunk up their checks and were just coming back to life again. At this time, Dad would force them to get up and get bathed and put some fresh clothing on. Momma would send up clean linens, and the cycle would begin again. The men would stay fairly sober and quiet until their check arrived, and then off they went on their "bender" drinking all their monies away. If it had not been for Momma taking up some plates of food once in a while, the men probably would have died from malnutrition, but Momma and Dad both seemed to understand their sorry plight in life and helped them the best they could. After several months of these drinking benders, Dad talked them into giving him a portion of their checks which he kept put away for when they needed monies to buy

245

food or such. Soon, they began to appreciate this matter of having some monies left when they came off their drinking benders.

To be truthful, I think it was Momma and Dad who brought these two men back to life or at least to a life that was somewhat better. They began to realize how nice it was to be clean, to live in a clean environment, and to have good food. They were able to cut down on their heavy drinking and keep it at a pint a day. They also like to come down and sit in the front shop and talk with Dad about various things in life and to just listen to Dad go on about things he had read in the classics or newspaper. Dad loved the attentive audience.

The two men were World War II veterans, and when they had returned stateside after the war, they just had not been able to settle back to civilian life and keep themselves in line. Thus, their life had fallen into heavy drinking and a general lack of responsibility. But I must add, these two gentlemen were always well-mannered and respectful to my Momma. It seemed that she was the only one or person who brought them back to their own memories of past years and perhaps their own mother. For whatever reason, they would always make sure to nod their head with manners long forgotten and proclaim "Lela" to be an angel placed on this earth.

November now in order, the announcement went out that the annual Turkey Shoot and Raffle would be held that Saturday. With the weatherman promising a sunny, somewhat cool Saturday, all interested participants gathered together that Saturday out on the dogcather's farm, outside Monett. I have mentioned the owner before with the Christmas story. He and his wife had a household of children, all sizes and ages. The house was small, the yard was mainly junk piles, overgrown grass and weeds, but the far corner of his land made a perfect area for the turkey shoot. Taking a light packed lunch, Dad and I headed out to the shoot early that morning. Dad had loaded up in the trunk of our Caddy some guns and rifles to take to the shoot. He planned to exhibit some of them and maybe trade or sell a few. Whenever the chance appeared, Dad did love to trade and barter. Also, Dad knew that Mr. Gunn would be there, and he always wanted to trade or haggle over some gun or rifle with Dad. So up we pulled at the house and parked on the side where some other cars or trucks had parked. One could see the children in the dusty front yard. I walked with Dad over to a group of men standing together by the bales of hay that had been placed there. I recognized many of the men there, Mr. Gunn, and Mr. Hall, our mayor and the sheriff. A few policemen, off duty, were looking at the guns. Mainly the participants were local businessmen and some farmers. All were thinking of taking home a fresh plump turkey for their Thanksgiving table.

Bales of hay had been set up for the target area. Three large sheets of bull's eyes had already been attached to the four-tiered bales of hay. An old cardboard table and a few chairs were over on the right where you could pay your admission monies per person. Many of the men had their guns or rifles with them. Some of them were sharing a sip of whiskey or gin from their carried flasks or pints in their jacket pockets. Dad was in his realm at this time. I moved over to the side of the area where I sat quietly on an old tree stump and proceeded to watch the events taking place. After some general talking and greeting, it was determined that there would be five shootings for the five live turkeys. Being of a more genteel nature, the men were using the bull's eye target for shootings. Long before they used to tie the bird to the bales of hay and the participants got to buy tickets to shoot at the turkey. Finally agreeing that it was not really a "sports" event to be shooting at tied birds, the participants agreed to shoot at target paper rather than the live bird. When a person won a turkey, they would take their awarded ticket to Monett's butcher shop and have the butcher prepare the bird for them to take home and bake for the coming holidays. I was glad it was a paper target or else I would not have been there.

The idea was to get a "dead shot" or bull's eye! The winner for each shoot had to shoot the bullet right smack-dab into the center or else they got no turkey. There could be no almost-there winners—it had to be right in the middle each time. So the shootings began. Then each person paid their money, and a bull's eye was in place on the bale of hay. Aiming the rifle or gun slowly, the bullet was fired. After about twenty minutes of this shooting and guffawing at each other, I was beginning to despair that anyone was going to get a free turkey. Finally, someone did hit the perfect bull's eye, and he was promptly announced as the new recipient of a fresh plump turkey for his Thanksgiving dinner. And so the day moved on. Drinking, shooting, trading, bragging, bargaining, and on it all went. I sat and ate some of the lunch and enjoyed being out in the lovely fall day!

I had moved over to the cardboard table to chat with one of the men collecting the monies and keeping the dollars in an old cigar box. At the end of the raffle, it was known that the collected monies would all be raffled off to the last shooter who won. Some of the men were getting ready to call the raffle shoot to an end and try for the monies so they could get on home. There was one turkey left to win, and everybody was pretty much winded and ready to just relax. Suddenly someone got the bright idea that I should try the turkey shoot. They asked me if I had ever shot a rifle before, and I told them that I had gone before with Dad and shot at some old cans in the junkyard. So to my surprise, I was lead over to the marked area for the shooter, and Dad gave me one of his rifles, all loaded and ready to shoot. Following instructions, I placed the rifle on top of the bales of hay, got into position to shoot, looked at the target, and fired the bullet. Luckily it was a small rifle, and I was only knocked back a few inches. Mr. Gunn gathered the rifle back from me and laughed as he handed it to Dad. Dad just smiled. And then a loud cheer went up, and Tom gathered the bull's eye from the bale of hay. There in the middle of the paper was one lone bullet hole, it was mine, and it was smack-dab in the middle of the bull's eye! Was I ever surprised. To my amazement, I had won a fresh turkey for our Thanksgiving table. All the men laughed and slapped me on the back with congratulations as they began to prepare for the last shoot for the collected monies. I stood in amazement rubbing my sore shoulder. I was given the ticket to give to Momma so she could take it to the butcher for our holiday meal. I couldn't wait to surprise her with my win!

To this day, I have always wondered about that shoot and the possibility that I could have honestly won the turkey. I guess I will never know for sure, but it was a highlight of my life. With all the gathered businessmen and fathers that I knew from town, it was a moment of highly prized attainment. I felt so jubilant I could have danced a jig right then and there. But I just smiled and thanked everyone for their fine best wishes. Dad gathered his guns and a couple new rifles he had traded for and put them in the trunk, and we got into the car to leave. We waited for a few minutes to see who won the monies and then headed home. I tell you, Momma was surprised when I showed her the ticket and told her of my earnings. Upon greeting Momma in the kitchen, I announced that I had brought home the bacon, or should I say turkey!

Well, that Thanksgiving, Momma invited both of our upstairs tenants down to our table for Thanksgiving dinner. Of course, being the only child and willfully disrespectful as all children of that age seem to be, I was mortified. These two old drunkards were going to sit at our table and eat with us, and I had to be nice to them. I was furious. I was the winner of the turkey, and I should be able to say who would be eating it and who would not!

I could not understand why Momma and Dad felt the need to bring these two men to join us at our small kitchen table filled with Thanksgiving food to eat. "Why not just send a plate up to them to eat in their rooms," I asked Momma. She smiled and told me that sometimes people need to be with other people, and this was one of those times. Much to my shame today, I stomped around the kitchen a lot and rolled my eyes in disgust when the two men arrived. Looking back, I feel such mortification that I have behaved in such an unmannerly way. The two men had bathed, combed back their rather long hair, and had even shaved, as evidenced by the piece of toilet paper stuck to one of their cheeks. Their shaking hands had denied them a clean, unhazardous shave. They were each wearing suits of some questionable fashion, style, or age. Their ties were probably the widest ties I had ever seen. But I admit today, they had tried to look presentable for the Thanksgiving dinner with their best friends and benefactors, Lela and Glenn. As to me, they just smiled and understood in their own shyness why I was acting as I was. They admitted that they probably would have acted the same way if they had had to sit beside someone like them. So we sat together, and Dad said a small prayer of blessing. Then we began devouring Momma's delicious cooking. I was amazed to see how much of the mashed potatoes, turkey, and gravy could be put away by two, rather skinny older men. I have to admit they were sure to thank Momma for each helping and saying, "Yes, ma'am," or "No, ma'am," to each question. After they finished eating, they wiped their mouths with their napkins and swore they had never eaten finer food in all their life. Momma laughed and offered them hot coffee and fresh pie. That was the actual cherry that could top the sundae. I swore I saw a few tears in those two gentlemen's eyes as they smiled a big "Thank you, ma'am," and they proceed to wolf down their pieces of pecan and pumpkin pies. At that, my own conscience began to prick my brain, and I decided I should settle down and show Thanksgiving kindness and manners to the two gentleman visitors.

When they left, to return upstairs, Momma gave each of them a heaping plate of food to enjoy later with the promise they would return the dishes to her kitchen. They sure seemed thrilled to have some more of that Thanksgiving dinner to take with them for later. I really do believe it was the best food they had ever eaten or at least, some of the best food. I was still grumping around as I cleaned up the table and helped Momma with the dishes. But I did admit later that I could see why Momma and Dad had invited them to our table. I confessed to Momma that I was sorry for the way I had acted. She told me to tell that to the two men who had visited. They would appreciate my apologies. Later, I did apologize to them, and over the weeks, we began to sit and talk, often outside, in the yard as we sat in our old lawn chairs. I found them to be simple men who had been destroyed in life through what they had witnessed in the war and all the bloodshed and killing. They had no particular family, just each other as friends. Over the years, as they continued to stay in our apartments, I learned new thoughts, kinder in deeds, from the two men as we sat and talked. I became appreciative of their smiles and continued interest in me. They often wanted to know about my studies, movies I was watching, or what I was reading. I listened to some of their stories about growing up on a farm and their army life.

Years later, when I was teaching in St. Louis, Momma wrote me a letter that one of the gentlemen had died from cancer. A short time later, the other gentleman died. Momma said she did not think he could live without his friend. Much to Momma and Dad's sadness, no family member came forward to claim either of the bodies. So Dad made arrangements for their burial with military honors in Springfield. My parents were the only people attending the funerals, and Momma told me they were very proud to receive a flag from each of the funeral ceremonies. Dad purchased two of those flag display cases and hung them up in the front of his shop. Neither of my parents could get over the fact that no one cared for either of the gentlemen. They were both proud to be keepers of the flags in memory.

The days were speeding along that Christmas of 1952, and I was looking forward to trimming our tree with Momma. Dad would usually go out to a farm and choose a midsized live tree. The farmer would then chop it down and bring it to us on his truck. Since Momma and I were going to decorate the tree the coming weekend, and it was Friday after school, I thought I would walk over to Priscilla's home to see if she had put up her tree yet. When I arrived at the house, things were rather quiet. Mrs. Evans was in the kitchen baking some cookies. Joey was sitting at the table reading comic books. Priscilla was in the living room taking out Christmas decorations from their boxes and getting things ready to decorate their newly acquired live tree. Soon, Priscilla and I were sitting on the living room floor together talking about our favorite songs when we heard a car door slam in front of the house. Mr. Evans was not home and had not been around home much lately. So when we heard a knocking at the front door, Priscilla went to open the door. To our surprise, there stood two policemen who asked if Mr. and Mrs. Evans were at home. Priscilla turned to me and told me to go home, out the kitchen door, and just go home now. I ran through the house and started through the kitchen door when I heard Mrs. Evans shout, "Oh no," and I saw her standing there by the kitchen table, holding on to the back of the chair as if her very life depended upon it. I ran outside and down the street to my home. Momma had just gotten home, and when I told her what I had just seen, she also said, "Oh no," and put her coat and boots back on. She told me to stay at home inside, and she was going up to the Evans home. When I asked why I could not come she also told me that this was not a time for young ones to be there.

Hours later, when Momma came home, she looked sad and tired. She sat down with me and told me that young Jimmy Evans had been killed in battle in the Korean War. I could not believe it. Jimmy, the silly boy with big ears, was dead and had been killed in battle? It was too much for me to understand, and it was so sad. I knew that Mrs. Evans and Priscilla were going to be so sad without their Jimmy at home with them.

Jimmy was buried that Wednesday, December 10, 1952, in the Monett cemetery. Born February 12, 1934, he was only eighteen years old at the time he was killed. In fact, he had just turned eighteen years old that year. He was an airman apprentice in the navy, and now he would not be coming home to be with us. I remembered that day he had left for service and how proud he had been wearing his uniform. It just did not seem possible that we would never see Jimmy again. After that, the Evans home changed so much. As a small child, I had sat on the curb and listened to all the happy activity going on in that home with all the laughter, noise, and wonderful cooking aromas. Now the house sat almost empty. Mr. Evans had gotten remarried. Roberta was married and living away. Jimmy was dead. Now there was just Priscilla, Mrs. Evans, and little Joey.

Momma would often bake an extra casserole or pie and take it up to visit her friend, Jessie, or for Mrs. Evans as I was always to call her. Momma would sit with her friend, Mrs. Evans, and listen or talk to her as she cried. Together they would look at old pictures in the family photograph book. I noticed that Priscilla wasn't in the house these days. She seemed to be off and away from the sadness.

The days of December passed through quietly. We had a small Christmas as Momma and I drove down to Grandma Clayton's house in Cassville to be with Aunt Rena and Betty and Maureece, my cousins. We played games and enjoyed lots of good home-cooked meals together. There were not many presents, but we did not really get upset. We felt we had a lot of toys already and were busy using our imagination to write funny skits to perform for each other or our family. We also loved to play various card games and would sit up as late as we could playing gin or hearts.

Chapter 27

Every Home Needs A Television

January brought the cold and snow to our homes. There is one sound I miss today when it is a snowy wintery day. I miss the sounds of chains turning on the wheels of the cars as they go by on the street or highway. When I was a child, chains were put on a person's car whenever we heard the prediction of snow. These chains gave better traction to our car's wheels on the snow, and then, when the snow was gone and melted, the chains should be taken off the car tires until the next predicted snow. Of course, one was not to drive the car with chains if the snow had all melted off because then the chains would cause damage to the roads. But on those days, with snow on the ground and cars driving to work and places, I loved to hear those chains turning and turning on the car tires as they passed by.

I had one continuous wish. I wanted a television for the living room. At school I heard the other kids talk about what they had seen on the television the night before, and I would listen to them and try to imagine what they were talking about, but I could not. It was beyond my realm of thinking. I didn't understand how the shows ran or commercials played. I had a lot to learn about television. And then I came to a brilliant solution. I would watch television at Viola and E.P. Beeler's home.

I knew they had gotten a large screen television for their living room to watch their evangelistic shows, especially Oral Roberts. They loved to listen to him pray, speak in tongues, and lead the audience in jubilant singing. I told Momma my idea and asked if I could go visit Viola and E.P. and present them with my question. Momma said I could.

So that afternoon, I made a Sunday call with Viola and E.P. As I had suspected, they were sitting in the parlor reading the Bible and talking about church that morning. When Viola opened the door and saw me there, she smiled and invited me in to read the Bible with them. I sat in the parlor, and we sat and read together and talked about various verses. I liked to listen to them. At this point, I felt the energy and strength to present to them my question regarding watching television. You see, I suggested that if I came up on Sunday early evenings to watch the *Oral Roberts Show* with them, I could then stay and watch the live theater shows later. There were such exciting live theater productions at that time on the television, and I was so excited that I might get to watch one of them. It was *The Loretta Young Show* (I loved to watch her enter through the door and swing around and flutter across the floor in some gorgeous chiffon dress or such), or the Lux Theater, or one of the many available. I loved to watch the live plays, often with famous actors and actresses. So I presented this idea to Viola and E.P., and as I finished, they both smiled at me and told me they would have to pray on the matter and get back to me soon. I told them thank you and went back home to await their decision. I was on pins and needles as I waited to hear of their decision. Imagine being able to watch one of the shows each Sunday night. It would be wonderful if they approved. After a few days, Momma ran into Viola downtown, and she told Momma to send me up Sunday early evening at 5:30 p.m. When Momma told me, I couldn't wait to go visit E.P. and Viola that coming Sunday.

When I arrived Sunday, Viola and E.P. told me that after thought and prayer, they were going to invite me in to watch television with them on Sunday evening if I also came and watched *The Oral Roberts Show* with them. I was rather dubious about sitting and watching Oral Roberts because he mainly scared me on his television show with his screaming and shouting from his pulpit. I will add also about his show that when the camera would close in and just show his head with flames of fire coming out around his head, it really scared me. Often he would speak in tongues, and I wasn't sure about that or when he claimed to be healing people. But I thought for a minute and decided I could watch his hour-long show to be able to watch the shows later on the television that I chose. So I agreed and thanked Viola and E.P.

Now I won't make light of the following Sunday early evenings as I sat with Viola and E.P. while watching Oral Roberts speak. Often they would get emotionally carried away also and would stand and speak in tongues or pray and read the Bible. But soon I became comfortable with the situation, knowing that neither E.P. nor Viola would ever hurt me, so I just sat quietly and waited until the hour was over, and then I would enjoy my choice of television.

When I watched my choice of show, Viola and E.P. would leave the room because they believed that I would be watching the shows of the devils. You know, after a few Sundays, much to my surprise, they came in and joined me, and Viola later told E.P., "You know, that play was interesting. I am sure that it would be okay if we watched some of those shows." So soon Viola and E.P. would ask me about the evening's choice and began to stay with me in the living room to watch also. They did enjoy the *Loretta Young Show,* and Viola thought she was a lovely woman.

Early summer brought another surprise from Dad. Without the use of credit cards, a person had to save monies to enable oneself to purchase an expensive item such as a television or air conditioner. I was dreaming of acquiring either one. They sounded super great to me. Of course, one could get credit in a store and purchase an item through the credit one had, but I am afraid Dad had a poor credit rating. He was always getting something and leaving Momma and me to pay for it. When we could not, we would have to let the store take the item back. Well, on this particular hot and steamy Saturday morning, Dad came in proudly announcing that he had two air conditioners that he was going to place in my bedroom window and the other in his bedroom's window. With that news, he proceeded to install the two air conditioners. As old fashioned as our wiring was on our house, I was not too sure the house would be supporting the voltage needed for the two air conditioners, but, to my surprise, the air conditioners came right on and began to instantly cool down my bedroom and the living room. The air conditioner in Dad's room made their bedroom like an iceberg. Momma was not too sure she was going to like sleeping in such a cold room. But the air conditioners were in our house, working, and we were not too sure how they had been obtained. In fact, Momma and I were rather leery of getting used to the air conditioners for fear they were going to be reclaimed back by whoever Dad had gotten them from. So we waited. To our amazement, the two air conditioners stayed our own. Somehow Dad had gotten the monies to buy them or else had gotten credit to use. I was afraid to look realism in the face! Momma and I soon became greatly attached to those two air conditioners and the coolness they lent to our home.

With these two miracles came yet another surprise a few hours later. Dad came in and told Momma and me that a television would soon be arriving to our home. A brand-new black-and-white television with a twenty-one-inch screen was soon going to be in our living room for us to watch. That was almost too much to bear for our excitement. Yet in walked Dad with two men carrying in the television to set in the living room, right in the corner, facing out, where anyone on the couch or Dad's chair could watch it perfectly. It was too beautiful to look at. I wanted to run out in the alley and scream for all to hear that we now owned a television too! Now I could watch all the shows that I heard the kids at school talk about. Each day, the kids would come to school all amazed with some show on television to talk about, and I could not ever join in because I did not know what they were talking about. And now we had our own television. I didn't question the two air conditioners or the television set. I was pretty sure I didn't really want to know the answers as to where they all came from. They could have been won in a poker game, or they might have "fallen off the truck." Sometimes it was just better not to know.

Dad placed a pair of rabbit's ears on top of the television on top of the embroidered linen Momma had quickly secured. She wanted to make sure that the top of the television was not scratched or scarred by anything that might be placed there, so she always kept a lovely embroidered linen on top of the television. Later, the most wonderful nightlight would be placed on top of the television also. This chalk figurine nightlight sat there on the television for the rest of the years and offered me comforting light as I lay in my bed. Dad had found the nightlight at a yard sale or estate sale, not really sure, and had brought it home to place on the television top. It was a statute made out of chalk, painted brightly green for the grass and hilltop where the large, snarling black panther stood, or maybe I should say poised, as if to make a large leap right off the chalk green hilltop. At first sight, one might feel a little queasy about the snarling panther sitting on top of the television set, but after I became used to it, the panther brought comfort in protection of me and the television set. There was the television set with the snarling panther in the corner of the room, couch on the left wall, and Dad's chair and small table across from the TV. I usually sprawled on the couch while Momma pushed her favorite platform rocker into the center of the room to watch TV.

The early shows carried a lot of Western shows, *Hopalong Cassidy*, *Wagon Train*, Roy Rogers, and Dale Evans, etc. We loved them all. We had quickly become television addicts, but with our busy schedules, we didn't really have much time to sit and just watch television. Over the years, Dad loved late-night television, sitting in his Naugahyde beige overstuffed chair with the small one-legged table sitting next to him holding his large ashtrays and many, many cigarette butts.

At this time, I wanted to enjoy the full realization of a television set in our home. First of all, I decided, we must get TV trays so we could sit in front of the television set at dinnertime and eat. That way, we could watch the news as we ate. No time wasted. So Momma ordered four beige flowered metal folding TV tray tables,with her Jewel Tea awards, and she and I would sit in the living room with our metal folding TV tray tables in front of us holding our lunch or supper. Soon, we could not fight the temptation to try out the TV dinners to eat on our TV tables. Momma bought two meat loaf dinners for us to try. One bite of those soon gave us way to return to Momma's own cooking. We both agreed that we did not need the TV dinners.

But then, a few weeks later, Dad had been at the local hardware store talking with customers and passing time that Saturday morning. He came in all excited with a package in hand and a promise to Momma and me that he had purchased a most amazing invention for our TV. When we asked what it was, Dad just smiled. And then he made the loud announcement that tonight we would be watching our black-and-white television in color, full color, just like in the TV shops. We stared dumbfounded at him and asked him endlessly as to how that would be possible. Dad would not answer. He just shook his head, smiled, and whistled a little tune as he walked back up to the shop.

Now this was exciting news. Color television on a black-and-white television. We could see the colors of clothes the people had on and all the other things that color would enhance in the programs on television. We were so excited that we decided to make it a special evening. Momma and I made a nice dish of chocolate fudge with handpicked walnuts.

These fudge pieces were our very favorite. We ate supper a little early, and then Momma popped some popcorn for us to eat with the fudge as we watched television. After supper, while Momma and I cleaned up the kitchen, Dad said he would go and ready the television for its surprise. It was to bring black and white to color. Momma and I could barely stand our curiosity as we worked in the kitchen while Dad was in the living room.

Timing it perfectly, just as we finished cleaning up the kitchen, Dad told us to come on in and see the surprise. Momma and I dried our hands and headed into the living room to where the television sat. As we looked at the set, there across the large glass screen of the television was a large piece of cellophane colored paper. Dad stood and told us to sit down so he could explain the process. After we sat down, he anxiously told us we might notice there were three color stripes across the cellophane paper he had taped to the front of the screen of the television. The top color was blue, the center red, and the bottom green.

It looked really silly to us, and we were not too sure how we would see the television show through the cellophane paper. When Dad turned on the television, "Color for you!" he exclaimed and stepped back as the *Hopalong Cassidy Show* appeared on the television, or at least we thought it did. We could not see it very well, for the three-color stripes seemed to cover across the set. Momma and I both looked at each other and then back at Dad, and I asked, "Where is the color?" Dad turned and looked and was furious immediately.

He adjusted the buttons on the set, but it still did not make the show any brighter, nor did the show suddenly become in color because of the three stripes. The set only showed the three stripes across the screen, blue for the sky, red for the flesh tones, and green for the grass or bottom of the land. It was an interesting idea but way before its time. The three colors on cellophane paper would not be the answer to a color television. Dad ripped the paper off the television set and stomped out of the house. He was going to see the owner at the hardware store where he had purchased this little gem and get his money back, all $3.98. Momma and I sat down in front of the television and ate our chocolate fudge and hot popcorn, laughing and enjoying our black-and-white television. It would have been nice to have a color television, but we just weren't really ready for one. We would just have to do with our black-and-white television until we had the monies to move on up to a real colored set.

Meanwhile, there was another problem with our television. Somewhere in her mind, my grandmother Clayton, Momma's mother, had determined that the local channel from Joplin, where we mainly listened to our weather and news, was owned and operated by Communists. Grandma even claimed that the reporters and announcers for the station were Communists. Now, as a God-fearing woman, Grandma would not have anything or ever be involved with anyone who were thought to be Communists or were Communists. Thus, she decided that the television station based in Joplin was not ever to be watched in her home nor in a home where she was standing. If she came to our house and found that our television station was on that channel from Joplin, she would turn right around and walk out of our house and wait for the channel to be changed or the television to be turned off. She would not or never be accused of being a part of any Communist agenda or plot. It did not matter if it was raining, snowing, freezing, or sunny; Grandma would go right out the kitchen door and stand in the alley by our house and wait for the channel to be changed or turned off. There was no enticing her back into the house with even the promise of changing the channel. She had to hear it changed before she would enter the house again. She would have been a joy to U.S. Senator Joseph McCarthy and certainly was one of his champions. There was never to be any doubt of her disloyalty in patriotism and her own affiliations to the United States of America.

If Grandma Clayton entered our home through the front door of the shop, Dad would holler, "Fire in the hole," and Momma or I would quickly walk into the living room to change the television station or just turn it off before Grandma could even know what station was playing. It was safer to do this. Many times Momma would miss her favorite soap opera in the morning because Grandma always seemed to arrive at our house just as the program would begin. I think Grandma had her own TV guide and looked forward to stirring up events in our own home. Whatever the reason, we knew not to be caught watching the Joplin station when Grandma was coming to visit.

As I had mentioned before, I had always found Grandma Clayton to be an unusual person for the years that I knew her. She lived meagerly on her Social Security checks and monies Momma and Aunt Rena helped her with. At Christmas, she would always have a small gift for me and my cousins, Betty and Maureece. We always told her that it

Three Women

Everytime I look at this picture I marvel at these three women - strong, wise and kind, good people. Having just walked somewhere down the street to see something, on the left is my Momma, Lela, with Aunt Rena in the middle and Grandma Ethel Clayton on the right. They are just past the Heim's Hatchery on their way back to our shop and home. Deep in conversation about something, they walk together in strength and family love.

was not necessary, but she enjoyed giving to us. To this day, I have to chuckle a little at the gifts she always gave us. Each of us received a tube of underarm deodorant and a small jar of menthol muscle rub. Grandma loved her menthol muscle rub and believed it was a deterrent to all illness and colds. She used the rub on her chest in cold weather and was always quick to dispense it to anyone near her who was ill. She always had a faint smell of the rub when you hugged or kissed her. To this day, I still use the menthol rub also during cold weather, and so does my daughter. I guess one could say the love of the item has been passed on through the generations of women.

Uncle Dink

Momma's youngest brother Raymond, or as he was always called, Dink, had come to live with Grandma Clayton.

Never one to settle down, Uncle Dink had finally gotten responsibility to maintain a job and he enjoyed being at home with his mother, Ethel.

He had gotten used to boxes all over the house, unpacked, moving many times but lots of good home cooking.

As he had aged he had come to the realization that comfort and warmth was a pretty good thing to have. I always found him to be a good, kind man with a happy sense of humor.

Chapter 28

Grandma Clayton

Grandma Clayton always seemed to march to a different drummer, one of her own making. One of my favorite stories about Grandma was when she was living in Monett with Uncle Dink. Now, Uncle Dink was my favorite uncle on my mother's side. The youngest of the family, Raymond became affectionately called Dinky because he was so little since birth and didn't seem to be growing much. Later, Dinky was shortened to Dink, and that was the name that seemed to stick. Well, Grandma had moved to Monett from the farm in Cassville because she could no longer keep up with all the work necessary and no one to help her, so she came to Monett to live where her daughters, Momma and Aunt Rena were living. She rented a small house and settled into the town to live away from the farm. Uncle Dink had never married. He seemed to have three loves in his live: whiskey, women, and cards. None of which seemed to do much in success for him. He would work at a job long enough to get some monies together, and then off he would go to enjoy days of drowning in whiskey, losing in cards, and definitely losing in women. He would move in with one of the women he met during his latest binging and live there for a few weeks or so. Sometimes the love only lasted a few months. Then the woman would get tired of Dink not working and lying around the house all the time, so she would get into a fight with him, and usually Uncle Dink would end up on the street with a large bump on his head where the woman hit him with the large iron frying skillet. Always seemed to be the same. So Uncle Dink

263

got tired of his raucous living and moved in with his mother, Ethel. We always said his head had gotten too many bumps on it from all the skillet beatings. Whatever. Uncle Dink was living with Grandma in a rented home in Monett, and it seemed to be good. Dink was handy in repairing things and kept Grandma Clayton in ship shape. He could not drive a car but could see to running errands, or sometimes Aunt Rena or Momma would take him around town to get some items needed. It was a good arrangement. Uncle Dink was even trying to sober up and to stay away from card games. As for women, I think Uncle Dink had just given up on that idea.

Now I must also add that Grandma loved to move. You may remember that I mentioned this matter when Grandpa Marion was alive and they lived on farms that they rented. Grandpa died when he was only in his sixties because everyone said he was just "worn out" from all the moves Grandma talked him into. She was always off to the next farm that she believed was nicer—"going to see the elephant" as used to be called by the early pioneers. Just over the hills, what might be even better! This seemed to be Grandma Clayton's mantra. Thus, she never unpacked anything so she was always ready for the next move. Each room in the houses she rented was filled with boxes and boxes of packed goods, ready for the next move. Of course, Grandma got out just the items she needed for everyday life, but all the rest of the things sat in the packed boxes ready to go. There were seldom pictures on the walls or knick-knacks on the tables or such because everything was packed. Over the years, we had gotten used to this matter and just left Grandma alone to live as she saw fit. Uncle Dink had soon gotten used to this life and lived around the boxes also with just his necessary items unboxed.

That specific morning, Uncle Dink got up to go to work. He was working on a construction site and glad to have some way to earn some monies to help with groceries and rent. He ate breakfast, said good-bye to Grandma, and off he went to a day of work. When he returned that evening to his little house with Grandma, he was surprised to find it empty and dark. Looking around he saw no sign of Grandma or any of their possessions. Concerned, he walked over to our home and came in to talk to Momma. Aunt Rena quickly came down also to figure out what had happened to Grandma. All had decided that Grandma must have moved and had forgotten to tell any of us, including Uncle Dink. So we took off in our car with Momma driving while looking

HOME AGAIN, HOME AGAIN, JIGGITY, JIG   265

for Grandma Clayton. Then Aunt Rena remembered a small house that had just gone up for rent and they drove over to the house. Sure enough, they found Grandma there, all just moved in, sitting at the kitchen table waiting with dinner on the table. Grandma was so mad at Uncle Dink for being late for dinner when we arrived. We laughed and went back home.

Later, Dink told us that after this incident, every morning when he prepared to leave for work, he would always turn to Grandma Clayton and ask her if she planned to move that day. She would always scowl her face and tell him that of course she was not moving. Uncle Dink would just laugh and make her faithfully promise that she would not move that day unless she told him what the new address would be.

I think Grandma did move during those years at least four or five times. She finally stopped and became stationary only because she had become ill and unable to oversee the moves. At this time, she went to live at Aunt Rena's home where she could be taken care of. Becoming almost an invalid through illness and old age, Grandma told Aunt Rena one morning that she knew her time was soon because she had seen a white owl sitting on the window. Aunt Rena shushed her replying that there were no white owls in the area and that surely it was just her mind. Each day, Grandma continued to report spying the white owl sitting on the windowsill as if it were waiting for her to die. A few days later, Aunt Rena found Grandma dead in her bed. She had passed on quietly in her sleep. We often wondered about that white owl and if Grandma had really seen it sitting and waiting in the window.

Grandma Ethel Clayton

After Grandma got older and she was no longer able to take care of herself, Grandma moved out to the home of Aunt Rena and Uncle Paul to live. Here she is shown in the kitchen reading her Sunday papers and enjoying her morning cup of coffee. Grandma Ethel never seemed to stop talking. It did not matter if she was alone or with someone, she was always talking about something. News events or something that happened fifty years ago, it did not matter, it was all mixed in together to become one story. Most of the time she just continued to talk and someone near her in the family would tell Grandma "yes or make some exclamation" and on Grandma would talk, of whatever matter she had thought of or what she knew about. We had become used to this and Grandma always seemed perfectly content. Oftentimes she had an interesting story of our family or a past happening. But most of the time we had no idea who she might be talking about. As she became bed bound and slept most of the time, her constant talking became quieter and quieter until soon she was mainly asleep. But, in her last few days she began to inquire about the white doves who were sitting on the window sill. We would look but never saw them. She always told us that the doves were angels who had come to take her to heaven. A nice thought for all of us.

Chapter 29

Election Day

Elections in Monett were always held in the Monett Public Library, across the street from our clock shop. When we first moved in and an election was held, Dad got the bright idea that it would be a good way to advertise his shop and services with clock and watch repair to the customers. To draw attention to his shop, Dad began to decorate the front of the building, all along the porch roof with small multicolored banners. Then Dad proceeded to walk over and talk to the voters as they came to vote. He would chat a few minutes and remind them of his shop across the street and wish them well in their voting. After the first few years, the election for mayor of our fine town came to be voted upon, and Dad took on further challenges regarding our shop and the forthcoming election day. He looked at the ballot and commented that V.B. Hall was the returning candidate for mayor and that no one else was on the ballot for the same position. He did not feel that was democratic, so he decided that he would run against Mayor V.B. Hall.

Now Mayor V.B. Hall was a special circumstance. He had started out his young life selling vegetables right off the back of a truck. As people began to know V.B. and to learn of his witty conversations and generally good disposition, they began to depend on him more and more for his produce and purchasing items from him. Working through the years, Mayor Hall had soon established himself as a fine aspiring gentleman in Monett with a staff and crew of many along with a staff of trucks that delivered and serviced various distributors of

267

vegetables and produce. He had become well-endowed in the business and a rich owner of a fleet of large delivery trucks. Along with all this, he had continued his fine, outgoing personality and proved to be a very popular community person among the Monett people. Thus, he had become Monett's mayor and was now up for reelection. After thinking the matter over, Dad had decided to take Mayor Hall on as a political opponent.

Come election day, and the election staff were busy setting up the little portable tent voting spots at the side of the public library and a table for registering and such. Dad had been up since daybreak, making his plans, after having delivered his regular newspaper route. First, Dad put out the colored banners all along the top of the overhanging porch roof. The banners made a colorful announcement to all passing. Something was going on of special interest at his clock shop at 508 Bond Street.

Then Dad carried out our old Victrola that he had hooked up to be played electrically. He then put the plug into a long extension cord that ran back into the house for electricity. Once this was accomplished, Dad pulled out his chosen records and began to play John Philip Sousa's selections from the marching bands. Now that certainly was a rousing round of music to be played. I was sitting on the front porch steps watching all of Dad's endeavors and work while wondering what the people across the street were thinking. The election polls were opened, and people began to appear to vote. All this time, there was Dad out in front, standing under the porch ceiling with many colored banners hanging down and surrounded by loud strains of Sousa's marching band playing all the favorites. It certainly made for a bright acoustical scene as people arrived to vote.

On the ballots, Dad had asked that his name be written in as a candidate for mayor also, running against the present mayor, V.B. Hall. Dad was pretty excited to see the printed ballots with his name present and was looking forward to a day of election proceedings. Of course, he wasn't just sitting in the front of the shop watching the voting people arriving to vote or leaving after having completed their voting ballot. Oh no, Dad had gassed up our powder-blue Cadillac and was driving around Monett and the outskirts to collect various friends and old cronies of his to come in and vote. Preferably to come in and vote for Dad so he would win and become the new mayor. Off Dad would drive in the Caddy, only to return soon with a man or woman, all of various ages and status. He would pull up and park in front of our clock shop and watch as the passengers descended from his car and walked across the street to cast their ballot. As I watched these people, chauffeured back and forth by Dad, I marveled that he knew so many people. Some were veterans of World War I or II. Some were just country folks who were living in various trailers, small homes and such. I did notice that often these people arriving in Dad's Caddy were a little unsteady on their feet, perhaps due to past addictions to alcohol or such. But I must admit, Dad had brought them to vote in a clean and sober appearance. And they were proud to be participating in the election with Dad. They all announced their endeavors and support of Dad as the mayor of Monett and would often loudly proclaim him to be the winner! Dad would just smile. Sometimes, these people came into the shop with Dad and sat for a small visit while passing around a pint bottle of whiskey or gin amongst themselves and chatting with Dad. Then Dad would usher them back out to the car and proceed to deliver them to their homes where he would then return to our home with more passengers to go and vote. And so the day would go with Dad driving back and forth with passengers to go vote, bright banners blowing in the wind from our porch roof, and Dad announcing the election across the street while asking for votes. Stirring stanzas of marching songs would be blaring from the old Victrola records with John Philip Souza. I can tell you, it was not a day to be easily forgotten. Most of the time I just stayed quietly out of the way and out of sight. I did not really want anyone to see me and recognize me as the daughter of Glenn E. Stone, candidate for mayor, or in any way connected to all these townspeople appearing at the election to vote, many with a long record of nonappearances at an election before. Today, I lack words to fully describe my many feelings during these election days! I know only that I would breathe a huge sigh of relief when all was complete, and Dad would take down the banners and carry in the old Victrola to be put away.

Sometime during all these proceedings of election day, Mayor V.B. Hall would always walk across the street and come into our shop to have a few words with Dad. Mayor Hall was a loud, boisterous man, and he would enter the shop with a loud "Hello, Stonie. How the hell are you?" Then Mayor Hall would offer Dad a cigar and tell him that it was a fine election day and that he was happy to see Dad adding his own contribution to the proceedings. He then wished Dad success in the election and left with an announcement, "May the best man win."

Dad would always answer with a loud, "Thanks, V.B. Thanks for coming by to say hello! Good luck to you, also, in your own election." Then he would remark to anyone listening, or not, that V.B. was a fine mayor and a good person. Adding a smile and a shrug of his shoulder, Dad would then continue to talk to the visiting friend or customer, take a swig of his pint of whiskey, and pass it around or just start puttering back with some broken clock. He seemed to just take it all in stride for the day. If he would have won, I am sure he would have been elated. But since he just seemed to have done all the electioneering and visiting for his own enjoyment, it really was not an interest to winning or not. It was just an electoral day that had been well met by himself and his friends.

Chapter 30

Under The Big Top

Early fall, school days were underway, and I felt once again, back in the path of everyday academic endeavors, how very much I liked the early fall days. A few weeks into school, Dad came from the shop back to the kitchen, and he was holding a newspaper. I was surprised at how excited he was to show Momma and me the page he was holding.

It seems that the page showed the itinerary of the coming Ringling Bros. and Barnum and Bailey Circus to Joplin, Missouri, that Saturday. At that time, the circus had begun to build several buildings across the United States where they could house the circus year round with no more costly traveling. It was becoming too costly to bring the circus to the people. From now on, the people would have to come to the circus. Dad said it would be the last time to see the old circus as it had been all these many years traveling by the railroad. He was excited and he announced to Momma and me that he planned to be there Friday morning at sunrise to see the circus move and set up for performances while there in Joplin.

Momma said she could not go to see the circus as she had to work. I had school that day, but Dad told Momma, "Susie can come with me. You can write a note to her teacher to excuse her that Friday and that she will make up the work. She will be seeing history in the making and enjoying the circus also." I could barely contain my excitement. I was going to the circus . . . at sunrise and watch it all unload. Although I

271

had to wait only two days until Friday morning when we would leave, it seemed forever. Thursday night, it took forever for me to fall asleep.

Friday morning, I was awake and dressed by 4:00 a.m., and that was the time Dad had said we were to leave. And so we did. I climbed into the backseat of the car, and off Dad and I went on our journey to Joplin to see the circus. I don't know who was more excited. He was like a kid again. I always thought that he would love to be employed with a circus and travel across the United States with it to see the states. Well, this time it was coming to us, and I was ready.

The drive was rather exciting and scary. Dad was driving fast and hitting the pint of whiskey already. He kept the bottle in the glove box in the car, but I could see him taking sips every once in a while. I knew it was going to be another interesting day. When we arrived in Joplin we drove on through and to the outskirts of town to an old field that belonged to some farmer. The circus had probably rented the adjoining acres of land also, and there they were unloading their supplies from the railroad cars and trucks. Despite being so early in the morning, and still dark, the day was busily beginning for the workmen as they readied the ropes, poles, and various tools they needed to put up the large center tent and the other tents for the sideshows and such. It was an enormous task. The circus manager had also hired many men from Joplin and the area to come and work for the day to help set up all the tents and such. It was a great chance for farmers and construction workers to get needed extra monies for working the day. Men of all sizes and age were arriving by car, by trucks, and by walking. They were anxious to begin their jobs and earn their monies.

When Dad and I drove in, he parked the car off to the side in some field and told me to get out and come with him. He then told me that he was going to go and meet with some gentlemen and would be gone for some time. He would be gone probably most of the morning, Dad told me. He then gave me one dollar in case I got thirsty or hungry and slipped his pint of whiskey out of the glove compartment in the car and into his jacket pocket in front. He then reminded me that I would be fine there watching the circus set up and that when he returned we would go see the circus. I laughed with glee and asked where we would sit. Dad replied, "It all depends on how I do at the poker gang. If I do well, we sit on the first floor and up front. If I lose a lot, we sit at the top." Without really understanding what he was talking about, I laughed and said that I hope he would win so we could sit downstairs and upfront.

Dad smiled and walked off to a group of men who were heading in the same direction. Standing there for a moment, I was surprised but then decided that I would just find a comfortable place to sit and watch the circus come to life with the many workmen. The circus workers had even brought over real live elephants to help lift the huge center poles and other heavy equipment. It was going to be an exciting morning as I looked around for a comfortable place to sit down and watch the proceedings. I felt perfectly safe, and I had a dollar in case I was hungry or thirsty. I settled down on an old tree stump and began to watch as the sun slowly rose over Joplin and the many perspiring gentlemen, eager at work.

I could have set there all day, just watching the work in setting up the center tent and the two surrounded sets. It was all interesting and busy with energy and action. But then I began to notice a pair of striped tents being set up on the side from the center tents. As I watched with interest, they also hung up several large signs that promised each person who could pay the grand entrance fee of one dollar that they would see the "freaks of the world"—the most famous freaks ever gathered under one large tent.

I was fascinated, mainly because I was not too sure what the word "freaks" meant—at least not in terms of what would cost one dollar to view. I walked over to view the posters they had placed around the tent entrance. There were pictures of a girl with no arms or legs. There was a picture of a midget that looked like a seal, half human and half seal. There was a woman with long hair all over her body pictured with an "alligator man." I was fascinated. I could not believe that these people were on view inside the tent. Also, I was not sure about how I felt to go in and stare at them. But then I thought it didn't really matter as I didn't have a dollar to spend. I would need my dollar later to buy some lunch or a soda.

While I was standing there reading the signs and looking at the pictures, a small group of people had begun to arrive and look around also. Out of nowhere, as if by magic, a gentleman in a suit and top hat appeared and began to set up a table and signs. Promising an act of magic and "magnification," the magician placed a small guillotine on the table and placed a carrot through the hold where normally a head would go for an instant "beheading." Announcing for all to watch, he pulled a lever and *wham*! The blade sliced downward and cut the carrot in half. The small audience gave some "hurrahs" and looked around, not really interested.

The magician asked then for an audience member to step forward to work some magic with him. No one stepped forward. The magician asked once again and then he looked at me and quickly invited me to step forward and help him with his magic act. Despite my several denials, he pulled me over and placed me behind the table, facing the guillotine on the table. He told me to place my finger into the slot where the blade could then fall and cut off my finger. I said, "No!" alarmed that he would even think of asking me to do such a thing. The audience laughed.

The magician laughed also, and with another promise of being safe, he placed my finger in the slot and readied the guillotine to fall, perhaps to cut off my finger. Believing in his "magic" and that it was all just a trick, but still a little worried, I shut my eyes and relented my finger to the magician. The guillotine blade fell swiftly and to my relief, no half of a finger fell on the table. He pulled out my hand and showed it to the audience. All five fingers were in place. I was relieved. Then he placed a carrot back into the guillotine and dropped the blade with the carrot top falling on the table. *Yikes*, I thought, *that was just too close to me*. I did not want to be the magician's assistant anymore. The audience began to wander off or to purchase tickets to see the coming "freak" show.

Then, the magician surprised me again. He asked me if I would like to go into the freak tents and see the "freaks." He further added that the tents were not open to the public yet, but I could go inside and maybe meet some of the noted "freaks." He asked about my parents. I told him that Dad was in a meeting with some men. The magician looked at me and smiled knowingly. And so, the magician finished his free show and promised more to see inside the tents when the show opened in thirty minutes. With that announcement and farewell, I helped him carry a few things behind the tent and then entered through a large flap into the advertised "freak" tent.

I had seen the posters outside of the tents announcing the "freaks" on display, but I was not ready for the sight that would greet me that special morning. Not really living in a society that the word "freak" was a customary word, I had not thought about such a matter or what a person would be that entailed calling him or her a "freak." It was not part of my vocabulary. And now, before me were all these special people walking around and doing normal things among themselves. They were all talking and laughing just like any other person I have known. But when I looked further, I realized they were not like "normal" people. There was a small man who looked like he was part-seal and a young girl who had no arms or legs. They were sitting and talking. There were more people in the tent, but just then, my attention was diverted by the arrival of the tallest, the largest man I had ever seen or imagined in my small-town life. My mouth dropped open with amazement as my eyes in my head traveled up, up, and up to his head where I stopped because the height hurt my head as I leaned back to stare at him. I was getting dizzy from looking up.

He smiled down at me and slowly walked over to this enormous chair made especially for him, and he sat down, gently as if each of his limbs did not really work together in one large package. He seemed to frown for a minute, and then he gathered his wits about him and leaned his head back on the back of the chair. He breathed a sigh of relief. I believe it was painful for him to walk or generate movement. Probably because he was so very large, it was too much for his body to support and move. Whatever the reason, he had a most kind smile, and he seemed to use it generously with the other people in the tent and with me. I slowly gathered enough courage to move closer to where he sat in the chair. I had read on the program that his name was Ted Evans and that he was nine feet tall. I wasn't sure about that matter, but I knew that he was enormously tall and big. Someone walked over with a box and sat it on the ground next to his chair. Then the person proceeded to open the box and hand one of the items up to Ted Evans. To my surprise, the item was a large silver ring. I could not believe what I saw next. To my amazement, Ted Evans took a large silver coin and placed it through the ring and then placed the ring on his finger. It fit. The ring was so big that a silver dollar slipped through it. I was amazed. With all my wishes, I wanted a ring like that to show the kids back at school. I could not believe how big his fingers were. Dad would enjoy seeing that ring also because he liked to look at jewelry. I drew a little closer to the giant to have a better look at the rings in the box.

They were for sale. Mr. Evans would slip a silver dollar through the ring and then place the ring on his finger to show that it fit him. Then he would sell the ring to a customer for one dollar. How I wished I had some money. I would certainly buy that ring. At that moment, it seemed as if the giant had actually heard me speak out loud in my absolute wish for one of those rings. Leaning down, he asked me to step over and look at one of the rings. I stepped near Mr. Evans and stood transfixed as he slipped the silver dollar through the ring and then placed it on his finger. I moved closer to look at the ring as he held out his hand for all to observe. Then to my transfixed surprise, the giant took off the ring and handed it to me asking if I would like to have it. I must have gasped or such because he gave a simple laugh and handed the prized ring to me. I took it in my hand and felt absolute amazement in how very large the ring was in my own hand.

I looked up in the giant's face and whispered a small, trembling voice, "Thank you!" He smiled and then turned to some other task he had with the person helping him.

With that, I felt like I had been dismissed, so I turned and walked a slight way from the seated giant and stood looking at the ring. Then I heard a small, wavering voice speak to me, "That was nice for Ted to give you the ring." I looked around for the voice speaking to me, and then I looked down, and there on the ground was a small kiddie pool with a small man lying on his back, floating in the water. Well, he was part of a small man, and the other part looked sort of like a seal or such. I was too afraid to stare or look too closely. I did not want to embarrass the man.

When he saw my discomfort, he laughed and said, "Come on over and say hello. I am used to people staring at me." I walked over and introduced myself to him, and he told me he was Charles Barent, or Sealo the seal boy. He was called this name by the audiences that came to look at him. He was the size of a midget and had arms that were not really arms but more like flippers. There was no shape to the arms; no elbow, hands, or fingers. And from his waist down, he had the body of a seal. I was afraid to look there. What kind of person was part-man and part-seal? He laughed his small tinny laugh and told me that really he was sort of playacting with the audience and wore a tailormade fish suit with a fish tail for the lower part of his body. Made him look more like a seal. Really, he assured me, he had legs, but the public liked to see Sealo the seal boy, so he complied. I smiled and pretended that I was comfortable with all that information, when really I thought I should walk over and sit down. It was all a little too much for me to take in so quickly. So I asked if I could kindly walk over and sit on the bench by the side. I was a little tired, I explained. Sealo smiled and said, "Of course," and then he proceeded to float a little more in the pool of water.

I sat down, holding my ring tightly in my hand and slowly raising my head to look around. That was when I saw a young girl sitting on a mound of pillows with a typewriter in front of her and boxes of pencils, pens, and notecards of some sort. I saw on the program that her name was Freda Pushnik, and she was not much older than me, probably seventeen or so. The program further explained why she was with the circus. She had been born without arms or legs. But to the amazement of her parents and doctors, she had disciplined herself to learn how to type, draw, and write with her mouth, holding a pen or pencil between her teeth. She could also type, at amazing speed, by placing a stick or such, the size of a pencil, in her mouth and hit the keys to write. She was amazing. I had to look at her work closer that she had had laid out around her pillows for all to look at. She had small notecards with envelopes packaged for sale and small drawings in frames also. I was amazed to see her delicate work and drawing in such careful detail. The notecards were just lovely. While I watched her, she began to type a letter on her typewriter, and the keys seemed to just fly under her guidance. Glancing up, Freda stopped her typing and smiled at me. She asked me my name, and I told her "Susie." She smiled again and asked me if I liked her notecards and drawings. I gushed all about how lovely her work was and beautiful her drawings were. I told her I wished I could be such an accomplished artist. She smiled and thanked me. Then to my amazement, she asked me if I would like a small package of four of her notecards that were for sale. I smiled and told her I had no money. But then, she really surprised me. She asked me to choose a set that I liked and to take it for my own. She felt sure I would appreciate her drawings and use the cards for friends. I was awestruck. Such absolute kindness was being shown to me by these people. Strangers I had never met and people whom I would not ordinarily meet in my hometown of Monett. I muttered something like, "I would love to have a package of your notecards." And then I leaned down to choose the package I wanted. When I stood back up, the young woman had already gone back to her typing, and her mind was on other matters. I stepped back and stood quietly with my two treasured items held tightly in my hands.

I felt like it was Christmas, and I had really been lucky this year with my new gifts.

Down further I saw the snake charmer with her snakes wrapped around her and in the boxes before her. I stayed far away from that area. I had no interest in any of those snakes, nor did I want to touch or hold any of them. After the kindness I had been shown by these other people, I was afraid the snake charmer might want me to join in on her act and hold some big snake or such. *No way*, I thought, as I shuddered with the mere thought of such a happening.

I could hear calliope music playing. To this day, the memory of the sounds of that huge calliope thrills me with the loud, energetic music it boomed out for all to hear. *What a happy sound*, I thought, smiling. Just then, the magician walked over to me and laughed when he saw the two items I was holding. He teased me that it seemed I had done pretty well for myself. I smiled and thanked him again for his kindness.

And then the magician told me there was a couple that I really should meet. They were Pricilla Bejano and Emmitt Bejano, the world's strangest married couple. You see Pricilla was called "monkey girl," and Emmitt was called "alligator skin man." Now I have to tell you, my mouth dropped open with this last piece of information. My head reeled—monkey girl and alligator skin man. Whoever heard of such a thing? *Not me*, I thought and shook my head and looked at the magician as if to say, "What?" Fred, the magician, laughed and said, "Come on over and I will introduce you to them."

We walked over the sawdust floor to a stage area where Pricilla and Emmitt were located. Emmitt, alligator skin man, was wearing just a pair of swimming trucks and was reclining back on a couch. He looked like a man all dressed up like an alligator. I could only stare at his skin and marvel at how scaly and dry it was. He was lying there with his eyes closed and seemed to be resting before the crowds began to arrive. Seated next to the couch was a woman wearing a white two-piece negligee. She was seated on a small stool in front of a dresser with a large mirror, and she was brushing her hair, on her head, and on her body and on her face. She had hair all over her body, like a monkey, and that was why she was called "monkey girl." And the magician assured me that they were married in real life. I stood staring before I realized my manners and said hello to the woman. She turned and looked at me and smiled back. She had a gentle smile, and her eyes lit up with humor.

The man and woman seemed very comfortable on the stage and being together. Later, I would read how many of these freaks, upon retirement, and the closing of freak shows, they all retired to two communities in Florida and made their homes there. Living in trailers mainly, and small homes, they would often hold festivals and invite tourists and visitors to come and look at them. During a documentary I watched recently, Pricilla spoke about her married life with Emmitt and how happy they were as a married couple. She was very sad that he had passed on and missed him very much. The person in the film asked her how she felt about people staring at her. She just laughed and replied, "Honey, if they pay me money, they can look at me all they want!"

Today they were in their middle ages and getting ready to meet the day's customers. I stepped back and asked the magician what time it was. I thought it was about time for the circus to begin. He replied that it was getting close to time, and perhaps I should head down to the large tent and wait for my father. As I began my walk back over the sawdust, I could see the sword swallower, Patricia Zerm, begin her act with large swords that she was putting down her throat. I walked a little faster with that sight and felt it truly was time for me to head on out to the circus. So I clutched my notecards and ring close to me and stepped outside of the large tent, faced the hot noontime sun, and began my walk over to the large center tent where the circus would be performing. I was really excited now to see the circus with all the clowns and animals.

As I neared the big tent, I saw Dad walking over to the entrance also. I was looking at him to see if he was happy or sad. He had told me that where we sat in the circus would all depend on how well he did in the game he was playing. Now I knew it was a card game, but I also knew he did not like to talk too much about it. So I hurried over to find out how the morning had proceeded for Dad.

As I got nearer to Dad, I could see that he was smiling. His gold teeth were shining in the sunlight; he was smiling so broadly and happily. I knew he had been a winner. So Dad called me over and said, "Come on, Susie. Today we are sitting right in front on the first level and enjoying the circus acts." And that was what we did. We walked into the large tent and went down to the very front rows and sat down. I couldn't believe my luck. I was right there where the clowns were and the animals walked by. There were prancing horses right next to my seat, and I knew elephants would be passing by later. I was so excited I could barely sit still. Dad never asked what I had been doing or what I had in my hands. He was too proud of his own accomplishments. But I was used to this matter and just enjoyed the present happenings with him, at the circus.

The circus matinee was too amazing to even describe. So much was happening. Three rings of performances were going on at all times. There were many animals and performers going and coming at the different entrances or exits. Music and color and beauty surrounded me. I felt as if I would explode with all that I was watching and listening to. All too soon, the matinee had ended, and the audience began their journey out of the tent to return home or to walk around the circus grounds. Dad wanted to head on back home now. He was feeling rather tired and needing to go home, eat a good meal, and take a nap. Personally, I think he was feeling a little too much of the whiskey he had been drinking all day from his flask and various other "sharings." I also felt a need for some good food and a long nap. I was just tired from all I had seen and enjoyed.

Walking back to the car, I was amazed to see a stand that was selling small lizards that one could wear on their shoulder. I stopped to look and asked Dad to wait for me. There they were. The man had small lizards in a box, and one could buy one for just fifty cents. The salesman announced that he would place a small chain and shackle on the lizard's leg so that you could pin him to your shirt or blouse. And then the salesman announced that as the lizards were chameleons, they would adapt to their environment and change their skin tones to match the color of your blouse or shirt. I was amazed. I couldn't believe my eyes. This little lizard would sit on my blouse and adapt to what I was wearing. I pictured the lizard sitting there all purple to match my favorite blouse. Wouldn't that be something to show the kids at school? It was too incredible to even think about. I had to have one to wear Monday to school. I would be so popular. Everyone would want to sit next to me and talk to me so they could look at my lizard on my shoulder. But I vowed to myself, they could not touch the lizard. Only I could touch the lizard.

I had to have one. I had to have the lizard to wear to school Monday. I felt as if my whole life depended on this one matter to make me popular, if only for a day. When I asked Dad for fifty cents to buy a lizard, he shook his head vehemently and told me that he would not pay money for some poor lizard to sit on my shoulder. He told me that it was cruelty to small creatures. But I didn't hear his words; I only knew that I had to have that lizard to wear to school. And then to my amazement, the manager said, "Look, I am going to give you this little lizard because I didn't sell too many, and I don't really want an overstock of them." And with that, he placed the small shackle and chain on the lizard's leg and pinned the chain to my blouse.

To my amazement, I had a lizard sitting on my shoulder. It was just sitting there and not moving. I didn't even notice, really, I was just too excited at the thought of wearing that little lizard to school Monday and having all the kids wanting to be my friend. So Dad walked on ahead of me, and I walked ever so slowly and gently back to the car parked in the backfield where we had left it that morning. I held my shoulder ever so stiff so as not to jar the lizard too much or further scare it. As we came to the car, I began to get into the backseat when the lizard fell off my shoulder and was just hanging from the shackle pinned to my blouse. It did not move at all.

I placed the lizard back on my shoulder, but it just fell off. I looked up at Dad, who was standing there watching the whole proceedings. He shook his head and told me that the lizard was probably dead. He reached over and unpinned the little thing from my blouse and examined it. "Yes," Dad told me. "The lizard is dead." Then he stepped over to a large clump of weeds growing near where we had parked the car, and he leaned down and placed the little dead lizard in the clump of weeds. "Poor little lizard. He probably never even got to see any grass or rocks in his short life. But now, he will be free to rest peacefully in this clump of weeds." And with those words, he walked over and got into the car to drive us back home. I hopped quickly into the backseat and covered my face with shame. I had been so involved with how I could be popular that I had forgotten that this was a small life involved in my own pettiness and popularity search. I had not even thought of the lizard and what it might think of being perched on my shoulder. Of course, it had been scared. It had no reason to want to make me a popular person. In fact, I thought, I had not even asked what it ate or if it had water. I just thought of it as a way to win popularity and friends. I was such a selfish person, I told myself.

I began to cry quietly and lay down on the backseat feeling huge waves of remorse for how I had killed that little lizard with my own selfishness. I heard Dad tell me "Susie, I know you feel bad, but that lizard was probably already dead or almost dead when it was pinned on your shoulder. The man had no kind thoughts for any of those lizards, and I am sure they are all dying quickly on him. Not a very clever way to make money, I would say." I agreed quietly with Dad. The thought didn't make me feel any better or to ease my conscience any, but it was food for thought in the future. I would try to be a better person and not think of pleasing the kids at school so I would be popular. I laughed—as if a lizard would make me be popular, I reasoned. It would take a lot more than a lizard to make me popular. But I was determined to never ever do such a heartless thing again to another live animal or lizard. Never ever again, I swore. That helped my sad conscience a little as Dad and I journeyed back home.

Chapter 31

Mary, Mary

That September, 1954, I was in junior high school, the seventh grade. It was pretty much like when I was in the sixth grade except we did not have recess, and we moved from class to class with different teachers. I was still shy and quiet with few friends. Definitely not Miss Personality. One Friday evening, during the first or second week of September, Dad arrived home from driving his bus route with a girl who was near my age, or a year or so older. I was in the backyard with my dog, Mr. Big Man, when they arrived, and he walked her back to where I stood. Dad introduced the young Indian girl to me as Mary and told me she was spending the weekend with us. I was sure surprised. Dad had never mentioned anyone that he knew on the route, and I had never met her when I visited the Indian Reservation near Oklahoma City, as I traveled with Dad on his bus routes. I stood staring at Mary in surprise as Dad turned and walked back inside. Mary smiled and knelt to pet Mr. Big Man.

She was a young Indian girl, with shiny black hair that she wore cut short. Her skin was dark brown, and she had a most beautiful smile with bright white teeth. She was dressed much like me in a summer blouse and skirt. We stood for a few minutes laughing at Mr. Big Man and making small talk. I discovered that she was two years older than me, around thirteen or fourteen, and was presently in the seventh grade, the same as me because she had not passed a couple of grades because of lack of attendance. She made no bones about telling me how she really

283

did not like school nor homework or any part of going to school. We walked inside to my room, and I showed her my books. I was presently reading Charles Dickens's *Tale of Two Cities*. I could barely put the book down. Momma came in and told us to wash our hands for dinner, and she said hello to Mary. We had an extra bedroom next to mine where Mary could spend the night. We then went in to eat dinner. Dad did not join us. He sat up in the shop and worked on a clock or watch and came back later to piece on chicken and potatoes from dinner, as he usually did each mealtime. Mary didn't seem to think that was unusual. I asked her if she would like to watch television as I had cleared up the dinner dishes, but she was not really interested in any of the programs showing that night.

We went outside and walked around the block with Mr. Big Man and talked a little about life. Mary lived on the reservation in Oklahoma City. I don't remember what tribe she was from. Maybe Mary had not told me. It seemed that she had a boyfriend and was very serious about him but could not see him much as he was in jail for robbery of some sort. That rather alarmed me. First of all, to have a boyfriend who was older, and then especially one who was in jail for robbery. But Mary didn't seem worried, so I didn't say anything about it either.

We went to bed early. Mary turned off her light and fell asleep immediately. I sat and read my book for a while. I couldn't wait to read all of it and then start on more of Dickens's writings. His characters were fascinating to me.

That morning, Mary and I awoke early, ate some toast, and dressed. Momma was going shopping at the store to get some food for the week. So we decided to accompany Momma and help her with the shopping and carrying of the bags. Mary seemed to enjoy walking through the stores and looking around. That afternoon, I took Mary to our local theater, and we watched a matinee showing of a Western. She enjoyed the movie and cartoons. The day dragged on, and I tried to find a way to entertain Mary as she seemed so disinterested in visiting with us or anything that I was interested in. After a quick supper, Mary and I walked back down to the theater and watched the evening movie. Sunday morning, we slept late and took a few walks and watched a few programs on television. It seemed the hours were dragging along. Then that afternoon, Mary and I were in the backyard sitting and talking when I suggested we become pen pals and write to each other. Mary had no interest in this matter, so we dropped that idea. Then I told Mary that if we did not write to each other, we could remember each other by becoming "blood sisters." Now Mary liked that idea. So I went inside and got one of Momma's sewing needles and pricked my finger to push out a little blood. Mary took the needle and did the same. We then said a few gibberish words as if we knew what Indians would recite and smushed our two fingertips together to try to get our blood transferred to each other. Pretending success or such, we then professed ourselves to be "blood sisters" and would always remember this day. It seemed to have cheered Mary up somewhat, so she was a little more talkative.

Monday morning, bright and early, Mary left with Dad on his bus route to return to her home on the reservation. As to where exactly she lived, I never knew. If she had parents or any family, I never knew. I only knew she had an older boyfriend who was in jail. She really was not very talkative and did not want to share any information of her life with me, nor was she interested in my life. When Dad returned that evening, he never said anything about Mary, and I never heard any further about her. To this day, I still am not sure why Mary came to visit us that weekend. I had gained a "blood sister."

School days were now becoming a little more busy with harder homework and more reading of textbooks. As for the students, I found that boys were even more silly and rude with their hormones literally bouncing off the walls. They just did not seem to know what to do with themselves. Girls were all serious with combing their hair and choosing the clothes they wore. I was not interested in any of that. I had no special boy that I liked. I enjoyed my teachers in the classes and worked hard on my assignments. I was disgusted by how the boys acted when they were around the girls. I tried my best to just ignore everyone, boys and girls alike. But the boys had come to knowledge about "monthly periods" and just could not keep their mouths shut about this happening. They were always speculating as to which girl had their "monthly visitor" as we used to say. And they loved to walk up to you as you passed by a class in the hallway and whisper a word or so in your ear. The word they loved to whisper in your ear was "Kotex." Honestly. Can you imagine anything more silly that a boy walking by you and leaning down to whisper "Kotex" in your ear. It was all so embarrassing. It would make me blush and get all nervous; thus, the boys liked to tease me even more.

I remember that in Miss Jones's history class, this one boy named Brock or such sat behind me and was always talking to me, often getting me in trouble with the teacher. This one time, he asked me if I would like to hear a "dirty" joke. I primly told him no and that I did not listen to those jokes. But he leaned up and told me the joke quickly anyway. "What did the vegetables say in the garden patch? Let us turn up and pea." And then he just laughed and laughed as if it was really funny. I was embarrassed that he had said the word "pea" to me as it really would be "pee" to make the joke funny. I was not used to a boy saying those words to me. I got so mad that I turned around and would not further talk to him. He kept telling me he was sorry and would not tell me any more jokes, but I was too embarrassed. A few weeks later, he moved with his family to another town, and I was no longer bothered by him or his "funny" jokes.

Ironically, years later, my senior year at college, during my last semester, I was attending the recently designed "new math" class for elementary grades. It had just been "created," and all schools were going to be teaching this style of math to grades 1–6. I had to pass the class to get my teacher's certificate. I was hopeless. First of all, I was poor in math and now this new math thrown at me, and I just could not get the gist of it. Every day after class, I would go to the teacher's office and sit in his office and cry about how I was going to fail, and my whole life would be ruined because I would not be able to be a teacher. Funny thing, joining me in my misery was another young lady who was in the same situation as me. She was desperate also to learn the new math so she could graduate and get her certificate. So each day after class, the two of us would sit in the professor's class and cry because we were not going to graduate. The poor professor. I know he truly got tired of seeing us in his office each day after class and was going to pass us just to get us away from him. But he kept persevering with us, and amazingly we passed the class and were all set to graduate and get our teacher's certificate. Graduation day came, and after the ceremony, I saw the gal who had been my fellow math partner in the new math, and I went over to say hello and wish her well. As we were talking, she told me she was getting married in a few weeks and turned to introduce me to her fiancé. I turned, and to my amazement, there stood the boy who had sat behind me in history class and told me the vegetable joke. I looked at him, and we both recognized each other and began laughing. I told the girl she must not marry this young man as he had told me a "dirty joke" in the seventh grade. They both laughed and assured me he had grown into a fine gentleman, and he promised no more rude jokes with ladies present. I laughed. Always seems to be a small world.

Ride 'em Cowboy

As I had said, I loved to travel with Dad in the summer on his daily bus route to Oklahoma City, Oklahoma. Oftentimes Dad would make a stop at one of the Indian reservations and we would walk around and talk to some of the natives and I would admire the jewelry they were selling. At one time I had some lovely beaded jewelry pieces made by the Indians to sell. On this day, one of the tribesman had a stuffed horse you could get on for a picture. So, Dad dressed me in chaps and his Stetson and up I climbed on that poor, dead, stuffed horse for my picture. Yahoo! I loved it.

Riding a Longhorn Steer

Along with the horse riding, I also posed atop this long horn steer. When my husband, Arthur, saw this picture he thought I had really ridden the steer! Hah!! Anyway, it was a fun day posing on the horse and steer and made for great fun to show at school. It was sad to visit the reservations as they were so dusty and poor - but all the tribes people were very nice and I enjoyed getting to know them.

Susie - Freshman High School

Betty, my cousin, took this picture of me on a lazy Sunday afternoon. We were outside in the parking lot across the street from our house.

Rena was probably in the kitchen visiting with Momma. We had Janice with us and she is seen walking back up to us from down the street. I had my long hair back and loved to wear it in a ponytail.

Betty was a couple years older than me but she would always come and have lunch with me at school. We liked to go over to the Cub's Den and listen to the juke box and the popular music.

At that time, Tennessee Ernie Ford had the popular tune "Sixteen Tons" - we loved to go to the Cub's Den and sit during our lunch hour. We usually bought a soda and french fries to share. We didn't have much money to spend.

Chapter 32

I'm Called Little Buttercup

During these years, my family consisted of Momma, Dad, and me. Betty, my sister, and Glenn, my brother, had moved on to Joplin where they had started their own married lives and homes. I often wished that I had someone who lived with us whom I could talk with and share my interests. Priscilla was older now and more involved in high school projects. I could understand that. She didn't want to listen to me when she could be sewing on her new clothes or listening to music and, usually, talking on the phone to her friends. So even though I missed Priscilla, I understood. Then a surprising thing happened. Rena, my mother's sister, who had been ill with tuberculosis years earlier when she lived in California and had been judged well, had become ill again. She had returned to Cassville to live with my grandparents Clayton, her parents, on their farm along with her daughter, Betty, and son Maureece. Newly divorced, Rena was trying to get her life back together and thus, was staying with her parents for the time being while she worked and supported her children Betty and Maureece. Now Rena was ill again with tuberculosis and was going have to be admitted into the TB sanatorium in Mt. Vernon. She was leaving for the sanatorium almost immediately because she was so ill. Grandma and Grandpa Clayton felt they could not take care of Betty and Maureece because of their own old age, so it was decided the two would come live with us. We had an extra bedroom next to my bedroom for Betty, and Maureece could stay in the single-bedroom apartment upstairs for the time being. It was all quite an adjustment. Suddenly we had two more people in the house and the

291

worry of how Rena was doing in the sanatorium. It seemed that she was very ill and was going to require surgery and lots of sunshine and rest for some undetermined time. I was sorry about Rena but excited because now I had gained friends to be with at home and to share interests and to talk to. I knew Betty and Maureece weren't too happy about the move. They had to leave their school friends and start a new school and make new friends. Also, of course, they were worried about their mother, Rena.

So Momma and I packed up their clothes and some personal items they wanted and moved them both into our home. Then Momma took them to the high school and registered them to start their high school education in Monett.

This additional family of Betty and Maureece proved to be a financial burden on my parents because it took more monies to raise two more people. Rena had no money as she was sick and unable to work. So we all kind of tightened our belt buckles and decided to do the best we could. Momma knew how to cook good nourishing food with a small amount of money cost, so we faced the new dilemma and worked to make it comfortable for Betty and Maureece. We also assured Rena that it was all just fine and that her problem now was just to get well so she could come back and be with her family.

Betty was several years older than me, and Maureece was three years older. But to tell you the truth, we all seemed to be the same age. We had the same interests in movies, music, and reading. We knew each other from the years I visited my grandparents' farm and they had lived there. We became avid card players; fish, old maid, gin rummy—we could play cards all night on a Saturday. We laughed and talked and were very competitive in the card games. It all became a lot of fun for me. I had someone to laugh and talk with. Although Betty was older than me, she acted the same age as me, so we were almost like twin sisters, talking and laughing about the same things. We also loved comedy shows on television and would act funny skits out after we had seen the show. We loved the *Sid Caesar Show* and would go on and on for hours about some funny scene or joke they had done on the show. We never tired of playacting. We also loved to perform together in music and singing. Often we would go into the spare room where my upright piano was located and sit and listen to the old electric Victrola Dad had fashioned into a 75 rpm record player. We had used 75s that had belonged to my sister, and we would play them for hours and listen to the songs of that

Maureece and Betty Come to Live With Us

When I was in the eighth grade and Betty and Maureece were just starting their freshman year in high school, Aunt Rena became very ill with tuberculosis and had to go to the sanitorium in Mt. Vernon, Missouri to live where she could get treatment to get well. As a result, Maureece and Betty came to live with us. Grandma and Grandpa were too old. They couldn't take care of them any more on the farm. So, they came to live with us. I loved having their company. Betty would always walk with me to and from school and we would meet for lunch in the Cub's Den during the week. I loved having the company. On weekends we enjoyed playing cards and various games together. Once a month, Momma would drive us up to Mt. Vernon to visit Aunt Rena on a Sunday. In this picture, Betty and Maureece are in our backyard with a neighborhood dog and my Pluto, a beagle.

time. Also, Betty or I would play the piano while we took turns performing. We loved to sing songs from Gilbert and Sullivan. My favorite was always "I'm Called Little Buttercup." That first summer, we decided to perform for the neighbors and put on an evening show in our backyard. But when Dad found out about that, he put a damper on that idea. He didn't want the neighbors to think we were looking for handouts by asking them for admission monies. We were angry about that and felt it was unfair of Dad to not let us perform for the neighbors. Actually, later, I was kind of glad we did not get to perform because it would have taken a lot of work to get ready to put on a show, and we had not been prepared to invite people to watch us. It was like in the movies where someone shouts, "Let's put on a play" and it all magically happens. Well, in real life, it doesn't just happen. It takes a lot of hard work to make a show happen if you want to make a good appearance.

For a while, Maureece played and talked with us, but as he was older and had begun to make some friends at school, he soon lost interest in time spent with the two of us and began to run around with his friends at school.

On school days, Betty would come find me during lunch hour at school, and we would walk over to the Cub's Den, next to the Monett High School. We loved to go in there and eat our lunch and listen to the jukebox music. It got really busy in there at lunch with lots of cheeseburgers and fries being eaten with cokes and malts to drink. Betty and I didn't ever really have much money, so we would often just go in and drink a Coke and listen to the music. Mr. Fly made the best cheeseburgers ever, and it was a popular hangout for the students. It was the place to be at that time in our life.

Rock and roll was beginning to roll, so to speak. We had heard the Big Bopper and loved "Chantilly Lace." When you heard the music, you just wanted to jump up and dance all over the floor. It was a new feeling that all of us kids had, despite the angry looks from parents and adults nearby. Our local radio station, KRMO, with Mr. Stewart, had Saturday hours where he took requests for the new rock and roll songs and Betty, Maureece, and I were avid fans. We would gather in the kitchen around the old radio sitting on top of the refrigerator and dance around the floor when Mr. Stewart played the new songs. Dad would often come back and holler at us to turn down the radio because the music was going to drive him crazy or deaf, or maybe both! Or at least we were going to go deaf listening to the music so loud. We would turn down the music on the radio for as long as we could stand it, and then soon the sound would creep back up to a high level. Meanwhile, we were jumping and dancing all around the kitchen. We often called in requests also. We loved "Rock Around the Clock." Feeling silly, we named ourselves Fish Net, Hair Net, and Aqua Net and would call in to request a song and tell Mr. Stewart our names and request. He would laugh at our silly names and play our requests. It was a lot of fun and excitement to us. There was a rebirth happening in music, and it was thrilling to be a part of it. I laugh now at how the adults would say, "This music will never last." Well, listen to the radio today; those songs are still playing, and the kids are still rocking and rolling to the music. Of course, some of those "kids" are in their sixties and seventies today, but they are still rocking and rolling.

As I had said earlier, Betty was a few years older than me, but she acted my age and was perfectly comfortable doing projects that interested me. Even at this age, Betty was never interested in boys our age. She would just make a face and tell me that she didn't really want a boyfriend. Although she was crazy about some movie stars that we both liked, Jacques Sernas was her favorite. He was a young actor in the *Helen of Troy* movie that we had seen in the movie theater. Betty went absolutely gaga over that man. She would buy every theater magazine that had picture or quotes about him. If he appeared on television on a talk show, Betty was there in front of the screen screaming and falling around on the floor. I couldn't believe how crazy she was for this actor. We didn't have too many opportunities to see Sernas on television or in the movies as his career never really shot to stardom. But Betty remained faithful to him for many years and swore he was her only love.

Dad and Maureece made fun of Betty's shyness around men. Dad often called her Olive Oyl—Popeye's girlfriend. When the Popeye cartoons came on television Saturday morning, he would call out for Betty to come on in and watch her twin sister. He thought it was really funny to call her Olive Oyl and make fun of her shyness. Betty was a good egg and put up with his teasing. She would just smile and pretend not to hear any of his teasings. I know that some of it must have hurt her, but she never let on that it did. Even though a few of the boys her age teased her, she just smiled and let it pass. Soon, all tired of the joke and forgot all about it. That was much easier for Betty. Sometimes, though, I did have to admit that Betty's actions were a lot like those of Olive Oyl. If she was walking in a corridor and a boy passed near her, she would press tight against the walls and wait until he passed. She preferred no contact with boys at all. Later, she was just called an old maid, and everyone seemed to have just settled the image on her. She kept it in her heart and never really said anything. Sometimes she even admitted she was an old maid and happy to be that way. But for now, she was busy being my friend and our growing up in Monett.

One very nice thing with Betty moving in to live with us was that she helped me on laundry day. Today women think they worked hard when they throw a load of clothes into the washer and then the dryer. Believe me, I grew up when things were much harder than that. When I was a small child, Momma would wash our clothes on the back porch while I sat on the rug or blanket and played. She had a large galvanized tub filled with water, a washboard, and a large bar of lye soap that she made herself. She would sit and scrub each piece of laundry on the washboard, wring it dry, and then walk downstairs to hang the clothes on the clothesline. In the wintertime, she hung the clothes on lines on the back porch and placed newspapers on the floor to catch the dripping water. All in all, it was a backbreaking project and took a lot of energy and time. Later, when we moved to the home Dad bought, we purchased a used wringer washer and had an electric socket in the wall in the kitchen. When laundry day arrived, every two weeks, we rolled the old wringer washer from the corner of the kitchen to a place by the kitchen door where the electric outlet was located. The hose to release the used water and soap was placed outside through the open screen and door to pour the waters out into the alley. You could always know it was laundry day at our home because the alley had soapy water running down the middle of the lane. Of course, one had to stand and run the clothes through the wringer, place the clothes into a waiting basket, and then run it outside to hang on the outside lines. In the wintertime, we hung the clothes on the lines in the spare room with newspapers on the floor to catch the dripping water. Sometimes, if you diverted your attention from the wringer washer while it was jostling around the clothes in its basket filled with soap and water, the machine on wheels would start a merry jig bouncing across the kitchen linoleum floor until it pulled the electric cord loose from the wall socket. It was a tough machine to handle and battle the laundry, soapy water, and actions. Laundry day was a full-day procedure. Momma was usually at work at the cleaners, so Betty and I did the laundry.

After we finished the laundry load, we cleaned up the machine and rolled it back to its corner in the kitchen. By late afternoon, we went outside to gather the newly washed clothes, fold them, and place them into laundry baskets to bring inside. Since Momma worked at the local cleaners, she steam-cleaned and ironed all Dad's clothes: shirts, pants, and jackets. The folded clothes brought inside from clothes lines were then set in the spare room to await ironing the next day. Should Betty and I not be able to iron the next day, the clothes had water sprinkled on them and rolled to await in the basket. No matter what plans, ironing needed to take place within the next day or so. The wrinkles became set in the laundry and made a harder ironing job if you did not. Of course, we had to iron every piece of laundry that had been washed. Momma liked the soft, unwrinkled look from an ironed piece. So we took turns all day or more ironing sheet sets, towels, handkerchiefs, our clothes—just everything! It was a tiring process. I can still see the old iron, the ironing board, and the Dr. Pepper glass bottle with the sprinkler piece attached in the mouth of the bottle. As we ironed, we sprinkled water on the object to help soothe out the wrinkles. I can tell you, I learned to be an excellent ironer from this weekly function. But let me tell you, I still cringe at the thought of having to go back to this procedure of doing laundry.

Years, later, around 1960 or 1961, I was home from college, and Momma told me she had something exciting to show me. She told me to hop into the car, and we would drive across the town for me to see the new addition to Monett. I could not imagine what Momma was so excited about. We drove for a few minutes and then turned to pull up and park on a graveled area. There in front of me was a small white one-level building, with a large sign in front reading "Coin Operated Laundromat." Momma and I got out of the car to go inside so she could show me her newly found joy. She could not get over the coin-operated washing machines and driers and how they made her life so much easier. She had even brought a load of my laundry I had brought home from college to wash. She then proceeded to place the clothes in the washing machine and added the coins necessary to start the washing procedure. Then we walked over and sat down in the chairs by the wall and watched the clothes bounce around in the machines. She was so happy with this new addition to Monett and so excited to have access to these miracle machines for the laundry. I had to laugh with Momma as we remembered earlier years of all the work it had taken to complete one load of laundry, and now we sat and watched it all happen. No lifting and carrying. Just sitting in the chair and awaiting the procedure to complete. It was a simple yet touching moment.

Returning to when Betty and Maureece were living with us, and I was in eighth or ninth grade, after a year or so, Rena began to improve in her health, and we could now go visit her in her room, in the lobby, and outside. Once or twice a month, Momma would pack a Sunday lunch, and off we would drive to Mt. Vernon—Momma, Betty, Maureece, and me—to visit with Aunt Rena. She was always so happy to see us come visit, and as she felt better, she would make us gifts in her craft classes. We enjoyed receiving the gifts she made. She loved having Momma's good fried chicken and salad with cake. It was good to see her with an appetite and eating food with energy. It made Betty and Maureece more hopeful that Rena would be coming home to stay someday.

One time, during a visit, Betty, Maureece, and I were asked to go to the car and get something to bring in for Aunt Rena. We thought it would be fun to have a race through the building and see who could beat the others out to the car. Rena's room was on the third floor, so Betty and I took separate elevators to return to lower level to race to the car. Maureece took the stairs. Somehow I pushed a wrong button and when the door opened, and I walked out, I realized, too late, that I had gone to the basement level, and I was in the morgue. Standing right there, in the darkened room, in the morgue where I could see covered bodies on the metal carts, I got so scared I could not even think of how to get out of the room and back to the elevators and up to the lobby and light. It was so dark and cold in that room. I was so afraid to even make one tiny noise for fear one of the covered bodies would suddenly sit up. I slowly walked out of the room backward and ran as fast as I could to the elevator and zoomed up to the third floor. I rushed out of the elevator and went running into the room and almost collapsed on the floor. I scared Momma and Aunt Rena. I scared myself. Of course, Betty and Maureece thought it was very funny about me getting lost in the morgue and teased me for days about the incident. It was not funny for me and left me with some nightmares. From then on, when we went to the sanatorium, I stayed with Momma and Aunt Rena. I was not leaving that floor alone.

Chapter 33

Tantrum For Two

Around this time, Betty got the wish of her lifetime. The manager at our local theater, Gillioz, gave Betty a job in the box office. At first, she only worked a few days a week, but as she got more experience there, she received more work hours. She was so happy. This was where she loved to be. Every evening she would get cleaned up and walk down to the theater and go into the small box office and start the evening's preparedness to sell tickets to the attending patrons. She took her job very seriously and would not even let me in for free. But I did only have to pay one dime as a member of my family was working in the theater. Betty also started smoking. Rena did not know or she would have thrown a fit and washed Betty's mouth out with soap as she would do when she was disciplining Betty. So Betty kept it hidden as best as she could. I knew but I did not tell anyone. How she did love to smoke. It was one cigarette right after another. She loved to just sit and read or listen to music and smoke her cigarettes. The ashtray would fill up to a large heap of butts and ashes before she would empty it and clean it. Of course, she had to hide that also from Momma, who would have told Aunt Rena on Betty.

Then, because Betty was such a hard worker at the Gillioz Theater, the manager asked her to also work on the books on the weekends. This was great for Betty. She would sit in the theater's office on the second floor, next to the projector room, and work on the books, smoking and drinking a Dr. Pepper. Betty had found her niche in life. She hoped to get more hours to work and planned to work there when she graduated from high school in a couple of years.

Meanwhile, Aunt Rena's health improved and was soon able to come back home. That was a great occasion. We were glad to see her well and back home. For the time being, Rena moved into the two-bedroom furnished apartment we had upstairs. Betty joined her, and Maureece stayed in the single room he had. It was great to have them all with us. At first, Rena was frail and had to take it easy. That was fine with Momma and Dad. They let her live upstairs and just relax and get rest so she could be well again. Maureece was not happy in school and wanted to leave and join the air force. He said he could complete his degree there and even get more education through the air force. Rena was upset and forbid Maureece to sign up. But as soon as he turned eighteen, he packed up and slipped away during the night and joined. He did not graduate from high school but was soon in active duty and traveling around the world. He loved it. Actually, he became a lifer in the air force and retired with his high school education complete and added a master's degree. Years later, he was married and raised a family. After retirement, when he came back to the area to live, he loved to tell stories about all the places he had traveled to and people he had met. It turned out to be a good decision for Maureece.

Betty had now graduated from high school and was working full-time at the theater in the box office and the office. She was handling the books, payroll, and ordering supplies. She loved her work and so enjoyed the staff she worked with. At this time, Betty had definitely found her niche.

Rena had more strength and was working in a diner as a waitress. That was where she met Paul, who was in town working with the telephone company. They married and moved to a house in Monett, and their daughter Janice was born. Betty lived at their newly settled home also. So when baby Janice arrived, Betty was thrilled to no end. She loved that little baby from the instant she saw her and every living moment she was not at work at the theater she was with Janice. As for me, well, I wasn't used to babies and didn't really know what to do with them. I was not one to goo-goo and giggle over the babies. Don't get me wrong, Janice was as cute as could be; it was just that I was not at the age or mind that I particularly wanted to spend time with her. I just watched from a distance. But one time, when Janice was older, a little over a year, Momma and I were at Rena's house for a visit, and I was told to take Janice upstairs to play with her in her room. So I went upstairs with her not really too enthusiastic or interested in the babysitting spot. I sat and watched Janice play with her dolls and such and even read a story to her, but Janice was bored. She wanted to go back downstairs and be with her mama. I told her no because Momma and Aunt Rena were talking. I told Janice that we were to stay upstairs. That was when Janice went into action. She had lately started this temper tantrum stuff where she would get real stiff and hold her breath until she got her way. Because she was so serious in this tantrum behavior and scared anyone with her that she was going to stop breathing, Janice usually got her way. Everyone gave in to her because they were afraid of what might happen to her.

Well, sure enough, when I said no to Janice, she began her little temper tantrum and threw herself down on the floor and proceeded to stiffen her body. She was amazing to watch; she lay there like a wooden child, all stiff, arms and legs stiff and straight with her eyes and mouth tightly shut. And thus, she lay there waiting for me to give in to her demand and take her downstairs to her mama. Well, this action by Janice caused great panic in my mind and body, and I didn't know what to do. I was afraid she was going to die on me, and that would be awful. The only thing I could think to do was to pick her up and carry her down to Aunt Rena for her to make her start breathing again. With that in mind, I lifted Janice up in my arms, and holding her very stiff body carefully in my arms, I began the short trip down the stairs, walking very slowly and softly because I was so afraid I would drop her. Halfway down the stairs, as Janice was hard to carry in the stiff position and my arms had grown tired, I dropped Janice. To my horror, I watched Janice roll down the few remaining stairs and then lie there on the floor, not moving or acting as if she was going to move.

I stood there in absolute terrified terror looking at the mute body of Janice there on the floor and was absolutely sure I had killed this small child. I admitted I didn't want to have much to do with her at the time, but I did not want to kill her. I didn't know what to do. I kept waiting for Janice to move, but if she wasn't dead, I must have knocked the wind out of her because she did not seem to be breathing. Wanting to get to the kitchen and to Momma and Aunt Rena, I grabbed up Janice and began to run toward the room where I heard them talking. As I was bouncing in my running, I seemed to have brought Janice back to breathing and awareness of the world and where she was. Janice came to and looked into my face. I was so relieved that she was alive, and I stopped moving and set her down on her own feet. Janice was just staring at me in disbelief. Then I realized, Janice thought I had thrown her down the stairs on purpose. She actually thought I had planned to throw her down the stairs to make her stop her temper tantrums.

Looking into her little face, I had to chuckle for a moment, and then I leaned down and whispered to her. I said, "Janice, if you ever do a tantrum on me again like you just did, I shall throw you down the stairs again. Do you understand me?" Janice nodded, and then I took her hand, and we walked into the kitchen to Momma and Aunt Rena. Janice ran over to Aunt Rena and stood by her chair. As far as I ever knew, Janice never told anyone that I had thrown her down the stairs, but I have to tell you, she never did one of those temper tantrums again. Aunt Rena would often ask me what did I do to Janice that made her suddenly begin to behave.

Of course, today I know that Janice should have been checked by the doctor. This was just in case she had been injured from her rolling down the few stairs. I should have told Aunt Rena or Momma about Janice's fall. But I was afraid to tell them in case they would believe that I did it on purpose. And Janice seemed fine with no bleeding or crying. So I figured all was well and just let it be. I will say, for years, Janice would always keep me in the corner of her eye, just in case I should run over and carry her up the stairs to throw her back down. She was a little wary of me.

Time had now brought me to the point where I had stumbled through junior high school and would be beginning my freshman year at high school the next year. But before that happened, in the fall of 1955, Dad decided he wanted to travel to Arizona. Just pack a suitcase and get in the car and drive to Arizona and spend a week or so there. Momma looked at Dad and just gave a small laugh. First, she explained, they had no money for such a trip. Gas, food, and lodging would cost too much, and there just wasn't any extra monies for such a thing. She added that we barely paid our gas and electric bills now as it was.

Monett High School

My old alma mater, Monett High School. I really loved that building. I didn't care much about my teachers nor my classes. I was not much in ways of popularity and not well known; but, I loved attending this school. Doesn't make much sense but that was the way it was. Mr. and Mrs. Tinklepaugh were probably my favorite teachers. Of course, Miss Jones was a teacher I highly regarded in history. Years after graduation and I was a teacher I came back to visit Miss Jones and tell her how much I had learned from her in regards to style of teaching, discipline, and regard of students. The lowest rating teacher on my scale was an English teacher who only had ears for our High School cheerleaders and football players. All the rest might as well not be in her classroom. I always wanted to tell her this fact but decided it was her own business. Most of all I remember and add my high regard for Jim Richardson for our Art teacher. He was a friend (he dated my sister Betty) but mainly he was a teacher who acknowledged all students, talented or not. He always offered leadership, confidence and friendship to all students he had in classes all the years he taught in Monett.

Chapter 34

Arizona Bound

Dad did not listen. He was going to go to Arizona, no matter what. Later, we learned that he was going with another couple and his own new girlfriend. So that would explain why he was so adamant about the trip and didn't care if there was money or not. He wanted to be the big shot and impress his new girlfriend and drinking buddies. So that Thursday afternoon, Dad went into the bedroom and got the old suitcase and began to pack his things for the trip. I was so mad about the whole matter that I went into the spare room next to their bedroom and began to play a song on the piano. Playing the piano, I accompanied the music as I sung as loud as I could "So Long It's Been Nice to Know You." Playing it over and over, I hoped to get it known to Dad how I felt about the whole matter. Momma sat and cried and asked me why I had to always stir things up more. I was too mad about the whole situation. I knew we did not have the monies for this trip, and I was furious that Dad was seeing this woman. I didn't know her but had only heard about her. You know how small towns are: they love to talk about someone else's problems.

Dad packed up that week in September and took off with our checkbook in hand. I made sure he could hear me playing the piano and singing the same song as he drove off. Then I stopped playing and sat down and cried. I was worried as Momma was about what we were going to do with Dad gone and no one to drive the bus route or work in the front shop repairing the clocks and watches. Dad had told us he would be gone four weeks or so, and that was a long time. Sure enough, a few days later after Dad left, he began writing checks to cover monies he needed on the trip, and they were arriving at our bank with no funds to back them. I was furious. We had no monies, and Dad was out joyriding and living high, leaving us to pay the bills. I begged Momma not to go to the bank and cover the checks. I begged her to let Dad be arrested for writing hot checks—that would teach him a lesson. But Momma would not let this happen. She didn't want Dad to go to jail, so she would gather enough monies to just pay off the checks as they arrived. That left us with no money to pay on the bills that came in each month or to buy groceries.

When our gas was shut off that week because we could not pay the bill, I went to Betty at the Gillioz Theater and begged her to help me get a job in the theater so we could get some extra monies to pay the bills. I met with the manager and explained the situation, and he hired me to work in the concession stand a few nights a week. As long as I worked seven in the evening and was home by ten, I could work there. Also, Momma gave her approval, and my school grades were satisfactory. The job didn't give Momma and me a lot of extra monies, but it did help us. I went to the gas company and the electric company and told them what was happening in our family and asked if I could pay so much money a week to keep us stay in good tabs with their business. Both the gas and electric companies agreed to help us in this matter and any monies that I made those weeks I paid onto the bills. Momma worked at the local cleaners each day, and she covered the checks Dad wrote and paid for our groceries with her salary. To our surprise, we just were able to keep above the waters and keep Dad's hot checks covered while he was out having his Arizona trip. Actually, I found the house to be wonderfully peaceful and enjoyable. My stomach didn't turn over with fear or get upset when I heard Dad yelling about something. The days were quiet and the evenings restful. Momma and I were working and enjoying our shared responsibilities. Momma even kind of relaxed and laughed more when she was talking to me. It was nice to see her enjoying our life, even if only for some weeks. It showed me even more how good it could be if Momma and I moved out and got our own little apartment. Momma would always just shake her head, and that was the end of that argument.

After four and one-half weeks, Dad returned one sunny afternoon. He just drove up to the house, parked the car in front, walked in, and went to bed. He didn't say a word to either of us about where he had been or thanked us for covering the checks he spent or told us how the trip had been. He just went to bed and slept for several days. When he got up, he dressed and came out and went up to the front and began working on the clocks or watches that needed repairs. He did not ever talk to us about his trip. He seemed to know that we didn't really want to listen to him. We didn't want to hear about his trip.

He did bring one souvenir home for Momma. It was a ceramic yellow bee that stood on four legs, and when you lifted the ceramic wings, there were four small bags of honey in them. Momma set the ceramic bee on a lace doily and placed it on a white teacart in the kitchen. She never said a word about the bee nor did I. But for the rest of my days in that house, whenever I walked by that ceramic bee, I would grimace and remember how scary those days were and just hate that little ceramic bee all the more. No one even ate the honey. It just sat there. Dad once asked Momma why she didn't eat the honey in the bee, but when he looked up at Momma's face, he never asked about the bee again. It just sat there as a reminder.

Many years later, while I was watching my ultimate favorite movie *Sleepless in Seattle* with Meg Ryan and Tom Hanks, there were a couple scenes of Meg Ryan in her little kitchen. To my amazement, there is a yellow ceramic bee, the exact duplicate of the one Dad brought to Momma from Arizona. I could not believe it. But there sat the little bee on top of the older refrigerator in the scene of the movie. I felt very nostalgic when I saw it in the movie!

As for Dad's girlfriend, well, she stayed around for the rest of his life I guess. I never knew her name or anything about her. Just that Dad was seen driving her around town, and sometimes she would come into the shop in the evenings when Momma and I were gone. She would sit with Dad and listen to him. It hurt me to no end to see her when I did. She wore all black and lots of rouge. I thought she was very ugly as compared to my momma, who had such a pretty complexion and hair. Momma was always dressed neatly and looked so pleasant. I never could understand what Dad saw in this woman, so I just left it alone and marked it as another reason I wanted to leave my home as soon as I could. I did not want to live around Dad, and I could not get Momma to leave him. So I was there in the house waiting my time and planning my life in the future. Years later, after Momma had died, I reminded Dad of this incident. I also reminded how I had played the piano and sung "So Long It's Been Good to Know You" just to hear what his reaction was to my audacity to do such a thing. He laughed and said he had always respected me the most because I would stand up to him. Later, in mulling over his answer, I had to reach deep inside my own self and respond with the answer that I wished I had been asked to stand beside Dad and not up to him. There seemed a needed response from Dad other than the fact that I was not afraid to battle with him. I had never wanted to battle with my father, just to find a way to understand each other and reach a conclusion of respect or love. I never felt either of these from my father. Just never meant to be.

So now, at this time in my life, I was working some evenings in the local theater in the concession stand. I loved it. I enjoyed the staff I worked with. Pop, as we called him, was the ticket taker and sometimes the projectionist. George worked sometimes as the ticket taker, and Brooks was also the projectionist. Betty was in the box office, and it was a nice group of people to be with. If the evening was slow, I could do my homework as I stood inside the concession stand. The pay wasn't much, but it brought in some extra monies to help Momma pay the bills.

I was fascinated with the projectionist's booth where they ran the films shown in the theater. There were two large film projectors and cans of film for each performance. The projectionist loaded the film onto the first projector and then the next reel on the second projector. During the film, a small butterfly clip would appear on the screen, seen only by the trained eye in the lower right side of the screen, which signified to the projectionist to change to the second projector, and back and forth it would go. It took skilled hands to run those projectors, load the films, and change the films smoothly and not even interrupt the viewer's attention as they watched the film. That small projector's booth was a world within itself. All was hot and full of light because you had to be able to see while you changed the projectors or loaded the film. Pop or Brooks would stand and sweat heavily as they worked in the booth. Usually they kept a towel around their necks to help wipe the sweat off their faces and arms. They also drank a lot of water or soda from the concession stand.

I was always fascinated when I went into the booth to watch them work. Years later, I read about the bulbs used in these projectors and the radioactive material used in the early lamps. When the projectionist was opening the door on the side of the projector, they often rested their hands on the area and were thus continuously exposed to the radioactive material from these early bulbs. Years of continuous exposure could endanger their health. I thought back to Brooks and Pop and the fact they both died of bone cancer and wondered if all those years of exposure in the hot, small projectionist's room, working those projectors had caused their cancer through that exposure.

Once in a while, Pop or Brooks would let me change a projector when I saw the butterfly clip in the lower right of the film. It was exciting to do but really scary. I only did a small part of the procedure as they worked along with me but it was a great responsibility. If one missed the butterfly clip, or was not smooth in their transition from one projector to the other, so many things could go wrong. For instance, the film could break or melt from the heat. I had seen that happen once in a while where the projectionist was distracted. The audience became very unhappy at this time because it broke their attention on the film, and sometimes it took a while to get the film repaired and back running. When this happened, the audience would become restless and boo out loud at the projection booth. Believe me, one did not want to get the theater audience annoyed. The ordinarily peaceful and kindly people in the audience tended to get ugly if they were not getting what they had paid for—the movie with no interruptions. I had learned a full respect for the projectionist and their work. Not everyone was born with the skill to handle the large machines of those days and keep everything smoothly running with the films to entertain the attending audience.

That winter proceeded with life marching onward each day and soon snow and ice was melting with warmer days of sun, and spring was soon to approach. At that time, I was working six nights a week with two matinees on Saturday and Sunday. It was great to me as I was able to add more monies into the daily budget, and I also so enjoyed being with the crew that worked there and to be away from home. I didn't have to listen to arguments or Dad's rudeness toward Momma and me. So I tended to blossom in my personality some and be more outward in my actions. Also, I so enjoyed going to Sunday attendance at our Presbyterian Church, as I had mentioned before. Our Sunday school teachers were very kind and attentive in their teachings. I sang in the church choir and greatly enjoyed Sunday participation with the kind members of the congregation. Each Sunday, I left the church to walk home feeling peaceful and truly blessed to know such good people and be able to attend the church for religious lessons and teachings. Sundays always brought me a feeling of love and peace. When I got home on those Sundays, Momma would have a lunch prepared, and we would eat together. As I had mentioned, Dad never joined us for a meal. He liked to "graze" for his meal, as Dad explained the matter. So Momma would prepare him a plate of our meal and set it on the countertop of the large kitchen cabinet Momma had on the right side of the kitchen wall. Then, later on, Dad would come back and put his teeth into his mouth and eat parts of his meal during the day until he had finished everything. He also enjoyed a large slice of cake each day for dessert, preferably homemade chocolate cake with icing. As for putting in his teeth, Dad had previously had his lower teeth removed because of the pain they caused him. When the plate had been made, he had ignored the dentist's instructions to keep his teeth in his mouth even though it was painful. Thus, the false teeth never settled and molded to his gums and were painful to wear. As a result, Dad began to wear shirts that only had pockets on the chest, and that was where he kept his teeth until the moment when he might need them to eat. Otherwise, the teeth sat in his shirt pocket on the right side, very seldom worn. After a time, Dad's gums became tough, and most of the time, he could chew his food without the lower teeth. I was surprised though by the fact that actually, Dad looked fine without his lower teeth in. You could not really see that there were no teeth and he spoke quite distinctly. It just always bothered me to see the outline of his teeth sitting there in his pocket waiting for usage on his meal. After Dad had eaten his complete plate of food and dessert, he would wash up his dishes and put them on the rack to dry. Momma and I enjoyed the peaceful meals together. The years before, when Dad joined us for meals, had not always been enjoyable. Oftentimes Dad would get mad at Momma and yell at her that she had added too much salt to the food and it was not edible. None of us could taste the added salt, but we kept our mouths shut. It was wiser to just stay quiet and let him rant on. When this matter of the salt came up, he would always holler, "Who are you mad at, Lela, that you got so heavy handed with the salt?" But you know, this matter never stopped him from eating the food. He would eat it all down and want more even. It was just something he enjoyed stirring up the table about.

One night, as Momma prepared supper and Betty and I were setting the table, Dad came back to eat and immediately began his harassment of Momma and her cooking. I had just finished this huge bowl of salad that Betty and I had been making and had walked over to place it on the table. No sooner had I placed the salad on the table, listening silently to Dad blabbing on and on about some matter regarding the cooking, when Momma just quietly walked over to the table and lifted the bowl of salad and walked over to dump it over Dad's head. Honestly, she dumped the huge bowl of salad all over Dad's head and upper body. There he stood with his mouth finally quiet, open wide in disbelief and looking dumbfounded at Momma. Lettuce leaves and many colored vegetables were sitting all over his head and shoulders. He just stood there in the middle of the kitchen with the salad falling quietly off his body onto the floor and stared at Momma. Betty and I stood in the corner huddled together ready for the explosion that was sure to follow. We did not know what to do. We had never seen Momma ever answer back to Dad let alone dump a salad on his head. We waited fearfully on what would happen next. Momma went right on with her cooking of the meat on the stove, never once looking at Dad or reacting in any way to the fact she had just dumped a full bowl of salad on Dad's own head. It was a moment frozen in my life.

To our utter amazement, Dad began to laugh. At first, it was just a low chuckle which then broke out into a huge uproarious belly laugh. While we watched in amazement, still both of us quiet and not really budging from our corner of the room, Dad slowly picked some of the lettuce and vegetables off his shoulders and ate them. He looked at Momma and said, "Dressing would have been better with the salad but will make do with this." He then walked over to the trash basket and wiped the salad from his shoulders and head. He walked quietly up to the bathroom, cleaned up his hair and face, and came quietly back to sit down at the table and ate all his dinner. Momma kept right on cooking until the meat was finished. She then set it down on the table and told Betty and me to sit down to eat. She also remarked that we would not be eating any salad that evening, but the meal would still be good. Dad never said a single word; he was busy quietly eating his supper. Betty and I sat down and began to eat, as quiet as a mouse, afraid to even move in the chairs. When Dad finished eating, he stood up and left the kitchen and went up front to work in the shop. We sat and finished our meal, and then Betty and I cleared the table. Momma went into the living room and sat down to relax. She never said another word about the incident to any of us. The salad was just never mentioned in our home except in whispers by Betty and me. Later, when Maureece came home and we told him what had happened he whooped with laughter for hours. We could not get him to stop laughing at what had happened. He kept lamenting the fact that he had not been home for supper to see the "salad bowl event" as it began to be called. We gained a new respect for Momma for finally standing up to Dad and just hushing him up for good. You see, after the "salad bowl event," Dad never said another word about the food, or too much salt, or any such matter. He kept his mouth shut and would come to the meal, eat, and then leave. Sometime later was when he began to stop eating with us and would have his plates to "graze" on when he decided he wanted to eat.

A few days later, we had driven up to visit Rena at the tuberculosis sanatorium in Mt. Vernon. Momma was visiting with Rena in the room, and we three, Betty, Maureece, and me, had stepped out into the hall to look out the large window at the lovely grounds below. I could just barely hear Momma talking to Rena, and then I heard a large gasp, "Oh, no, Lela, not really," followed by minutes and minutes of stifled giggling and more giggling like two young teenagers. Momma and Rena sat and laughed for a long time. It felt good to see Momma acting young and carefree during those moments with Rena. She had finally stood up to Dad in the only way he could understand. She had, in her own way, told Dad to sit down and be quiet or leave the table. Dad understood her actions completely. As for me, well, I was somewhat sorry to have lost the salad. Betty and I had worked especially hard on the salad, and it was a shame not to get to eat it. But it had served a good matter at hand and helped to win a few points for Momma.

Chapter 35

A Kiss Is Just A Kiss

I was going into my fifteenth year, a freshman at high school that fall, and working every evening at the Gillioz Theater downtown. Summer was arriving, so the staff began to close the downtown theater and open the summer outdoor theater. I was so excited. I loved the outdoor theater, and it looked like it would be fun to work there. Betty had been out at the drive-in those days working and cleaning, and she invited me out that Saturday to help. I spent the day setting up the concession stand with Betty and Pops. We were busy that day cleaning and getting the concession stand all spruced up and filled with the many necessary items. There were two ramp boys, Phil and Hank, with George, who worked the concession stand also. All three boys were pulling weeds, spraying poison on the weeds, and cleaning the areas of trash and debris. The drive-in had sat empty all winter, and it was ready to be placed back into action and activity for the summer nights. Since the theaters were not air conditioned yet, the drive-ins were the perfect place to go see the movies in the summer. A family could pack up a food basket, with drinks of soda and water, and place the children in the backseats. It made a fun night out, watching a movie together, while enjoying the moon and starlit skies.

I had talked about the ramp boys. In explanation, the ramps were the rows at the drive-in where the cars parked. Each row had an entrance for the cars to drive down to a chosen area on a row of ramps. The ramps were an inclining row of dirt and gravel that the car would park the front

312

of a car on top. The driver or passenger then could reach over and take a speaker from the hook on a pole by the parking space and place the speaker on the open window of their car. This way, they could hear what the movie was saying. The ramp boys walked the ramps with flashlights and helped the audience members in their cars, or anyone needing help, and escorted cars out of the drive-in when the movie was over. In many ways, they were like an usher in a movie house. The ramp boys were Phil and Hank. George was to work in the concession stand with me. Betty was in the box office. Pop or Brooks were the projectionists. It was well set up.

Opening night was set for the coming Saturday night with a three-movie lineup of cowboy movies, newsreels, and cartoons. Our manager had arranged for a drawing to be held for all attending that night, winning free tickets for another Saturday night show. There were also balloons and a clown at the playground area to be with the children where they played before the movies started. It was a festive opening night for the drive-in for all attending.

Betty and I arrived for work a little early so we could get all set up for our jobs. While I began to slice tomatoes and onions and gather the condiments to set out on the small tables in front for the customers, Betty gathered her paperwork, tickets, and change bags and left to walk down to the box office to get ready for arriving customers. Pop was in the projection booth setting up the films, and the two ramp boys were out on the ramps waiting for the customers to arrive. George and I were busy in the concession stand getting our area set. Placing cups for the drinks, making sure the soda fountains were filled and ready, napkins and condiments in place. It was a busy thirty minutes or so. Then we took a breather and looked around and realized all was in place and in clean shape. Now all this time, George and I had not said one word to each other but just gone about our jobs. Once in a while he would remind me to place something where it belonged, but we had not really talked. George had worked a previous year in the concession stand, so he knew what all was needed to be set up. He was very courteous to me, and it was an easy preparation for the evening's business.

I had gone over to the sink in the backroom to wash my hands several times because they smelled of onions to me when George walked into the backroom. He then closed the door that led out to the concession area and proceeded to close the window flaps where the large wall fan was. I thought to myself, *What's going on? George had just made sure that no one could see in the room where we were.*

I was standing there wondering what George was doing when he stepped back and leaned against the old refrigerator there. He then reached out, and taking me by my hand, he gently led me over to him, placed his arms around my waist, and bent his head down to softly kiss me. I can tell you I was so surprised that I didn't even move for a minute. I just stood there dumbly kissing George. Well, I wasn't really kissing George. I was just standing there while George gently and sweetly kissed me. I remember thinking that George had the softest lips I had ever known. Not that I had anything to compare his lips to as this was the first boy I had ever kissed, but they sure seemed sweet to me. This tender and soft kissing proceeded for about fifteen minutes—no rough or panting moves, just slow, sweet gentle kissing, George and me. Then, he took his hands away from my waist and walked over to open the window for the fan and opened the door to the concession stand. I stepped back, puzzled and not really too sure all this had really happened. George stepped outside to have a cigarette, and I walked, or should I say wobbled, unsteadily to the restroom with my purse in hand to apply lipstick back on my lips and to comb my hair.

In the restroom, I walked on steadier feet over to the wall mirror and stood there looking into the bathroom mirror with a dull shock. This had been my first kiss. Absolutely my first kiss I had ever had, and I could not believe how it had all just happened. It had really been a sweet kiss plus some more kissing, just as I had always dreamed it would be. George was a tall, slim young man with blond hair and blue eyes. I smiled at myself. *Well, this might be a very interesting summer,* I thought. *At least it had certainly started out to be!* And with that thought, I went back inside the concession stand, and George and I began the evening of serving the customers and working in the concession stand. Never once did George nor I look at each other, wink at each other, hold hands, or touch each other's waist or shoulder. We worked together just as if we were two employees and busy at our job. After the concession closed, we cleaned up the area, said good-night, and Betty arrived for us to leave with Pops. It had been arranged that Pops was giving Betty and me a ride home that night. George had his own car, and he took the ramp boys home.

I never mentioned to Betty what happened that night. Amazingly, I went home and did not even think about the kiss with George at work. I did not moon around about how sweet it was, question what I thought about George, or listen to music and dream about his kisses. I just went home, read some of my books, said my prayers, and went to bed. I was tired.

The next night, Sunday, I went to work with Betty and proceeded to set up the concession stand as I had the night before. Betty walked down to the box office, and George worked alongside me setting up the concession. After we finished, and all was prepared, I had gone over to wash my hands when George closed the door to the concession and shut the window to the huge wall fan, shutting out any way for someone to look into the room. He then leaned against the refrigerator and pulled me over as we slowly began to kiss softly and sweetly for the next ten or fifteen minutes. Then George proceeded to open the door and windows and go outside for a cigarette. I went to the bathroom to comb my hair and reapply my lipstick. Once again, I stared in the wall mirror and shook my head in amazement. *Well, what the heck!* I thought. *No one was being harmed, and it sure was fun kissing George.*

The evening again proceeded without any talking or recognition of our kissing. Pop again took Betty and me home, and George drove home with the ramp boys.

Amazingly, I have to say, this proceeded in the same way each evening for about a week. And then something else happened. As George and I were quietly kissing and standing together, George did a very strange thing. He put his tongue in my mouth while we kissed. I was so taken aback that I could not even breathe. I pulled back and was gasping for air when the backdoor opened and Betty came into the room. When she walked in she saw me in George's arms, mouth open and gasping for air with George just standing there smiling. Betty ran over and shouted, "Susie, what did George do to you?" I was too embarrassed to say anything, and I turned and ran out of the door and into the bathroom next door. Betty followed. When we were both in the bathroom, Betty grabbed me by the shoulders and demanded to know what George had done and if I was hurt or anything. I got my breath back and mumbled to Betty that George had been kissing me when he had stuck his tongue down my throat. I told Betty I had never known about such things, and I was so scared I wasn't able to get my breath when she had walked in and caught George and me.

Betty said, "Oh, well, if you are not hurt, I guess that all is okay."
But she continued in a very angry manner wanting to know why George
and I were kissing and how long this had been going on. Embarrassed,
I told her about our evenings of kissing and how it had been going on
since opening night, but now his tongue in my mouth had changed
everything, and I was not too sure I wanted to continue. Betty explained
to me that it was called French kissing and was quite popular with
many. I thought quietly to myself, *Hmmmm, so that is French kissing
that I had heard about. Honestly, if I had known it was going to happen I
might not have gotten so embarrassed when it did happen. I had to think
about this. It was kind of nice after all.* Betty was flabbergasted and
tried to get me to promise that I would not kiss George anymore. I
told her I would not promise that, and I threatened her sincerely that
she had better not tell her mother, my aunt Rena, or Rena would tell
my mother, and that would get me into a lot of trouble. I made Betty
promise most sincerely that she would never talk about George and me
kissing. Betty promised, but I knew that she had hated to do so.

So George and I continued with our secret kissing each night all that
summer when we both worked in the concession stand. Of course, now
we had added the French kissing to our repertoire also. I found that it
was most enjoyable. George just grinned.

The funny thing, I worked two more summers at the drive-in.
During those nights, George and I had our secret kissing sessions. The
kissing was always just sweet and soft, no passion with grabbing or
huffing and puffing. Just soft sweet kisses. In the winter when we went
back to the indoor theater, George and I never kissed or really talked.
Well, several times George did grab me in the storage closet for the
concession, and we did kiss and hug for a few minutes. But nothing
ever happened at the Gillioz Theater. It happened only at the drive-in
in the summer. My senior year, George did ask me to the senior prom,
but I told him no. I had already made plans. I was no longer working
at the theater my senior year and was surprised George had asked me
to the prom. It would have been nice, I am sure, but I decided I should
stay with my original plans with the girls, and they were staying over at
my house that night after the prom. Years later, during my college days,
I was home for the summer and I was with friends when we went to
this Western bar in some small town practically out in the country. We
had gone in for some beer and some juking (listening to the jukebox

while drinking beer). To my surprise, George was working there as a bartender. You know what, we didn't even say hello or acknowledge each other. To this day, I still call it a very strange relationship. I do have to admit, George taught me a lot about kissing. Later I was told at times by other young men that I was a "sweet kisser."

Don't get the wrong idea. Working in the summer at the drive-in was not just about kissing. Many other funny and interesting things happened at the drive-in those starlit nights and filled my memory book with delightful stories.

Our concession stand offered many gastronomical delights including buttered or plain popcorn, soda, hamburgers or cheeseburgers, hotdogs, candies of many colors, sizes, and flavors with one most popular choice by the females a "chilly willy." I still laugh when I think about this culinary delight for the gals and actually for the guys. Very low in calories, a "chilly willy" was a large sour pickle that was served on a stick and kept ice cold in a container of ice until purchased. These "chilly willies" looked cold and inviting there in the ice, if you liked sour pickles, but I would rather have the popcorn.

Now what I had observed was that when a young couple entered the concession stand for treats, the guy ordered everything available, soda, buttered popcorn, cheeseburgers with everything, and candies. Then, when he turned to his own true love, his girlfriend, to ask what she wanted to order, the girl would smile demurely and whisper to him that she just wanted a "chilly willy." Well, I can tell you that I have seen big, bulky football players break out in a cold sweat when his gal ordered a "chilly willy." You see, the girls were making a big show of watching their calories which made the boyfriends smile proudly, but also the girl was heightening his attention with the purchase of the "chilly willy." For some reason, as if you can't guess by now, the boys loved to watch their sweetheart eating the large cucumber-sized pickle, ice-cold, on the stick provided. So as I had said earlier, the "chilly willy" was our most popular item, and we often ran out of the icy packed "chilly willies" during the night and had to open new jars of the sour pickles. When Pop and I were working the concession stand, and a "chilly willy" was ordered, he would always smile and holler, "Susie, I need a 'chilly willy' over here for this customer." I had to hide my smile because Pop was teasing the couple without their realizing what it was all about. Sadly, I haven't seen this item sold in the theater for years. I guess their popularity faded with the changing times. Now where's a "chilly willy" when you need one?

Speaking of sexual innuendos, as I guess they have been, we had a most unusual Wednesday show lineup that evening at the drive in. It had been advertised that for one Wednesday evening only, and no others announced, two movies would be shown followed by a live discussion about birth control methods. We, as the staff members, were very surprised and somewhat shocked that our manager would line up such an evening of entertainment, but he seemed rather excited about the prospect of a packed night of customers. He was sure that the lineup would bring in customers from all around. The first movie was to be what is now a cult classic, the 1936 movie titled *Reefer Madness*. This was a short propaganda film presenting melodramatic events that would ensue should a high school student try marijuana as it could lead to manslaughter, suicide, rape, addiction, and madness. The second film was 1953's *Glen or Glenda?* which was an exploitation film and docudrama about cross-dressing and transsexuality. This film also later became a cult classic. Then the manager told us that the speaker who traveled with this show would speak to the attending audience and talk for about forty-five minutes explaining natural family planning.

I can tell you now, we had more than a few laughs about the lineup for this evening of films. First of all, we could not figure what a film about marijuana usage and a film about transsexuality had to do with birth control. The three information topics seemed to be unrelated. Granted we were a small-town community and none of the issues were ever discussed out in the open, which would seem to be all the more reason not to present any of these ideas to our expected audience. If anyone wanted to know about these areas, they should see a parent or church minister—certainly not come to a drive-in theater and listen about this information from a complete stranger. What did we know about the credentials of this person who traveled with the show? How did we know how educated he was in the matters at hand? But our arguments did not prevail. The manager was determined to set up this evening and had complete belief that it would be a big night for revenue and attendance. Then comes Wednesday evening with the lineup that I had previously talked about. Brooks was in the projection booth, Pop and I were in the concession stand, and George, Phil, and Hank were working as ramp boys. The manager felt he needed three ramp boys out keeping the large attending audiences settled.

Gillioz Drive-In Theatre

Every summer we would close the downtown Gillioz Theatre and open the Drive-in. I loved it when we traveled there in the summer to work. So much of my life transpired there! I was first kissed, Momma was almost poisoned, I was robbed there, and amazingly enough, we all worked there! The days of the drive-in are gone now but I believe it was an important era in our lives and I am sorry to see them gone.

Pops at work at the Drive-in

One of our most respected workers and friend at the Drive-in was always Pops.

He was mainly our projectionist but he could also take tickets, work the concession stand and usher.

Everyone knew Pops. In this picture, left to right, are Nora, Pops and Hank, ramp boy.

Pops was the authority on all subjects and he knew what he was talking about. He was a good and kind person and loved his family very much.

To our amazement, there was a large turnout that evening. Teenagers mainly, with some young couples. No one really got out of their car to come to the concession stand because they did not want to be seen attending the films or a speaking lesson about birth control.

So, Pop and I were standing in the concession waiting and wondering about customers and if they would be coming in or not. The speaker who traveled with the show was standing in the projection booth speaking to the audience through the sound system about the various details on monthly birth control planning. I could hear some of his information and found it way too detailed for me to figure out. Just then, a young man walked into the concession stand and called for Pop to please come over to him so he could speak to him. Pop walked over to the young man and leaned down to hear what he was whispering in his ear. Pop listened for a few minutes and then stood up and said, "Too late now," and the young man walked back out the door. I walked over to Pop and said, "Hey, Pop, what was that about?" With that, Pop smiled and said, "Well, the young man told me that he and his girlfriend had gotten a little frisky in the backseat from listening to all this talk about abstinence and birth control. While they were being frisky, the rubber had broken. So the young man came in to ask me if there was anything they could do." Pop smiled and said, "I told him, 'Too late now.'"

Today, when I tell that story, I always have a few chuckles or two about the showing of the propaganda films along with a discussion and learning program on birth control, which only seemed to have led to more difficulties than were known before. Oh well, as Pop once stated, "It's too late now."

Chapter 36

"Oh, Say Can You See..."

I might add that, as will show in some of my stories about the drive-in, our manager loved to plan special shows, events, and evenings of movies. He was always looking for a way to pack in a larger audience, sell more products, or present special events. Right now, the manager was looking at the calendar for the Fourth of July and was talking about some plans for the evening.

The manager was always looking to make a buck while spending a quarter. He was the happiest when he got something for nothing. I admit many of us are like that, but I can tell you the manager was truly an advocate of "a penny earned is a penny saved" or such as that. Anyway, Fourth of July was just around the corner, and the manager was lamenting the fact that we were sure to lose the audience to everyone who would be attending their local firework displays. The manager wanted the possible audience to come to the drive-in theater for Fourth of July instead of going to their town's local festivities. He was pondering how to accomplish this matter when George popped up with the following suggestion, "Why not have our own fireworks display?"

Everyone turned to him and looked as if he had just suddenly sprouted a second head or such. Having a fireworks display would be just about as crazy as if George grew another head. Pop just laughed and said to George, "And who is going to set up the firework display?" George thought for a minute and then said, "Why, I would set up the fireworks. Why not?" he asked.

Pop shook his head and said, "No way, George. You have no experience in such matters, and it can be quite dangerous." To which the manager held up his hand and asked George, "Wait a minute, do you have experience in setting up fireworks?"

George pondered a moment, looked back at the manager, and said, "Listen, I have not ever set up a huge firework show before, but I have been doing fireworks since I was a small kid. Come on, how hard could it be?" George laughed and shirked his shoulders. Pop and I just shook our heads and stared in amazement at the way this conversation was all turning. The manager might really consider doing a huge firework display that Fourth of July night and let hapless George be in charge along with Phil and Hank, ramp boys, helping. "Heaven help us," Pop said aloud and kind of walked away from the circle of the manager and the rest of us. He shook his head and added, "I want absolutely nothing to do with this madness. Absolutely nothing." I nodded my head and said I did not either. But I would check to see if the fire department would be available in case the whole place goes up in flames. My humor was not really appreciated at this time, and only Pop and I smiled.

So despite Betty, Pop, and me arguing with George and the manager about the idea of letting George set up the firework display for the attending audience on Fourth of July night, the whole matter began to take shape, and action was calling for there to be a fireworks display manned by George with help by Phil and Hank.

The manager made up flyers announcing plans for that Fourth of July evening promising a gigantic fireworks display that would far outshine all local town displays. The flyer also announced the lineup of movies to be shown with cartoons and a clown with balloons for the children attending. It all sounded great to the untrained ear because Betty, Pop, and I knew who was planning to make all this happen, and we just were not sure about the ability of George to safely make the evening a success. The manager was all excited about the planned possibility of a packed audience at the drive-in and selling lots of concession to the people as they watched the super spectacular fireworks in the sky! The flyers were distributed everywhere, and the manager even ran a half-page advertisement in the local town paper. Everyone knew about the planned festivities at the drive-in for the Fourth of July, and it was sounding good to them. The manager was striving to make more monies that night with a packed audience and to bring them in with a fireworks show that he didn't have to pay as much money for since he was hiring George to do the setup. He was sure to pay George less money than what a trained professional would have charged for such a deed. To George, though, it seemed like a lot of money, and he was excited to begin the setting and designing of the fireworks. The day before the planned event, July 3, the manager and George drove over to a large fireworks stand near Monett and began to buy an enormous amount of fireworks. George was just buying things left and right, and the manager let him because it was still cheaper than if he had hired a professional. George was like a kid in a candy factory; he wanted to buy two of everything. Finally, they settled on their purchases and were pretty well excited about what would be offered in the display. They brought all the fireworks back to the drive-in and stored them in the warehouse after the drive-in had been shut for the evening and we had all gone home.

That following evening, Betty and I arrived early at the drive-in for work because we were excited to see what the events were going to bring for the Fourth of July evening. Betty would be working the box office and was going to close a little early so she could come up and see the fireworks at the concession stand. Brooks was coming in to work the projectionist's booth. Pop was with me in the concession stand, and George was out setting up the fireworks with the manager present. Phil and Hank were helping also until they had to go and assume their jobs as ramp boys. I had told Momma about the planned events of the night, and she was going to come to the movies also so she could see the fireworks. I told her to park near the concession stand so she could walk over and watch the show with Pop and me. She was looking forward to the evening. George continued to set out the fireworks down at the end of the row of ramps, in the back of the drive-in, nearly out in the cow's pasture. He needed lots of space to work and set up all the display for the night. I could see him back there at the ramps, and he had on his usual short-sleeved white shirt and white slacks with black cowboy boots and a black Stetson on his head. If I wasn't so worried about the night's events and what might happen to him, I would have thought that George looked rather sexy that night in his cowboy boots, Stetson hat, and white shirt and slacks.

Then it was show time, and Betty announced that the ticket box office was nearly sold out. The drive-in was packed to almost full capacity. Who would have thought that the people would rather come to the drive-in than go to attend their traditional Fourth of July fireworks show in their own town? Of course, the manager was absolutely thrilled and was running around rubbing his hands together in glee as if already anticipating all the monies he was going to make with the extra purchased tickets and rush for food and drink at the concession stand after the huge fireworks display. It was all coming to fruition just as the manager and George had planned, and I can say the manager was all smiles and jokes. Meanwhile, our thoughts kept swaying over to George, where we saw him standing out in the far corner of the drive-in's cow pasture, awaiting the full setting of the sun and the ensuing darkness of the night. Children were still playing on the playground and enjoying the antics of the clown with the balloons. Momma had come over to be with Pop and me. Betty was soon to follow from the box office. No one was really interested in the concession stand yet. They were all waiting to purchase food and drinks after the fireworks show. I could feel the vibrations in the air of oncoming excitement. It was the wonderment of questioning if it would be successful or end up a flop. Pop and I were pretty certain it was going to be a flop, but we really didn't know what to expect. Momma and Betty were just thinking good thoughts and hoping for the best.

The manager then walked over to the projectionist's booth and took the microphone to announce over the loudspeakers there about the approaching event with the fireworks display. He suggested that the children should be rounded up and taken back to their car so they could watch the show with their parents. The clown was closing his balloon display and would be leaving shortly.

So all was in preparation for the event. The attending audience was mainly sitting in folding chairs they had bought and had placed them on the ramps beside their cars. Some had spread blankets, and children were sitting on the blankets. All had turned and were facing to the back of the drive-in and looking at the location where George was standing, ready to spring into action at any moment. The tension was so thick in the night one could cut it with a knife. And then it happened. The first colorful and bright rocket soared into the air quickly followed by another and another. There was a moment of absolute Fourth of July wonderment while watching the rockets burst into color and vibrated through the air with their loud booms and bangs. Pop and I looked at each other and smiled; maybe it would be okay after all. Maybe we were wrong, and George knew what he was doing. But as the moments that followed show, we had spoken too soon. Way too soon.

Even today, after all these years, the following events are still hard to describe. Within the next few minutes, as we were standing there with shocked faces and our eyes not really believing the sights we were seeing, it all really needed a video camera to detail the following events for future generations to follow. I know we had a hard time following what was going on.

Somehow, with the rockets blazing and whizzing into the dark skies and all the excitement with these first firework displays, one was not prepared to behold what followed. Suddenly the night grew in noise, color, and enrichment in the skies with fireworks getting louder and larger and larger while going higher and fuller. It was incredible to behold. Everywhere in the sky, fireworks were blazing and banging. The night was filled with thunderous noise the like of which had never been heard. It became louder and louder and larger and larger for the next three to five minutes with people shouting at their cars and honking their horns in pure excitement at such a spectacular display of fireworks. I tell you, it was fantastic to see. Pop and I kept shaking our heads in wonderment while oohing and aahing at the filled night sky with color and sound and beauty. It was a thunderous success. It was amazing. The manager was practically dancing on the ramps. And then came one enormous boom, thunderous beyond any sound heard in our little town before. The boom was earth-shattering. John Philip Sousa could have marched around our drive-in and not even been heard by this enormous boom of color and sound. It was deafening.

Then came absolute silence. Silence as if one had just lost their hearing. No sound, just a few sizzles, a few bangs, followed by lots of smoke that rose and floated from the site and into the sky. There were no more fireworks to be seen. Nothing. No sounds, no colors, just absolute silence and a descending cloud of smoke and ashes beginning a descent on the attending audience. But after one gained back their hearing and sight from all the smoke and previous sounds, one could just make out a singular figure that could be seen running across the ramps toward the concession stand. Let me tell you, I do not believe in all of George's life he had ever ran this fast. It was as if the devil himself was fast in pursuit. I do believe at that moment, George believed the devil was in pursuit. Or at least, in a moment he would be, in the guise of the manager.

For a stunned moment, the silence continued in the air as blackened soot and smoke began to waft over the ramps and down over the field and on to the sitting audiences. People were coughing and making gagging noises as they covered their faces with napkins or such.

Until the summer breezes began to disperse the smoke, it was a threatening atmosphere. It took a few minutes as people began to talk to each other and ascertained what had just happened. Then began the loud, incessant honking followed soon by screaming and abusive words that I really do not wish to repeat at this moment. It was an event of sounds that I would rather not ever repeat. I could add that certainly George and the manager's names were being taken in vain. I might add "very loudly in vain." When we looked around, we did not see the manager by the concession stand. Where he had been once dancing around in glee on the ramps as the fireworks flashed brightly in the sky, now he was hiding in the back office behind the concession stand. He did not want to meet any of his once-adoring public at this moment.

Pop and I went inside and began to set up the concession stand. Momma went over to the outside deck and sat down to watch the evening of shows until Betty and I finished our work. Just then, Pop and I heard the backdoor of the concession stand open and close, and we looked around in the back to see who had come in. There stood George. At least we thought it was George. I still have to giggle a little when I think of how that boy looked at that moment with his blackened face and clothes. Once dressed in white shirt and slacks, George was covered with black ashes and soot from head to foot. Even his blond hair was not recognizable. His black boots and black Stetson hat were covered in soot and ashes. He was a downfallen young man with ringing in his ears from all the loud bangs and whizzes of the ensuing fireworks that had literally exploded practically in his face. Pop took one look at George and told him to quickly step into the office and shut the door and lock it. He warned George that it was a sure matter that he would not want any paying customer to get ahold of him right now. They were all pretty mad at the lack of Fourth of July events and some even threatened to punch George in the nose. Quivering and shaking, George sat down in the office chair and rested his head on the desk. Let me tell you, he was scared. I brought him iced soda and told him to just rest, that he was safe now. Well, safe at least until the manager got ahold of him.

The concession stand did fill up with customers, and lots of food with soda was sold that evening along with much hollering about the poor Fourth of July festivities and questioning who exactly had planned this event. Pop and I just smiled and kept serving them their orders. As in most cases with people, especially small-town people who have known each other all their lives, people began to joke about the night's events and predict that soon people would all be bragging that they were there the night the firework display lasted all of three to five minutes. There were some funny stories beginning to build as more people began to talk to each other about the events. The movies started, and people drifted back to their cars and chairs to watch the shows. It was going to make a good memory in their scrapbooks of life. But most of them all agreed that next year, no matter what was promised, they were going to go back to their usual celebration of Fourth of July and attend their own town's festivities where the professionals knew how to handle events. We smiled and said it sounded like a good idea.

The manager had already quietly snuck out and left for the evening. George waited in the back until we closed the stand for the evening. Pop took him home. Betty and I rode home with Momma. The next day, George, with help from Hank and Phil, went out to the drive-in and cleaned up all the mess. It honestly looked like a small war zone with definitely no acknowledged winners. Did the manager learn any lessons from this fiasco? Not really. He still continued to plan events at the drive-in or downtown theater. Some were successful, and some were not, such as Elvis Presley's movie *Love Me Tender*, which was shown at the indoor theater that following fall.

Chapter 37

Elvis Has Left The Building

Having closed down the drive-in, we made our seasonal migration back into town to the Gillioz indoor theater and were all looking forward to another winter at the movie house. Come late November, the manager waltzed into the theater lobby all excited about a movie he was showcasing that coming Sunday afternoon matinee with showings that Sunday night and all the rest of the week. It seems that a new teen idol Elvis Presley had made a movie, *Love Me Tender*, with Richard Egan and Debra Paget, and Elvis sung in the movie. The manager announced with great gusto that the theater would be packed with screaming females that whole week, and the sales profit would be sky high. He was truly excited about the whole matter. Pop and I looked at each other and shrugged our shoulders. Unbelievably true, Pop, George, and I were not aware who Elvis was and had not heard his music. Betty shrugged and announced that she knew who Elvis was and had heard his music, but she didn't think he was all that great! She much more preferred Eddy Arnold and his soft crooning voice. She added that all the screaming teenagers could have their Elvis and that she didn't want him. Well, this made us curious as to whom Elvis was and we said we were looking forward to seeing the movie *Love Me Tender*.

Then the manager explained his plans for this special showing of Elvis and his first movie *Love Me Tender*. The manager had ordered one hundred 8×10 black-and-white pictures of Elvis, and he was going to give them free to the first one hundred girls to enter the theater that

329

Sunday afternoon for the matinee. He showed us the picture, and we all smiled and said that his plans sounded great! Then George volunteered for the event and the privilege to hand out those precious photos of Elvis to all the young screaming females. "Sounded like a project that only he could handle," George added to his offer to the manager. The manager smiled and said that he had been hoping George would offer to hand out the pictures. The manager and George then left to further discuss the matter of handing out the pictures that Sunday afternoon. Betty went into the box office to start opening; I was already in the concession stand, so I began to pop some popcorn, and Pop, who was taking tickets that evening, walked through the house to make sure all was ready for the Saturday night cowboy movies. I think Hopalong Cassidy was to be the featured star that evening in one of his cliffhanger movies. Last Saturday, we had watched Hopalong knocked unconscious and then tied onto a table by the unseen villain. Before leaving the cabin where Hopalong lay unconscious on the table, the villain had left an opened jar filled with black hairy tarantulas. As we rejoined Hopalong, who was now awake and facing the creepy tarantulas who were walking menacingly all over his body, the camera slowly pans over to where we see a bomb that is about to explode in the small deserted cabin and kill Hopalong. What a predicament. Of course, Hopalong always got undone, away, or out of the situation and into a new one, but the audience loved these cliffhangers and especially the ones with Hopalong. The movies were Western thrillers usually pitting the cavalry against the Indians in battle.

At the end of the Saturday movies, we closed the theater, and all announced we were excited to see this Elvis tomorrow. George was extra excited.

Sunday afternoon arrived, and we were all at work at our stations when George arrived for his special job. To our surprise, George was wearing his Sunday church suit, complete with a tie and dress shoes. He had slicked his hair back and looked quite dignified. The manager was in the lobby to hand the small box of 8×10 pictures of Elvis to George. All one hundred of the pictures lay flat in the gray cardboard box, ready to be passed out to each entering female. George had placed himself squarely in the center of the lobby where he was facing the front doors where the arriving customers would be arriving through. The manager had gone upstairs to stand in the balcony overlooking the front lobby so he could be sure to see all the exciting moments as the audience arrived to see Elvis. Betty was a nervous wreck because in the last fifteen minutes or so the audience of young girls arrived to be sure to be one of the one hundred entering the theater so they could be given a free picture of Elvis. They wanted that picture. Betty hollered back to us that there must be two blocks of girls lined out there waiting for the box office to open. Pop walked over and opened the front door to look out to see the line for the box office, and to his wonder, the line did go down the full block and almost on to the next block. We had never ever seen such a lineup of people, let alone girls, to see a movie. These girls must have been from all over the towns and communities because there were certainly more than the ones who lived in Monett. It was incredible to see. And of course, the boys were driving by in their cars whistling and taunting the girls with shouts and ridicule of Elvis, the scream king!

The girls did not care. They were there to see the movie and to get a picture of Elvis, no matter what they had to do. Suddenly George was not so sure of himself, and he began to stand on one foot and then the other, twisting uncomfortably in his suit and tie and looking like he just might be sick at any moment. Where he had thought he was going to be the big hero and glory in handing out the Elvis pictures, now he was hoping he could just survive the onslaught of the screaming and shouting females.

Betty shouted she was opening the box office. Pop opened the front doors and then ran quickly to the place where he stands to take the tickets. I was behind the concession stand, and our manager had retreated to his office to await the results of this venture. There, in the center of the lobby, stood George, who was now slowly backing toward Pop as if he no longer wanted to be standing out there alone holding only those 8×10 pictures which were going to be soon grabbed by all the entering females. He was beginning to sweat and tremble a little as the door opened and with a huge waft of air, screaming and shouting young ladies were all running into the lobby and heading right toward George. But you know, I have to hand it to George, he held his ground. No matter how scared he might have felt as he faced those descending females or the incredible frailty of his body that he might have been feeling, George stood right there, eyes squeezed shut tightly, lips pursed together, body clenched in rather a tight defensive stand with his arms outstretched to the arriving females, offering them their 8×10 picture of Elvis. I watched in pure amazement as did Pop. We saw the door open, the numerous tall, short, thin, fat, screaming, crying females descending on George, and then we saw the pictures all fly up into the air, and we no longer saw George. There was just a large crowd of female counterparts, legs and arms flying, pieces of the torn box in the air and sometimes a suited leg or arm of whom we believed to be George. Then, just as quickly as all appeared, they disappeared. Like a flying horde of locusts upon an acre of grain, the ladies arrived and then left, each clutching an 8×10 picture of Elvis. It was all amazing.

We looked back again toward George, and there he was, lying in a crumpled heap on the floor of the lobby—tie in a crumpled mess around his neck, shirt unbuttoned and hanging out of his belted waist. One shoe on and one shoe off lying on the side of the lobby. Hair all tumbled and rather looking like a poor raggedy doll, George was attempting to stand back up and gather himself together into one piece. After ascertaining that George had not been hurt, Pop and I began to laugh uproarishly at the whole afternoon proceedings so far. George had survived the onslaught but was rather shaken up from the incident. Pop gave George a flashlight and told him to go watch the corridors and usher the theater. I don't think George was too excited about going back into the darkened theater with all those girls again.

Then we heard the music in the movie begin. Elvis was singing the title song "Love Me Tender," and to our amazement, we heard loud screaming and shouting coming from the attending audience, the girls! They were screaming over Elvis. The manager came down and told me to close the concession stand, and Pop grabbed some flashlights. We were told to walk the aisles of the theater with George and help keep the girls in their seats while we tried to stop their incessant screaming and shouting for their hero, Elvis. When Pop and I arrived at the back entrance to the theater, we found George standing in the hidden corner. He was not going down into that den of ladies alone, he told us. So Pop, George, and I walked the aisles that whole movie as we hushed screaming, shouting ladies, or we ordered them to please stand up and not roll up and down the aisles. It was incredible to see these ladies so completely throw all options and thoughts to the wind as they watched their beloved Elvis. These were all fans of Elvis, that was for sure. The amazing thing to me was that I knew these girls. I went to school with them, and I certainly never thought I would find them rolling in the aisles or shouting in hysteria for Elvis. I was thunderstruck at how the girls were acting over Elvis in the movie. Personally, I found Richard Egan more to my liking. I thought Elvis looked like a petulant, spoiled young man who certainly could not act.

Then, at the end of the movie where Elvis rises out of his grave and sings again, that was the end of all attempt at calming any of that gals! They were screaming, stomping herds of Elvis fans, and that was all there was to it. They were not going to settle down or be quiet. They wanted to celebrate Elvis's triumph in the *Love Me Tender* movie in a loud, uproarious behavior, and that was all to the matter. After the movie ended, all the girls left the theater quietly and demurely as if the previous two hours had never happened. Joyful were the gals holding their 8×10 picture of Elvis close to their bosoms as they left the theater. The girls who did not win a picture stared disdainfully at the winners. Of course, the winning girls did not care; they were going right home to frame the picture and place it in their bedroom so they could look at Elvis each night before falling asleep. Pop and I smiled. The manager left for home. Betty closed and locked the theater doors for the afternoon, and George sat down to shakily light up a cigarette.

The rest of the performances that week were watched quietly and respectfully. It was as if the girls only let loose that one Sunday afternoon. The rest of the performances were watched as any other movie. I was glad because I don't think any of us could have handled another episode like Sunday's. At least I know George could not have.

Chapter 38

Gorgeous George

My life continued through high school and home and the theater that year. At school, I attended regularly, participated a little, and eagerly awaited each night to return to work. It seemed that the theater was the only place that I felt fully comfortable and welcome. The staff members were my friends, and I loved to watch the people as they entered the movie house to go watch the performances. Many people I knew, and it was nice to say hello to them. I also worked on my homework and enjoyed sharing some of my written work with Pop or Brooks. They always enjoyed hearing stories I had written. My schoolwork was mainly at the medium level, nothing spectacular, just chugging along. Teachers did not seem to take particular notice of me. I had no favorite teacher. I didn't have much in the line of clothes and mainly wore the same outfits. The other girls at school were always dressed in clothes from the expensive clothing stores in Monett, but most of my clothes were hand-me-downs or from outlets. I seldom was able to get brand-new clothes. It was okay at the time because I wasn't really concerned about my clothes or shoes. I did not have boyfriends or anyone wanting to date me. I was friends with four girls, and we enjoyed being together in class, walking the halls, or walking home together. But we were not exceedingly close. I always seemed to be waiting. My main thoughts were to finish high school and head on, away from Monett, and go to college. I wanted to be a schoolteacher. That was all I could think about. I had no idea at that time as to how I would accomplish this matter of going to college, but that didn't stop me from dreaming about it. Truthfully, attending college seemed like a dream that I shouldn't even hope for. I would only be heartbroken when I could not accomplish the matter.

At this time, Momma came to my attention with regard to her sudden absolute fascination with wrestling. Not just any wrestling, I might add, but with anything that included the famous Gorgeous George from the 1940–1950 wrestling days. I could not believe my ears nor eyes when quiet, calm, and reserved Momma watched television and Gorgeous George was on the set wrestling. She became like those women you see in movies shouting, "Throw da bum out!" at the television set or jumping up and down in her seat at the wrestling episodes she watched with her dear George in gloried costume and action on the television set. Dad and I became fearful that one of the times she was going to throw some item at the television set in excited fever over the action of Gorgeous George. She might break the screen of our television. We were amazed to watch the shy demure housewife and mother transform to a screaming, yelling tiger whenever she watched the wrestling matches and George was performing. Who would have thought the change to be possible?

Bearing the original name of George Raymond Wagner (1915–1963), George created his name Gorgeous George when he overheard two women say, "Isn't he gorgeous?" as he entered the ring. Shortly after that, he grew his hair long and dyed the hair platinum blond. He had long, elaborate capes designed to wear with the name Gorgeous George emblazoned on the back in gold letters. He designed entrances fit for a king, marching in to "Pomp and Circumstances" surrounded by chosen members of his entourage. The public loved it, including my mother. I read that his days on television drew more audiences than Milton Berle ever did. Amazing. He knew how to collect the fans and hold them to him. Momma never missed one of his wrestling matches and always enjoyed fully her hours spent yelling and clapping for the wrestler. Then, one day, the Joplin paper announced that Gorgeous George would be appearing in person in Joplin to wrestle. Well, I can tell you, Momma planned to be there to see him. Dad was going to attend with her to keep her in line, or else we had no idea what she might do in the excitement of the moment.

Now Gorgeous George further pleased his lady fans by wearing gold-plated bobby pins in his hair and when he walked by the ladies, he would take them out of his hair and hand them to the awaiting ladies. He called them "Georgie Pins." So the night Gorgeous landed in Joplin to perform, there was Momma waiting at the entrance to the wrestling ring as Gorgeous George walked by. When George saw Momma, he stopped and pulled two "Georgie Pins" from his golden locks and handed them to her. Let me tell you, Dad said he thought Momma was going to faint. She was so excited. Dad also added that at the wrestling match that evening he thought he was going to have to get a policeman over to help him take Momma from the arena. She was screaming and hollering, "Throw da bum out!" to George's adversaries and even threw an empty Dr. Pepper bottle at the wrestling ring. It was like a doppelganger had taken over my mother. It sure was an exciting night for Momma, and I was so glad she was able to go see her idol Gorgeous George perform in life. She continued to watch him on television until his early retirement and later death of the age of forty-eight. She loved to get those two "Georgie Pins" and show them to whomever she was talking about her experience and sharing the night of excitement. Years later, I found those two gold-plated bobby pins among Momma's own bobby pins in her small jewelry box on the dresser. Those two "Georgie Pins" were worth their weight in gold to Momma.

When I had talked about laundry day and how much work it took to accomplish the chore, I had forgotten about my colorful, full-tiered petticoats we wore. How we loved those petticoats and how much work it took to wear them successfully is what I most remember about fashion of those day during my last few years of high school in the late 1950s. Our skirts were in wide swing style with length to below the knees in colorful cotton patterns for summer and felt or corduroy for winter. If you were lucky and had a brand-new petticoat, it was usually full and bouncy enough to be worn as a single under your skirt. As the petticoat got older, you had to add more petticoats to keep the same popular choice of bounce and fullness under the skirt. Sometimes I would have on as many as three to four petticoats under a skirt. Believe me, that is not easy to do because the elastic waist would also get stretched with wear, and it would be hard to keep all the worn petticoats up and beneath the skirt. If I had two to three petticoats on, I would sometimes have to wear a belt to keep the petticoats all in line. Then on top of the petticoats and belt, I would wear the skirt with another belt to cinch in my waist. It could be very cumbersome at times. Most of all was the pressure of sitting in the school desks where you had so squeeze into the seating area between the writing area of the desk. Once you got in the desk, with all the petticoats stuffed in around you, you felt like a caterpillar sitting inside a cocoon. But we loved it! Made us feel all feminine when we walked down the school hallway with our ponytails on our head swinging and our skirts on our hips swaying. The boys loved it. On top, we usually wore a blouse with a buttoned sweater and in the winter a short-sleeved sweater with a buttoned sweater also. They were fun outfits along with our white socks and penny loafers or saddle shoes. I mainly wore white or blue petticoats. I never liked to wear the other colors and especially not red.

Adding to that problem was the upkeep of these petticoats. Once a month, I would set up a large galvanized tub on the floor in our spare room with newspaper underneath to protect the floor. Then I would pour in a bottle of starch and water and lay the petticoat in the mixture letting the starch fully soak the petticoat. Then I would lift the petticoat up and let it drip for a few minutes in the tub and then spread it out on the floor on newspapers. That way, the petticoat dried in a round circle and would be stiffer to wear. It was a messy job, and all had to be coordinated so that you had petticoats to wear while the others were drying. Sometimes, after the petticoats were dried and you were wearing them for the first day or so, small flakes of starch would fall out of the petticoats leaving a trail of sparkling flakes where you walked or sat. Could be embarrassing to girls as the boys pointed out the trail of dried flakes of starch following a girl as she paraded down the school hallway.

We wore these petticoats pretty much our junior and senior years in high school. Years later, when I was away in the college dorm and was getting dressed for my first day of classes, I was informed by a college friend to ditch the petticoats—they were no longer in fashion—and to grow up! So I sadly packed them up in a box, and Momma later packed them away on my first trip back home. Actually, it was good to be free of the petticoats and wearing the skirts plain. One could certainly get around easier and sit more comfortably. Straight skirts came back into fashion to wear with blouses and sweaters. That was a great return in fashion. Thank goodness there would be no more days of tubs of starch in the spare room filled with soaking petticoats or watch the petticoats dripping on newspapers placed on the linoleum floor.

Chapter 39

Pellet With The Poison
In The Vessel With The Pestle

That summer of 1958 brought a return to the drive-in and opening of the concession stand for the summer. Some things had changed. Momma now worked with me in the concession in the evenings. Pop was the projectionist. George and two other young men worked the ramps and general area. Betty worked the ticket booth down at the front. It was a good lineup. I enjoyed the evening hours working with Momma in the concession. On very busy nights, George would join us during the breaks and help serve the customers. That particular summer, as we prepared the concession to be open again, Momma was filling the soda dispensers with the chosen liquid syrup for flavor and adjusting the carbonation lines to connect to disperse the soda from each machine. Now Momma loved Dr. Pepper, and she had just begun to fill the Dr. Pepper soda machine so she could have a soda to drink as she worked. It was a hot afternoon. She asked one of the ramp boys to go get a bottle of the Dr. Pepper syrup so she could fill the machine. The boy returned with the bottle and placed it on the front counter. Busy at the time, Momma told the boy to pour the bottle's content into the Dr. Pepper canister, and she would hook up the carbonation. The boy lifted the large glass gallon jug and poured the liquid into the correct opening. Pop was in the room visiting and taking a break from his work in the projection room. The manager had entered the

338

HOME AGAIN, HOME AGAIN, JIGGITY, JIG 339

room. He had just driven up and was carrying some paper products to be placed in the serving areas. I was polishing the counter and doing general cleaning jobs.

The ramp boy poured the whole jug of Dr. Pepper syrup that he had brought in from the storage room into the container, and Momma went over to connect the carbonation line. The Dr. Pepper was set to be served. Momma announced that she was going to get a large paper cup and fill it with cool ice and then get a big drink of Dr. Pepper. Since Momma was such an avid fan of Dr. Pepper she had elected herself to be the tester on the product to make sure it had been correctly dispensed and had the correct ratio of syrup and carbonation. Just as she reached for a paper cup, the manager stepped forward and announced broadly that he would be the official taster of the Dr. Pepper. Although my mother might be the connoisseur of Dr. Pepper, he was the manager, and the testing of any product for flavor and taste should be his call. Momma backed away from the dispenser and handed the paper cup to the manager. It was to be his call.

The manager walked over to the soda dispenser and placed the iced cup under the fountain to disperse the first taste of soda. He filled the cup and, raising it to his lips, took a hefty swig of Dr. Pepper. He swallowed, and as we all stood waiting for his announcement, the manager began to groan loudly and grab his throat. We laughed and all said, "Oh come on, no playacting. The soda could not be that bad." The manager again grabbed his throat and motioned that he was going to be sick. With that, he fell to the ground with a loud thud. As we stood there, all in complete amazement, staring, the manager groaned even louder. Pop ran over and grabbed the now-empty glass jug and shouted, "What was in this jug? Had it been a new jug?" Pop turned to the ramp boy and asked him where he had gotten the jug in the storeroom. When the ramp boy told Pop he ran out to the storeroom to look at the jugs placed there on various shelving. To our surprise, Pop came running back in and grabbed the ramp boy, questioning him, "When you were spraying weed killer on the areas on the ramps, where did you put the leftover weed killer?" The boy listened, thought about it, and then shrugged. He guessed he had put the weed killer into an empty gallon jug. Perhaps an empty Dr. Pepper glass gallon jug, he answered. "Oh my gosh," we all announced. The manager had been poisoned with the weed killer that had been accidentally poured into the Dr. Pepper container. He had drunk pure weed killer. The manager was really sick and was not just pretending to tease Momma.

Momma gasped. She had nearly drunk weed killer. The manager had drunk weed killer. Pop loudly announced he was taking the manager to the hospital and that George was to come with him to help. The manager was now screaming with pain, and they helped him up off the floor to slowly walk out to Pop's car parked right by the concession stand door. They placed the manager in the backseat so he could lie down, and off they raced to the hospital. George later said it was a very scary ride to the hospital with Pop driving over speed around the corners and such and the manager screaming in the backside. George said he was glad to arrive safely at the hospital. Pop and George came back to the concession stand later to tell us that the manager had had his stomach pumped and that he was resting now. Pop said the manager's family, wife and son, had been called and they were with the manager now in the hospital room. The manager was going to spend the night in the hospital room to make sure all weed killer had been removed and thrown away.

Momma was in shock. She had almost drunk weed killer. I was terrified. Momma might not have been so lucky as the manager who just had to have his stomach pumped. Momma might have gotten sicker and died. And then we all realized, what if no one had tested the Dr. Pepper soda? It might have been served to the awaiting customers. It could have really been a catastrophe. Someone might have died. The guilty ramp boy was now crying. He felt so awful about what he had done. Pop was shouting at him, adding to the boy's guilt. He admonished the boy about not placing a label on the jug to announce that the glass jug now contained poison weed killer. Pop took George and the guilty ramp boy into the storehouse and began to clean out the area. Any stored gallon jugs that had broken seals on them were tossed into the trash. That way Pop made sure that *no* weed killer was ever served in the concession stand again. Momma and I cleaned out the dispenser with very hot water and lots of soap. We had to get it ready for opening the summer drive in and service to the customers. I was so thankful that Momma was safe. That had really been a scare for all of us. A few days later, the manager came back to work and arrived at the concession stand to see how business was going. Momma asked him if he wanted a Dr. Pepper to drink but he quickly declined. He said he had lost all desire for any sort of iced soda to drink.

Chapter 40

We Are All Rainbows

The summer had also brought a surprise with Priscilla, my friend. She had gotten married quietly to a fellow high school classmate and was now a married woman at the age of eighteen. Momma and I were in shock. We could not understand why Priscilla had gotten married at such an early age. But then, we reasoned she had always talked about having a home of her own and being a mother. That large home I had once envied so much as a child had really changed over these years of my life. Where once I had watched the home filled with laughter, noise, and activities, only Mrs. Evans and her son, Joey, lived quietly in the home. The oldest sister had married and was with her family. Jimmy had been killed in the Korean War and was buried in the Monett cemetery. The father, Mr. Evans, had left his wife, Jessie, and family to be married again and lived away. And now Priscilla was married. I missed my friend Priscilla and all the others in her family who had once lived in that envied large white house. I seldom saw Priscilla now.

As I thought of Priscilla now married, I remembered how I had joined the Rainbows last year and Priscilla was a member also. I liked attending the meetings and she was there. She always had a lovely smile for me and friendly greetings for me when we had a moment to talk. My father was an avid Mason and loved being a member. It was only natural that I would become a Rainbow when I came of age to join. Later, I had planned to become a member of the Eastern Stars when I became older. Most of my high school female classmates were also members

341

of the Rainbows. Some of the boys were members of the DeMolay Organization. Now a member of the Order of the Rainbows for Girls and a daughter of a Mason, my dad, I was proud to become a member. When I had been accepted into the order, there was a ceremony to participate in, and we ladies all wore long evening dresses and were specially gathered together for the welcoming ceremonies. I was proud to see that Priscilla was a high-ranking member in the organization. Rumors abounded about the welcoming ceremony about things we would have to do such as ride a greased goat. I laughed when I heard that one. Now why on earth would they have us dress up in evening dresses and then tell us to ride a billy goat. It was too silly to even think about, but there were whispers that it happened. Of course, it did not, and we were all welcomed to the ceremony by the older members of the Order of Rainbows. Lovely flowers and lit candles decorated the large room as we gathered into the hall for the service. The girls all looked so lovely in their dresses. I was wearing my cousin Betty's gown. We did not have the monies for me to get a new evening dress, so I wore her evening gown. It did not fit me very well, but it was a dress. Priscilla was very kind and remarked to me about how nice I looked. During my years of attendance at the Rainbows, we shared in teachings about the formation of us as young ladies with the proper way to dress and behave. We were taught to cross our legs at the ankles and not at the knees. We were instilled with lessons on leadership, patriotism, and the love of home and family and a service to humanity. The Bible was often read, and we learned various quotes to heart. We also had a secret handshake and password that we must use each evening we attended the meeting to gain attendance. Well, one night, the inevitable for me happened. I forgot the secret password. I tried to stumble through the word and pretend like I knew it, but I was denied that luxury. I had to go to the center of the assigned seating and be admonished for not remembering the password. Priscilla, with kindness and friendship, stood in sponsorship for me, and I was able to be joined back into the fellowship. After that, I made sure to always remember the password. To this day, I remember the time in the Order of the Rainbows as a dear time in my life. Dad was always proud of being a Mason, and I believe he was proud of me as a Rainbow. Today, these organizations have fallen into low memberships and poor attendance. I still believe in the importance of my years with the Rainbows and the bonding with other members. My second year in the Rainbows, Dad surprised me with a beautiful blue full-length evening dress to wear to the special ceremonies. He told me that I needed a lovely dress to wear because I was his daughter. It was such a beautiful dress and had assorted glitter in the netting that fell lightly on the ground when I walked. I felt rather like a sparkling fairy when I wore this dress and looked back to see the glittering trail I left behind. I doubt that the cleaning people agreed, but that did not matter to me at the time. Priscilla always complimented me on the dress and how lovely I looked.

The school year of 1958 had just started. I was in my sophomore class, and the fall days were before us. I was still the same person. Shy and quiet in school. Mainly walking the school halls alone and sitting alone. There were students I spoke to, but I mainly was a loner. I loved to sit and read. Art class was my favorite. Jim Richardson was the teacher. Ironically he had been a classmate of my sister, Betty, and had often been at our house to pick her up for a date. Now he was the art teacher, and I loved to be in his classroom and listen to his talk and share his knowledge of the arts. He was always kind to me and helped me in my art projects. He often praised me in what I was accomplishing and identified my many talents in the arts. He made me feel important and resourceful in my skills and knowledge. I probably had a huge crush on Jim also. He was just gorgeous to look at and single during these years. Always tan and slim, Jim was popular among the young girls. My developing interests in the arts helped me also to become a little more outgoing in classes. Whenever Jim had his students working on a project, he would let us have open discussions on our thoughts and interests. Those were great days in class, and I enjoyed Jim's humor and guidance immensely. I remember we were once talking about old age, and I announced emphatically that I did not want to get old and would probably kill myself before I got too old. Jim chuckled and asked me what I considered to be old age. I thought and then announced thirty-five was a very old age to me. Jim laughed aloud and said, "Well, Susie, let's think about that a little more, and someday when you are thirty-five, come to me and tell me if you still believe you are too old and should commit suicide." Sad to say that when I reached thirty-five, Jim died of stomach cancer at a much too early age. We were not together to later talk about growing old and the blessings of aging in life.

I now reach a very sad point in my young life. An incomprehensible moment in my life—the passing of a very dear friend. On this day, I had just come home from school and had gone into my bedroom to put away my books and rest before leaving for work with the theater. Momma came into my room in silence and sat down beside me on the bed. She had been crying. I looked at her with growing alarm and further queried, "What is the matter, Momma?" The following moments surrounded me with questioning thoughts as Momma prepared to answer me. She told me simply. Priscilla was dead. She had died that fall day, September 9, 1958, in the St. Vincent's Hospital in Monett. She had been just 18 years, 9 months, and 23 days old. A beautiful young married woman and she was dead. She had committed suicide by slitting her wrists and taking rat poison. She was dead. We were now left with only memories of yesterday and questions for today. We asked why she would kill herself. And yet, as she was dying in the hospital, Priscilla had reached out for her mother and screamed that she did not want to die that she wanted to live. But it was too late. The poison had already worked, and the doctors could not save Priscilla that day. She was dead. My mind was filled with raging questions. Why? I kept asking myself over and over this question. What would make kind and dear Priscilla do such a horrible savage act? I could not imagine the grief of not being able to see or talk to Priscilla again. Not to hear her laughter or see her sweet smile again. I would not know her as a mother with children in her home. I could only sit and stare at Momma.

Later, I cried and cried. Betty covered for me at work, and I stayed home and sat on my bed trying to understand what had happened to Priscilla. Momma told me that Mrs. Evans was just distraught with grief. She had now lost two children to an early death. Momma further explained that she had fixed some food to take to the Evans home and asked me if I would like to go with her. I said that I would and straightened my hair and dress to go outside and drive up to the Evans home with Momma. Momma felt that Mrs. Evans would be needing company.

When we arrived, Mrs. Evans was at home with other friends and neighbors. Many had come over with food and prepared help for Joey and his mother, Mrs. Evans. A once loud, boisterous house now sat in silence. Momma and I sat in the kitchen at the table and talked with Mrs. Evans. We mainly listened as she sobbed heartbreaking tears and spoke of her losses with Jimmy and now Priscilla. It was hard to bear. Everywhere I looked, I saw memories of my days visiting in the house and shared secrets and friendships with the family and especially with Priscilla. I looked around the house in wonder at the loss of two such fine young people.

The next few days were unbearable with the funeral, the burial ceremony, and later the gathering of family and friends with Mrs. Evans at her home. Priscilla had been a popular young lady in school with her classmates. She was a cheerleader. Academically she had exceled with her teachers and was remembered fondly in her high school classes. She had so much in life to enjoy. Friends, classmates, and faculty attended the funeral and later came to visit the Evans' home. Many had contributed food and thoughtful items at the time of this grief, and the kitchen table was fully burdened with food and drinks. I stood in disbelief and remembered how small and forlorn Priscilla's grave had looked when we had arrived at the cemetery with her casket. Flowers had decorated the grave and lay over the mound of dirt, but I still couldn't believe that we had to leave this young woman behind. We all left together and drove away in life, but Priscilla stayed alone in her grave in death. It was all so desolate and sad.

For a while, the days were filled with incomprehensible sad thoughts and memories. Although I had not been seeing Priscilla much because she had been married, I still missed my occasional hellos and greetings to each other when we did see each other. I missed her sweet smile and happy laughing. It took some time, but slowly the days became more regular and back to the usual. Momma often stopped by the house and visited with Mrs. Evans. She always made sure to take something by for Joey and his mother. She worried that they might not be eating right because of the intense grief felt in the house. Soon, again, life became more normal and continued with the everyday happenstance of life. I missed Priscilla.

We would never know what happened in Priscilla's life to bring her to want to die. She had never been a depressed or a sad person. She had loved life and the joy of each day. Yet she had stood in some dark corner of her mind and shouted the need to leave all of us. I missed Priscilla.

The Presbyterian Church

When I was twelve years old, I woke up that Sunday morning and knew I wanted to attend this church. I dressed myself in my good clothes and woke Momma to ask for some money to take to church for donation. I walked up the block to the Church, walked in and introduced myself to Mary and Harold Rooney, who would later become mentors to me all through the next formative years. I so loved this church and was active in the Church for as long as I lived in Monett. My favorite time was always when we had the Christmas Pageant.

Choir Members

This is a picture of the Presbyterian Church choir members with the lovely organ behind them. That organ amazed me - so many pedals, stops and keys. It was amazing to play. Absolutely lovely. The choir members pictured are before I joined but I would be singing with most of them during my high school years. I served in many capacities in that church, all filled with love and comfort. The members were all like a huge family to me - always caring and helping.

Chapter 41

Strictly Robbery

Life continued in its journey. The holidays arrived and left. A new year—1959. I attended school and worked at the theater. Dad sat in his shop and worked on the clocks. People came in to sit in the shop and talk with him. Momma worked at the local cleaners in the day. She loved to attend yard sales. It seemed that truly "one man's junk was another man's treasure," and these yard and estate sales had become widely popular during the last few years. People cleaned their attic, garage, and basement; tagged the monetary value onto the item; and set the item out in the yard to sell. Momma could not pass up a yard sale. She often bought children's clothes and laundered them and gave them to young parents she knew. She always found surprises for me in records, jewelry, and clothing. She soon began to box and pack items she purchased and place them in storage in our closet for a possible yard sale of her own. She loved to find an item and later sell it for a higher price than she paid. She had become a real expert on items of worth for resale.

In fact, it was about this time that Momma opened a store she had leased in Neosho to sell these items she had purchased at yard sales. Dad had helped her lease the building and set up the used-clothing and houseware store. Momma kept the store open several days a week and soon had a busy little yard sale of her own—in this rented room in Neosho selling items she had purchased at other yard sales. She loved it. The shop lasted about a year when Momma soon tired of all the extra work and decided to close the shop. She had a huge sale and later

348

donated and gave away all nonpurchased items to needy people. It all made for a good purpose. But she did continue to attend yard sales to purchase items for those she did know. When they printed the sign "I brake for yard sales" to place on one's car—that was just what Momma needed on her Cadillac. She could never pass up a yard sale. Later when I was married and living in St. Louis, Momma would plan a trip to visit and stay with Melissa and me for a week or so. When Momma arrived to my home, I would have newspapers with circled listings of coming yard sales and maps to help me find the areas. The listings would be awaiting her arrival and a planned travel to all the yard sales we could find during her stay. She always brought an empty suitcase with her on her visits so she could take it back filled with items she would purchase on her visit. Actually, during the early days of my daughter Melissa's life, Momma dressed her almost exclusively from those yard sales. I seldom had to purchase an item for her. I financially appreciated Momma's endeavors, and Melissa loved her surprises. My aunt Rena told me she always got a chuckle listening to what Momma had purchased at a yard sale and the many clothes she had purchased for Melissa.

Even today, Melissa and I reminisce about Momma's arrival to visit and how we would plan our yard sale journey the next day. We would get up at 6:00 a.m. because Momma liked to be early at the sales, and off we would drive on our journey for the day. I always had cold Dr. Peppers to drink in the car waiting with a bag of doughnuts and sandwiches. It was an adventure each time.

Changes were beginning to arrive on the horizon. I was getting older. Thoughts were now looming in question of what I was to make of my life after high school. I still really wanted to be a school teacher, but I was not sure I was going to accomplish this matter. I was not academically driven, and my grades were medium. I loved the arts. I read a lot. But mainly there were no monies for college. At this time, I had never heard about government loans or scholarships for attendance in college. I found no special help in planning for school. The guidance counselor told me I should plan for employment in an office as a secretary or such. I was not given a large boost to want to further educate myself. I had the dream but no real way to attain this dream. I was feeling rather deflated in life and not sure how to attain becoming a schoolteacher. Many things would change in my life that would alter my life and happenstance to attain my goal.

Once again, we were out at the summer drive-in. I was a senior in high school, and this would turn out to be my last few days working at the theater. I didn't know this and only foresaw my regular school days and another year with the theater. The days to come would not bring this to fruition. Changing times were ahead for me. Betty, my cousin, was going on a vacation with Aunt Rena and Uncle Paul to Arizona, and I had been asked to work in the box office. Momma would be working in the concession stand with George. The next two weeks would bring me to working nights in the box office, and I was not really looking forward to the job. I didn't like being down at the box office alone; I always felt so vulnerable. The box office was stationed a few miles down from the theater concession stand and building. The box office was glass on all sides with a concrete bottom half. It felt sort of like being in a large fishbowl.

That particular night, the manager was really excited because we were showing the movie *The Nun* with Audrey Hepburn, and it promised to be a large sellout. When I arrived to work, cars were already beginning to line up at the box office. As I readied the change bags and paperwork to take down to the box office, the manager pulled me over to the side and, for some reason, reminded me of some rules we all already knew when working with monies. He reminded me that "should anything happen, the money was not important but my life was!" He told me that money could be replaced, but I could not. I was in a hurry to get to the box office and get the evening started. I picked up my belongings and began the walk down the gravel road to the box office. Leroy, the ramp boy and younger brother of George, was with me.

Leroy stood outside the box office while I set up the change and tickets. When all settled, he signaled the cars could start driving up the graveled road to the box office to buy their tickets. We both remarked how long the line was coming up to the box office. We were really going to be packed that Sunday night, that was for sure. So the long continuing lines of packed cars slowly dwindled as people drove up to my box office window to purchase tickets and go in to see the show. Everyone was excited to go see the movie and had brought the whole family. The next thirty minutes was very busy with getting all the cars into the drive-in and parked. Leroy stayed by my box office and pointed the direction the cars were to drive to continue their journey up into the parking spaces to get settled in for the night. We had a lot of people passing through that I did not even know. I figured they had driven over to see the movie from other towns like Pierce City or Aurora.

Slowly, the line of cars began to lessen. It seemed that we had gotten all attendees into the drive-in and settled down to watch the movie. It had been a strenuous beginning to the evening with so many people arriving. They had had to open up the back area of the drive-in that we never use. It was almost at the end with the fence where the cows were kept. There were probably a few cows at the fence watching all the strangers in their cars and the movie also. Some people complained that the cows sometimes mooed over the sound of the movie! We were really packed. At that time, Leroy and I were standing and talking at the ticket window. I was inside the box office counting change and putting ticket monies in bank bags for deposit later that night. Leroy was standing outside the box office window leaning on the window ledge and talking to me. We just could not believe how many people had arrived to see the movie. We did not think we had ever had that many people. I told Leroy that the manager was really going to be excited to see this money I would be bringing to the office later. I had never handled so much cash before.

Just then, we heard a noise some short distance from us in the grassy section past the graveled road that ran aside the box office. There was a small water stream that ran past on the adjacent land to the box office entrance, and often there were frogs and birds there. Leroy threw a rock at the noise, and I cautioned him against doing that. I was afraid he might hurt a frog or such in the water stream there. He laughed at me for being such a softie. Then Leroy said he should get up to the concession stand and get in station for directing the cars as they would be leaving from the theater. He knew it was going to be a large effort to get all the cars out and back on the road without some altercation. People always got so eager to get back on the road and return home they would sometimes zoom out in front of other lanes of cars or honk their car horns to hurry the ramp boys in their work. The ramp boys always tried to direct the cars out in an orderly fashion, but some nights it was just impossible to manage. So Leroy left to walk back up to the concession stand and continue his work.

I turned back to the monies before me and continued my paperwork and ticket counting. The monies all lay in the bank bags on the counter and on the floor beneath my feet. Just then, I heard someone running over the graveled road by my box office window, and as I looked up, there was a man standing there at my window with a gun pointed right through the window. The gun was pointed at my head. I could look right down the gun barrel. I could also see that he had his finger on the trigger and had pulled it back. The gun was all ready to be shot at his slightest whim. I looked up from the gun barrel at the man before me, but I couldn't really see him. He stood about five feet seven or so, taller than me for certain, and I had to look up at him. He wore a Stetson cowboy hat on his head and had a colored bandana tied over the lower part of his face. I could only see his eyes, and I really didn't want to look there. He wore a dress tweed jacket, and he either had a hunch back or he wore a small pillow on his back to create a deformed back. It made him hard to distinguish in shape. I was not aware of his lower half. The concrete lower half of the box office obliterated any sight of him from my angle. I looked back into his face or what part of it I could see.

The man kind of shook the gun at me again and said, "Give me all your money, Susie, and be quick about it." He had certainly gotten my attention with those words and the movement of the gun. I was certain I was going to be shot to death at any moment. I could barely stand straight and not just fall over in a fainting spell. I was shaking a lot.

He handed me a Gillioz bank bag and told me to start filling it up. I opened the box office money drawer and began to pull out the dollars and stuff them into his bag. I gave him all the coins wrapped in bank wrappers and was busy filling up his bag. While busy working to fill up his bag, I did not mention the money bags beneath my feet. I knew my feet were covered from his sight by my full checkered skirt and the three petticoats I had on that evening, so unless he knew about the bagged monies, he would not be able to see them. I also kind of smiled to myself as I thought how this robber did not know the assigned colors of bank wrappers for coins. Each color stood for the denomination of coins—for instance, brown for pennies, green for dimes, etc. So despite my fear of the man and the gun, I found myself quickly filling up his bank bag with rolls and rolls of pennies. I figured he was going to be pretty mad when he got to his hiding place and opened all those coin wrappers to find so many pennies. My humor always got me into trouble, and I was already sorry I was pulling this trick on the robber so I gave him all the pennies and began to give him quarters and dimes and nickels.

Just then you could hear the honking of cars, which meant the movie was over, and the cars would soon be coming out of the drive-in on the opposite side of the box office's graveled road. They would be coming out and heading back onto the main road and on to their homes.

The robber shook the money bags and zipped them close. He then twisted the gun a little closer at me and began to walk away from the box office to the front of the building. Then to my surprise, he turned, and pointing the gun right at me, he hollered, "Get on the floor, Susie, and don't get up for ten minutes." And let me tell you, with him standing there, pointing that gun full at me through the glass front, that is exactly what I did. I got down on the floor among the bank bags of monies and stayed, shaking and crying. I was so scared that he was going to realize I had not given him all the monies and come back and shoot me. He asked for ten minutes, well, I was going to give him all the time he wanted to get away! That was for certain. So I lay on the floor, very scared and vulnerable, as I heard cars driving away while honking and passengers hollering at each other, for a good ten minutes. Then, as the sounds subsided some, I slowly sat up on my knees and took a small gander around the box office and outside the glass windows. The robber was gone. I was alone in the box office. All activity was happening on the graveled road on the other side of the drive-in.

Cautiously I stood up. I saw the cars driving away, but I had no way of telling them I needed help. We had no phones in the box office and no connection to the concession stand a mile or so up the graveled road and in the drive-in. So I gathered the bank bags left on the floor and a flashlight, my keys, and my purse and positioned myself to walk out of the box office and back up the road to the concession stand. I just wanted to get with people and feel the comfort of safety. I was so frightened by what had just happened and my own close brush with possible death by gunshot. It was just all beginning to formulate in my mind as to what had taken place and how completely vulnerable I was. So on very shaky legs, I gathered the previously mentioned items and turned off the box office light and shut the door while locking it behind me. When I stepped out of the building, I looked up the road in the dark and saw how far away from me the concession stand really was. I had to walk alone in the dark to get to help. Let me tell you, that was a very long mile to walk in the dark, starlit evening to get to the concession stand to find help and be able to tell what had happened. Somehow I made the walk on my shaking limbs. The last few minutes to the stand, I began to run. I wanted to be inside that building as fast as I could and have people around me to comfort me and make me feel safe again. I ran to the office door and jerked it open to run inside. As I slammed the door shut, I was crying and shaking while hollering, "I have been robbed!"

My mother, who was working the concession night, and Pops stepped around the corner from the front and looked at me in shock. Momma walked quickly over to me to comfort me, and Pops was screaming at me "What are you talking about, Susie?"

I quickly told them what had just happened as they sat me into a desk chair. Pop got on the phone to call the state police while he shouted at the ramp boys to stop all cars from leaving right then. It was an emergency.

As I sat and talked to Momma and Pops and drank some iced soda they had given to me, I was still crying and shaking. Telling them the story had made me realize even more how life-threatening this robbery had been and how close I had been to being shot or killed. I just wanted them near me and to not leave me. Just then, the manager came pounding through the office door hollering, "What is going on?" and then he saw me. Leaning near me, he listened as I told him about the robbery and what had happened. That was when we heard the sirens of arriving local police and state police. Officers were talking through their bullhorns to the passengers who wanted to leave and telling them they had to wait. There had been a robbery! That brought a stunned silence to the passengers, and they quieted down in their cars and sat there.

The officers arrived into the office and came over to me. They listened quietly as I summed up the happenings of the robbery and answered their questions. They left several policemen by my side and began to walk around the drive-in lot to look into the cars parked or on the exit road. After they searched through the cars, they would signal that they could leave, and Leroy or George signaled their exits with flashlights.

I sat terrified at the desk from all the police around me and their questions and looks. They assured me that I was now safe and they would be with me to keep me further protected. Momma sat down with me and Pops went out the shut down the concession stand.

After having listened to my description of how the robber had been dressed, the officers gathered a cowboy hat, a bandana, and a jacket with a small pillow. They then proceeded to escort various young men into the backroom dressed in these clothes for me to look at and listen to them speak. Let me tell you, there were some young men shaking in their boots that night as they spoke my name and pretended to threaten me. I had to smile to myself at their frightened look at me and almost startled plea for me not to identify them as the robber.

I laughed for a moment and turned to the state policeman and told him that I could probably marry the young man and never know he had been the robber. His disguise had been just too good, and I could not give any identifying remarks about him. I could not really even remember the color of his eyes. I think they were brown, but I was not sure.

The state policeman shook his head. And then, just when I thought I could not get any more upset, shocked, startled, or otherwise devastated, my father arrived at the scene, in the concession stand. I could hear his voice and the stern answer from the policeman and state policeman. And there was Dad, walking around the corner of the entrance, pushing past the policeman standing there. I looked at him and there he stood, all five foot six inches of him, standing there in his summer slacks, beige summer shirt, his favorite beige Stetson hat, and his two six-guns slung over his hips in holsters. A gun hanging on each side of hips, and he had his hands on the guns as if he was going to pull them out of their nestling places in the holsters. It was like looking at a bad Gene Autry movie. Dad looked around at the policeman and then over at me and said, rather loudly, "Nobody messes with my daughter. What is going on here?!"

The two policemen stepped back, and I swear I saw a smile on one of their faces, when he said sternly, "Now, Stonie, no need to get yourself all riled. Susie is fine now, and we are looking out for her. She was robbed. The robber got away with some money. But as you can see, she is here now, with us, protected and safe, and we are going to make sure she stays that way."

Then the policeman stepped over to Dad and, talking to him, made sure he was proper in his ownership of the guns and had needed licenses. Then he stepped back, and looking down at Dad, he said, "Stonie, you are going to have to take off those guns before you shoot one of us or yourself. Give them to us or put them in your car's trunk. We can't have you marching around here threatening these people. What if someone got hurt? Right now you are more of a threat than the robber was. Are you listening to me, Stonie?"

Dad nodded in agreement and mumbled, "I was just making sure my daughter was safe. I see what you mean, officer, I do. I'll go and put these guns and holsters in the trunk of my car, but I want one of you officers to stay with Susie."

The policeman agreed, and much to my relief, Dad left the room to put the guns in the car. You see, everyone knew Stonie in Monett, and the policeman knew Dad was not a threat. He just needed to make sure that all precautions were covered. Dad knew that and respected the policeman's request. As for me, well, I just wanted Dad to put up the guns before he shot himself in the foot or shot one of us. Also, I was a little embarrassed at Dad showing up at the concession stand dressed with the guns in their holsters on his hips standing there in front of all the policeman. I didn't want them to be laughing at him. But I think they all understood his fears for my safety and respected him in the matter. Whatever. The building had quieted down. Cars had all been removed from the drive-in, and the customers had gone home. I had not identified anyone the police had brought in for my inspection, so they figured I might as well go on home also. I thanked them all, and they told Dad they would be driving by the house during the night to make sure all was settled.

Momma drove us home, and Dad followed. When we got home, Dad called Dr. Kerr and told him of the night's events, and the doctor came quickly to the house to talk to me and check up on me. I had gotten out of my clothes and into my pajamas when Dr. Kerr arrived. He looked me over and opened his large black satchel to take out a hypodermic needle to give me a shot. He told Momma and Dad it would settle my nerves and help me to sleep.

I tell you, despite my nervous crying and shaking, I was asleep as soon as my head hit the pillow. Momma slept beside me in my bed to make sure I was okay during the night. Dad thanked Dr. Kerr, and he left after telling Dad to call him should he be needed further.

That morning when I woke up, Momma was already in the kitchen making breakfast. She wanted me to stay home, but I insisted I should go to school and that I felt just fine. That was a mistake. When I got to school, I realized how shaken I still was, and I was feeling a little dizzy and nauseous. Of course, the kids weren't helping either. They all thought it was tremendously funny and kept jumping out from behind lockers and doors and hollering, "Bang—you are dead!" and such. It all had me a nervous wreck, and by noon, I decided I should go home. The principal agreed, and Momma came to pick me up. I went home and took a nap for the afternoon.

That evening I was to report to work back in the box office. I told Momma that I really did not want to go there to work. When we got to the concession stand and the office, the manager was already there. When I saw him, I asked if the ramp boy could stay at the box office with me that evening as I really did not want to be alone. It all made me feel so nervous to think that the robber could just jump out of the dark again and have the gun to shoot me. To my surprise, the manager said that he could not spare the ramp boy and that I would have to work that evening alone in the box office. I was furious and very scared. I did not want to go down there alone this night. It was all still too fresh in my mind, and I was scared that the robber would return.

Momma was furious, but I went down to the box office to work. I got the office open and had all set up for customers to arrive. We had a fairly good showing of cars arrive for the second night of *The Nun Story*. Then, slowly, all became quiet, and all cars had driven through. I was alone in the box office, listening to all the night sounds of crickets, frogs, and various things that go "bump in the night." I was feeling very vulnerable sitting there in a half-glass building where anyone could see me from any angle nearby. I just wanted to fall on the floor and stay hidden from anyone who might be watching me. I couldn't bear to be sitting there alone in the night. Finally, I could not bear it any longer. It was close to closing time anyway, so I packed up the monies, tickets, and paperwork, locked up the box office, and began my lone journey back up to the concession stand. I was terrified walking back up there in the evening dark. I felt a little better as I got to where the cars were parked and I could see the concession stand and the lights.

When I arrived at the stand, I went inside to the office and set my things on the desk. The manager was there working on various reports. I told him how scared I had been down in the box office alone. I asked him if I could have a ramp boy the next night as I had two more nights to work before Betty returned from vacation and she would be working there. The manager shook his head and told me no. I was furious.

I stood there silently thinking and weighing my choices—and then I told the manager that I was quitting. I told him that I could not go down there to the box office another night and work alone. It was too scary, and I felt too vulnerable. It was a hard choice as I had been working there since I was fifteen. Three years and I had hoped to work at the theater through my senior year so I could have monies for my savings for college. The manager was steadfast in his rulings, so I had no alternative but to leave. I went out to the car and sat until Momma came out, and we went home.

The manager worked the box office those two days until Betty returned home. When Betty heard about what had happened, she came right over to our house to see me. I told her the whole story of the robbery, and to my surprise, Betty was mad because I was the one who had been robbed. She was going on about how she had worked there all those years, but when the robbery was held, she was gone and I was the one robbed. She would have wanted to be there. She told me she would have known how to act. I just laughed at her and told her she was very lucky it had not been her and how scared I had been. She left to go home, and I could tell she was really mad. Momma just laughed and said that it was just Betty's little oddities and told me not to pay any attention to her. She was just jealous of the attention I had gotten from everyone and the news on television, radio, and papers. I replied, "Trust me, she could have had any of it. I didn't want any more of it at all. I just wanted to feel normal again." Momma smiled, and so did I.

To this day, some fifty years later, nothing was ever found out about the robbery. Nothing. I seem to remember that the robber got a total of about three hundred dollars that night with a lot of pennies. I did hear later from a very small article in the newspaper that someone had held up the box office at another drive in. It could have been in Aurora or near. I am not really sure. I also think that the ramp boy was shot. Not seriously, but he was wounded because he tried to fight the robber. Whatever happened, I figured I had been lucky enough in my robbery. No one had been hurt, and all was over.

So there I was. No work and the year seeming to move along although only a week or so had gone by since my leaving the work at the theater. Betty was still rather miffed with me, but had gotten back over her anger. She now realized how scary the adventure had all been, and she felt sorry it had happened to me. The manager was just happy to have Betty back in the box office.

Then the minister at my church stopped by the shop to talk to me. He said that he had a lot of correspondence that he needed to keep up with and general filing and such in the office and wondered if I would want to work in the church's office to help him and the congregation. I was so excited. It was just about the same pay I had received at the theater, and it was in the afternoon, after school, and Saturday work. No night work. I could stay home and watch television, read, get my homework done, or just rest and enjoy being at home. It was the perfect solution. With a paycheck, I could continue saving for college and help with family bills.

Of course, I always had a feeling that the church's congregation and minister had seen my own plight and had pooled their resources to help me get a job. We had never had a secretary in the office before to help the minister and didn't resume so, later, after I left for school, but whatever, it was a lifesaver for me. I was very blessed by this church and the members. They always seemed there to help me when I needed some extra help in my life.

Working for the minister was a delight. He was kind, thoughtful, and a good boss but extremely forgetful. There were times that he would be dictating a letter to me and just put on his hat and walk out of the building leaving me sitting there holding paper and pen. After the first incident, I became used to the matter, and I would just put down the pad and pen, and the next time he was in the office working, we would get the letter finished. Oftentimes he was not in the office when I went there to work. At this time, I would answer the phone and get the Sunday bulletin ready for the congregation. I loved to be in the church in the afternoons. There was such peace and love there that I could feel it surround me those days. I felt the church building to be a home of safety and comfort. I was also extremely thankful for the job that would enable me to continue my saving monies in my bank account for that hopeful day when I could enter college. It was a determination for me, and I was trying all the ways I could to make it come true for me. I wanted to be a schoolteacher.

Chapter 42

Driving With Miss Daisy

At this time, I decided I wanted to learn how to drive a car. I took driving lessons at school with Mr. Tinklepaugh, who was a delightful, funny, and kind man. He was always willing to spend some time sitting and talking with me about my plans and showed interest in what I said. During the driving lessons, with the other student sitting in the backseat, I am sure that I greatly tried Mr. Tinklepaugh's nerves and concern. It is not that I was a careless driver. I just did not concentrate on driving like I should. I was too easily distracted; thus, I missed stop signs, turned at corners, was a lousy parker of the car, and never did learn how to parallel park. Oftentimes, as I drove, the student in the back, usually a young man who was just panting to get behind the wheel, would be shouting at how stupid I was and all the mistakes I was making. Mr. Tinklepaugh would just hush him and remind me that I needed to concentrate harder and follow the driving rules. He never got upset when I missed a turn at the corner or when I missed the stop and drove right into the gas station. When the backseat student began to laugh and make fun of my mistake, Mr. Tinklepaugh would just smile and remark upon how I was just thinking of the needs of the car and that it did need some gasoline. I would smile and thank him for supporting me.

Again, Mr. Tinklepaugh was a very kind man and was always a great supporter for the students, often the ones who were not as popular and needed extra guidance. He seemed to be the only one interested in my wanting to be a teacher and encouraging me to try my very best. The school advisor and counselor had met with me one afternoon and told me that I should not waste my endeavors in going to college but instead should settle for a secretary job there in Monett. She recommended the shoe factory, which was always hiring. When I told Mr. Tinklepaugh about this matter, he just smiled and told me that I should aim for what I wanted to do and not to listen to any other person. He laughed at the idea of working in the shoe factory and reminded me that I had much higher dreams to attain—that of becoming a schoolteacher. His kind words often encouraged me and inspired me to continue in my efforts. After college graduation, I returned to Monett to go visit first the advisor/counselor to show her that I had attained all A's in my major in college and that I had received various awards for my accomplishments at graduation. She just smiled at me and acted as if she had always been in support of my thoughts. When I talked to Mr. Tinklepaugh, he really smiled and was so happy for me. That was a proud achievement for me.

As for my written driver's test, I failed the eye test. Yep. Seemed I was very nearsighted and could not read the letters on the eye test. When I went home to tell Momma, she shook her head and said she could not help me. We did not have the monies to buy me eyeglasses, and I would just have to do the best I could. I had managed all these years, and she was sure I could continue. Ironically, the next year, when I was working that first summer at School of the Ozarks in Branson, Missouri, where I attended my first two years of college, I was able to work extra hours in the night at the canning factory peeling tomatoes and was able to purchase my first pair of eyeglasses through those monies. I was amazed to see all I had been missing when I put on my first pair of glasses. I could see blooms on the trees—it was amazing to me!

Did I ever get my driver's license? Well, yes, I did. After graduation from college, Julie and I were moving to St. Louis to teach school in September in schools where we had been hired. Julie wanted me to be able to drive so we could take turns with her car. So there I was again, facing the task of getting my driver's license, only this time I had one advantage: I had glasses so I could pass the eye test. But there was one other matter. I did not have a car to use for the test. I could not use Dad's pink Cadillac because he was on probation for some trouble he had gotten into, and he could not risk any car accidents happening with his car. He could get blamed and be hauled off to jail. So there

I was, desperately wanting to get my license and not able to get a car for the test. At this time, I was working at Lakeland Restaurant during the summers, and one evening I had been talking to a friend about my dilemma. Some men were sitting at the counter drinking coffee and sometimes listening to me talk about my need to get my driving license. Julie was adamant that I had to have my license before I could move with her to St. Louis. I was in a panic.

Suddenly, a man at the counter called me over and said, "Hey, do you need a car to take the driver's test with?" I nodded yes and wondered who he was. He smiled at me and explained that he had a car dealership just down the road and that he had just the car for me to use for my test. It was almost brand-new and guaranteed to pass the driver's test inspection. I was so surprised to be offered the use of this man's car and that he would so trust me. He further told me to meet him tomorrow afternoon, and I could have the car from his lot and go take the test as the driver's licenses were being given that day. I quickly agreed. Meanwhile, I told Dick, my friend, that I was really worried about this because I had not driven a car for years since high school and that I had not done too well then. I did not know how I was going to pass a driving test. Well, Dick thought for a minute and then he said, "Listen, let's go driving after you get off this afternoon from work. You can drive my little jalopy around town and get used to turning and driving a car." I thought it was a great idea. I did not tell Momma or Dad because they would be hollering at me as I did not have a driver's permit and I could get into a serious accident.

Anyway, Dick came by with his Ford jalopy he had built and rigged to be started by touching two wires together. It also had an old stick clutch on the floor, which I had never, ever driven. But you know how the young are—nothing is impossible to them. We can accomplish anything—or so we believe. So there I am chugging around town in Dick's old jalopy, ripping the gears as I try to go higher in speed. It was a horrible experience. And then, just as we are bouncing along Bond Street, in front of my house, Dad steps out of the shop and is standing in front where he can see me driving Dick's car. I scream at Dick, "What am I going to do? I can't let Dad see me driving your car!" I didn't know how to turn the car around, so we had to keep traveling down the street to our house and shop. So as we get closer to where Dad is standing, Dick hollers to me to just scrunch down, keep driving the car, and go right by Dad. As we go by, Dick waves to Dad, who has a startled expression on his face as we drove by. I am sitting down low in the seat, driving, or trying to drive with Dick guiding me, trying not to laugh at the imagined sight of me sitting almost on the floor and driving. We drove a little more and decided we should go out to the dealership to get the man's car and I go take the test. I was so scared I could barely sit still.

So we pull up to the car lot, and there is this incredibly shining, almost new Cadillac for me to use in my driver's test. The man hands me the keys, and Dick drives off to meet me at the town hall to take the test. I sat behind the steering wheel and, to my amazement, realized that the car is all push button. But there is nothing written to tell me what button to push to make the car work. There I am, alone, in the parking lot. Dick has left. The kind man has left for the afternoon. No one is around, and I have to start up this gorgeous push-button car to go take my driving test! I sit there in tears. How was I going to accomplish this? So I begin to test the buttons. I have the windshield wipers going and the horn honking. Windows were going up and down, and the radio was blaring music for all to hear. I was terrified. My appointment time has arrived, and I knew I had to get to the town hall to take my test.

Somehow, on a wing and a prayer, I drive the car, horn honking, windshield wipers moving, etc., down Main Street and up to the town hall to park to take my test. I see Dick over talking to Dad. When I get out of the car after parking it in front of our shop, Dad is telling Dick, "It was the most amazing sight I have ever seen. Your car drives by me down the road with no one behind the steering wheel and you are sitting there on the passenger's side, waving to me with a silly grin on your face. What's going on?" Dick just shrugged and grinned.

I then told Dad what I was going to do, and he said, "This I have gotta see." So Dad and Dick walk across the street and station themselves on the fence there to have a front row view of me driving the borrowed car for my driving test. Both are laughing at me at how I probably will not even get the car started.

I walk inside the town hall and go over to take my eye test and written exam. This time, I pass both of them and am notified that I may now take my driver's test. I walk out to the parked car and get in on the driver's side. The exam person walks around the car checking the tires and such. I have the windows up, and he hollers for me to turn on the windshield wipers. I am frantically trying to figure out which button to push, and before I know it, I have the horn honking, windows going up and down, windshield wipers going back and forth, and the window wash spraying the car's windshield. The exam person just stands there looking at me with this amazed face while I shrug my shoulders and try to use the various buttons as he asks for them.

And then it happens. He gets into the car and sits down. Did I mention that it was the hottest day ever in our town of Monett? It was one hundred degrees in the shade and definitely no cooling breeze. The day was a killer for heat. And there I sat in this wondrous fairly new car, with all the buttons to push, and I had learned the most needed button of them all—the air conditioner. Did I further mention that this air conditioner in this car probably had the most powerful and cooling wind to press over one's hot, sweaty face? As soon as the examiner sat down, that huge waft of Arctic cooling air hit him full on his face and body, and let me tell you, he just melted in pure, unadulterated "coolness." He could not even speak for a few minutes; it was all so delightful! Like sitting in the freezer of one's refrigerator. It was tremendous to watch that man expand and collapse with one huge swelled breath. He was mine!

He told me to pull away from the curb and drive slowly forward. I did and then in pure panic, as I was in terror of my own driving, I slammed on the brakes, squealing the tires and throwing gravel everywhere in the parking lot. To my surprise, I even watched the examiner, in slow motion, fall forward and strike his forehead on the front glass window. I knew it was all over! I could see Dad and Dick standing there with their mouths open with concern and wonder.

I turned to the examiner expecting him to tell me to pull back over and park the car, but he did not. He just asked me if I could turn up the air conditioning even higher. I could and did—filling the front seat even further with the most frozen Arctic air I had ever felt. The front windows were even frosting over. The examiner just wiped the windows clear with his elbow and told me to drive off. As I drove past Dad and Dick, I could see Dick picking himself up off the ground where he had been laughing so hard he had fallen off the fence he was sitting on. I pulled off quietly, examining the person in the front seat, sitting back in the comfortable, leather-bound seats, cool to the touch, and relishing in all the luxury that almost new Cadillac could offer. I swear I could almost hear the man purring!

HOME AGAIN, HOME AGAIN, JIGGITY, JIG   365

We drove slowly around town. I won't tell you it was a pretty picture. I ran a stop sign. I missed a turn and ran over a curb. I almost ran a red light. I threw the gentleman examiner several times against the windshield, but we kept on driving. Cold Arctic air was felt pulsating through those car vents covering us both with bone-chilling, pure cold air. Finally, the gentleman told me to head back to the town hall. Of course, in the final endeavor, I still could not parallel park, but the examiner told me to not mind and just pull over to the curb so we could have a few minutes and enjoy a little more of the Arctic air.

I did. I put the car in park and turned to the examiner and waited for the bad news. I figured he was going to ban me from ever driving during my entire life and that there was no way I would ever be able to move to St. Louis with Julie and drive to work. My life was over before it even began.

So I sat there, behind the wheel listening to the wafting Arctic air pulsating through the vents. One could not even see out of the windows because the car was so steamed with cold air. We were literally sitting in a car of cold, pulsing wind. I was beginning to feel like a threatened Eskimo about to be eaten by a whale. My life was over. And then the examiner turned to me and said, "I am going to pass you and give you a driver's license but only if you promise me to never, ever drive in Monett again or anywhere that I may be on duty. You pack up and head on to St. Louis to teach and let the troopers worry about you there."

Then, as I sat in stunned silence, he leaned back further in the seat and told me to hit that air conditioner button one more time for a few more minutes of luxurious cool air before he had to go back out into that horrific sweltering hot day! I obliged and sat quietly, smiling and thinking, *I had gotten my driver's license!*

After some more minutes, the examiner slowly got out of the car and handed me my passing exam. He walked away from the car and into the town hall, with one final pat on the front of the Cadillac. He really loved that car. Dad and Dick came over and were talking with me about how there could be other times to try for the license. I laughed and showed them my approved exam. I had passed. I had my license. It was a miracle!

When I returned the car, I told the car dealer about my test and how the air conditioner had saved my life and my driver's license. He just laughed and responded that he was happy to have helped. I tell you—he was my hero!

Chapter 43

Truman, Can You Spare A Dime?

Moving back to my high school days, I have mentioned that my father was an avid Harry Truman fan. The first piano piece I was to learn was "The Missouri Waltz" because Harry Truman played it on the piano in the White House. Dad had pictures of Harry Truman framed and hanging on the wall all through his clock shop. Dad loved to tell stories of Truman and to quote him. All in all, he idolized him. Well, around this time, there were rumors that Harry Truman would be attending the 1960 Democratic National Convention in Los Angeles, California. It wasn't really acknowledged, but Dad got all excited to read that Truman might be there. My graduation from high school was near, and I was now working at the church as a secretary to the minister, and a few nights during the weekend, I would work at the local ice cream shop on the main street, across the street from the Monett Hotel. It was not even a block from our house, and it was ideal for me to work there to pick up some extra monies. I liked the lady who owned it and the two people I worked with. Actually, I never did really learn how to run the soft ice cream machine where one filled the cone with the soft ice cream ending with a curl on top. I could never get the cone to be evenly filled nor the curl to be on top. I always made lopsided cones which tended to fall right over to the side. Maurice, a high school friend who worked with me, would always come over and square off the cone with the curl, and then I would serve it to the customers.

HOME AGAIN, HOME AGAIN, JIGGITY, JIG   367

Anyway, I was working in the ice cream shop and at the church and going to school to finish up my senior year. All seemed comfortable and peaceful. One day, Dad came storming back into the kitchen where Momma and I were, and he was all excited. He had just read in the paper that Harry Truman might attend the Democratic Convention in Los Angeles after all. He was adamant that he wanted to go see Harry and attend the convention. Momma and I just shrugged it all off as we did most of Dad's ideas or thoughts. We knew we had no monies for such a trip, and Momma and I both had jobs. We could not take off from our jobs to drive across the United States from Missouri to Los Angeles on the one hope we might be able to see or meet Harry Truman. Dad went on ranting about his plans, and Momma and I just kept on busy with what we were doing. It didn't make sense to argue with Dad. It was better to just ignore him, and soon he would just wear down.

I decided to go in and read in my book and rest as I had work that night. Momma wanted to drive out to see Aunt Rena for a few minutes. I soon fell asleep in my bedroom, and Momma was gone to see Aunt Rena. That was when Dad began his plans to go see Harry Truman. Without our knowledge, Dad walked over to the newspaper office just down the block from our home. He met with the owner and editor and announced to them that Mr. and Mrs. Glenn Stone and daughter, Susie, would be leaving on Monday to drive across the country to Los Angeles where they would be attending the Democratic National Convention. He also informed the editor that when they arrived at the convention, they would be speaking with former president Harry Truman, who had announced his plans to attend the convention. He then proceeded to walk back home and go into the kitchen to use the telephone to call the Democratic National Convention in Los Angeles. He wanted to tell Harry Truman that we were arriving at the convention and he would like to be able to meet with him. So he called the operator and asked for her to dial the Convention Center in Los Angeles and to ask for Harry Truman who was supposed to already be there in attendance at the convention. Well, the operator put Dad through to the center, and someone answered the phone, and Dad asked to speak to Harry Truman. Apparently, the person who answered then set the phone down on a desk or table and walked off to find someone to talk to this person calling long distance from Missouri. Soon, Dad got tired of waiting and apparently laid the phone receiver down on the kitchen table. Then he proceeded off to his bedroom to pull down the shades, shut the door, and go to bed to sleep off the high from the whiskey he had been drinking all day.

I was asleep in my bedroom. Momma came home some thirty minutes later to wake me up so I could get ready to go to work. She then asked me who was on the phone. She said the receiver was lying on the kitchen table and when she picked it up to say hello, no one answered. I told her that I had no idea who was on the phone as I had been asleep. Momma then noted that Dad was passed out in bed, so she just hung up the phone.

I got ready for work and was about to leave when I heard Momma call my name. "Susie, come quick," she said. I walked into the kitchen to see what the matter was and saw Momma standing there in the center of the room holding the local newspaper *The Monett Times*. "Look at the front page," Momma said as she handed the paper to me. I glanced over the page when my eyes suddenly stopped to take in a better view of the small column pasted there on the front page. Right there, for all the world to see, was a small one-column posting on the front page that talked all about the trip Mr. and Mrs. Stone and daughter, Susie, would be taking next week when they journey by car to Los Angeles to attend the Democratic National Convention and to speak to former president Harry Truman. Dad further added to the small article, on the front page of the newspaper, that he had called Harry Truman personally to tell him that we were coming. That would explain why the phone receiver was lying on the table.

"Oh no." I gasped. Dad had called Los Angeles long distance. "Oh no," I said again. Dad had told the whole world that we were going to Los Angeles when we both would just be going to our usual work and Dad was passed out in bed. I was so mad. "How could I face my friends in Monett or anyone for that matter?!" I could see red—a bright, bright red. I was so angry. Dad had just wandered down to the local papers and told them that we were going on the trip. He had then proceeded to call the convention and then just gone off to bed leaving Momma and me to deal with all the results of his actions, as usual. I was so angry.

Momma just stood there. What could she do? I decided I should calm down as I was only hurting Momma. So I wiped my tears from my face and asked Momma, "What are we going to do?" Momma smiled and folded up the paper. She laid it on the table and said to me, "Don't

HOME AGAIN, HOME AGAIN, JIGGITY, JIG   369

worry, Susie. No one really pays much attention to what your father says. They will laugh about it for a day or so, and then something else will happen, and it will all be forgotten. By then, Dad will be up from his nap and will just go on as before. He will have forgotten all about Harry Truman and his proposed trip. It will all be forgotten and never spoken about. Just go on to work, and don't pay attention to what people may say. On the whole, they know we had nothing to do with all this and will leave it alone."

So I got ready for work at the ice cream shop, and Momma got ready to work at the theater in the concession stand. Momma drove off to work in the car, and I crossed the street to walk down the block to work. As I started to walk down the hill to the shop, I looked over and saw all the firemen sitting out in front of the station. They were sitting and smoking and reading the newspaper. Of course. It was too late to turn back and such, so I just kept on walking. As I was in front of the station, several of the firemen looked up and feigned surprise I was there. "Susie, why are you here? I thought you would be on the way to Los Angeles with your parents." As the fireman spoke, he nudged the other one near him, and several of the men looked up at me. I stopped and gave everyone a sweet smile and replied, "Oh well. Guess we won't be going to Los Angeles. I have to work, and so does Momma. Too bad I would have loved to meet Harry Truman."

I think my calmness and my reply made the firemen ashamed for teasing me as they knew we weren't really going on the trip. So they all smiled at me and wished me a good night. I walked on down the hill with my head held high. Later, I read in the news that Harry Truman did not attend the convention, but he certainly made his ideas known regarding the Democratic nominations. He was definitely against the young senator John Kennedy.

Several weeks passed on, and as Momma had said, people soon forgot about the column in the newspaper and about Dad's planned trip to Los Angeles. No one mentioned it in the shop, and Dad never mentioned it to us. It was all forgotten. And then the phone bill arrived. Long distance, person to person, from Monett, Missouri, to Los Angeles, California, the bill was two hundred fifty dollars. Oh my gosh. It took our breath away. That was like telling it cost two hundred fifty thousand dollars. We did not have monies to pay that bill. In fact, we could not imagine ever having monies to pay that bill.

Of course, the telephone company came and took our telephone away. We could get it back when we paid off the bill, and Momma was determined to pay off that bill. I tried to add a few dollars to the bill when I could. We both knew it was going to take a long time before we had a telephone again. So we made arrangements to drive out to Aunt Rena when we needed to use a phone. Actually, we didn't really use the phone much. So at that point, we found that we could just do without the phone. It was convenient to have when we had it. But we could do without it. I would have loved to have had a phone to call my friends, but I was always working or busy at home, so I didn't have a real need for the phone. I just liked the idea of gabbing with my friends.

Chapter 44

Graduation

Life continued somehow. We became used to not having a phone. High school graduation was near. But I had a really big worry now. How was I going to be able to attend college? I did not have enough monies saved. My parents had no money to give to me. I was on my own, and the future was looking bleak for me. Prom night arrived. George had asked me to attend with him, but I said no and stayed with the agreement to go with my three high school friends. When we had made plans, we had decided that we would go to the prom, and they would then all come to my house to change, and then we planned to go out and drive around until time to go to the breakfast given to us as graduating seniors. It all sounded like fun for us.

Prom night was fun. The theme was Cinderella, and our souvenir was a small glass slipper. Of course, I broke mine almost immediately. None of us had special boyfriends, so we weren't really into the night's events. It was pretty and it was exciting, but we were not feeling all romantic and teary-eyed as many other girls were. We attended the prom and then went back home to my house and changed into comfortable clothes, and then out we went in a friend's car when she came by to pick us up. We drove all over Monett and near towns—sometimes meeting other cars of friends or sometimes just driving in the country and talking. It was our very last night together, and we all seemed loath to end the night. Soon, we would all be going our separate ways as we headed out to our individual, chosen lives. It was daunting to think about.

371

Around two in the morning, we decided to head back to my house and talk about the night's events. Actually, we arrived back home, said good-night to Paula, and soon fell asleep on the bed, all rumbly tumbly, like little puppies, exhausted with the day's events and sharing old memories and new thoughts in all that was coming to fruition in our young lives. Morning came quickly, and parents arrived at my house to pick up the girls. After they left, I went back to bed and slept most of the day. That felt good. I was almost a graduate—a free person!

Graduation arrived Sunday, and we wore white dresses under our graduation robes. Momma came with me to attend the ceremonies. I can still remember the thrill of marching into the high school auditorium for the ceremony. The music brought reminders of all the days of growing together, laughter, and memories shared. I said good-bye to friends and joined Momma. It was just the two of us, and all my friends had families with them. After we returned my robe, Momma and I decided to go out and have a nice early dinner together and talk about summer plans. Momma would get easily emotional about thoughts that I might be going away to some faraway place for college. I got emotional that I might not be going away. With both of us tearing up as we laughed at some incident we were remembering about the past years, it did not make for a pleasurable evening to celebrate my graduation. It was too emotional for both of us. Suddenly, I did not feel like that graduate, eighteen years old and ready to decide what I was going to do or where I would be going. I just felt the need to go home and snuggle down in my bed and go to sleep. It was too much to take that I was now free to face new endeavors and actually make my dream of attending college come true. It would be so much easier to just stay home and do what I was doing. No changes. No traveling. No new places. I wanted to be a little girl again and just be with my momma. Lots and lots of sleep sounded awfully good to me. But of course, life had other plans for me, and I was soon going to be facing all the new plans and decisions I would have to be making in my "older" life.

For many years, the Jewel Tea man had come to our home to visit with Momma and sit and show her his catalog of sale items and coupons. It was Momma's favorite time of the month, I believe. First of all, she used that little Jewel Tea catalog as a wish book each and every day, looking through the pages and marking items she might be interested in, as well as counting the little Jewel Tea stickers she received with each purchase, placed lovingly in the many Jewel Tea booklets to be saved for future items to be obtained. I loved to watch Momma sit and count her Jewel Tea booklets and mark items in the catalog she might be able to purchase. Momma and my aunt Rena were always looking at the catalog together and contemplating what item they might get for their book of stamps. They were like happy little children, giggling together and counting. Those Jewel Tea coupons were magic coins that could be spent to obtain some item that was truly wanted by Momma or some member in the family. Most of the time, the gifts were to be for me. It was a way for Momma to get me special gifts without spending monies we did not truly have. It made her feel benevolent with the gifts for me and yet prudent as she did not have to spend monies. Besides, she received the coupons from items that she purchased that we needed. She always purchased all her spices, teas, salt and pepper, flour, and sugar from Jewel Tea. That was a known agreement. By graduation, Momma had saved very diligently with her Jewel Tea stamps and mounted the stamps in her collected coupon books weekly. That Sunday, after graduation, when Momma and I returned home, she proudly presented me my gift of a matching three-piece suitcase. Most extravagant with a makeup case, middle and a large suitcase. They were really lovely in soft pale blue. They were the first pair of suitcases that all matched that Momma or I had ever had. Before, we had a couple of old odd-matched brown suitcases. We never traveled anywhere overnight so one never needed to have suitcases. But as I had high hopes of traveling away to college someday, Momma thought it would be a sensible gift for me at graduation. I was thrilled. I set the three suitcases carefully at the end of my walk-in closet in my bedroom. I gave the three suitcases each a little pat and made a wish that I would soon be packing those suitcases for my trip away to college.

We all fell back into our everyday life. I worked weekends at the church in the minister's office and then during the night or evenings at the local ice cream shop down on Broadway Street. I wasn't making a lot of money, but it was a steady work, and I was saving all the checks in the bank in my savings account. All I could do was wait now.

Chapter 45

College Bound

Actually, that first week after graduation, Momma, Aunt Rena, Betty, and I had driven down to Point Shirley, Missouri, to look at the School of the Ozarks campus and to meet with various people to discuss my application to the college. We were all so excited. Betty was glad to be returning back to School of the Ozarks as a student after being home for a week's vacation. She had the lucky job of working in the CX on campus where the students could socialize, listen to the jukebox, have snacks, and buy books. Betty loved working there and was a very popular gal—she was always in some chess game with one of the guys! In fact, she had garnered some acknowledgment from classmates for her skills in playing chess.

Betty walked around campus with me while Momma and Aunt Rena rested in the CX. It was a hot day. I loved the open air of the campus and loved seeing all the busy students and workers on campus. Betty showed me her room on the first floor of the dorm and told me I would probably be housed on the third floor as all freshmen start there until they get assigned to a room and a roommate. Sounded great to me. Everyone was so friendly acting, always saying hello to Betty and me and stopping to talk about something. The boys looked cute, and I could feel myself getting excited with the thought I may have just found what I was looking for in attending college. When the four of us went into the admission's office and met with the dean, I knew this was what I wanted. We talked with those available to meet with me, and I filled

374

out the necessary papers. It all seemed like a dream to me. I could go to college just by working on campus at a job assigned. Wow! It was a dream come true.

I hated to leave. I wanted to take my three suitcases and just move right into the dorm, third floor and all. I was ready to take the big adventure! But we returned home to await what God had planned for me in my life. Then it was my choice as to whether I would be doing it or not. Several weeks later, I remember it was a Sunday lazy afternoon, Momma and I had gone out to the diner for lunch and had just returned home when Aunt Rena pulled up in the alley by our house and beeped the horn in her car. I walked over to the kitchen screen door and hollered out to Aunt Rena as to what she needed. Aunt Rena rolled down her car window and, leaning out over the window, said, "Quick, Susie, tell your momma to come with you and drive up to my house." The School of the Ozarks had called. Aunt Rena had told the Dean of Admissions when she called that Momma and I were out for lunch but would be returning soon and that I would call as soon as I returned home. The lady told Aunt Rena that she would call right back in about ten minutes. So Aunt Rena had jumped in the car and driven down to get us. Aunt Rena looked at me and winked her eye with a huge smile on her face. "Susie, this may be the call you have been waiting for." I clapped my hands for joy, and I hurried Momma for us to go and get out to wait for the phone call at Aunt Rena's house.

Riding in the car with Momma, I could barely sit still. This might be the phone call I had been waiting for. Aunt Rena had driven on ahead. She had a cake in the oven that Sunday afternoon and knew it was just about ready to be taken out to cool for icing and then dinner. When we stepped into the back kitchen, it all smelled so good. There was a large ham in the oven cooking with white potatoes, and some sweet potatoes were cooking in the oven also. It all smelled so good. Hot white biscuits sat on the window ledge cooling on a plate. They would sure taste good later with the ham and potatoes.

I waved hello to Uncle Paul, who was sitting in the living room watching some sports show on the television. Janice was not to be seen. She must have gone out with some of her high school friends at the pool or such. Momma sat down at the kitchen table to have a visit with Aunt Rena while I walked quickly over to the telephone in the living room and sat down in a chair by the little table that held the telephone.

Betty and Susie at School of the Ozarks

Betty, my cousin, with me, are shown out on campus at The School of the Ozarks.

Betty was already enrolled and would be an incoming freshman. My mother, Aunt Rena and Betty had driven down with me on a Sunday afternoon to look at the campus. I was so excited because this School of the Ozarks offered me my one chance to attend college. I could live on campus, work and attend college. My employment on campus paid for my classes. It was an answer to my prayers. Later, when I was accepted and moved on campus, I worked in the Office of the Treasurer, Dr. Davis, handling the fruitcake orders which are sold worldwide. Then a year later, I was placed in the office of Dr. Mace, the minister for our new Church on campus. Talk about wonderful, sweet luck! I was truly blessed.

Touring the School of the Ozarks

I am sitting on the stairs of the newly completed Williams Memorial Chapel, on campus of the School of the Ozarks, talking with one of the guides who had been showing me the campus. I loved this church and was amazed to hear the bells ringing from the Hyer Bell Tower as they played various hymns and songs. I knew that I loved this campus and school and could not wait to attend classes there and live on campus. This opportunity was an answer to my prayers. I was college bound!

I found myself sitting there staring at the phone as if I could will it to ring. And then, to my surprise, the phone did ring. I could hear everyone get very quiet in anticipation as I lifted the phone receiver up to my ear. Trying to sound very adult and confident, I managed out a squeaky "hello" into the phone receiver and then waited for a response from the other end. I could hear Momma, Aunt Rena, and Uncle Paul strain forward so they could get a better earful of my conversation.

A woman responded to my "hello" with an introduction of who she was and her position at the School of the Ozarks. As I tried to listen with full concentration, over the buzzing in my ears because I was so excited, I could hear the woman tell me that a student had changed their mind and had dropped out of the school. Thus, she informed me, there was room for me to attend to get my college degree. Of course, she went on to explain to me, as I had not been down at the school during the summer to work the needed hours to pay for my fall tuition, I would have to report to the school to work a job assigned all that fall term and then in the winter term I could begin my classes and work my assigned job also. It was too amazing to believe. Then she said, "So Susie, what do you think—will you be joining us at the School of the Ozarks?"

I sat there for a moment, trying to catch my breath and slow down the thumping of my heart from all the excitement. Just as I was about to answer the woman, the dean of admissions, I caught a glimpse of myself in the mirror on the wall by the telephone table. Oh no, I gasped, I had completely forgotten. I shook my head and slowly opened my mouth to give the dean my answer. "I can't come down next week to begin my assigned job at the school. You see, thinking that I would be going down in January, I had gotten a very short haircut and a permanent. I never usually get permanents, and this definitely proves that I should never do so again. I can't come down to attend the school until my hair has grown out and the permanent is more manageable. This just is not how I had planned it at all." I finished what I had to say and sat there waiting for her response. I could hear everyone behind me take in their breaths sharply. What was I talking about? Was I going to waste this whole opportunity because I did not like my hair? Yes, that was how I felt. I had to do it as I wanted it to happen.

There was a moment of quiet on the other end of the phone and then I heard the loudest burst of laughter. To my amazement, the laughter continued for a few minutes. Then I heard the dean of admissions gain control of herself and speak back to me. "Listen carefully to me, Susie. We all do things to our hair or clothes or such that we regret, but it is all able to be corrected. In other words, Susie, your hair will grow out and be back as you like it, *but*," she stated most emphatically, "you will not receive such an opportunity again like this one, short hair or not! Do you understand, Susie? Your hair will grow out, but you may not be able to get into college another day. It must be now, today, that you make your decision!" And with that, the dean concluded, "Now, Susie, you go home and begin to pack your clothes you are bringing to the school. And report here in one week, on a Sunday afternoon. Your dorm room will be waiting for you." And then she continued, "And Susie, be sure to drop by my office Monday. I want to meet you and see your short permanent hair!" With that, to my surprise, she hung up, but I swear I could still hear her laughter as she placed her phone receiver.

I sat in shocked silence. I was leaving in a week for school. I was going to college. I had found a way to get my further education and become a teacher. It was all possible!

Everyone was just grinning and grinning as I told them about the phone conversation with the dean of admissions. I was leaving in a week to go to college. It could not be happening. I told Uncle Paul to pinch my arm as I just could not believe my luck. Maureece, my cousin, shouted out he would be glad to pinch me. Aunt Rena invited Momma and me to stay for supper with them to celebrate my good luck. The food baking in the oven smelled so good, Momma and I quickly agreed to stay. It would be fun to celebrate together. But out of the corner of my eye, I could tell that Momma was feeling a little sad. She was happy for me but knew she was going to be so lonesome with me gone. Later, I promised her that I would write as often as I could, and it would be wonderful to get letters from her. And even packages of "goodies" would be welcome. Momma smiled at the thought of fixing the surprise packages to mail to me.

Thus began a week packed with many errands and plans to make for my travels to college. I guess Momma told Dad that I had gotten accepted into college at the School of the Ozarks because I did not. He seemed to know about my plans, but he never alluded to this fact. He went on about his own business in the front shop as though nothing had changed and life was continuing as it had been. But then, that was the usual way our life was lived. Dad was never really a part of my life, and he never really seemed to want to be such.

Monday afternoon, Momma and I were going to walk downtown and look at some clothes at the Bon Ton. They had advertised some fall clothes on sale, and we wanted to see if I could afford any of their lovely items. As we stepped outside, I saw that Johnny's van was parked in front of their hatchery, and I asked Momma if we could stop to say hello to Johnny and tell him my good news. She answered, "Of course."

We walked into the cool, dark building and saw Johnny sitting in the back at his desk in his wheelchair. He waved us over, and we went back in the office to sit down and talk to him. As I had expected, he was thrilled for me about my attending school. He kept repeating what a lovely thing it was to have happened and how proud he was that I would be able to go away to college. I sat there quietly and listened to Johnny's voice talking to Momma and thought about what a kind person he was. Despite his own personal loss with the crippling polio, he never failed to be happy for someone else's good luck or fortune. He was so kind and generous that he just naturally was happy for others and their achievements.

Then I realized that Momma had begun to cry. I was surprised and asked her what was the matter. Momma sat there for a moment and then explained to Johnny what her sadness was about. You may remember how I had told you about our loss of the use of the telephone because Dad had such a large phone bill when he called President Harry Truman. So we were still out of the use of a phone while Momma slowly and steadily paid the looming phone charge. She knew that we had another year or so before we could get the bill paid and have the use of the telephone again. Before it had not really mattered, but now with me going off to college, Momma would have no phone to call me, nor could I call her during the day. Momma was so upset.

Johnny listened and then he spoke quietly to Momma and me so that the other guys in the office did not hear us. He said, most emphatically, "Now, Lela, don't you worry about a thing here. You are always free to use our phone here in the office during the day should it be necessary to call each other. We can take care of that matter without one single problem. If you have to call Susie, Lela, well, you come over here, and I will dial her dorm phone number and ask for a person-to-person call to Susie Stone. The dorm mother can call her to the phone,

HOME AGAIN, HOME AGAIN, JIGGITY, JIG 381

and then she can call you here in my office where you shall be waiting so that you two can talk. And vice versa—she can call here on a person-to-person call, and I will have one of my workers run over to your house to get you Lela, and you can both talk. As for the charge, don't worry about that. It shall be my contribution to Susie's education."

And that was how the problem was solved so that Momma felt she could call me whenever she needed to call me or I could call her. We would call each other through Johnny at the Hatchery. It made Momma feel much better. Of course, Momma added, on weekends and the evenings, she could call me at Aunt Rena's. It would be just fine. But mainly we would write lots of letters back and forth to each other so that we could keep up in our news together. In the meantime, Momma was trying to pay off that phone bill as soon as she could spare the extra money.

To this day, I still remember the kindness that was offered to us by Johnny that day. He understood that it was just a way to offer Momma an opportunity to not miss me so much, and it calmed her more about my leaving home. Plus, as Johnny offered, he could keep up with all my goings-on also and hear all the gossip about who I was dating and how my grades were in class. I had to laugh at the dear friend. He always shared so much goodness with my mother. After I left for college, through the years, I always made it a point to stop by and say hello to Johnny in his office and tell him about my college escapades. He loved to listen to my stories and would just giggle right along with me. This continued until later when he left the Hatchery to be at home for his health and then died at an early age.

There was another problem I needed to solve with my college duties. I knew that when I came home on weekends, there would be times that I would have homework or projects assigned and papers to write. I did not have a typewriter and had a small chance of getting one. Then Momma told me she had heard L.G. Jones was renting out typewriters for students at his Texaco gas station. That would be a great idea. So Momma and I drove over to the station to see L.G. and how it worked to rent a typewriter when I was home to do papers.

It just so happened that L.G. was in his office that day. I had known him since I was a small child. He had ice cream for sale, and Momma and I would sometimes go out on a Sunday evening drive and stop by in the cooling to enjoy a cone while sitting on his wooden bench there in front of his building. Sometimes L.G. would sit with us and enjoy a vanilla cone. When L.G. saw Momma and me, he came over to say hello to us and asked Lela what was going on. Momma explained to L.G. about my leaving for college and how I would be needing a typewriter to use when I came home to write papers and wondered how much they would cost to rent. L.G. looked at me with a smile and congratulated me for my good fortune. He said that the future students that would be having me as a teacher were going to be very lucky as he was sure that I would be a great teacher! It was nice to hear those kind words from L.G. I smiled and thanked him.

L.G. sat for a moment, and then he asked me if I saw the typewriter over there on the table by the window. I replied, "Yes," and waited to hear what he had to say.

L.G. thought for a minute and then turned to Momma and said, "Lela, I am going to help Susie the best way I know how to continue on with her college studies. When Susie calls or writes you that she is coming home and will need a typewriter for the weekend, well, you just call over to me and tell me that the typewriter is needed. I will have one of the boys run it over to your house for use that weekend or for however long she needs it. Then, when she goes back to school, just call me, and I will have one of my boys come back and get it. Of course, I shall always give that one sitting on the table to Susie to use. It is good and solid and always seems to get the work done. I will keep it clean and a typewriter ribbon in it all set for her to work. Now, even better, I am giving this as a gift to Susie. No charge for the renting of the typewriter or use. You have to furnish your own paper, but I think you can handle that. Just call me when home, and we shall make sure you have a typewriter to use while needed." And with that, he said good-bye and wished me luck in my school days.

For the next four years, whenever I needed a typewriter for my school work, that typewriter, free of charge, and with a new ribbon would be sitting at home, waiting for me to come back and start on a new project or report. I always appreciated that kindness so very much.

The week was drawing to a close with Sunday looming there ahead for the day I would leave. My clothes were washed, ironed, and packed gently in my two new suitcases. I had boxes packed with towels, sheets, and things I would need in my room for the term. Momma told me that she did not expect Dad would be traveling to the college with us.

He had shown no interest in the matter, and she did not want to drive by herself if she did not have to. The roads were very curvy and hilly for the trip to the school and back. Aunt Rena could not go as she had been sick, and Uncle Paul was on an assigned job. We were not sure how I was going to arrive at school. I had not really worried about this matter, but now I had this problem to solve.

As you may remember I had spoken earlier about Mary and Harold Rooney from my church and how they had often taken me out for trips, dinners, and shopping. They were always there to help. So I called them and asked if they would drive Momma and me down to Branson, Missouri, and return the same day. I explained that Dad would not be attending, and Momma did not like to drive along on the trip.

With great kindness, Harold and Mary immediately said they would be honored to escort us to the school and asked when we should leave. We both agreed that Sunday around eleven o'clock would be a good time as it takes about two hours for the trip what with all the curvy and hilly country roads.

Sunday quickly arrived, and I had everything packed, was bathed, and was all dressed for my big adventure. I had not spoken to Dad as he did not seem to want to talk about it, so I just left it at that. Momma and I placed my new blue suitcases inside the kitchen by the door, and the three boxes were placed there also. We decided we would take a quick drive out to Aunt Rena and tell all who were home a fond farewell there and then return home to leave with Harold and Mary. It all seemed so good. I could not believe my luck. As we left from the back kitchen door, I could hear Dad up front in the shop puttering with some clock or such. There was no one in his shop with him.

It was good to see all at Aunt Rena's home. I always enjoyed a visit there. We shared a glass of cold iced tea and then felt we should get back home to meet with Mary and Harold when they arrived. We drove back home and parked the car in front of the house. I mentioned to Momma that the house looked dark and empty as we got out of the car. I did not see Dad in the shop.

We walked around to the side of our home to the kitchen. There, in the alley, was a surprise to Momma and me. Dad had thrown my suitcases and boxes out into the alley there by our home. Some things had spilled out of the boxes and were spread around on the ground. I was so embarrassed. I told Momma that we needed to get things all straightened before Harold or Mary arrived. I did not want them to see my things in such disarray. How could I explain it all to them?

As I cleaned up the area and got all back together and neatly packed for our trip, Momma tried the kitchen door and walked around to the other doors. All were locked from inside, and Dad had pulled down the shades in the rooms. We figured he had done this deed in anger and then gone to bed, as he often did, with all doors locked and everything dark and closed. I started to cry in my worries about Momma and my sadness that Dad could act this on such a joyous day for me. But then, that had always seemed to be the way with Dad. He never seemed to enjoy my good fortunes. I always felt that he was jealous that I was accomplishing what he had never been able to do in his younger life.

"Ah well," I told Momma. We had gotten used to Dad's behavior on these days. We just let it pass on and forget about it. Momma knew that by the time she returned home, Dad would be up and about and all open and lit up. They would never mention the incident, nor would he ask about how I was. It was just his way. I worried about Momma as I would not be there to help her or defend her if necessary. Momma smiled and told me she would be just fine. Dad would forget all about it very soon.

Then Harold and Mary arrived to take us on my journey to a new life. They were excited as we were for the happenings! Despite a small twinge of sadness that Dad would make this my memory of leaving home for new beginnings, I was soon laughing and smiling at the jubilant behavior of Harold and Mary. It helped Momma feel better also.

We talked and sang songs on our journey, and when we arrived in Branson, we stopped to have dinner at a fine restaurant there in town. Mary told me I had missed dinner at school, so we had better eat this meal. We all ate plates of fried chicken, not as good as Momma's, but it was all good. Then we headed on to the School of the Ozarks and my new beginnings.

Years later, I asked Dad why he had thrown my things out into the alley and locked up the house on the day that I was leaving for school. He told me, "I had to do that. I was afraid you would not leave and head on to college. That you would want to stay home and never leave." I looked at him and replied, "But Dad, all my life I had never had another thought in my head except that I was going to leave home as soon as I

HOME AGAIN, HOME AGAIN, JIGGITY, JIG   385

could leave. Why would you think that I was now not going to leave?" Dad turned and looked at me and replied, "Because of your mother. She needed you."

Maybe he thought that was the answer, but it did not work for me. It was better not to dwell on it for too long. It would never be clear to me. It was just Dad and his ways as Momma always said to me.

Slowly I heard the voice of Janice talking to Arthur, and I was pulled back to the present from all my various thoughts I had just faced through my memories while standing there on the corner where it had all began. In front of our small apartment, facing my little Presbyterian Church, and the Beeler home, and across the street, that large home where Priscilla and her family had lived—my memories had traveled through the years as I had listened to my Momma's voice or my thoughts about life, and all else that had transpired on that very spot so many years ago. I looked around me at the faces of Doug, Janice, Nathan, and Arthur and thought once again about how I had enjoyed my little visit back home and all my many memories. Yes, I had been right. I could not go home again. There was nothing left there that had been made from my earlier memories. My home had been sold and bulldozed down to make way for an office building. So many friends and family members were now dead. Nothing looked the same to me nor felt the same. It was not possible to go home again, I responded to Arthur. Yet there was some kind of tug at my heart. I felt such joy at thoughts of past days and years, thoughts and memories—my yesteryears. I suddenly came to a conclusion. I had gone home again only I had not even needed to leave my own present bed. My home was in my heart, filled with memories of yesteryear, friends, and moments. Sadness and happiness. Kindness all lived there in my heart, free at any time to be reached for and kindled back to life again. I was not alone. I had my family and loved ones. I had led a most incredible life of adventurous travel, met so many people, and had been blessed with so much love and friendship. I was home again . . . I was home again.

CPSIA information can be obtained
at www.ICGtesting.com
Printed in the USA
LVHW090504300719
625842LV00001B/38/P